Deliberate
Prose

The Visions of the Great Rememberer (with Visions of Cody,
Jack Kerouac), 1993

Journals Mid-Fifties: 1954–1958, 1994

Luminous Dreams, 1997

Deliberate Prose: Selected Essays 1952–1995, 2000

Photography
Photographs, 1991

Snapshot Poetics, 1993

Vocal Words & Music
First Blues (Smithsonian/Folkways FSS 37560), 1981

The Lion For Real (Mouth Almighty/Mercury Records),
1989, 1996.

Howls, Raps & Roars (Fantasy), 1993

Hydrogen Jukebox, opera w/Philip Glass (Elektra Nonesuch), 1993

Holy Soul Jelly Roll: Poems & Songs 1949–1993
(Rhino Records), 1994

The Ballad of the Skeletons, w/Paul McCartney, Philip Glass
(Mouth Almighty/Mercury), 1996

Howl, U.S.A., Kronos Quartet, Lee Hyla score (Nonesuch), 1996

Howl & Other Poems (Fantasy), 1998

Deliberate Prose

SELECTED ESSAYS
1952–1995

ALLEN GINSBERG

EDITED BY
BILL MORGAN

HarperCollins*Publishers*

HarperCollins books may be purchased for educational, business, or sales promotional use. For information please write: Special Markets Department, HarperCollins Publishers Inc., 10 East 53rd Street, New York, NY 10022.

FIRST EDITION
Designed by Joseph Rutt

Printed on acid-free paper

Library of Congress Cataloging-in-Publication Data

Ginsberg, Allen, 1926–
Deliberate prose : selected essays, 1952–1995/Allen Ginsberg. — 1st ed.
p.   cm.
Includes index.
ISBN 0-06-019294-1
I. Title.
PS3513.I74D45   2000
814'.54—dc21   99-41360

00 01 02 03 04 ❖/RRD 10 9 8 7 6 5 4 3 2 1

To Allen Ginsberg's readers

If it isn't composed on the tongue, it's an essay.
—Allen Ginsberg

CONTENTS

ACKNOWLEDGMENTS

Thanks to hospitable editors, variants of these writings were printed first in the publications listed immediately following each essay. In addition, special thanks are extended to Bob Rosenthal and Andrew Wylie, Peter Hale, Simon Pettet, Gordon Ball, Judy Matz, Ellen Saltonstall, Terry Karten, editor now, and all editors past.

Prose from Allen Ginsberg's published books was not used in this collection; for example, essays from the *Annotated Howl* and introductions and cover blurbs for books like his *Collected Poems*. These are easy to find and quite naturally belong with the books that they annotate. Journal entries, correspondence, captions to photographs, interviews, and speeches were generally not used; a few exceptions are noted where they were rewritten for publication. Letters to the editor, in particular, often seemed to be more essay than letter and were included, if important in content. Light editing was done on some of the essays to bring them up to date or to correct errors.

FOREWORD

What a wonderful book is *Deliberate Prose*, the selected essays of Allen Ginsberg! It is the work of a great poet, a great American, and a great friend of literature who more than any bard in history helped shape social thought and political change in his era. Brilliance suffuses the collection, beginning with the opening essay, his prophetic "Independence Day Manifesto" of 1959, directed to "an America, the great portion of whose economy is yoked to mental and mechanical preparations for war," as prophetic in the twenty-first century as it was in the years following Ginsberg's early masterworks, *Howl* and *Kaddish*.

The 124 essays in *Deliberate Prose* read like the burning signposts of our age. In them we are amazed at the wide range of his mind, the evidence of his wild curiosity, his goodwill, his dedication to a better world, to good causes, to a new kind of openness and truth emblemized by his watch-sentence: "Candor ends paranoia."

Of particular pleasure in *Deliberate Prose* are the essays on literature, especially his exquisite 1980 illustrated lecture on *Leaves of Grass,* and his remembrances of Michaux, Auden, Robert Creeley, William Carlos Williams's short poems, and his quick insight into the meaning of Andy Warhol, for instance, for Warhol's festschrift. Other gems include how he calmed down the Hells Angels in '65 when they were threatening violence against a big antiwar rally, and a number of important essays calling for expanding personal freedom, including the freedom to use psychedelics, and in opposition to what he saw as an encroaching American fascist police military state.

A love of verse was at the core of his spirit. No other bard ever matched his dedication to poetry. "I am ready to die for poetry and for the truth that inspires poetry. . . . I believe in the American Church of Poetry," he wrote in an essay in 1961.

He was one of the most generous poets of any era. "Learn a little Patience and Generosity" is a line from one of his songs. No other bard ever appeared at so many benefits or raised so much money to help his friends. He helped get hundreds of books published. When he was young he would carry the manuscripts of his Best Minds friends on his frenetic literary rounds. One example was in the fall of 1956, after *Howl* had been published, when Allen swept into New York City with manuscripts by Gary Snyder, Phil Whalen, Robert Duncan, Ed Dorn, Robert Creeley, Philip Lamantia, Denise Levertov, Michael McClure, and even Charles Olson, trying to get all of them into print pronto. *Mademoiselle*, thanks to Allen, published Levertov and even some Burroughs. Around that time he approached *Time, Life, Esquire*, the *Hudson Review, Partisan Review, Kenyon Review, The New Yorker*, and *New Directions*, et al., demanding ink for himself and the Best Minds group. It is that notion of Generosity which permeates the essays of *Deliberate Prose*.

He also brought a wild eroticism into poetry in a way not seen since Catullus. This he accomplished in a country known for its strong streak of Puritanism. There is a section in *Deliberate Prose* called "Censorship and Sex Laws" whose essays give evidence of his lifelong effort to expand the types of verse and writing available over the airways, in the concert halls and coffee shops, and on the shelves of libraries. Allen Ginsberg also brought a vast curiosity to the world of poetry. No other bard ever asked so many questions as Allen Ginsberg. Look at all the question marks, for instance, in his books of verse. The essays in *Deliberate Prose* are the sum of the answers he created from his quenchless searching.

Allen Ginsberg refused to be isolated from his times, however controversial the stances of his poems and public statements. He thrived in the hot debates of the media arena, while refusing to get boxed in. Early in his career he isolated a core group of social and literary passions and then became intensely proactive. That was not so easy to do in the chaos of moiling egos, the anger of a war era, and the lure of fun and eros.

Nevertheless, the bard was able to establish an agenda of passions and issues that stayed with him during his forty-two years of almost round-the-clock intensity, beginning, say, with the writing of *Howl* in San Francisco in 1955. The message, complicated and lifelong, was one of reacting to suppression and oppression through insistent nonviolent action, candor, openness, and love. He was like a bacchic/bardic/Buddhaic/Judaic Gandhi in that regard.

Allen Ginsberg made it his business to know the intricacies of his nation, more so than any other bard in our history. It was another aspect of his refusing to be denied his voice. He once called Henry Kissinger, then secretary of state, and got through to him: he wanted Kissinger to meet with Dave Dellinger to talk about ending the war in Vietnam.

He took on the excesses of the military-industrial complex in a multi-decade campaign unmatched by any other bard in world history. It was a heavy, time-consuming struggle, some of which obviously had to be done obliquely, an ironic feature of a life so totally open and candid. Just as William Blake set up his own "system" in order to go about his work in the unpleasant atmosphere in England after the French Revolution, so Ginsberg developed his own "Blake path," growing out of lines of his own poetry such as "Now is the time for prophecy without death as a consequence" (from "Death to Van Gogh's Ear"). Ginsberg's "Blake path" was a fantastically complicated course from which he addressed the entirety of American civilization, urging it up a path which glorifies nonencroaching dreams of personal fulfillment, retards fascist insect robotic right-wing police statism, and spreads around the wealth. The struggle is "against native fascist militarization of U.S. Soul," he wrote in the same essay as the statement that he was ready to die for the truth of poetry.

He studied early the enormous hypocrisy and even dishonesty in official government-intelligence circles on the issue of drugs. He spoke up for forty years against many stupid American drug laws, which only enrich the military-industrial-intelligence-agency-organized crime coffers, and which unjustly stigmatize millions of productive Americans.

He was always cynical about big government, and though one might label him as left-liberal, he was critical of almost all socialist formations so far created. What other bard could have been tossed out of both Communist Cuba and Czechoslovakia in the same era as when he made a bet with the head of the U.S. Central Intelligence Agency that the CIA was involved in drug running?

He loved to teach. If he opened his refrigerator door, he gave a lecture on the rice milk and organic food on the shelves. These 124 essays are some of the emblems of that passion to teach. He had a spiritual side and was a practicing Buddhist. Meditation, sitting, and formal Buddhist practice were important to him, beginning in the 1970s. It was a method for dealing with the hubbub of public debate, personal turmoil, and anger, one result being some interesting essays in this book in the section called "Mindfulness and Spirituality."

I loved reading *Deliberate Prose*, for not only does it show how the burning issues of Allen's years are still very much with us, but it also demonstrates the "prose" side of his mind. He had a unique style whose strength holds up all the way from the 1957 introduction to Gregory Corso's *Gasoline* to the essays on Gary Snyder from the 1990s.

These essays are news that stays news, to paraphrase another great poet. They are the "emblems of conduct" of Allen Ginsberg, great bard, great friend, great American.

Edward Sanders
1999

EDITOR'S NOTE

Who knows what form these essays would have taken had Allen Ginsberg lived a few more months? My project had begun two or three years earlier. I was to put together all his prose pieces so that he and I could sit down and organize a book. Allen had worked on the project off and on for the previous twenty years but had never gotten very far in the work, just too many demands on his time. I assembled everything that even remotely resembled an essay, cut it down to only the clearest, most succinct diamonds, and presented him with a 574-page manuscript just a few months before the end, but Allen was in such weakened health that he had little time to do anything more than thumb through the pages of my selections.

I had envisioned late night sessions sitting up with Allen at his kitchen table arguing whether such and such a piece deserved inclusion in this book. My determination was to keep this a lean and trim selection to which Allen would add countless gems that I had excised, but that was my intention. He had once described the project as a collection of his essays that he would sprinkle with shorter blurbs and epigrams, "like stars scattered through the heavens," as I recall he put it.

His model was to be Norman Mailer's *Advertisements for Myself,* which he had always known would be the best way to display his own work. Had Allen lived I think this volume would be significantly different. It would certainly be much longer, it would certainly include a few essays specially written to fill in gaps, and it would certainly include his introductions to many of the pieces. As it stands, it isn't any larger. Only Allen would have known which small, obscure blurbs were of special importance to him— only Allen would have been able to annotate his essays with the autobiographical precision of Norman Mailer's work—only Allen would have been able to write the unwritten essays on friends like Neal Cassady, Amiri Baraka, and others. These oversights were caused only by Allen's sudden illness; he would have responded to the needs in each case. At one point ten or twelve years ago, Allen began making notes on each essay and detailing how and why each one was written. The dozen or so that he annotated thus are included with an "Author's Note" following the essay. Certainly he would have annotated each and every item, given the time. Also, at that long-ago moment, he pronounced the collected essays *Deliberate Prose*, a wonderful title and the one used for this completed volume.

After Allen's death I didn't look at his copy of the manuscript for more than a year. When I went back to it, I found that he had scrawled "The End" on that last 574th page of the manuscript and drawn his detailed little picture of the three fish with one head, symbol of Buddha's footprint. His last note to us, encouraging us to come to The End of the project and yet still observe the details of the fish.

If Allen were alive it would be his job to exert his personal preferences over the book and make it his own. As he is gone, it is the editor's job to stand back and let Allen's voice be heard without interference. He still speaks to us directly in each of the essays that follow. His writings on drugs and politics were never more clear than in this new-century world. The work is informative, timely as well as historic. We're still confused and Allen is still confidently straightening us out.

Bill Morgan
New York City
1999

PART 1
Politics and Prophecies

POLITICAL LIFE

Poetry, Violence, and the Trembling Lambs
or
Independence Day Manifesto

Recent history is the record of a vast conspiracy to impose one level of mechanical consciousness on mankind and exterminate all manifestations of that unique part of human sentience, identical in all men, which the individual shares with his Creator. The suppression of contemplative individuality is nearly complete.

The only immediate historical data that we can know and act on are those fed to our senses through systems of mass communication.

These media are exactly the places where the deepest and most personal sensitivities and confessions of reality are most prohibited, mocked, suppressed.

At the same time there is a crack in the mass consciousness of America—sudden emergence of insight into a vast national subconscious netherworld filled with nerve gases, universal death bombs, malevolent bureaucracies, secret police systems, drugs that open the door to God, ships leaving Earth, unknown chemical terrors, evil dreams at hand.

Because systems of mass communication can communicate only officially acceptable levels of reality, no one can know the extent of the secret unconscious life. No one in America can know what will happen. No one is in real control. America is having a nervous breakdown. Poetry is the record of individual insights into the secret soul of the individual and because all individuals are one in the eyes of their creator, into the soul of the world. The world has a soul. America is having a nervous breakdown. San Francisco is one of many places where a few individuals, poets, have had the luck and courage and fate to glimpse something new through the crack in mass consciousness; they have been exposed to some insight into their own nature, the nature of the governments, and the nature of God.

3

Therefore there has been great exaltation, despair, prophecy, strain, suicide, secrecy and public gaiety among the poets of the city. Those of the general populace whose individual perception is sufficiently weak to be formed by stereotypes of mass communication disapprove and deny the insight. The police and newspapers have moved in, mad movie manufacturers from Hollywood are at this moment preparing bestial stereotypes of the scene.

The poets and those who share their activities, or exhibit some sign of dress, hair, or demeanor of understanding, or hipness, are ridiculed. Those of us who have used certain benevolent drugs (marijuana) to alter our consciousness in order to gain insight are hunted down in the street by police. Peyote, an historic vision-producing agent, is prohibited on pain of arrest. Those who have used opiates and junk are threatened with permanent jail and death. To be a junky in America is like having been a Jew in Nazi Germany.

A huge sadistic police bureaucracy has risen in every state, encouraged by the central government, to persecute the illuminati, to brainwash the public with official lies about the drugs, and to terrify and destroy those addicts whose spiritual search has made them sick.

Deviants from the mass sexual stereotype, quietists, those who will not work for money, or fib and make arms for hire, or join armies in murder and threat, those who wish to loaf, think, rest in visions, act beautifully on their own, speak truthfully in public, inspired by Democracy—what is their psychic fate now in America? An America, the greater portion of whose economy is yoked to mental and mechanical preparations for war?

Literature expressing these insights has been mocked, misinterpreted, and suppressed by a horde of middlemen whose fearful allegiance to the organization of mass stereotype communication prevents them from sympathy (not only with their own inner nature but) with any manifestation of unconditioned individuality. I mean journalists, commercial publishers, book-review fellows, multitudes of professors of literature, etc., etc. Poetry is hated. Whole schools of academic criticism have risen to prove that human consciousness of unconditioned spirit is a myth. A poetic renaissance glimpsed in San Francisco has been responded to with ugliness, anger, jealousy, vitriol, sullen protestations of superiority.

And violence. By police, by customs officials, post-office employees, by trustees of great universities. By anyone whose love of power has led him to a position where he can push other people around over a difference of opinion—or vision.

The stakes are too great—an America gone mad with materialism, a police-state America, a sexless and soulless America prepared to battle the world in defense of a false image of its authority. Not the wild and beautiful America of the comrades of Walt Whitman, not the historic America of William Blake and Henry David Thoreau where the spiritual independence of each individual was an America, a universe, more huge and awesome than all the abstract bureaucracies and authoritative officialdoms of the world combined.

Only those who have entered the world of spirit know what a vast laugh there is in the illusory appearance of worldly authority. And all men at one time or other enter that Spirit, whether in life or death.

How many hypocrites are there in America? How many trembling lambs, fearful of discovery? What authority have we set up over ourselves, that we are not as we are? Who shall prohibit an art from being published to the world? What conspirators have power to determine our mode of consciousness, our sexual enjoyments, our different labors and our loves? What fiends determine our wars?

When will we discover an America that will not deny its own God? Who takes up arms, money, police, and a million hands to murder the consciousness of God? Who spits in the beautiful face of poetry which sings of the glory of God and weeps in the dust of the world?

WRITTEN: ca. July 4, 1959

FIRST PUBLISHED: *San Francisco Chronicle* (July 26, 1959) This World, p. 27. Reprinted: *Village Voice,* vol. 4, no. 44 (Aug. 26, 1959) pp. 1, 8; Thomas Parkinson, ed., *A Casebook on the Beat* (New York: Thomas Y. Crowell, 1961); Donald Allen and Warren Tallman, eds., *Poetics of the New American Poetry* (New York: Grove Press, 1973).

Back to the Wall

The individual soul is under attack and for that reason a "beat" generation existed and will continue to exist under whatever name rosy generation lost or as Kerouac once prophesied found until it is found. The soul that is. And a social place for the soul to exist manifested in *this* world. By soul I mean that which differs man from thing, i.e. person—not mere mental consciousness—but feeling bodily consciousness. As long as this tender feeling body is under attack there will continue the expression in art of the scream or weep or supplication the EXPRESSION in one form or other of that infinite—Self—which still feels thru the smog of Blakean-satanic war mills and noise of electric sighs and spears which is twentieth century mass communication.

Uniquely the art work is of one single hand, the mark of individual person: thus in prose developed thru Kerouac Burroughs Selby the nervous transcriptive spontaneous faculty. Thus in poetry the individualized metre reflective of eccentric breathing William Carlos Williams thru myself Corso Kerouac Creeley Wieners Snyder etc.

How difficult to sustain this in the USA presently occupying its deepest energies in wars (not against communism, for peace has been made with Russia) against the yellow and other races.

Though ten years ago it may have been inconceivable that the great sweet "casaba melon" as it was called of "American Century" prosperity was really a great psychic hoax a mirage of electronic mass-hypnosis, the real horror, the real evil latent in America from the days of Poe to the days of Burroughs is clearly visible in the faces of the hate-gangs that crash thru newspaper and television at last to lay their Ahab curse on the Negro, as they have already laid their Ahab curse on Communism. The spectacle of supposedly respectable elders—Eisenhower the leader of the country himself—sustaining a bid for power by an Android like Goldwater! The choice given—or CHOSEN?—by us between an old-fashioned politician like Johnson, which is to say conservative and an outright authoritarian right-winger? We never had a choice between middle and left, we were always stuck between middle and right. Finally it becomes too much to fight. But the stakes are too great to lose—the possession of one's feelings intact.

There has been an outrage done to my feelings from which I have never recovered though I've talked to Blake and bowed at the feet of many an Indian guru.

To live in a country which supposedly dominates the entire planet and to be responsible for the outrages of one's own country! Woe to the Germans silent under Hitler woe to the Americans silent now.

Sitting in a park in Saigon, the strategic bombing expert in civilian clothes drunk at three AM said "I've got the Eichmann syndrome."

Not a matter of policy, rational discourse, etc. A total discontinuity between my deepest feelings desire for acceptancy tenderness and the military machine non-person rage that dominate the thinking feeling mass media family life publishing life universities business and budgetary government of my nation.

You DON'T have a $60 billion military budget without the EMOTIONS being affected. Maybe the majority feels well means well? I hope so. Actually the majority don't "feel" anything at all personally, where it comes to politics, just like the Germans. Total indifference to the Vietnam War. I feel a little since I been there. But the war goes on. Few American lives lost, myriad of Yellow, it makes no difference here. The suffering the suffering the suffering yet all unknown unaccounted for—the vomiting grimacing bleeding myriads in rice fields? The commuter train pulls in air-conditioned: packaged news. The *New York Daily News* last month proposed that the U.S. Government attempt to promote a war between China and Russia in which they supposed at least 300,000,000 lives would be lost. Modest Jno. Swift![1]

Things no longer merely out of proportion, things are UNREAL. Manipulating the unreal from centers of power—how can the soul endure? Which is to say, what happens to real bodily feelings confronted with inhuman response? The feelings and the response become seeming unreal. Total disorganization. Eisenhower kneeled before Dulles to take the wafer.

Oh well, what about the avant-garde? It's the only thing (aside from family, childbirth, etc. day-to-day common sense)—it's the only social-public manifestation that makes much sense—because it's an attempt to push forth outward feelers of feeling. In public, tender shoots of private sensibility, private understanding, rapport, giggles, delicacies, amens, awareness of what is underneath all the pre-packaged money oriented murderous blather. Movie blather, news broadcast blather, slick magazine blather, newspaper blather, school board blather, politics blather, courtroom blather, social blather of a totally maladjusted tribe engaged in struggle to retain power-dominance and control over an entire planet (nay an entire solar system!).

Poetry: the renaissance of individual sensibility carried thru the vehicle of individualized metrics—individually differentiating not conforming—that's accomplished.

Prose: the vast project of total recall begun by Kerouac continues as he's a saint to that task. English readers by this time also know Burroughs and though he's typically "controversial" in his own time (Is he or is he not an artist? What a stupid argument!) he already influences the thinking processes of a whole generation of American and English boys.

But what's happening now in the U.S.? Amazingly enough, MOVIES. After having been absent from the land for three years, I found on my return an excitement, a group, an art-gang, a society of friendly individuals who were running all around the streets with home movie cameras taking each other's pictures, just as—a decade ago—poets were running around the streets of New York and San Francisco recording each other's visions in spontaneous language. So now the present moment is being captured on film. This is nothing like the commercial film of banks distributors money-stars etc. This is the film of cranks, eccentrics, sensitives, individuals one man one camera one movie—that is to say the work of individual persons not corporations. As such naturally it's interesting depending upon the individual behind the camera—Ron Rice, Harry Smith, Jack Smith, Brakhage, Mekas, Anger, Connors, others. Jonas Mekas is the genius organizer of encouragement and showings, and there is a Film-Makers Cooperative—which naturally has been attacked by the police.

Police, another problem. Police and John Birch societies together ganging up on the avant-garde. Goldwater almost, not quite, in reach of power. To make a long story short, laws were sneaked thru in New York requiring licensing for poetry readings in coffeehouses. The State attempted to close down all coffeehouses where poetry was read, one year later. As well as threatening theater cafes, banjo-art cafes etc. A "synchronistic putsch." Film showings of the new cinema were stopped in New York and Los Angeles. No student riots or sit-ins took place (unlike our more bold brotherhood behind iron curtain) (nor were there protests by Congresses of Cultural Freedom). Sculpture has been seized in San Francisco. Editor of Oregon University mag. was bounced for printing Antonin Artaud's *To Be Done with the Judgment of God* (as several years ago editor of *Chicago Review* was bounced for Burroughs). Wichita police closed down local coffeehouse, seized City Lights books and one-shot poetry magazine *NOW*. Lenny Bruce comedian arrested in New York City. All this a sort of white backlash possibly temporary, for myself I've lost my mind and am immersed in legal calculations and artistically sterilized screaming at newspapermen and college professors IT'S HAPPENING HERE. I don't suppose this phase will last too long with me and I trust my own genius to carry me thru to tears somewhere else.

WRITTEN: Independence Day weekend 1964

FIRST PUBLISHED: *Times Literary Supplement* (Aug. 6, 1964) pp. 678–679. Reprinted: *Now*, no. 2 (1965) pp. 35–36; Jeff Berner, ed., *Astronauts of Inner-Space* (San Francisco: Stolen Paper Review, 1966).

AUTHOR'S NOTE: Requested by *London Times Literary Supplement* to write a brief essay on literary-cultural life contemporary U.S.A., flattered by their consideration, I thought to pen some thing of the reality information I saw rather than moderate sugarcoated and plump essay self-satisfied by my own apparent social acceptability.

Demonstration or Spectacle As Example, As Communication
or
How to Make a March/Spectacle

EDITOR'S NOTE: In Nov. 1965 a demonstration march was planned in Berkeley in support of peace in Vietnam and to protest the draft. Allen Ginsberg was to be an active participant. The Hell's Angels vowed to beat up demonstrators if such a parade were held and so a committee met to prepare for the threatened violence. These were Ginsberg's suggestions to that committee.

If imaginative, pragmatic, fun, gay, happy, *secure* Propaganda is issued to mass media in advance (and pragmatic leaflets handed out days in advance giving marchers instructions) the parade can be made into an exemplary spectacle on how to handle situations of anxiety and fear/threat (such as specter of Hell's Angels or specter of Communism) to manifest by concrete example, namely the parade itself, how to change war psychology and surpass, go over, the habit-image-reaction of fear/violence.

That is, the parade can embody an example of peaceable health which is the reverse of fighting back blindly.

Announce in advance it is a safe march, bring your grandmother and babies, bring your family and friends. Open declarations, "We aren't coming out to fight and we simply will not fight."

We have to use our *imagination*. A spectacle can be made, an unmistakable statement OUTSIDE the war psychology which is leading nowhere. Such statement would be heard around the world with relief.

The following suggestions manifest or embody what I believe to be the conscious psychology of latent understanding of the majority of the youth and many elders who come out to march.

And once clearly enunciated by the leaders of the march will be clearly understood and acted upon by them. Necessary to TRUST the communal sanity of the marchers who already demonstrated that community when they first SAT DOWN.

Needed: an example of health which will paralyze the Angels and also manifest itself thru mass media reportage.

N.B. A negative psychology, of becoming scared by threats, adrenaline running in neck, uprush of blood to head, blind resentment, self-righteousness, fear, anger and active return of violence is exactly what the [Hell's] Angels' "power structure" press and fuzz THRIVE ON what the young people who come [to] march don't want and are dragged by what will decrease the number who come and discourage the great many on the fence who would come to a good scene.

The following are specific suggestions for organizing march and turning marchers on to their roles in the demonstration.

1. Masses of flowers—a visual spectacle—especially concentrated in the front lines. Can be used to set up barricades, to present to Hell's Angels, police, politicians, and press and spectators whenever needed or at parade's end. Masses of marchers can be asked to bring their own flowers. Front lines should be organized and provided with flowers in advance.

2. Front lines should be the psychologically less vulnerable groups. The Women for Peace or any other respectable organization, perhaps a line of poets and artists, mothers, families, professors. This should also be announced (publicized in advance).

3. Marchers should bring crosses, to be held up in front in case of violence; like in the movies dealing with Dracula. (This for those who use crosses or Jewish stars.)

4. Marchers who use American flags should bring those: at least one front row of American flags and myriad in the spectacle.

5. Marchers should bring harmonicas, flutes, recorders, guitars, banjos and violins. (Those who don't use crosses or flags.) Bongos and tambourines.

6. Marchers should bring certain children's toys (not firecrackers or balloons which cause noise hysteria) which can be used for distracting attackers: such as sparklers, toy rubber swords, especially the little whirling carbon wheels which make red-white-blue sparkles, toy soldiers.

7. In case of heavy anxiety, confusion or struggle in isolated spots marchers could be led in
    > Sit Down
    > Mass Calisthenics
    > In case of threat of attack marchers could intone en masse the following mantras
    > The Lord's Prayer
    > Three Blind Mice (sung)
    > OM (AUM) long breath in unison
    > Star Spangled Banner
    > Mary Had a Little Lamb (spoken in unison)

8. More interesting Zen/Spectacle SIGNS
    > As In Oakland So In Vietnam
    > Everybody's Made Of Meat
    > Nobody Wants To Get Hurt—Us Or Them
    > Everybody's Wrong Including U.S.
    > Hell's Angels   Vietcong   Birch Society
    > > DON'T FLIP
    > > We Love You Too

9. Candy bars carried by marchers to offer Hell's Angels and police.

10. Marchers encouraged to carry copies of the Constitution if they have them; or can buy them.
11. Little paper halos to offer Angels, police and spectators and patriots.
12. A row of marchers with white flags and many white flags in mass.
13. Those who have movie cameras bring them and take pictures of spectacle or any action. (To combine for documentary film which could be used in court in case of legal hassles later, and also to circulate for propaganda and profits.) Monitors who can should have cameras.

OTHER MORE GRANDIOSE POSSIBILITIES.
14. Corps of student newsmen to interview newsmen, propagandize and soften and charm TV crews etc.
15. Small floats or replicas in front:
    > Christ with sacred heart and cross (invite church groups to prepare)
    > Buddha in meditation (invite Zen people to come march and meditate on floats)
    > George Washington, Lincoln, Whitman, etc. (float or living masquerade)
    > Thoreau behind bars[2] (float)
    > Hell's Angels float—with halos, happy, praying (no ugly provocative caricature)
    > Birch Society float (old ladies in tennis sneakers)
    > Dixieland Band float dressed as Hitler Stalin Mussolini Napoleon and Caesar (See "Universal Soldier" song).[3]
16. At first sign of disturbance, public address systems swing into vast sound to loud *Beatles* "I Wanna Hold Your Hand" and marchers instructed to dance (if not doing calisthenics or Lord's Prayer). (These could be schematized as strategy 1, 2, 3, etc for diverting crowd and angels from violence.)
17. The Mime Troupe[4] in costume a block down the march, walking doing pantomime.
18. Sound tracks with Bay area rock 'n' roll bands every 2 blocks, Jefferson Airplane, The Charlatans, etc. (These bands have their own sound systems.) Family Dogg people might be able to arrange this. This scheme to pick up on the universal youth

rockroll protest of Dylan, "Eve of Destruction,"[5] "Universal Soldier," etc. and concretize all that consciousness in the parade.

19. Front (or toward front)—toy army in costume, Civil War or Revolutionary War or WW I uniforms and signs.

>   NO MORE
>
>   LEAVE ME ALONE

Addenda: Pre-March Propaganda

1. Muslims, unions etc. all invited to join *inside* the masses.
2. Leaflets with above instructions to marchers how to channel their anxiety and respond to attack.
3. Daily delegations to Hell's Angels to talk to them, pestering them in advance.
4. Petitions and letters and news releases to papers setting tone of march: Petitions to [Gov.] Brown, open letter to Hell's Angels one news release (We're NOT going to fight); open letters to Young Republicans, Democrats, Birchers, Army, Johnson etc. All the propaganda suggested at Tuesday meeting—conferences with Oakland police to force them to keep peace.
5. Emphasize in propaganda TRUST THE MARCHERS to be hip, calm and tranquil with a sense of humor and not get sidetracked into frustration/personal violence.
6. Perhaps as propaganda, an imaginary ladies corps to pull down Hell's Angels pants in case of attack, or a (theoretical) corps of trained fairies to seduce them in mid-battle. This is a sort of press release joke to lighten the atmosphere.

WRITTEN: ca. Nov. 1965

FIRST PUBLISHED: *Berkeley Barb* (Nov. 19, 1965) pp. 1, 4. Reprinted: *Liberation,* vol. 10, no. 10 (Jan. 1966); Massimo Teodori, ed., *The New Left* (Indianapolis: Bobbs-Merrill, 1970).

Coming to Terms with the Hell's Angels

I think Peter Orlovsky and I came to San Francisco some time early in mid-'65. And the Haight Ashbury cycle was forming, which was—incidentally—similar to the North Beach cycle: a lot of young kids coming in and creating a culture and prosperity coming with them. At that time Haight Ashbury was just rising and becoming more charming. Kesey was around . . . and Neal Cassady was in town visiting at my house. Peter Orlovsky was there, I was there with a Buddhist girlfriend, and a young fifteen-year-old boy Buddhist acid-head who was illustrating *The Tibetan Book of the Dead* on a 150-foot scroll. Dylan was about to come to town before Christmas to give concerts at Berkeley.

Around October there was the beginning of a series of demonstrations at Berkeley, following the Free Speech Movement. There was an air of expectation and apocalyptic demand, which was quite beautiful and at the same time unrealistic. I remember this one kid kept climbing in the window of my poetry class demanding a revolution. He was demanding that I lead an immediate revolution right then and there, and he wasn't able to define it.

The first demonstration that I remember taking place was a march from the Berkeley campus through the black district of Oakland to downtown Oakland, I guess. And I was on that daytime march. And we were maybe four or five rows from the front lines. The police stopped us from entering at the Oakland border. And so everybody sat down on the street and a sound truck was put in place and there were some speeches; at that point a fellow named Tiny—one of the Hell's Angels, who'd been behind the police lines on the Oakland side—and about seven Angels rushed out from behind Oakland police lines and tore down the big "Peace in Vietnam" banner that was being held up in front of the march, and ran over to the sound truck and cut the wires; nobody could make any speeches to be heard under the vast sky. Then there was a little scuffling with the police and one of the Angels broke his leg. I'm not sure here.

Now, the reason that we were going to march through Oakland was that there were so many disadvantaged blacks—it was at the height of the black movement and we thought we could pick up a lot of marchers, particularly among poor and blacks who *were* against the war.

That's why we were stopped at the border by a straight line of what looked to us like storm troopers, the Oakland police. They were standing out there, with, I think, tear-gas masks—they had guns with them, though not drawn or pointed at us.

The October march was blocked, frustrated, so there was still the need to carry it through in a democratic fashion and "exercise Privileges"— which meant organizing another march for November. So there was a mass meeting to decide on the policy for the next march. One guy got up and said that the appearance of the Hell's Angels was parallel to the appearance of the Brown Shirt storm troopers in Germany who broke up Left democratic marches and demonstrations. He said that all the young men should march with long sticks and black-and-white armbands.

I printed up a handbill entitled "How to Make a March/Spectacle," which proposed a march as "Theater." It wasn't just a political march where people were supposed to run and march angry, shouting slogans; it could be seen as theater, as almost all political activity was. And given the situation, the best kind of theater would manifest the peace that we were protesting. Pro-test being "pro-attestation," testimony *in favor* of something. So if we were going to be a peace-protest march, then we should have to be peaceful, and being peaceful took skillful means under such anxious circumstances.

My handbill outlined the possible "acts," suggesting that the march should be like an old-fashioned parade with floats and clowns, with grand-mothers carrying flowers, babies in their arms, followed by all the girls and maidens dressed up in pretty costumes, followed by a corps of trained fairies to rush up and pull down the Hell's Angels' pants and blow them on the spot if they gave any trouble, followed by a big float showing Lyndon Johnson with his pants down or something, naked virgins and beautiful boys advertising peace with flower garlands, big papier-mâché caricatures of the war, floats which would dramatize the issues: a half-naked Vietnamese girl attacked by American soldiers all dressed up in robotic battle gear; airplanes, gaily painted dummy bombs—make a Max Reinhardt spectacle, Fritz Lang's *Metropolis*–inspired perhaps—Charlie Chaplin! Have someone disguised as W. C. Fields in the march, people dressed up as George Washington, and incense sticks in everybody's hands, harmonicas and guitars and funny poetic signs. Poetry March! I think probably the majority favored that attitude, a minority was noisy, at the end they voted a modified form of "manifestation": invite everybody to a community march.

Also, before the march there was another grand meeting with the

Hell's Angels. It was at Sonny Barger's house. Now, the Angels'd threatened to come out and beat up the marchers if they marched. Kesey made a date to have a party at Barger's house and also discuss political social community developments with the Berkeley student movement. And so Cassady, myself, Kesey and several of Kesey's Prankster friends gathered together with about twenty Hell's Angels at Barger's house with his wife, in Oakland, and all dropped acid—except me. I was having bad trips and I didn't want to lay my bad trip on myself or anyone, not under those circumstances. I was scared, but they were all gung-ho for it. I brought along my harmonium and everybody was in a relatively excited state. The house interior was like some strange giant puppet theater, the Pranksters in the strange Prankster costumes and Angels in their Angel costumes. We did finally get into a discussion of what to do about the march and I was trying to discourage Barger from attacking; so was Kesey, very manfully, trying to talk sense to Barger. He told Barger that it wasn't really a communist plot, the main thing that he kept telling him was that it wasn't *just* communists. The Angels' argument was we gotta fight 'em here or there. Our argument was we don't have to fight them anywhere; why fight at all? We went over there—Americans invaded there, they hadn't invaded us. There's no point in picking a fight on their territory or turf.

And it was beginning to get a little acrimonious because it was somewhat blocked, although I think Kesey was making sense to them. He was succeeding, but there was still a great deal of resistance. So I pulled out my harmonium and began chanting the *Maha Prajnaparamita Sutra,* which is a text basic to both Tibetan and Zen Buddhism ("Highest Perfect Wisdom" Sutra).

So I started chanting the *Prajnaparamita Sutra,* which was not an argument, simply a tone of voice from the abdomen. I kept up this monosyllabic deep-voiced monochordal chant for a few minutes, and pretty soon Tiny joined us. I was sitting on the floor playing my harmonium and chanting, and Tiny joined me and began going, "Om, om, zoom, zoom, zoom, om." Pretty soon we had a gang of about twenty people and then Neal and I think Kesey joined in—pretty soon the whole room was chanting. It brought the whole scene down from the argument to some kind of common tone—because they were desperate too. They were just arguing because they were desperate; they didn't know what else to do except argue and maintain their righteous wrath. It settled everybody's breath there in a neutral territory where there was neither attack nor defense.

I was absolutely astounded, I knew it was history being made. It was the first time in a tense, tight situation that I relied totally on pure mantric vocalization, breath-chant, to alleviate my own paranoia and anxiety, resolve it through breathing out long breaths. Well, the upshot was that several days later the Angels issued their newspaper edict, saying that it would *demean* them to attack the filthy marchers, they wouldn't touch 'em with a ten-foot pole, dirty communists. They sent a telegram to Lyndon Johnson offering to fight against the commies in Vietnam and offering themselves as G-O-R-I-L-L-A soldiers, they spelled it in the telegram, printed in the *S.F. Examiner*—it was funny because the last publicity image the conservative, middle-class pro-war right wing wanted was the Hell's Angels as a bunch of gorilla allies: it showed up the bestial nature of the war, to begin with. Also it resolved the temporary march situation and it also saved face for the Angels! Their cover story was that the marchers were too icky to attack. That "happy ending" came mostly from Ken Kesey's statesmanship and his common sense, because he'd been the one enlightened person on the scene—he wasn't on the left or right. Instead of banning and denouncing the "outlaw" Angels, he socialized with them and let a little light into the scene.

It was December then, and Dylan came to town for his West Coast tour. I saw a lot of him, and he gave me thirty or forty tickets for opening night. A fantastic assemblage occupied the first few rows of Dylan's concert: a dozen poets, myself, Peter, Ferlinghetti, Neal, and I think Kesey, Michael McClure; several Buddhists; a whole corps of Hell's Angels, led by Sonny Barger, Freewheelin' Frank and Tiny; and then came Jerry Rubin with a bunch of peace protesters. Fantastic.

Afterwards, I took Barger, McClure and several Angels to Dylan's dressing room. Barger pulled a joint out of a cellophane bag of forty to offer Dylan, but Dylan wouldn't mess with it. Then he got into a very funny conversation with Barger, saying something like "Look, you guys got something to say, don't you? You want to talk to the people, saying something to the nation? Well, what's your act? Why don't you come to New York and we'll put you on at Carnegie Hall. But you gotta get your show together, get your shit together. Do you have any songs? Can you recite poetry? Can you talk? If you want to extend yourselves, you can't make it by hanging around Oakland beating up on your own image."

They were stunned or stoned, but at the same time they realized that they had nothing to say, or else if they did, they hadn't found the right theater. And we'd had the same realization: our march had to get its theater together, just as the police and the government did. I think that was the beginning of our realization that national politics was theater on a vast scale, with scripts, timing, sound systems. Whose theater would attract the most customers, whose was a theater of ideas that could be gotten across?

Dylan was in town during the debates about the march, so I told Dylan about this, you know, all the scenes I'd seen and what was going on, and he thought; then he said Jerry Rubin had sent a message to him, would he join the march, lead the march? He wanted Dylan to lead the march, and they were still arguing whether it would be an angry chain march or what.

So Dylan said, okay—paraphrase—"Except we ought to have it in San Francisco right on Nob Hill where I have my concert, and I'll get a whole bunch of trucks and picket signs—some of the signs will be bland and some of them have lemons painted on them and some of them are watermelon pictures, bananas, others will have the word Orange or Automobile or the words Venetian Blind, I'll pay for the trucks and I'll get it all together and I'll be there, and we'll have a little march for the peace demonstration. What they're doing is too obvious, it's a bad show, chickenshit poetry, they don't know what the kids want, who's their public?" His image was undercurrent, underground, unconscious in people . . . something a little more mysterious, poetic, a little more Dada, more where people's hearts and heads actually were rather than where they "should be" according to some ideological angry theory.

So I reported Dylan's ideas back to Jerry Rubin and the Vietnam Day Committee marchers, and they didn't act on it, they didn't realize what was being offered them on a silver platter. I think Dylan offered it somewhat ironically, but I think he would have gone through with it. I think he was *interested,* he wanted to do *something,* but the terms of the march were too negative, not good enough theater, not even effective as propaganda, it never would have penetrated through to the young kids who didn't want to get involved in a crazed anger march.

And that always was the trouble with the marchers, before and after. There was too much anger marching, we'll come to more sublime calm theater in the next decade.

WRITTEN: 1977

Unpublished.

The Fall of America Wins an Award

EDITOR'S NOTE: This was Ginsberg's acceptance speech for the National Book Award in Poetry. It was delivered by Peter Orlovsky at Alice Tulley Hall, Lincoln Center, New York, on April 18, 1974.

Poem book *Fall of America* is time capsule of personal national consciousness during American war-decay recorded 1965 to 1971. It includes one prophetic fragment, written on speakers platform of May 9, 1970, Washington DC Peace Protest Mobilization:

> White sunshine on sweating skulls
> Washington's Monument pyramided high granite clouds
> over a soul mass, children screaming in their brains on quiet
>   grass
> (black man strapped hanging in blue denims from an earth
>   cross)—
> Soul brightness under blue sky
> Assembled before White House filled with mustached
>   Germans
> and police buttons, army telephones, CIA buzzers, FBI bugs
> Secret Service walkie-talkies, Intercom Squawkers to Narco
> Fuzz and Florida Mafia Real Estate Speculators.
> One hundred thousand bodies naked before an Iron Robot
> Nixon's brain Presidential cranium case spying thru binoculars
> from the Paranoia Smog Factory's East Wing.

Book here honored with public prize, best proclaim further prophetic foreboding that our United States is now the fabled "damned of nations" foretold by Walt Whitman a hundred years ago. The materialist brutality we have forced on ourselves and world is irrevocably visible in dictatorships our government has established thru South and Central America, including deliberate wreckage of Chilean democracy. From Greece to Persia we have established police states, and throughout Indochina wreaked criminal mass murder on millions, subsidized opium dealing, destroyed land itself, imposed military tyranny both openly and secretly in Cambodia, Vietnam, and Thailand.

Our quote "defense of the free world" is an aggressive hypocrisy that has damaged the very planet's chance of survival. Now we have spent thousands of billions on offensive war in decades, and half the world is starving for food. The reckoning has come now for America. $100 billion goes to the War Department this year out of $300 billion budget. Our militarization has become so top heavy that there is no turning back from military tyranny. Police agencies have become so vast—National Security Agency alone the largest police bureaucracy in America yet its activities are almost unknown to all of us—that there is no turning back from computerized police state control of America.

Watergate is a froth on the swamp: impeachment of a living president does not remove the hundred billion power of the military nor the secret billion power of the police state apparatus. Any president who would try to curb power of the military-police would be ruined or murdered.

So I take this occasion of publicity to call out the fact: our military has practiced subversion of popular will abroad and can do so here if challenged, create situations of chaos, take over the nation by military coup, and proclaim itself guardian over public order. And our vast police networks can, as they have in last decade, enforce that will on public and poet alike.

We have all contributed to this debacle with our aggression and self-righteousness, including myself. There is no longer any hope for the salvation of America proclaimed by Jack Kerouac and others of our Beat Generation, aware and howling, weeping and singing *Kaddish* for the nation decades ago, "rejected yet confessing out the soul." All we have to work from now is the vast empty quiet space of our own consciousness. AH! AH! AH!

WRITTEN: April 17, 1974

FIRST PUBLISHED: Allen Ginsberg, *The Fall of America Wins a Prize* (New York: Gotham Book Mart, 1974).

Nuts to Plutonium!

by Allen Ginsberg and Col. Sutton Smith[6]

Albeit political and social projections change year by year, I still form public theories. The 10,000 things of the present world appear as follows:

The interesting characteristic of fellows I imitate has one theme, a generous hopelessness of view, close to Rimbaud's despair, "The world marches forward! why doesn't it turn around? . . . Slaves, let's not curse life!" I've heard Burroughs say the "world problem" was hopeless overpopulation, and sex addiction was a disease virus, curable only by the classic remedies: plague, war and starvation. Thus his recently finished magnum opus of the '70s, the novel *Cities of the Red Night*, features a plague in which the red-buttocked citizens die in frenzies of orgasmic delight, policed by an army of junkies who alone are immune to the sex virus.

Gary Snyder speculates that Earth can support only a tenth of its present human population without disturbing the long-evolved balance of eco and atmosphere systems. Thus he practices meditation and right labor cultivation of woods in his particular Sierra locale.

Chögyam Trungpa's Vajrayana system applies specifically to those who have escaped the world's rage, and abandoned common "social" worlds as lost in samsaric[7] passion aggression and ignorance. This Tibetan-style Buddhist practice is a bodhisattvic[8] candle in the world's darkness; but redeeming the world in its own terms, or present American terms, is a lost cause. I agree with these views; the saving grace, as Kerouac said, is that "it doesn't matter" and any sensible secret soul would agree; there's no Soul anyway, all you have to do is read Dostoyevsky. Free from hope and fear, the great liberation doesn't deny our delight in the "sticky little leaves of spring," a green insight that once saved the despairing hero of a Russian novel. This "Hopelessness" is not the same as pathogenic despair, it means freedom from egocentric preconception.

The social thinker Timothy Leary, oddly in concord with the above sages, wants to get off the ruined eggshell of earth in an immortal sperm ship through Heaven.

Regarding Flower Power of the '60s in perspective after a decade, understanding emerges. If Flower Power's interpreted not as emotion or "idiot sentimentality," but as reference to green millennial agronomic stability, it makes enduring sense. Many folk emerged from the spiritually politicized sixties with a doubt of their own sense and nature's sense, internalizing the FBI-CIA-Time-Life Luce-Army Intelligence "primitive view of reality" as containing Original Sin, some ineradicable evil as an eternal component of nature, human or floral. This is nonsense from the "soul-less" Buddhist point of view. How people were hypnotized into believing this ignorant nonsense is now a matter of public record with the release of U.S. police agency documents under the Freedom of Information Act. In sum, there *was* a vast bureaucratic conspiracy to brainwash the public left and right, separate the generations, project obnoxious images of youth, divide black and white citizens, abort and blackmail mental social leadership of black citizens, set blacks on each other, provoke whites to murderous confusion, confound honest media, infiltrate, prevaricate and spy on reformist multitudes, becloud understanding and community, and poison public consciousness. These generalizations are proved if one examines Xerox facsimiles of government intelligence documents, more extensive and detailed in paranoid system than most seekers ever guessed.

The notorious black-white split of the sixties was a workable neurotic situation resolvable in the natural course of mutual action, but the intervention of the FBI's Counterintelligence Program, and the CIA's Operation Chaos, among other army and navy secret plots, escalated the difficulties, magnified them to crisis, and orchestrated original community difficulties to unworkable cacophony for awhile. That paranoia between black and white activists is now somewhat dissipated. Same for other neurotic problems of aggression, passion and ignorance in the peace "movement." "Kill the Pigs" was also an FBI provocateur party line, as well as "lily-white honky middle-class intellectuals."

One freak fact turns to pleasant surprise. From the 10,000-page public file of CIA's LSD operation, MKULTRA,[9] it now appears that this astounding psychedelic catalyst to U.S. cultural revolution was launched inadvertently from 1953 on by CIA and army intelligence secret bungling experimenters. The CIA and army intelligence turned on more people (without telling them) in uncontrolled experiments than Timothy Leary ever did giving Cambridge adults psylocybin pills in their hands. Ken Kesey, myself and Peter Orlovsky among others were initiated to LSD in experiments at Stanford Institute of Mental Health. Unknown to us, these programs were secretly funded by army intelligence. Henry Luce himself had been turned on earlier to psychedelics by an intelligence-contractee doctor, and the comic history of the psychedelic soul-bomb followed due Karmic course. Six years later *Life* magazine's hysterical cover-slogan was "LSD—The Mind Drug That Got Out of Control." Out of *whose* control? Leary seems to have been a scapegoat for all these "respectable" controllers, government secret operators, horrified by what they half-realized *they themselves had let loose* in the early fifties. Delightful, poetic justice!

Early secret government experiments were bent on mind control, including development of involuntary amnesiac assassination personnel, and this Project ARTICHOKE[10] seems to me to symbolize the vast messianic FBI-CIA infiltration of media (newspapers movies cartoons television publishing) now evidenced in an increasing flood of Congressional committee reports, investigative researches, and Xeroxed FBI, CIA, and Narcotics Bureau files now available to public eye in various open libraries.

Many of these themes converge in the nuclear energy debate now prominent in public argument. As Marxists observe the means of production determining cultural superstructure, so the great ENERGY argument may be interpreted. If the energy is a centralized and poisonous nuclear base to our culture, a monolithic surveillance state will result. Unknown to the literate public in 1978, the Rockefeller Group, that "Black Hole in American Politics," is the largest single investor in nuclear fuels (as it had been in petrochemical economy). Thus Nelson Rockefeller is proposing a one hundred billion dollar government subsidy to his own failing "high-risk energy ventures" in the nuclear industry. (Charts and figures for 1976 are set forth in the unpublished text, *Nuclear Energy, Rockefeller, and Big Business,* by Peter Salmonson, Goddard College.)

What alternative energy technic would decentralize and democratize our civilization, encourage sanity? The best I've heard was proposed at a meeting with the late economist-philosopher Fritz Schumacher and representatives of New Alchemy, the astronaut Rusty Schweickart, the agropoet Peter Orlovsky, and others present with William I. Thompson at Lindisfarne Association in the stone heart of Manhattan, February, 1977.

Schumacher said his "Bible" was a book he'd read, written in 1929 by J. Russell Smith, *Tree Crops, A Permanent Agriculture* (reissued by the Devin

Adair Co., Old Greenwich, 1977). The book proposed renewable protein and energy source through massive tree crop agriculture. Nature
should be brought into the cities, and the cities brought into production, Schumacher said, through universal tree rows on streets, rather
than cities abandoned in a "return to nature." Nut trees should be
grafted to produce "genius walnut" varieties, among others (a much
neglected area of research and development). Hill soil above 15-degree
angle shouldn't be ploughed, it leads to erosion but is proper for "three-
dimensional" tree agriculture. The tree is "the most efficient form of
solar collector ever developed." Energy, stewardship, food protein, fuel
alcohol and beauty were obvious advantages. Labor-intensive recycling
of city wastes can provide appropriate compost immediately available,
thus resolving problems of garbage, anomie, unemployment, alienation
and hunger. In Western man's earliest written epic, the hero Gilgamesh,
"builder of cities and walls" had killed the forest god in his journey to
visit the Land of the Dead and regain company of his lover Enkidu, now
covered with dust. This myth of "inappropriate technology" accounts for
the decertification of many old and new civilizations. Schumacher
added that J. Russell Smith's main ideas would be found in the first thirty
pages of his book, helpfully, for the benefit of contemporary speed-read-
ing death-defying Westerners.

Given the vast unemployment and city illiteracy in America at the
end of the '70s decade, tree-crop agriculture can provide productive
employment for metropolitan multitudes as well as for uneconomic
small-farm country citizens repelled or unemployable by soil-killing
petrochemical agribusiness. Where would the money come from to subsidize such a national Civilian Conservation and Production Corps?
Switch Rockefeller's proposal for one hundred billion dollars for "high-
risk energy ventures" from nuclear to tree crop energy base, and money
will be found where it was to be found, in the public treasury, with the
additional advantage that this less risky venture applied to peaceable
industriousness can create more jobs than the famously electric-inten-
sive low labor-intensive nuclear industry can provide.

What of the dangers of a welfare state? Is employing the populace in
decentralized labor-intensive handy production any more welfare state
than subsidizing elitist petrochemical and nuclear industries, or military
corps? Citizen's welfare state versus Capitalists' welfare state? Agronomic
welfare state encourages people to work in infinitely variable "ecological

shelves," and doesn't concentrate bureaucratic power in centralized and monolithic military-style power centers. The objection to welfare state was begun as an objection to laziness, paper shuffling, and government police bureaucracy, drags which a nuclear-energy state requires.

While cleaning air over cities, we can encourage street stewardship in tree care activity, beautifying urbs, suburbs and countryside. Progress toward law and order in the cities would be near-completed by sending all junkies to doctors for maintenance treatment with more natural, less synthetic opiates, "medicalization" of the opiate problem. Shifting the vast parasitic and corrupted narcotics bureaucracy (a billion-a-year business at present) to planting tree crops would solve another unruly unemployment problem.

Flower Power versus Nuclear Power are alternative blueprints drawn by the nature of things for our civilization. The obstacle to steady-state of Edenic clarity of social air seems to be, as ever, ignorance (of means and ends), passion (for poisonous indigestible synthetic possessions) and aggression (to defend raw materials, territory, and markets, for petrochemical-nuclear economies). Granny wisdom both Marxist and Capitalist has defined foreign policy (imperium and war) as territorial struggle for raw materials and products. Such struggle is necessary only if one assumes a petrochemical and nuclear base for energy. Without that energy base specific, cause for imperial self-protection declines. Why fight over Iranian territory if the oil's no longer central as a power base? Philosophies and rationalizations for "defensive military might" atrophy as the material causes diminish.

Psychological inertia remains, the conditioned complex of indolence, fear, luxury and cultivated dependence on robot energy, anxiety over survival, un-disciplines characteristic of our long-developed petrochemical-nuclear addiction.

The speed-freak greedy psyche of the Industrial Revolution has its appropriate remedy in the slowdown, patience, generosity and clear-mindedness of meditation practice, which also works well in conjunction with tree cultivation, gathering of protein-rich crops, "appropriate technology," unharried right labor. I hope that Mobilization for Survival in the '80s decade will feature this means of pacific protest. Gary Snyder and a handful of friends began sitting meditation practice at the gates of the Oakland Army Terminal in 1965, when that facility was used to ship armaments to escalate the "serious" futile Indochinese war. On May 27, 1978 a phalanx of 40 experienced meditators manifested their individual awareness and concern at the U.N. disarmament session's popular Mobilization for Survival in a special area set for them by War Resister's League organizers. Those who wish to bring meditation practice to future assemblies, and call mindfulness to the occasion, should bring pillows or blankets to cushion the concrete.

2

Submitting this plan to an old gentleman in Boulder sitting on a park bench with his cane, the familiar Col. Sutton Smith, I noted these comments: "Trouble with this is there's no one to implement it. Now we're ruled by people whose hands are tied, nothing's going to be done. It's hopeless because it's been *made* hopeless . . . They tie their own hands . . . the whole fucking bureaucratic system. They're all a bunch of worthless shits. Maybe they need someone like Hitler: the leader principle, one person in power to *do* something . . . You can't take a hopeless situation and say what you are going to do with it . . . Democracy is a farce, nobody asked us about the atom bomb, they just dropped it without telling anybody. What we've got is a fucking bureaucracy, all they want is to keep their jobs.

"Where are we going now? We're going nowhere. Can anyone get a job done in this mess? No! Not without firing a lot of lazy sons-of-bitches . . . the whole Narc thing. Give heroin to addicts and appropriate money for research into endorphin . . . cures . . .

"Faced by a situation like that, what can a person do? Nothing . . . If a flying saucer came I'd get in and say, 'Let me out of this whole fucking solar system!'

"Any bad situation just gets worse and worse and worse. That's the way the planet's going—worse and worse and worse—unless something drastic is done and nobody's in a position to do anything drastic. We're just a tiny minority of privileged people sitting here in comfort on sufferance . . . and we don't have any power—I don't foresee anything except that things get worse.

"This stupid proliferation principle—as if we needed more people to sell products to. The whole goddamn thing started with the Industrial

Revolution: the more people the better to buy your fucking soap . . . It's all based on quantitative money, you can't have too many people if you're selling toothpaste or soap.

"Protect Sentient Beings? We don't want any more beings now, we got too many beings, we don't *want* any more. Of course the Pope is there: 'You can't deny people the right to the banquet of life.' What does that banquet consist of? A banquet of radioactive garbage . . . a sort of phosphorescent blue metallic gunk in troughs . . . Quite suddenly you reach a saturation point . . . There's nobody to implement anything. I've got to a point where I just don't give a shit. If there's nothing going to be done, why bother?"

I questioned the irritable old gent further: "Your message seems to be, we need less bureaucracy not more. Can you particularize on that?"

"Abolish the FDA![11] Consider the modest beginnings of this pestilential agency like a tiny wart that will grow into a ravening cancer. Now back in the good old days before addicts were criminals by act of Congress, folks was brewing up medicines in their attics and basements and selling them through the mail or any other way. Patent medicines. And they was making various curative devices like magnetic coils and brain breathing machines. So the fledgling FDA says that some of these preparations contain harmful ingredients like opium and any preparation sold to the public should have the contents stated on the bottle, and somebody has to make sure the stated contents are the actual contents, right? And people should not be allowed to make money selling worthless curative devices thus battening on their fellow creeps, right? Sounds reasonable, don't it? Starting with the hypocritical excuse of controlling and purifying the profit motive they became its most dedicated representative. Next step is the drug has to be tested before it is released to the public, that what we're here for is to protect the natives . . . To protect the public interests . . . Alright, here is a young medical student back in the '40s, he's read the early experiments with mold for infections. Working in his basement laboratory he comes up with penicillin . . . Millions and millions of lives there in that white powder he hopefully delivers to the FDA. Of course it has to be tested, you know. And these wondrous tests often take ten years, and this looks like a dangerous cure-all . . . He is an eccentric paranoid old man when they finally tell him that because of certain adverse effects on the animal experiments, the drug cannot be released. Later, of course, the big drug companies pick it up. The whole set-up is designed to protect the big drug companies from any basement lab competition or any medium-financed competition. You're going to start a drug company with $20,000,000 dollars like Tucker and his car that never got into production. All he had to face was General Motors and the other car gangs, and they broke him. Couldn't get materials, etc. You can't win against a stacked deck. And the drug company deck is double stacked by the big drug companies and their company cops, the FDA. Yes, that's exactly what those bastards are. Company cops."

WRITTEN: June 3, 1978

FIRST PUBLISHED: *CoEvolution Quarterly*, no. 19 (1978) pp. 13–19.

Introduction to "Smoking Typewriters"

What is now proved was once only imagined.
　　　　　　　—William Blake

The reader of this PEN[12] Freedom to Write Committee document on government harassment and attempted destruction of the underground press will glimpse only the top of the pile of press clippings, court records, word-of-mouth testimony and anecdote, vast rooms full of FBI files and congressional hearings, whole libraries that substantiate the cases cited, and document them hundred-fold in detail and gruesome effect.

Though the account compiles reliable data on harassment, arrests, beatings and jailings of journalist-citizens, trials and much waste of money on unconstitutional prosecution of workers in dissenting media, it should be clearly stated that not one agent of the government engaged in these nationwide criminal (legally illegal) activities has ever been punished by jail, and very few by prosecution. Two heads of the FBI involved with these nefarious terrorisms who were tried and convicted for only one obvious case of illegal surveillance among the many crimes committed (in this instance, harassment of ill-mannered Weathermen[13] groups) were immediately pardoned in 1981 by the very President whose conservative campaign philosophy promised to "get the government off our backs."

If the secret police bureaucracies of the government, illegally operating to torment and terrorize legal dissenters, are not precisely those bureaucrats who should be kept off our backs, then what is meant by this pious slogan? Our Bill of Rights was adopted to limit the pushiness of such police spies, government gossips, agents-provocateurs, kinky bureaucrats, and double agents who smoke pot and lush, scream "pig," and then try to frame idealistic citizens for the same crimes they are hired to commit. Such "COINTELPRO"[14] terrorism is, after all, an invention of the police in all countries, including U.S.A.

What ignorant hypocrisy has so reversed conventional usage that now citizenly Thoreauvian pacifism (i.e. nonviolent antinuclear action) has been called "terrorism" and actual government-inspired bombings, beatings, thievings and lies have been excused by the President of the U.S. as patriotic action "on high principle" in pursuit of government interest?

What hypocrisy this presidential actor dares display to large minority of affronted citizens. How many see thru this Orwellian twist of language that says "War is Peace"? Government terrorism is "Internal Security," and "Get the government off our backs" are buzzwords for increasing the military bureaucracy and for turning the government treasury into a pig's trough of military expenditures.

How dare the aboveground press of America allow this continuous hoax to maintain itself, like a public hallucination, a doublebind extreme enough to freak the entire nation into schizophrenic crime in the streets—one half of the brain screaming No More Government Interference in the Private Sector! and the other half yammering for More Military! More Electric Police! More Funds for the Pentagon's Brass Bands! The chutzpah of those scholars of war who chatter endlessly their priggish syntax in praise of a "free market" of goods and ideas! Half the national budget enslaves us for life behind the bureaucratic iron of a military industrial reformatory equipped with radioactive showers.

Who had the guts and courage to see this Imperial Roman fraud for what it was and protest out loud? The underground press among others. Who served it up in the language of the people, private news of civilization's waste, terrible news for youth, not "fit to print" in middle-class media that for generations had averted eyes from domestic race blood-shed, sex persecution, political persecution, eyes glazed over with American imperial murder in Latin America, yet hypnotized by Red imperial murder in Siberia? The underground press saw that much.

While J. Edgar Hoover denied for decades the existence of organized crime, he devoted the energies of his intelligence agency to eavesdropping on Martin Luther King, Jr.'s bedrooms and to myriad-paged surveillance of white Negro Abbie Hoffman's psycho-political gaga. This sex blackmailer and dryhanded public virgin was lunching secretly each week with the east coast spokesman for organized crime, Frank Costello, in N.Y. Central Park's Tavern on the Green (according to the *Time* magazine obituary).

Take a look at the documents reproduced in the PEN report—a plan to cut down the charismatic influence of black leaders and organizations including the Student Non-Violent Coordinating Committee and Nobel Peace Prizewinner Martin Luther King, Jr., a twelve-point plan to ridicule, misinform, blackmail, dissolve, destroy, discredit, infiltrate, jail and make ugly images of the bewildered New Left and its shoestring press. A plan to set black man against white man. After you have read these FBI documents you realize that all through the Sixties the notion of Race Separation and Race Nationalism—"Tough bad blacks can't work with punk liberal whites"—was escalated by FBI double agents and poison-pen letter-writers and orchestrated to produce national paranoia. What are we to say of these criminals paid by FBI, state and local Red Squads? What are we to say to their bewildered victims? Punk New Wave conservative alike, stereotyped as incapable of political action because they saw in the "friendly mass media" "obnoxious" photos of peace protesters? ("Naturally, the most obnoxious pictures should be used.")

What to say to the millions of blacks who've known all along—moaned and wept under the August 25, 1967 "COINTELPRO" plan to deprive them of their political consciousness, their constitutional rights of assembly, their press, and some of their leadership?

Why did the FBI lay off the Mafia and instead bust the alternative media, scapegoating poet LeRoi Jones, ganging up on Jane Fonda, Tom Hayden, Martin Luther King, Jr., anti-war hero Dave Dellinger, even putting me on a dangerous subversive internal security list in 1965—the same year I was kicked out of Havana and Prague for talking and chanting back to the "Communist" police?

"The fox condemns the trap, not himself," Blake wrote in *Proverbs of Hell*. Remember that Mr. Gallup, our national pollster, reported back in 1968 that the majority (52%) of the nation did feel that the Vietnam War "all along had been a mistake." This tipping of the national mind balance occurred just at the time U.S. police networks were teletyping out their August 5, 1968 grand master plan for counterintelligence to disrupt the New Left coalition and press opposed to an undeclared war—a war which ended exploding more bombweight than all previous modern wars and crippled Indochina for the rest of the twentieth century. Then America had its nervous breakdown, the 1970s.

If America goes more totalitarian (and we've got a good beginning, for a bunch of jerks who advertise ourselves as the "Free World"), won't it be because the media allowed sadistic police hypocrites to stink-bomb and beat up spokesmen for a majority of the U.S. populace?

Poet Robert Duncan observed that under the mask of American violence lies all the grief we feel for our "unacknowledged, unrepented crimes."

Slowly the poison the whole bloodstream fills;
The waste remains, the waste remains and kills.
—William Empson

This document can enlighten The Establishment in America as to a cause of its own grief. The federal, state, and local police bureaucracy censored the youthful frankness of the alternative press. William S. Burroughs (an American novelist widely published and interviewed for decades in the underground media) remarks: "What the American alternative press did in the 1960's under considerable pressure is of inestimable value. Many of the gains in freedom that we take for granted in the 1980's were won due, in great part, to the efforts of the alternative press—among others: 1. Ending the Vietnam War. 2. Decriminalization of marijuana. 3. Abolition of censorship. 4. Recognition (if not complete realization) of minority rights. Poets, writers, journalist, editors, and publishers—all did their work in a concerted effort." There was an international breakthrough of cultural insight in the '60s that amounted to a world revelation. The "Youth Movement" came out on the streets not only in New York, Chicago, and San Francisco but also in Singapore, Budapest, Belgrade, Paris, London, in cities on both sides of the Iron Curtain.

A 1984 American generation may glimpse here the trauma and jail-helplessness, the unconscious blood-fear they've inherited, that's hexed many a mouth to imitate the same bland singing-in-the-dark doubletalk they hear on commercial television in the course of being sold more gasoline war.

WRITTEN: June 17, 1981

FIRST PUBLISHED: Geoffrey Rips, ed., *The Campaign Against the Underground Press* (San Francisco: City Lights, 1981).

AUTHOR'S NOTE: Special thanks to Attorney Ira M. Lowe, Esq., for his prophetic accuracy in legal pursuit of literally related Freedom of Information Act files thru all secret branches of the government.

Outline of Un-American Activities

A PEN American Center Report

What I would like to report concerns the harassment and sabotage of the underground press in the United States during the years 1968 to 1972, and up to the present, by the FBI, the CIA, the army intelligence, Narcotics Bureau agents, the state police and local police, local red squads. Around 1968 there was a large movement of underground intel-lectuality, and there was an enormous press: 400 to 500 newspapers scat-tered all over the country from Florida to San Francisco to New York, and in Canada also. Some really great newspapers, the *Georgia Strait,* and the Montreal *Logos,* which was one of the most beautifully printed. It was obvious to anybody who was involved with the underground press that there was also a large-scale campaign of harassment, a government con-spiracy to suppress the alternative media. And so as a member of the New York Chapter of PEN—I am a member of the Freedom to Write Committee from the mid-sixties—I asked for authority to begin assem-bling information on the harassment of the underground press by the FBI and other agencies.

I began collecting newspaper clippings, anecdotes, copies of the underground press that were busted, larger-scale surveys from the University of Missouri journalism school. I interviewed a lot of people and circulated an open letter asking for information to be sent to the PEN Club through the Coordinating Council of Literary Magazines. So actually there was a network to receive information, and one central place to get it. The book called *Un-American Activities: PEN American Center Report: Campaign Against the Underground Press* is primarily a white paper by the PEN Club; it has that weight and authority.

The reason PEN was interested was that the underground press, of course, is writing, but the underground media in America serve as a vehicle for avant-garde literature as well. Amiri Baraka published a great deal, and was also under attack by the FBI, both in his print and in his person. Charles Bukowski first published in the underground press; he is not perhaps so well known here, but is a giant literary hero in Italy and in Germany. William S. Burroughs was first interviewed extensively in the New York *Rat* by Jeff Shero (later known as Jeff Nightbyrd) who, having been driven out of New York by the FBI, founded the Austin [TX] *Rag*. Gregory Corso published in the underground press, I published extensively, both poems and prose, Norman Mailer published in the alternative media. And Ed Sanders, who had earlier had the rock 'n' roll group The Fugs, edited and published in the underground press. So actually, there was a large-scale literary movement representing subculture, or what was called "alternative culture."

What we found when we actually surveyed the field and took individual case histories and compiled and compared them was that there *was* a systematic campaign of harassment, though it needed very little encouragement, because J. Edgar Hoover (FBI Chief) already was willing to use force and violence and subterfuge and illegality to stamp out what he thought were un-American opinions.

The methods were as follows.

First, there was harassment of distributors. The distributor for the New York *Rat* was called into the FBI and told it was a subversive newspaper and that he would be in trouble if he kept distributing. So distribution was curtailed. That was one example; it happened all over the country.

There was harassment of printers. A fellow in Milwaukee who printed underground newspapers for the entire Midwest was constantly harassed by the FBI. They would also call up his above-ground clients and send anonymous letters to them, forcing him to move from city to city to continue printing. He held out, and finally, years later, there was a long exposé in a bunch of magazines, because his case was so singular and the harassment had been so official and so blatant.

There was harassment of vendors in almost every city. While regular newsboys were selling newspapers on the street corners, stands where the underground newspapers were distributed were seized. Vendors were arrested on charges of distributing obscenity or vending without a license or blocking traffic. In no case were any of these vendors ever convicted of anything, but it was a harassment by constant arrests.

Then there was harassment of publishers. Older people in the community who were publishing the newspapers would be the subject of anonymous letters written to fellow businessmen, chambers of commerce, university trustees, parents, city councils. Usually they were signed "An Outraged Taxpayer" or "An Outraged Citizen" or "An Outraged Alumnus" or whatever. And these outraged alumni, citizens, taxpayers, were a stereotype for a sneaky FBI agent, on government time, with government money, writing poison-pen letters.

Harassment of advertisers was another technique—poison-pen letters written by an annoyed or "anguished citizen," or "outraged taxpayer," to advertisers to discourage them from contributing to the underground press coffers. Or FBI agents would simply visit an advertiser and say that it was acting un-American by supporting the Milwaukee *Sentinel,* or the Atlanta underground newspaper, which had the most brilliant title of all: *Great Speckled Bird.*

There were FBI conversations with trustees and presidents of colleges, urging the college to ban the distribution of such smut and un-American matter as was supposed to pervade the underground newspaper. So there was a constant battle, especially in Austin, Texas, to get student rights to read the newspapers and have them circulated along with *Playboy* and the *National Enquirer,* which were left alone.

Then there were constant prosecutions by local prosecutors, very often instigated by the FBI, for obscenity. Since there was a breakdown of old-fashioned obscenity laws to admit the literature of Jean Genet, William Burroughs, myself, Henry Miller, Lord Rochester, D. H. Lawrence, and other authors, by the late sixties, porn satire had become a funny kind of underground joke and language. Samples of that were constantly seized and the newspapers were prosecuted, including a lot of Canadian underground newspapers, specifically *Georgia Strait,* which went through *enormous* problems with that kind of censorship. Once some copies of *Logos* from Montreal had been sent to me in New York. I was so pleased with them, I brought them when I went to Canada, and they were seized by Canadian customs for obscenity. That was one of the major ways of persecuting the underground press. Very few convictions resulted—I don't know of any long-term convictions that held—it was just a method of harassment and also of draining the finances of the newspapers, because they were shoestring enterprises in any case. An obscenity accusation could involve getting lawyers, getting involved with litigation, with evidence, having to look up all the old obscenity laws, maybe even printing long articles about it in the newspaper, which then would be busted again as a sort of feedback.

A major way of harassing the underground newspapers was on drug charges. Very often the Narcotics Bureau would send an agent provocateur to hang around and inveigle everybody into giving him pot or smoking his pot or buying pot from him or selling him pot. If they couldn't, they would hide pot in a typewriter drawer, and then that night raid the office, seize all the files, destroy all the machinery, take everybody down to jail, and ultimately the government would lose their case, because it was generally a setup.

There was sabotage of the large-scale news services—Liberation News Service and the United Press Syndicate (the UPI and AP—of the underground network) in the late sixties and early seventies. They would be raided for either drugs or obscenity or conspiracy, and files would be taken, machines would be destroyed, legal papers taken. The late Tom Fourcade of the United Press Syndicate told me that back in '69 in the Midwest, where UPS had its office at the time, they were raided by the local police and the files they had kept on the harassment of the underground press were seized. So a huge body of evidence on harassment of the underground press from 1965 to 1969 was destroyed by the police. He said that there were about four hundred underground newspapers, and that 60 per cent of them had been sabotaged or harassed or busted illegally or framed, or the vendors intimidated or publishers intimidated or printers intimidated or distributors intimidated. Or *landlords* intimidated. That was another way of dealing with the underground press: the FBI would visit the landlord and say, "You got a subversive newspaper here, and you'd better make them move, or *raise their rent*." That happened in a number of cases—San Diego, Ann Arbor, New York, and Austin, Texas.

A major way of harassment was, as I mentioned, the use of spies. Their role would be to incite violence, to write excessively nutty, violent copy so that everybody was offended, to delay business, and editorial conferences with all sorts of left-wing harangues—"Bring the War Home," "anybody who isn't as revolutionary as we are is a petit bourgeois white honky creep"—or just to act stupid and clog the pipelines of intelligence, so that a lot of editorial meetings were hung up for hours on minor ideological debates instigated by FBI agents chosen for their familiarity with left-wing competitions and animosities, and encouraged to escalate animosities between left groups as much as possible. That was one of the major techniques: to take advantage of the already existing arguments and escalate them to a point where nobody would be talking to each other.

There was *dis*information spread by the FBI. An underground newspaper would be called and told that a march called for noon was really scheduled in a different place at 5 P.M.

There were midnight raids, both by the FBI and local police, *and* by vigilante groups ostensibly unconnected with the government but secretly paid, or armed, or working in close cooperation with FBI or local red squads. That involved bombings—fire bombings as well as auto bombings. It involved destruction of machinery—typewriters, typesetting machinery—desks, lists of subscribers, lists of contributors, thefts of lists or burning of lists of all kinds.

One constant practice was the theft of legal papers, as with the United Press Syndicate. During the Chicago Seven Trial, both newspaper and lawyers' offices were burgled by vigilante groups actually working with Chicago police. Legal papers pertaining to the trial were stolen by the vigilante groups, passed on to army intelligence, and then to the local D.A.s in Chicago.

There were wiretaps, that was customary; there was harassment of subscribers, that was customary; there were threats of bombs when there were no actual bombs. There were conspiracy charges formulated and brought into court. One group, the Juche Cooperative which worked a great deal with Denise Levertov, the poet, in Cambridge, was actually set up on a charge of armed conspiracy to start a revolution because they found guns in the house. The case was ultimately dismissed because there was a license for the guns, which had been purchased by the Juche people to defend themselves against vigilante and Nazi threats that had been pouring into the office with the collaboration of the local cops. There were physical assaults: cop cars pulling up to a vendor or a reporter and cops threatening to beat him up or actually beating him up. There were insults, which may be ultimately the most mentally violent form of harassment: the distribution of obnoxious photographs and satirical cartoons by the FBI, making fun, satirizing the people involved with the alternative media.

Those are the generalizations. To back them up, what I'd like to do is 1) print one FBI directive, which will give you the whole master plan by the FBI against the entire underground movement of newspapers, and 2) give a few anecdotes about situations where I was involved.

The twelve-point master plan was issued July 5, 1968, just before Nixon was elected, or around the time of the Chicago Convention and the mass protest there. It was from the director of the FBI; this copy to the FBI office in Albany, New York, with a footnote: "This to all field officers," which means all the officers all over the country.

Counterintelligence Program Internal Security Disruption of the New Left

Bulletin of May 10/68 requested suggestions for counterintelligence action against the New Left. The replies to the Bureau's request have been analyzed and it is felt that the following suggestions for counterintelligence action can be utilized by all offices.

1: Preparation of a leaflet designed to counteract the impression that Students for a Democratic Society and other minority groups speak for the majority of the students at universities. The leaflet should contain photographs of New Left leadership at the respective university. Naturally, the most obnoxious pictures should be used.

2: The instigating of or the taking advantage of personal conflicts or animosities existing between New Left leaders.

3: The creating of impressions that certain New Left leaders are *informants for the Bureau* or other law enforcement agencies.

4: The use of articles from student newspapers and/or the "underground press" to show the depravity of New Left leaders and members. In this connection, articles showing advocacy of the use of narcotics and free sex are ideal to send to university officials, wealthy donors, members of the legislature and *parents* of students who are active in New Left matters. (*So this is not only interfering with free speech, but interposing government obnoxiousness between father and son, mother and daughter. Actually interfering with family life.*—A.G.)

5: Since the use of marijuana and other narcotics is widespread among members of the New Left, you should be alert to opportunities to have them arrested by local authorities on drug charges. Any information concerning the fact that individuals have marijuana or are engaging in a narcotics party should be immediately furnished to the local authorities and they should be encouraged to take action.

6: The drawing up of anonymous letters regarding individuals active in the New Left. These letters should set out their activities and should be sent to their parents, neighbors, *and* the parents' employers. This could have the effect of forcing the parents to take action. (*Heartless, I'd say, that one.*—A.G.)

7: Anonymous letters or leaflets describing faculty members and graduate assistants in the various institutions of higher learning who are active in New Left matters. The activities and associations of the individual should be set out. Anonymous mailings should be made to university officials, members of the state legislature, Board of Regents, and to the press. Such letters could be signed "A Concerned Alumnus," or "A Concerned Taxpayer."

8: Whenever New Left groups engage in disruptive activities on college campuses, *cooperative press contacts* should be encouraged to emphasize that the disruptive elements constitute a minority of the students and do not represent the conviction of the majority. The press should demand an immediate student referendum on the issue in question.

9: There is a definite hostility among SDS and other New Left groups towards the Socialist Workers Party (SWP), Young Socialist Alliance (YSA), and the Progressive Labor Party (PLP). This hostility should be exploited whenever possible.

10: The field was previously advised that New Left groups are attempting to open coffeehouses near military bases in order to influence members of the Armed Forces. Wherever these coffeehouses are, *friendly news media* should be alerted to them and their purpose. In addition, various drugs, such as marijuana, will probably be utilized by individuals running the coffeehouses or frequenting them. Local law enforcement authorities should be promptly advised whenever you receive an indication that this is being done.

   (*And this is the one that I think was actually the most effective, in terms of intellectual or emotional or* propagandist *counterattack—this next point is what has settled in on the somewhat traumatized college era of the seventies and driven them a little bit off any participation in political activity.*—A.G.)

11: Consider the use of cartoons, photographs, and anonymous letters which will have the effect of ridiculing the New Left. Ridicule is one of the most potent weapons which we can use against it. (*Very intelligent. And it's also a method used in Germany on the Jews and used in communist countries on dissidents.*—A.G.)

12: Be alert for opportunities to confuse and disrupt New Left activities by misinformation. For example, when events are planned, notification that the event has been canceled or postponed could be sent to various individuals. (*The final comment:*—A.G.) You are reminded that no counterintelligence action is to be taken without Bureau approval. Ensure (*and William Burroughs liked these next sentences as being inspired Burroughsian, Swiftian comment*—A.G.) that this program is assigned to an agent with an excellent knowledge of both New Left groups and individuals. It must be approached with imagination and enthusiasm if it is to be successful.

There was also, a year before, a directive about black nationalists, which said that "the purpose of this new counterintelligence endeavor is to expose, disrupt, misdirect, discredit, or otherwise neutralize the activities of black nationalist hate-type organizations and groupings, their leadership, spokesmen, membership and supporters, and to counter their propensity for violence and civil disorder." Among the groups that they were going to expose to this treatment were the Student

Non-Violent Coordinating Committee and the Southern Christian Leadership Conference. Those were groups that Martin Luther King worked with. At that time, J. Edgar Hoover was collecting as much obscene information as he could on Martin Luther King, including tapes of him making love in hotel rooms, and he tried to peddle it to UPI, the *New York Times,* the *Washington Post,* and so forth.

In Detroit there is a rock and jazz impresario named John Sinclair, who was a poet much beloved of Charles Olson. In 1965 we had a big poetry meeting in Berkeley, and Ed Sanders, Anne Waldman, and John Sinclair were invited specifically by Olson to represent the younger generation. Sinclair had an organization in Detroit called the Artists' Workshop, which published huge mimeographed volumes of local poetry, as well as pamphlets by correspondents. He put out a long anticommunist manifesto (*Prose Contribution to Cuban Revolution*) that I wrote in 1960 about the Cuban Revolution, a sort of challenge to the spiritual foundations of it saying that it was too materialist. So he wasn't exactly a riotous red. His main thing though, his main "schtick," so to speak, was uniting black and white in the otherwise tense, riot-torn areas of Detroit, through the Artists' Workshop, because there was collaboration between black jazz musicians and white jazz musicians, black writers and white writers, black poets and white poets. It was a kind of heroic effort, actually. He had a newspaper, and after a while he had a thing called the White Panther party, sort of in collaboration with the Black Panthers, or in defense of the Black Panthers, who were also being subjected to this kind of double-dealing and harassment by the government.

So the narcotics police sent in a young married couple to hang around with John Sinclair and wash his dishes and do mimeographing and distribute papers, and they were constantly harassing him: would he please give them a joint, would he give them some grass? Which he didn't do, fortunately, for a long long while. Finally, one late night, they were really on his back to give them some grass, so he gave them a stick of marijuana. He was busted several weeks later, set up for a long trial, had to pay a lot of money for that, was convicted of peddling marijuana, and sentenced to nine and a half to ten years. Of which he spent several years in the federal penitentiary in Marquette. That was an FBI attempt to silence a dissenter and a poet. In jail he wrote a really interesting poem. He said, "My books wait for me on the shelf, myself, my typewriter sits empty, urging me onward. Nine and a half to ten years is not enough!" So actually, he was a sharp poet. And a worthy citizen. He's now the chief impresario of black and white jazz in Detroit, and has rock 'n' roll, jazz, and old blues concerts.

Yoko Ono and John Lennon, working with Jerry Rubin at the time, 1969 to 1971, decided that they would go on a tour of all the persecuted areas, the hot spots as they called them: to visit Lee Otis Johnson, who was in jail in Texas for thirty years for a joint, John Sinclair, Angela Davis, and others. So they formed a giant touring group and went to Ann Arbor, where they had a giant Free John Sinclair concert while he was still in jail. They had Phil Ochs, myself, Ed Sanders, Anne Waldman, reading poetry; they had John Lennon and the New York Street Band and Yoko Ono to sing; they had limousines—all the luxury of rock 'n' roll turned to political agitation, propaganda, entertainment, education, illumination. They had an itinerary: they were going to wind up in 1972 at the Republican Convention in Miami. So the concert was actually a very powerful political gesture. Based on pacifism, actually, that being Lennon's and Yoko Ono's obvious bent. It might have resulted in enormous cultural changes, a sort of cultural revolutionary shot. The consequence for Lennon was that the FBI and Immigration and the Narcotics Bureau got together to try and expel him from the country. Lennon—and Yoko Ono, who was a citizen—had to drop their whole political campaign, not go to Angela Davis' trial; not go to Lee Otis Johnson's domain in Texas. As for John Sinclair—the concert was on a Friday night. By that Monday, the state legislature had altered the draconian law of "ten years for one joint," and John Sinclair was out of jail by that Monday. So it was actually an effective cultural-political instrument that they had devised. Aborted, then and there, by FBI and government conspiracy. Lennon was not, ultimately, deported, because the method for deporting him was that he had been busted in London on a pot charge, and the Sergeant Pilcher who busted him on the pot charge actually had planted the grass, and was himself later indicted for selling hashish. He was a celebrated narc in England who had busted Mick Jagger personally, as well as Lennon, as well as McCartney; he had some kind of love for the counterculture musicians and went around busting them for narcotics charges. There was actually a campaign against the Beatles in the United States, to make sure that every single one of them got busted on narcotics charges. I know, because a federal narcotics agent in New York tried to get someone to bring marijuana to my house to set me up for arrest, and this guy was asked did he know me, and did he know Ringo Starr? (Ringo Starr being the only Beatle that was never busted.)

The harassment and the busts of the Beatles and other rock 'n' roll candidates for immorality is paralleled in Czechoslovakia by the harassment of the Plastic People of the Universe, the great modern/new jazz/new rock 'n' roll/punk/new wave group, that was inspired by American contemporaries—Ed Sanders and the Fugs, and Frank Zappa and the Mothers of Invention, and Tuli Kupferberg. So on both sides of the Cold War, there seems to be a hatred of youth/music/speech.

Actually, I don't think the ruling elites hate each other as much as they hate their dissidents. They need each other in order to burgeon and prosper. When I was kicked out of Czechoslovakia in 1965, as I was on a security list, within a year there was an attempt to set me up for a marijuana bust. I went into Robert Kennedy's office, and also to my local congressman's office—Charles Jolson, from Paterson, New Jersey—and complained, and tried to put the heat back on them, and so got a little story in the *New York Times*[15] and *Washington Post* and *Life* magazine. My congressman wrote to the Narcotics Bureau asking them what kind of hanky-panky was going on? When I got my Freedom of Information Act papers several years ago, I found that they had translated a scurrilous article from the Prague youth newspaper accusing me of being a homosexual, a narcomane, and, in addition, an alcoholic! And had sent my congressman that information! So that the police bureaucracies both inside the socialist countries and in the capitalist countries use each other's material and use each other's scripts, and have a working relationship against the dissidents of both.

There was further complication in the John Sinclair case—which is a nexus in a way, because it was in the Ann Arbor-Detroit area, which was a center of underground, alternative, counterculture activity. An agent provocateur, who was a nut employed by the FBI, came to John Sinclair saying that he wanted to blow up the CIA office in Detroit. Sinclair said, "No, for the love of God, no! Out!" So the guy went and blew it up and then accused Sinclair of encouraging him to do it. Sinclair was indicted on a conspiracy charge; the main witness was the crazed agent provocateur. Sinclair obviously won the case, because it was flimsy, but it also occupied his time and legal attention, with William Kunstler and others, for many months—about a year and a half.

A further complication relating to Sinclair and this Detroit–Ann

Arbor nexus came from Washington. The antiwar mobilization was going to have a giant national meeting in Washington in the early seventies. All the different groups under the umbrella of the War Resisters' League would be there: pacifists, Trotskyites, women's groups, gay groups. But David Dellinger and others who were organizing the Mobilization in Washington were told by the Black United Front in Washington that, although they as middle-class liberal honkies thought that it was so important for them to gain their egos by going to Washington and demonstrating, it was going to create a lot of unsettlement in Washington among the black population, and those blacks were the leaders who were going to have to clean up their turf after them with the outraged police. So if the antiwar movement wanted to have its meeting, it should give the "just" contribution of twenty-five thousand dollars to the Black United Front in Washington to fee the grass-roots war, because that was where the war really was, not in Vietnam. As it turned out later, the spokesman for the Black United Front who wanted to do this was an FBI agent trying to harass the antiwar movement. As part of his maneuver, an anonymous letter was sent to the *Michigan Daily*, the Ann Arbor student newspaper, and to Black Panther leaders in Detroit, telling them to put pressure on John Sinclair and the White Panthers to put pressure on the white liberals in Ann Arbor that they should accede to this "just and honorable demand" from the Black United Front. The commentary under this FBI directive said: This will cause trouble between the White Panthers and the Black Panthers, as well as between the White Panthers and the liberals; will offend all the liberals; and will have the ultimate effect of putting the entire community into dispute with itself, as well as draining it financially.

Copies of these demands were sent to all radical groups and were printed in the *Michigan Daily* newspaper. Naturally, all the white liberals were either intimidated or astounded or put off; it caused a tremendous amount of controversy. And one of the centers that was used for dissemination of this kind of double-dealing was the *Michigan Daily* newspaper. In fact, the FBI directive said the *Michigan Daily* would be glad to print such a radical letter.

The result was that my dentist, a white liberal in Washington who worked with blacks, threw up his hands and said, "If the blacks in Washington are so nutty, how can we whites work with them, so I'm just dropping out of the whole problem of black-white relationships."

So, all within that one nexus of Ann Arbor you get a picture of FBI sabotage and disruption of race relations. Throughout the sixties the celebrated black-white paranoia was fanned by the FBI. And a lot of poison-pen letters were written by supposed blacks denouncing white participation in the black movement. For those of you who do remember the paranoia of the sixties between white and black, you should understand that though there may have been a seedbed for such a neurosis, its escalation into unworkable psychosis, miscommunication, and lack of direct face-to-face working it out, emotionally and intellectually, was the result of FBI manipulation. It was a large-scale thing, which still has a hangover: black and white are still afraid of each other on the political front because of that old trauma.

What was accomplished was simply a kind of discouragement, a duping, a hypnosis of a kind, of the general public, or the kids, who were told that they were "creepy jerks who couldn't get their act together." There was a kind of cultural discouragement, or a *propagandist* discouragement. But basically, there is an alternative media now, and if Reagan has to send troops into El Salvador this winter—as was prophesied by reporters for *Newsweek,* United Press International, the *Washington Post,* and Knight-Ridder newspapers, in round-table conversation in Mexico City three weeks ago—I'm sure there'll be an underground press springing up to oppose that.

Actually, the alternate press has a great present and future, because its stylistics and its outrageousness affected the aboveground press. Many people working today in the aboveground press, and in the other media also—television, radio, public radio, private channel, cable, the *New York Times*—started with the underground press, and they have that inoculation of understanding. Its visual style affected a lot of the aboveground press. Certain big publications have survived, like *Rolling Stone,* which is relatively radical in terms of its investigative reporting, and there is the *Real Paper* in Boston. There is the *Distant Drummer* in Philadelphia; there is still the Vancouver newspaper, now called the *Sun,* edited by Dan McLeod, the same as before. There are lots of presses, and they have quite an influence.

FIRST PUBLISHED: *The Writer and Human Rights*, edited by the Toronto Arts Group for Human Rights (Garden City, NY: Anchor/Doubleday, 1983).

VIETNAM AND POLITICAL CONVENTIONS

Statement Written for *Authors Take Sides on Vietnam*

1. US intervention in Vietnam was always a mistake because the motives were wrong from the very beginning and the consequences of our actions have compounded the original miscalculation to such a tangle that no one in his right mind or wrong mind could follow all the threads anymore. Bad Karma, bad Karma for the States.

   The original mistake was the Dulles-Eisenhower apocalyptic barroom brawl hysteria psychology aided and abetted by three Catholics namely Max Lerner Cardinal Spellman and Henry Luce and one Negro the head of Freedom House Leo Cherne. Now they all got together in the mid-fifties and broadcast to everybody some very complicated series of doctrines which wound up in my poor father's mind—he reads television—that in order to "contain" China—see, everybody wanted to "contain" China—we had to surround China with Christian capitalist Western-oriented governments such as the Diem government which the above-mentioned gentleman promoted. By the time all this thinking got formulated consciously so that it arrived in my brainpan it came in the form of this sort of language: that in the struggle between China and American freedom power, neutralism was unacceptable. Only those guys on OUR side were acceptable, to form governments surrounding China, to contain China. Active people, who were really *against* China and with us. Now, we really insisted on that, we spent money, sent spies, armies, etc. It was announced officially in *Life* magazine; everybody read it at the dentist. *Time* magazine had big discussions about neutralism unacceptable. Everybody insulted India for a year. Everybody had to be with us or against us.

   Naturally such a humorless foreign policy, smacking of outright paranoia if not, at the least, total lack of self-control, could lead to nothing but more and more reality-complications, an escalation of aggressive hysteria to jabberwockian heights limited only by the physical nature of the universe.

What's really disgusting is the tone of perplexed sincerity adopted by *Time* and *Life* senior editors A.D. 1966 to explain that we're in it too deep to pull out now even if we shouldn't be in it. Meanwhile the Peking Universe is also swept by winds of paranoia emanating from Henry Luce's brain. Mao Tse-tung and Henry Luce both think the root of the struggle is a geopolitical mystical struggle between the emanations of the yellow virus life form and the white virus life form, and that it makes a difference if their own side wins.

US intervention in Vietnam was always a mistake because the motives were wrong from the very beginning and the consequences etc.

2. The way to end the war has less to do with the situation in Vietnam than it has to do with the situation of internal propaganda, attitudinizing, brainwash, image-manipulation, news control etc. within the United States. How the entire communications and media apparatus have been able to sustain a sympathetic myth rationalization for our part in the two-way paranoia for over a decade, is a little mysterious. It took a lot of doubletalk, from the mid–50's on, to make the whole dream of Vietnam seem like normal everyday waking consciousness. It would be necessary to bomb out the entire public consciousness of the USA with LSD or some therapeutic equivalent like Burroughs' cut-up method[16] before we could expect the beginning of self-examination on the part of the majority of our populace who are, after all, enjoying some artificial prosperity as byproduct of hostility to China.

I mean we don't want to share what we got so we'll overeat a little.

Elections in South Vietnam, as reported in the *New York Times,* excluded all candidates who proposed reconciliation with Vietcong or Neutralism. One step toward resolving the armed conflict would be to promote elections which would lead to a government which would want to end the conflict.

We could even do what the Buddhists proposed, stay in Vietnam to help a neutralist government sympathetic to Vietcong, or even pro-Vietcong government, reconstruct the country.

If we still are concerned with containing China, we might let Ho

Chi Minh do that for us, instead of driving him into dependence on China. After all we're not fighting "Communism"—we made peace with that in Europe—we're really fighting the Yellow Life Form Virus, specifically the Chinese one.

If we're worried about betraying all our "friends" and allies in Saigon, I would be in favor of inviting them—millions if necessary—to share these States with us. A larger dash of oriental style has always been desirable here.

All in all the problem is not how to manipulate the situation in Vietnam—common sense would show a way; ways have been shown and rejected for decades. De Gaulle and the Pope could show the way if we asked them. The problem is here in America, how do we get out of ourselves, our own minds. "A new world is only a new mind."—William Carlos Williams.

FIRST PUBLISHED: Cecil Woolf and John Bagguley, eds., *Authors Take Sides on Vietnam* (London: Peter Owen, 1967).

1968 Chicago Democratic National Convention

Allen Ginsberg's Answer to Claude Pélieu's Questionnaire

As of August 1, 1968 I'm confused about the Youth International Party plans to hold a be-in during political convention time in Chicago; as above so below—confusion of assassinations, resignations, changes of terminology, police violence, make the purpose of me or younger people going to Chicago unclear and I worry about it at night. I don't want to go or attract anyone else to go and get their heads busted. If there were several thousand people in white clothes who knew intuitively how to say Aum[17] from their bellies I would feel in safe company, who had the soul intelligence to cut thru hysteria and violence instantly. Or several thousand people who could be naked and completely calm. As it is, there are giant verbal plans for assemblage of youths in Chicago—plans in which I'm sentimentally involved not really knowing what I'm doing.

And I feel as if I'm up a dead end street. I should not be involved in Party politics like this. I'm talking now about a specific U.S. event not generalizing about International Worldwide Idealism.

One month it looks like America will have a psycho-political breakthru, the next month image-amnesia sets in again and giant wars get worse, heavy metal gets heavier, and authoritarian impasses seem permanent and unresolvable except by apocalypse, like the population explosion.

Same breakthrus, repressions, generational atrocities police violence and revolutionary realization as well as hysteria seem to take place in Europe, Americas, and in and out of the Iron Curtain. My cousin got an elbow cracked at Columbia[18] [University] and that "radicalized" his entire middle-class schoolteacher family. So there's this enormous growth of horrible insight into the impersonal bureaucratic violence of the machine-state which has made robots out of masses of well-fed citizens. That's a major breakthru in places of "education." Conceiving, blueprinting, imagining an alternative anarchistic humanistic spiritual yet technological and over-populated State or No-State, present (much less future) social form is a proposition now so gigantic I have little to offer except in tiny particularities wherein I'm experienced, like sexual *upaya*[19] or language skills or narcotic-mystic-educational programs. Charles Olson (who suggests that in the U.S. all police be blacks or women) and Timothy Leary (who has experience in psychedelic educational communes) or William Burroughs (who in essay "Academy 23"[20] set forth curricula for non-stereotype i.e. non-conceptual citizen wisdom schools) or Paul Goodman (who proposed specific subsidies for youths engaged in organic farming in country communes, rural reconstruction his ideal) and others all have specific fragmentary propositions. But new nations (fresh planets) twentieth century and technology may need giant Orwellian master-plans, self-correcting with IBM Univac feedback unified field physiologies. Every 5 years you'd need a new master-plan. I drove along oceanside south of San Francisco this morning and saw whole box-house cities and populations that didn't exist last year. Giant Gandharva[21] cities risen overnight! No parks no ocean left. People multiplying like rats. I don't know where my own thought-stream is wandering, much less the living surface of the entire planet or even one pretty city San Francisco. Crisis communes restore liberty and human contact, but there's still the Heavy Metal Megalopolis proliferation to deal with—or not deal with—leave the sinking ship, or get together for a new revolutionary WHAT? At least we all, the young, have a clearer sense of what is *wrong* with present structures. That's clearer after the 1968 uprisings.

July 1968 I arrived at Nuevo Laredo, Texas, bordertown between U.S. and Mexico with my brother's family, 5 children, in a mini-bus. Customs guards at desks told me the family could go thru but not me. "You'll have to take a bath and shave or you can't go in, official government regulation, no existentialists or hippies allowed to enter Mexico, it give a bad impression of tourists." Literal quote. I had passport and $600 in travelers' checks so it wasn't only indigence that was forbidden. U.S. Consulate at Nuevo Laredo confirmed that it was official immigration regulation on Mexican side for previous six months, not just arbitrary moment. I got thru border after 3 hours on approval of local *jefe* of immigration, because of fame identity. Returning thru U.S. Customs a week later I was stopped searched and my tape machine switched off by police fingers as I was being asked if I wanted to register as a narcotics offender. Previous return from England I was stripped, U.S. customs looking for marijuana in the lint of my sports jacket.

San Francisco Diggers'[22] proposition to abolish money as well as frontiers is obviously healthy future, if there is any technological future; restudy of Ezra Pound's explanation of socially degenerative nature of private banking (exploiting money as a commodity instead of a measure) would be useful, as long as a medium of exchange is in use.

Pound says the trouble with money system is not money as a measure, but private monopolistic manufacture of money (credit i.e., checks) by banks, and their use of money to multiply their own money monopolistically, even though they perform no productive service to earn their increase. Like, they skim the cream off everybody's work. Whereas all the credit they give out and take interest on really belongs to the community, commune, state, i.e. *demos*. So how come the State licensed the banks to loan out our money? Of course a State Bank would lead to monopolistic authoritarian dictatorship of money too.

Suppression of sensory awareness, alteration of ratio of senses, stereotyping of conscious awareness in language formulae, homogenizing of communal imagery via mass-media, creation of mass hallucinations (headlines) are present condition of megalopolis. Burroughs provides counter-brainwash techniques and leads the reader to examine conditioned identity. Provides modern TV-den yogic means for examining

Mind. Such liberation leads to recognition of alternative social and affective universes. Naturally that leads to changing material conditions. "An efficient police state doesn't need police" (*Naked Lunch*), because citizens are conditioned not to imagine anything different from houses, streets and labor they're already exposed to. Burroughs' theme and practice is de-conditioning. That's the liberty required for imagining a twentieth century re-invention of social forms. The word revolution, permanent revolution, is OK in some mouths though some mouths make it sound sadistic, so it still depends on how it feels and not the language label, or slogan.

FIRST PUBLISHED: Mary Beach and Claude Pélieu, eds., *Liberty or Death* (San Francisco: City Lights/Beach Books, 1968).

All Is Poetry

Statement on 1968 Chicago Democratic National Convention

All is Poetry, the political convention's fake images, mobilizers conspiring with reason to demonstrate American unconscious, hippies chanting Aum the first word of the universe under cloudy newmoon light and brilliant sun. When the arms of the police were filled with flowers and their mouths filled with AUM there was civic order. Authorities of the city are authors of loud-mouth bad poetry—noisy pistols put into police hands not wise flowers, tear gas substituted for the vital breath. I got gassed chanting holy AUM with a hundred youthful voices under the trees, Jean Genet a little gassed wandering among crowds of children at night. We wanted to sleep on the grass all night, not confront tired historical phantoms armed with tear gas revolvers acting definite roles written for them by egotistical poets in the City Hall. The Daily Mayor[23] has written a bloody vulgar script for American children.

WRITTEN: August 1968

FIRST PUBLISHED: *New York Free Press* (Sept. 5–12, 1968) p. 13.

Television Address

My name: Allen Ginsberg, responding to this station's editorial denouncing violent behavior of some protesters at Republican Convention proceedings at Miami Beach late August 1972.

A small minority, anti-war movement protesters, fringe-group of hysterical kids, attacked cars and buses carrying North Carolina's Nixon Republicans to Miami's convention hall. Some few delegates were directly struck. The war-protest majority sanely sat on streets Gandhi-style, non-violent, offering their bodies for arrest. Half-dozen pacifist organizers fasted a month. There were sit-ins, speeches, street theater, and marches; an elephant dragged a black coffin to the convention hall.

Did any of you see Dave Dellinger's starved saintly face and sensible voice on television? You saw kids trashing instead, right? Dellinger fasted for forty days through Miami to protest Replication Indochina war violence, the greatest single episode of man-made violence ever wreaked on earth! Did you hear bony faced Dellinger remind us of the four million tons of bombs (twice the weight of all bombs dropped in World War Two) dropped on Indochina in Nixon's last three and a half years?

The righteous Nixon Republican conventioneers didn't renounce a four-year-old policy of guava bomblets and vomit gas! Propane incendiary super bombs! Dragontooth plastic pellet gravel mines! Flechette barbed-nail cluster bombs! Napalm-phosphorous-thermite anti-human splash-bombs! Project Igloo White, the automated electronic computerized air battlefield that's already murdered half a million people! Mostly innocent peasants in ricefields, 80 percent of Vietnam's bombs were dropt on South Vietnam! Over a million injured! More than five million homeless refugees from U.S.A. bombing in Nixon's three and a half years!

Did the proud Nixon North Carolina delegates know these facts? Did they care? Wasn't it our own official government violence that washed half-way round the world and touched us with a wavelet of horror?

I was teargassed sitting on the street praying AH! A few police-infiltrated peace protesters spoiled the scene for many more sane anti-war fold. But what of the bland double-think of the North Carolina delegates who came accepting Nixon's "handling of the war" including four million tons of bombs. This is science-fiction style, dehumanized, remote control mass violence.

Spoken in Charlotte, NC, 1972

INTERNATIONAL

Declaration of Three
Joint Statement on Nicaragua

The following text, composed together and signed by Eugenio Yevtuchenko, Russian poet, Allen Ginsberg, American poet, and Ernesto Cardenal, Nicaraguan poet and Minister of Culture, declares a common ground between the three cultures, and defines the prospect for a liberty for Nicaragua independent of ambitions by either Cold-War superpower to dominate the Nicaraguan national scene. The occasion was a centenary meeting in Managua to celebrate the Nicaraguan poet Rubén Darío's Modernist proclamation of cultural independence.

Declaration of Three

We are three poets of very different countries. One of us is a Catholic poet, son of an underdeveloped country. The other two are sons of countries called superpowers: one from a capitalist state, and the other socialist. But we are all sure that the one superpower which must exist is the human spirit, that there is no state bigger than the human soul. The human soul must be the Church of all—religious, or non-theistic in all parts of the world.

We don't want to see Nicaragua become a puppet in anyone's hands. At this moment we are witnesses that here in Nicaragua, which suffered so much under tyranny, misery and ignorance, there is an intent on the part of the people to defend their economic and intellectual independence. Nicaragua is a big experimental workshop for new forms of get-together wherein art plays a primordial role. Many Nicaraguans—not only intellectuals but also workers, farmers, the militia—write verse today, with hands tired of weapons. Let's give them the possibility to write poetry with ink and not blood.

We call the world's writers to come to Nicaragua to see with their own eyes the reality of Nicaragua and lift their voices in defense of this country, small but inspired. They'll be welcome and can acquaint themselves directly with the true character of this revolution, of the efforts of the people to create a just society exempt from violence, a revolution whose image is being consciously distorted by those who have an interest in destroying the alternative which it proposes.

The Damocles' sword of aggression now hangs in the air above these people.

We trust that if the writers of the world get together, their pens will be mightier than any sword of Damocles.

WRITTEN: Jan. 26, 1982

FIRST PUBLISHED: *Soho News* (Feb. 16, 1982) p. 11.

China Trip

I went through China asking everybody I met what they really thought—and found the general atmosphere is one of an opening up, of reform and new breath. In individual conversations, the Chinese are completely clear and Mozartean-minded, very friendly, and tell you everything they can about themselves. But you can only have a subtle, real, frank conversation on a one-to-one level.

If you talk with three people, they'll be somewhat inhibited because it is considered anti-state activity to criticize Deng Xiaoping, China's paramount leader, or the socialist basis of the state, or to say anything funny about China's occupation of Tibet. When people talk about the Gang of Four, for example, they lift up their hand with five fingers as they say "Gang of Four," meaning Mao Tse-tung was actually behind the four leaders blamed for the excesses of the Cultural Revolution, although that is still not officially said.

In class, students ask very few questions except technical ones. They told me that anybody who asked too much, or too curious a question, would stand out as too individualistic and it might be noted in his dossier. They are also inhibited by a cultural timidity and traditional Confucian respect for authority. Sometimes they surprised me. One student near Shanghai borrowed a book and translated a large number of my erotic poems. When I asked him who he would show it to, he said, "My girlfriend." I asked him, "What's your pleasure in that?" He said, "I'm young and I enjoy love. I'm interested in love." But he said he couldn't show it to very many people; maybe one or two friends.

The Chinese I met were thirsty for some kind of real emotion and frankness and feeling. They denied there is any sex life until people get married at 28. One guy told me, "Well, people go to the park and rub elbows for hours." If a student is caught just making out, it could mean a mark in his dossier. If he is an English speaker, instead of being sent to the United States or Oxford, he might be sent to teach high school in the Gobi Desert or assigned to a provincial town and stuck there for the rest of his life because he didn't measure up to the moral standards of the community.

So mostly they take showers or do Boy Scout exercises. Every morning they're up at 5:30, running around the soccer field, doing *tai chi* exercises. It's like the Moral Majority is running China.

I was in China with a literary delegation sponsored by the University of California at Los Angeles and the American Institute of Arts and Letters, and invited by the Peking Writers Association to meet leading writers in China at a four-day conference. The subject of the conference was "The Source of Inspiration," a tricky title designed to dodge the doctrine of art as revolutionary propaganda and give Chinese and American writers a chance to talk about individual sources of inspiration and for them to air their ideas of liberty of expression.

The best conversations were in private, on the side, and we Americans, being polite, didn't probe too deeply into Chinese censorship but made speeches about freedom of expression as a basis of art, hinting by example rather than criticism.

The excesses of the Cultural Revolution (1966–76) are still very much a part of their lives. Some Chinese are worried that the "open door" and the new free market might close down again, worried about whether the recent reforms are permanent, worried about what effect they will have on Chinese culture. Some intellectuals fear that the new technology China is buying might lead to a high-tech computer control system over the population, more efficient than the paper-shuffling bureaucracy.

I spent a lot of my time among the intellectuals at the foreign languages departments of universities, so everybody had a story about the Cultural Revolution, about how they were sent out to the country as a Red Guard, or how their parents were fired from their jobs as translators or physicists, or their mothers sent off to the countryside, or how they themselves were exiled to clean latrines. Elderly physicists were forced to stand bowed over wearing dunce caps, answering questions from a bowed position day and night. Intellectuals were humiliated by such job assignments as cleaning latrines. And in China there are innumerable latrines. So instead of being chairman of the English faculty, a person was assigned the job of cleaning night soil out of the "streetside water coffin."

While I was there, there was a big self-examination within the party. Each party group had to check out the validity of the rumors about members' activities during the Cultural Revolution, rumors that somebody had used undue violence or zealotry in persecution of so-called "bourgeois stinkers"—their neighbors.

I went to a meeting of freshman English faculty. It was all discussion of the latest purification of the party, of all the miscreants and how to deal with the fact that half the faculty was not at the meeting and can't teach anyway because they don't speak English, having gotten their jobs for the "correctness" of their Maoist views during the Cultural Revolution when Red Guards reigned. Now they are dead wood but still occupy positions, so the faculty is only limping along on half the number of proper instructors and having to feed and house obsolete political hysterics.

Almost every city in China was involved in the Cultural Revolution, so it's like a giant family problem as well as a political problem. In conversation, the Chinese express different emotions about the decade of upheaval. They feel bewilderment that China, which was the greatest civilization in the world, went through this period of self-degradation. Many people I spoke to remarked that the people who made the Cultural Revolution—the Red Guards, the professors who were informers—are now working side by side with their "rehabilitated" victims.

A typical comment was, "The man who led the investigation of me and interrogated me for months on end in 1967 now has a lesser post than me: he's a clerk in the English faculty. I see him every day in the office." I asked him how he accepted that, and he told me, "What should I do? Where is he going to go? Where am I going to go? I can't ask that he be sent to jail; there'd be too many. We don't want to start another reign of violence. We're trying to get on with the future."

A lot of the Chinese knew my work from a translation of "Howl" in the foreign language magazine. And they knew about the Beats—there was an essay on the Beat Generation by Fan Yi Zhao, a former Red Guard who had been burning dictionaries in the '60s and who is now taking his Ph.D. on Edmund Wilson at Harvard.

The Chinese think of the Beat Generation very differently from Americans. They see it as a literary movement in rebellion against capitalism, or American imperialism, and partly in rebellion against simple government repression and censorship. They don't understand all of it, but they got a whiff of liberation, of Bohemian openness and freedom of speech, and that fits in with their current phase of getting rid of the heavy bureaucracy that controls literature.

The Chinese are heartbreakingly in love with Americans. At a literary conference in Shanghai, Chen Nai-Sun, a very good young lady poet, was asked by the elder writers to be the first speaker. Talking about her ideal, she said that as a young girl she always dreamed of Gregory Peck and his movie adventures. "I had colorful dreams of youth about him," she said.

There's an ambiguousness among the Chinese. The people are trying to sort out how much of the sexual repression, how much of the travel limitations, how much of the hyper-organization is really a support system for keeping the whole society together, and how much is a control system to keep power at the top. But they rely on some kind of basic socialism to keep the country from falling back into the dog-eat-dog time when the European nations' free market—including Western nations peddling opium—dominated Chinese politics.

In Shanghai, I supped with the president of Fudan University, a specialist in molecular physics. She had been locked in her office during the Cultural Revolution, given a menial job, kicked and left slightly crippled. Now she is a member of the ruling Central Committee. I told her, "I have heard students everywhere and they all tell me they don't believe in communism, they're disillusioned." She said, "Not all think that way. It is a difficult problem. It's true many of the students are disillusioned with socialism. We have all suffered a great deal. We have to work together, we have to find solutions. I think things will change for the better."

•   •   •

I spent three weeks teaching at Baoding University in the provinces. It's not an open city, so there is no facade created for tourists, no international hotel, no marble-floored bathrooms, no heat in any of the houses—even in the teachers' houses—and soft-coal dust everywhere. There's soft-coal smog throughout China; it is the industrial energy source and used for cooking.

Chinese students laughed or tittered whenever I said something outrageous. American teachers in China are allowed to say anything they want—presumably you wouldn't go so far as to denounce Deng or the Communist Party, but you can make jokes at their expense.

I read students a William Carlos Williams poem, "Danse Russe," that goes,

If I in my north room
dance naked, grotesquely
before my mirror
waving my shirt round my head
and singing softly to myself
I am lonely, lonely.
I was born to be lonely,
I am best so!
If I admire my arms, my face,
my shoulders, flanks, buttocks
against the yellow drawn shades,
who shall say I am not
the happy genius of my household.

I explained that, despite the notion the Chinese have of American conformity, despite their view of the American businessman, this is what people are like at heart.

After I finished teaching at Baoding, they held a farewell banquet for me and another teacher. An old cadre member at the dinner—whom I'd thought was a spy bureaucrat—turned out to have managed a Chinese opera company on tour in the mid-'50s. He sang to us, and then sentimentally recited a famous heroic poem by Mao that goes in part:

The mountains are dancing silver serpents,
The hills on the plain are shining elephants
I desire to compare our height with the skies.

We were Americans, we were going away and he wanted to manifest his great feeling for China. Our farewell was warm with tipsy embraces.

WRITTEN: 1985

FIRST PUBLISHED: *San Jose Mercury News* (Feb. 20, 1985) pp. 10, 40.

Statement to *The Burning Bush*

I think Jews should start making it with Negroes. My Jewish family in New Jersey doesn't have any Negro friends—and they think they are big liberals . . . and they would really get upset if one of their daughters married a Negro—when I was twenty-three I had a Negro girlfriend and my home training was such that I hesitated to take her home to papa for fear of the hysteria fallout—I wound up secretly *making* it with men that year—and when my brother brought home this Southern Baptist minister's daughter as a bride then my grandmother, God rest her soul, took him aside into the bathroom and started pinching his arm in anger. In other words Jewish race consciousness is built upon the same stuff that killed President Kennedy, to the extent that it excludes other human images as clan to its family consciousness.

It's time for everybody's image to be bankrupt so we can all enter the New Jerusalem, which has already arrived on earth. It's the Space Age—is everybody going to complain that the Martians aren't Jewish or Baptist or Marxist? No doctrine but complete acceptance of the softness of the living can teach anybody soul in the pocketbook era. Furthermore it must be understood that Jahveh is identical with man; in man: man is God now. Man has seized power over the universe, whatever that means . . . or as Swami Vivekenanda so rightly observed in chorus with myriad rabbis, the proper worship to God is devotion and service to suffering men.

As long as the Jews keep God invisible they will prolong their suffering in human form, ask Martin Buber!

Tears rolling down the eyes of the colored minister in San Francisco show the Bay Area Jew how lonely he is. Whether this separation is implicit in the structure of Judaism or not, that's how it is working out. So everybody should stop worrying about being Jewish or being Negro and live in that one place where we have *common* suffering identity which is this nameless planet we are on . . . behave a Jew on the planet Earth.

And the trouble with the Israelis is that they are *Jewish,* they were hypnotized by the Nazis and all the other racist magic hypnotists of previous eras. Astonishing mirror image resemblance between Nazi theory of racial superiority and Jewish hang-up as chosen race. They didn't desire it—any of them. Any fixed static categorized image of the Self is a big goof. Open wide the doors of the future! Hurrah! Messiah has come!

WRITTEN: November 1963

FIRST PUBLISHED: *Burning Bush,* no. 2 (Sept. 1964) pp. 39–40.

AUTHOR'S NOTE: I met black bearded Lee Meyerzove thru younger poet friends in San Francisco when I returned from India. He was founding *Locales,* a Jewish "little magazine." It seemed a forerunner of that study now called Reconstructionalized Judaism, i.e. reconstruction of Jewish practice (*shabbat, Midrash* etc.) with twentieth century space age postnuclear spiritual liberation as ground: the 60s decade already begun. Text is explained in following note by *Burning Bush* editors:

> Note by editors of *Burning Bush:* The above statement was given to *The Burning Bush* by Allen Ginsberg during his stay in San Francisco. Leland S. Meyerzove, editor-in-chief of *The Burning Bush,* met with Ginsberg at Vesuvio's, in San Francisco's North Beach, four days after President Kennedy was assassinated. Ginsberg dictated his statement to Meyerzove as the two of them sat in Vesuvio's. The contents of the statement were based upon an earlier four-hour non-interview discussion that Meyerzove and Tsvi Strauch, Hillel advisor-editor to *The Burning Bush,* had with Ginsberg about (among other topics) the Jew and the Negro, Ginsberg's visit to Israel, and his discussions there with Martin Buber.

The statement was given in reply to two basic questions put forth by Meyerzove: what should be the Jew's relationship to the Negro and what did Ginsberg think about American and Israeli Jews. Originally these remarks were to be used as a part of Meyerzove's review-essay; but we feel that Ginsberg's statement stands by itself as part of the universal Judaic theme of brotherhood.

Thoughts and Recurrent Musing on Israeli Arguments

I was struck as with my own unconscious spoken when I first read report of [Daniel] Berrigan's speech attacking Israeli—and Palestinian—military politics and psychology. The complete text seems clear and serious, raising many hitherto undebated points regarding modern-style military and nationalist chauvinism I do find, albeit from distant news report, characteristic of Israeli Government. Israeli support of US war in Indochina made me question the whole mentality of Israeli nationalism—the more so that I think probably a majority of US Jews or Israelis have ever completely realized consciously the extent of their own approval or use of violence—Meyer Lansky's guns in fact—in the course of securing Zion's physical territory from Palestinian inhabitants. My friend Peter Orlovsky in 1961 Palestinian refugee camp met one family who had been forced to walk away down the road from their Holy Land coffee shop at the point of a Jewish, or Zionist, gun. The apparent amnesia or desensitization to this human problem on the part of pro-Israeli argumenters, including members of my own family, seems to be covered by a general attitude toward Arabs that they are a mob poor, dirty, uncivilized, and hysteric. This image as carried in many political Jewish minds is, really, what's called "racism"—it enables disputants to treat the other side as not-human-like-us—whose problems are disposable by force.

I have no doubt that Arabs view Israelis the same. But here we are discussing the neuroses of our own side—Jewish family, or Western modern middle-class white. We can clarify our own minds; once our own hypocrisy is straightened out there is hope for straighter action, signaling for clarification from the supposed "enemy." There is much to be said. Very little has been said. In fact I was afraid to say anything, lest my

family and friends in Israel look wounded, exasperated, uncomprehending—HOW COULD YOU! like a Jewish Momma! *O mine Hertz, mein
Hertz!* But Berrigan has spoken, clearly as I said, almost bravely, perhaps
a touch of resistance-rousing anger in his generalizations showing influence of a God in his mind—I myself as Buddhist Jew don't believe in a
monotheistic God, who exhibits self-righteous egoism in Jewish, Moslem
and Christian faiths. Probably that centralized authority figure is the
cause of such concentrated conviction of divine mission on every side.
But the problem is, I am told, in human terms, much different—namely,
the bodily health and survival and mental calm of Israelis and
Palestinians competing with each other for the same space. Holy land
indeed! In a sense any one who projects holiness on to a piece of territory, land, earth, dirt, outer geography, is deceiving her/himself with
what Tibetan Buddhist friends call "Spiritual Materialism" . . . i.e. mistaking one's inner awareness for any of the outer forms our body passes
through on the way to death. So the problem is one of reassuring living
Israelis and Palestinians of a place in the sun. Jewish fright is too great to
resolve with anger, and more violence. I know less of Palestinian fright
but it must be the same as Israeli, human.

I understand that an orthodox position has always been that a political state should not be established by Jews till the Messiah's return sig-
nals the tribes' readiness. Having established a secular state, Jews are
prey to the same power politics of all states, and subject to the materi-
alisms and arrogances of power of modern states, and dehumanization
caused by nationalism, and also subject to the traditional criticisms
thereof. Yet I among others was afraid to criticize lest I be accused of
genocide. The recent episode of war was seen by some of my family as
"Victory or Buchenwald." Was this a true appraisal? I didn't think so.

Yet there is a funny kind of Jewish browbeating, nobody should say
anything embarrassing to Israel, it's ungracious, it's turncoat, it's neurotic self-denigrating Jewish anti-Semitism, go see Dr. Rose Franzblau, a
psychiatrist could analyze a Jewish radical's self-hatred and identification
with the *goyem,* not even *goyem, schwartzas.*

Do I identify? Yes, no. I identified with Martin Buber visiting him at
time of Eichmann trial debate—to kill or not to kill? Israel could find no
answer but death at that moment of marvelous opportunity. (Put him in
a Kibbutz was my thought at the time.) The Holy Land? Everyone should
have one. Put the UN building there, internationalize Jerusalem. I don't

know if it's practical, but it's more practical than "driving the Israelis into the sea" versus "a Jewish atom bomb."

Dan Berrigan's speech began good debate, necessary debate, breakup of stock-in-trade illusions, opened space to talk and think about Israel's identity in a way that space had not been opened for me by any Jewish or Arabist commentaries that I'd encountered. I understand that some of his notions were long ago voiced by Israeli socialists. I must say that I am considerably ignorant of the long history of Mid-East polemics. It may be that the tone was too smug and vicious on all sides, so I kept away. Or the problems insoluble. Or the reality too horrible for me to face, or my thought blind. I don't know what precisely "theological anti-Semitism" is, the history and color or the term. It's a specialized phrase. I doubt if it means anything in this situation, and seems to be a catchphrase applied to Berrigan for no good reason. It distracts from consideration of the problems raised by Israel's military life, confronting an Arab armed camp, both groups believing themselves God-bidden or historically destined to humiliate their neighboring tribes, or perish in shame. I don't believe these are incurable neuroses, in that the root problem is more homely, the physical safety and comfort of actual family people both Jewish and Arab, a great bulk refugees, in the middle of the earth.

FIRST PUBLISHED: *Liberation,* vol. 18, no. 6 (Feb. 1974) p. 14.

Statement Concerning Dissident Human Rights

Lately I heard that some Buddhist teacher said, "Don't take sides." It's true, I don't think it's good to take sides in fights, too much aggression's roused, especially in fights between Russia and America. Nor between Jews and Gentiles, nor between Jews and other Semitic tribes.

Still it seems the Soviet bureaucracy has taken sides against Jewish artists and citizen dissidents who don't agree with the Soviet bureaucracy's pattern of taking sides against Jewish artists and citizen dissidents in USSR. As a dissident Jew in USA who doesn't like my own U.S. government bureaucracy, I sympathize with Jewish artists and dissidents in USSR who have a bad time with USSR government bureaucracy, which won't even let them get out of the country.

At least I can get out of the USA to go to Russia to talk with Russian writers and artists, and I hope to do that with mouth open in Moscow this year.

WRITTEN: July 9, 1985

Unpublished.

An Indirect Encounter: India

I never met Shri Nehru[24] in the 14 months I spent in India, though as a high school boy I had read his jail books and was always happy to know that at least one nation on the planet had as its chief politician a soul of great sensitivity and "idealism" and learning, dressed in white, with a long interesting face. I felt that had I met him there would have been no barrier to communication, with humor, with talk, with poetry, with sentimental appeals to the heart, with mad appeals to divinity, with eccentric personal truthfulness, with gaiety, with irresponsibility, with fantasy, with whatever is in the human heart. Within limits, one look at the streets of old Delhi and I realized he was busier than I was so there'd never be any chance to talk.

So I trusted him, or his image, as one trusts Man, if one is human. But after long time in India I realized he too was lost, India was so large, I lived half a year on Dasaswamedh ghat,[25] Varanasi, and daily saw men and women dying in the street near the little park—months of malnutrition followed by several days swift attack of dysentery perhaps. What could Shri Nehru do? Far up at the top of the vast bureaucracy in New Delhi? Down below in the lowest echelons of that bureaucracy, a hundred paces away from the dying man sat a paid employee of the Benares Municipal Health Bureau in his office. When I rushed in to ask for help for a beggar (who I saw had only hours to live without immediate attention) I was told to come tomorrow, he'd have to ask his chief. Returned tomorrow in behalf of another dying woman, the bureaucrat was not there. A week later he explained he was new in his office and had simply put me off out of confusion. Meanwhile several people were dead.

Meanwhile I'd seen the Mayor of Benares and gotten a polite run-around. Meanwhile loudspeakers over Dasaswamedh ghat were appealing for courageous gold to drive the Chinese back beyond Tibet. Meanwhile young lassi-drinking[26] lawyers hanging around the tea-stalls gave me this advice: "Nobody starves here. Pious pilgrims give them plenty of food." Meanwhile the Marxists at Godowlia coffee shops cried angrily: "You are attacking the problem wrongly. Only complete change of the system will help." Meanwhile the beggars groaned and screamed and cried all through the middle of the night. All trapped in a vast sagging disorganized civilization where, for self-protection, elementary compassion is withheld and the eyes look the other way.

Nehru trapped also, and must have suffered. Yet one thing to his credit, that though he did not, could not, single-handedly, control and order the vast—almost cosmic—bureaucracy of India, his presence seemed to affirm the hope, if not the actuality, of the survival of a democratic compassion. And if one were properly connected (alas!), in cases of great injustice, there was the possibility of an appeal. I can imagine him at the center of vast lines of broken communication, 400 million appeals merging in his brain. How did he retain his sanity?

At one point in our stay (I was with poet Peter Orlovsky) we were much harassed by local, almost illiterate, agents of the CID.[27] Having been suspected variously of immorality (we wrote modern poetry and talked freely of personal matters) or spying (we wore Indian clothes and lived near the ghats unlike U.S. tourists so we were obviously paid Chinese agents and/or as monks in disguise for the American CIA), we were given ten days to leave India. I sent a telegram to Shri Nehru asking him to invite us to tea so we could explain. I never got the tea, but the telegram was handed down efficiently, inquiries were made, *literate* inquiries finally, and our visas were extended.

"Oh I see you are here on the *intellectual* level," exclaimed the official in the Home Minister's Office. Finally we had found a safe pigeonhole in the bureaucratic desk. And without Nehru's sophistication and carefulness and generosity in the bureaucracy, I don't think that affair would have ever been straightened out. Now he is gone, the vast bureaucracy looms more gigantic, and is there anyone to appeal to?

WRITTEN: 1964

FIRST PUBLISHED: *The Illustrated Weekly of India* (Nov. 22, 1964) p. 39.

PART 2
Drug Culture

U.S. Senate Statement

Statement of Allen Ginsberg, Poet, New York City Hearings Before a Special Subcommittee of the Committee on the Judiciary—U.S. Senate

I am here because I want to tell you about my own experience, and am worried that without sufficient understanding and sympathy for personal experience laws will be passed that are so rigid that they will cause more harm than the new LSD that they try to regulate. But with some sympathy, and if possible, kindness and understanding, it might be possible for all of us to get together and work out the riddle of LSD as it is approaching our society.

I hope that whatever prejudgment you may have of me or my bearded image you can suspend so that we can talk together as fellow beings in the same room of now, trying to come to some harmony and peacefulness between us. I am a little frightened to present myself, the fear of your rejection of me, the fear of not being tranquil enough to reassure you that we can talk together, make sense, and perhaps even like each other—enough to want not to offend, or speak in a way which is abrupt or hard to understand.

I am 40 years old now, a poet, this year with the status of Guggenheim Foundation fellow. I graduated from Columbia College, curiously enough, and had a practical career in market research before I went to writing full time. When I was 22 I had a crucial experience—what is called a visionary experience, or "esthetic" experience—without drugs—that deepened my life. William James' classic American book *Varieties of Religious Experience* describes similar happenings to people's consciousness. What happened to me amazed me—the whole universe seemed to wake up alive and full of intelligence and feeling. It was like a definite break in ordinary consciousness, lasted intermittently a week; then disappeared and left me vowing one thing—never to forget what I'd seen.

Now maybe that doesn't seem important, surely it's "subjective." But remember we are not machines, impersonal "objective" figures. We are subject, person, most of all we are feeling—we are alive, and this aliveness that we all know in ourselves is just that feeling of individual, unique, sensitive person. And this nation was made to be an association of such persons, and our democracy was framed to be a social structure where maximum development of individual person was to be encouraged.

I am taking the word from our prophet, Walt Whitman. This is the tradition of the Founding Fathers, this is the true myth of America, this is the prophecy of our most loved thinkers—Thoreau, Emerson, and Whitman. That each man is a great universe in himself; this is the great value of America that we call freedom.

Now in the twentieth century we have entered into a sort of science fiction space age: massive overpopulation on the planet, the possibility of planetary war and death, as in Buck Rogers, like a Biblical apocalypse, a network of electronic intercommunication which reaches and conditions our thoughts and feelings to each other, spaceships which leave earth, loss of our natural green surroundings in concrete cities filled with smoke, accelerating technology homogenizing our characters and experience. All this is inevitable, especially since presumably we have come to value material extensions of ourselves, and don't want to give those up.

We all know and complain about the drawbacks; a feeling of being caught in a bureaucratic machine which is not built to serve some of our deepest personal feelings. A machine which closes down on our senses, reduces our language and thoughts to uniformity, reduces our sources of inspiration and fact to fewer and fewer channels—as TV does—and monopolizes our attention with secondhand imagery—packaged news, and we are having it packaged now, and entertainment hours a day—and doesn't really satisfy our deeper needs for communication with each other—healthy personal adventure in environment where we have living contact with each other in the flesh, the human universe we are built to enjoy and grow in.

Maybe you already know about experiments with infant children's absolute need for contact with living bodies. If babies are totally isolated from human touch, warmth, contact, caressing, physical love, various studies have shown that they turn idiot or die. They have no life to turn to, react to, relate to. Human contact is built into our nature as a material need as strong as food, it is not an esthetic desire, it is not a fancy idea, it is an absolute fact of our existence, we can't survive without it. And this gives us an idea of what we all need, even all of us in this room grown up. We can't treat each other only as objects, categories of citizens, role players, big names, small names, objects of research or legislation—we can't treat each other as things lacking feeling, lacking sympathy. Our humanity would atrophy, cripple and die—want to die. Because life without feeling is just more "thing," more inhuman universe. There is certainly one thing we can all agree on, we all want to feel good, we don't want to feel bad basically.

What I am trying to do is articulate the common body of feeling that we all have together in this room, and I hope you will not reject my feelings of wanting mutual friendliness and communication here now—scared as my feelings are to make themselves known to you.

I had just begun to explain a vision that I once had, and immediately feared your dismissal of the idea of someone coming up in Congress and saying, "I had a vision 20 years ago," something so personal and nonobjective I want to explain why that very personal thing has a place here now.

The LSD experience is also a personal experience that can be listened to with sympathy. Then we can make up our mind how to act on it, how far it feels all right to go along with it, how far it feels bad to go along. Please follow my presentation as long as it feels all right to you.

After having had a sort of vision, as I called it, I later took some peyote, the Indian cactus, in my house in Paterson, in the presence of my family. They didn't know the changed state of mind I was in—I watched them with new eyes—a family argument became extraordinarily sad, it seemed that they were as lost, or isolated, as I was, from the depth of my strangeness, watching them. I found that speaking to them tenderly pleased them, and drew us closer. Most of the day I spent in the backyard watching the cherry tree in bloom, and writing down my observations of the blue sky as seen through changed eyes—that day the openness of the sky seemed oddly like what it was—a giant place in which I was on a planet. So this is an area of consciousness that psychedelic drugs bring to awareness.

Now, this kind of feeling is natural to us, but because of stereotypes of habit and business and overactivity and political anxiety we have been conditioned to put these feelings off. How deeply these feelings had been buried in me is measured by the fact that the first vision I had, and the peyote vision, felt so strange and familiar as if from another lifetime, that I thought they were eternal—like the myths of all religions, like the graceful appearance of divine presence, as if a god suddenly made himself in my old weekly New York universe. So that I used the word "vision" when it might be better to say I had come back to myself.

Where did I come back from? A world of thoughts, mental fantasies, schemes, words in my head, political or artistic concepts—mostly a world where language itself, or thoughts about reality, replaced my looking out on the actual place I was in, and the people there with me, with all our feelings together. A world where, for instance, you can look at death on television and not feel much or see much, only a familiar image like a movie.

I took peyote a few times again. It is nauseating and difficult for me to hold it down, and there is always a thrill of fear at returning to a larger, more detailed world than the normal mind—a world where I became conscious of being a brain and intestines and mysterious sensations called Allen Ginsberg, a lonely heart also, a world at war with itself, with unresolved conflict and fear leading to massacre between nations and neighboring races, a world which has police states, and my own nation engaged in war as well.

In 1955 I wrote a poem describing this, a text which is now taught in many universities—a central part of the poem called "Howl" was written while I was in a state of consciousness altered, or enlarged, if you will accept that, by peyote. I have the poem here and will leave it with the committee if it wishes.

The second part of the poem "Howl" was written under the influence of peyote in San Francisco.

In succeeding years I experimented with mescaline, not often, once in a while, once every few years. In 1959 I took LSD twice under controlled experimental circumstances at Stanford University. I wrote a single poem on each drug, while still high, trying to articulate the insights that appeared. I tried to keep track and make public communicable record of those moments—and continued in South America where I had the opportunity of living for a month and working with a *curandero,* that is an herb doctor, who used a psychedelic vine ayahuasca, the Latin name is *Banisteriopsis caapi,* in weekly meetings with members of his community.

Use of this drug has been common for centuries all over the Amazon area, and appropriate traditions for institutionalizing the experience and integrating it into community life have been worked out so that there is minimum anxiety and little incidence of stress breakdown caused by sudden changes of feelings of the self. This is possible in some cultures, with the psychedelic "mind-manifesting" drugs. Peaceful tribes, savage tribes, the headhunters, use it as well as the Chauma, a calm, peaceful group.

One effect I experienced in Peru I would like to explain, for what it is worth in your consideration. From childhood I had been mainly shut off from relationships with women—possibly due to the fact that my own mother was, from my early childhood on, in a state of great suffering, frightening to me, and had finally died in a mental hospital.

In a trance state I experienced in the *curandero*'s hut a very poignant memory of my mother's self, and how much I had lost in my distance from her, and my distance from other later friendly girls—for I had denied most of my feeling to them, out of old fear. And this tearful knowledge that had come up while my mind was opened through the native vine's effect did make some change—toward greater trust and closeness with all women thereafter. The human universe became more complete for me—my own feelings more complete—and that is a value which I hope you all understand and approve.

I also had had "trips"—sensations of fear, much like the feeling in nightmares—mainly the realization that one day I was going to die, and was not ready to give myself up. Later I traveled to India and sought out respectable yogis and holy men and brought my fears to them, and was reassured by their attitude of tenderness to the living community, and their attitude toward visions—"If you see something horrible, don't cling to it; if you see something beautiful, don't cling to it." So said Dudjom Rinpoche, a head of the Nyingmapa sect of Tibetan Buddhism, a celebrated group which practices intensive visionary meditation. "Your own heart is your teacher," one Swami, the famous Shivananda, advised.

I had not taken LSD for several years by now, and no longer wanted to pursue self-realization through drug means, but rather through trust in my own heart's feelings. By 1965 I felt secure enough from death anxiety and last fall went to a secluded place on the Pacific Ocean coast to see what I would feel with LSD again.

I was sympathetic to the Berkeley Vietnam Day march students, who were preparing for their demonstrations at that time, and there was great anxiety in the air. There was a great deal of hostility, too—the nation was not as understanding or sympathetic to political dissent that season as it is now. We were all confused, the Oakland police, the marchers, the nation itself—many angry marchers blamed the President for the situation we were in in Southeast Asia; I did, too.

The day I took LSD was the same day that President Johnson went into the operating room for his gallbladder illness. As I walked in the forest wondering what my feelings toward him were, and what I would have to say in Berkeley next week—the awesome place I was in impressed me with its old tree and ocean cliff majesty. Many tiny jeweled violet flowers along the path of a living brook that looked like Blake's illustration for a canal in grassy Eden; hug Pacific watery shore.

I saw a friend dancing long haired before giant green waves, under cliffs of titanic nature that Wordsworth described in his poetry, and a great yellow sun veiled with mist hanging over the planet's ocean horizon.

Armies at war on the other side of the planet. Berkeley's Vietnam protesters sadly preparing manifestoes for our march toward Oakland police and Hell's Angels, and the President in the valley of the shadow—himself experiencing what fear or grief?

I realized that more vile words for me would send out negative vibrations into the atmosphere—more hatred amassed against his poor flesh and soul on trial. So I knelt on the sand surrounded by masses of green kelp washed up by a storm, and prayed for President Johnson's tranquil health. Certainly more public hostility would not help him or me or anyone come through to some less rigid and more flexible awareness of ourselves or Vietnam.

On the second Vietnam Day march that November the public image of a violent clash between students and Hell's Angels escalated in everybody's minds—like a hallucination. That is, the extremists among the marchers saw the Hell's Angels as swastika brown shirts. Hell's Angels mistook the Berkeley students for Communists, because that is what it said in some papers. The newspapers were excited and reported everybody readying for a massacre. Paranoia everywhere, some marchers thought the Oakland police would back the Angels.

Actually the majority of marchers appreciated the Hell's Angels as romantic space-age cowboys. We got together for debate at San Jose

College and the majority of students there in the cafeteria actually called for violence, voted aloud their hope that marchers' blood would be spilled.

The Hell's Angels chief diplomatically vowed not to begin violence and to obey police. But this wasn't reported in the newspapers, and the violent image the Angels had to live up to was resistance in case of violence. Two days before the march nobody knew what to expect.

At this point, Ken Kesey—a man whom you may have heard of as a major contemporary novelist—who lives near San Francisco and sympathized with both marchers and Angels, intervened. We all had a party at the Hell's Angels' house. Most everybody took some LSD, and we settled down to discussing the situation and listening to Joan Baez on the phonograph, and chanting Buddhist prayers.

We were all awed by the communication possible—everybody able to drop their habitual image for the night and feel more common unity than conflict. And the evening ended with understanding that nobody really wanted violence; and there was none on the day of the march. The LSD was not the whole story—there was desire for communion and fear of endless isolation—but LSD helped break down the fear barrier.

Now I would like to address myself to the social riddles proposed by LSD. If we want to discourage use of LSD for altering our attitudes, we will have to encourage such changes in our society that nobody will need it to break through to common sympathy. And now so many people have experienced some new sense of openness, and lessening of prejudice and hostility to new experience through LSD, that I think we may expect the new generation to push for an environment less rigid, mechanical, less dominated by Cold War habits. A new kind of light has rayed through our society—despite all the anxiety it has caused—maybe these hearings are a manifestation of that slightly changed awareness. I would not have thought it possible to speak like this a year ago. That we are more open to hear each other is the new consciousness itself; reveal one's vision to a congressional committee.

So I have spoken about myself and given you my direct experience of psychedelics under different conditions; in my family house, in formal research setting, in South American Indian traditional ceremonies, in solitude at the ocean. I accept the evidence of my own sense that, with psychedelics as catalysts, I have seen the world more deeply at specific times. And that has made me more peaceable.

Now I would like to offer some data to calm the anxiety that LSD is some awful mind-bending monster threat which must be kept under lock and key. There are three main ideas I would like to clarify for the committee:

1. There has been a journalistic panic exaggeration of LSD danger.[1]
2. There is negligible danger to healthy people in trying LSD and comparatively little danger to most mentally sick people, according to what statistics we already have.
3. Research already has verified the appearance of religious or transcendental or serious blissful experience through psychedelics, and government officials would be wise to take this factor into account and treat LSD use with proper humanity and respect.

Footnote 1. The 1966 case that imprinted fear in most people's minds was that of a 5-year-old Brooklyn girl who accidentally swallowed a sugar cube left in the icebox. First, here is a quote from a reliable, authoritative medical document saying flatly that nobody dies from LSD. Next a highly hysterical and inaccurate version of the story in the *New York Post.* Then a follow-up story 24 hours later which continued to exaggerate the terror and death fear. Last, a week later in the *New York Telegram and Sun* giving the actual facts—the little girl began to "behave normally again within hours."

The Pharmacological Basis of Therapeutics, ed. Louis S. Goodman, M.A., M.D. (chairman, Department of Pharmacology, University Utah College of Medicine) and Alfred Gilman, Ph.D. (chairman, Department of Pharmacology, Einstein College of Medicine, New York), Macmillan Co., New York, third edition, 1965, page 207, Toxicity of LSD: "In no man, no deaths directly attributable to the drug are known. . . ."

That is a flat statement. That was the information available to everybody including the newspaper reporters at the time that this story was reported.

The *New York Post* of April 6, 1966, Wednesday, no byline:

GIRL, 5, EATS LSD AND GOES "WILD"
A 5-year-old Brooklyn girl, et cetera . . . people who have swallowed LSD went berserk. Some have killed—several deaths have

been reported, sometimes because of the toxic effect of the drug and sometimes because of the hallucinations that lead to suicide.

New York Post, April 7, 1966, Thursday:

LSD GIRL, 5, CLINGING TO LIFE
By Ralph Blumenfield

Five-year-old Donna Wingenroth fought for life today after swallowing an LSD-coated sugar cube she found in the family refrigerator. The blond little Brooklyn girl was reported still in "very critical" condition 18 hours after doctors pumped her stomach and treated her for convulsions at Kings County Hospital . . . said a Kings County Hospital aid, not a doctor . . . "Right now it is at the grave or serious state . . . very critical. Silent and in an apparent coma, her face pale and drawn. . . . Glucose was being fed intravenously into her right arm and both wrists were tied to the crib-bars with gauze so she could not thrash about.

New York World Telegram and Sun, April 14, 1966, Thursday:

LSD GIRL HOME, CONDITION SEEMS NORMAL
By Lynn Minton

. . . was released from Kings County Hospital in apparently normal condition . . . Donna began to behave normally again within hours after her arrival at Kings County, according to Morris Kelsky, assistant hospital administrator. Despite this she was placed on the critical list. She was kept under close observation by pediatricians and neurologists to test her reflexes and all her functions before she was released . . . Kelsky explained that cases of accidental poisoning of children are not rare at the hospital . . . Candy-flavored children's aspirin is one of the biggest dangers, said Dr. Achs . . . "We have had several deaths a year in this community from children's aspirin."

I think that these quotations speak for themselves as to how all of us were imprinted with a death fear, and through the use of an inaccurate language in dealing with a deplorable situation that the girl had had LSD accidentally and was suffering from a sense of consciousness that needed care, tenderness, reassurance, understanding, not the hysteria with which it was treated.

The key thing with LSD is that a hostile environment precipitates psychosis. A friendly environment cuts down the anxiety and cuts down the psychosis. So we have now to deal with statistics on breakdown through the use of LSD, which is crucial, because in reading earlier statements to this committee, Mr. Tannenbaum's statement, I come across language like this:

> One of the most common recurrent reactions to LSD is the psychotic breakdown.

There is no evidence that all users of LSD become temporarily insane.

The reason I am quoting that is to put these generalizations in the language used here in relation to the actual statistical information that we do have so far.

One of the main causes of medical and legislative worry (particularly in New York State where legislation was taken without any kind of hearings on the actual scientific or sociological implications of LSD or the actual facts of the situation) have been reports issued on Bellevue LSD "psychosis" via the New York County Medical Society's report of May 5, 1966, and auxiliary papers detailing a few case histories in the *New England Journal of Medicine.*

New York County Medical Society report:

> Seventy-five people in 12 months admitted to Bellevue with "acute psychoses induced by LSD." Most "recovered within a week. Five remained in mental hospitals a longer time."

I would like to comment on the presuppositions of the language used and on the statistics.

As some schools of psychiatry are aware, a "flip-out" (here termed acute psychosis) may be a basically positive experience if rightly handled. This means there is a breakthrough of new awareness, temporary social disorientation as a result, and an "up-leveled" reorientation to slightly richer awareness with more variable flexible social role-playing as a result. Some of the hospitalized may qualify for this description. I have spoken to a few of those who were in Bellevue and who did feel positive about the whole experience.

And laws witch-hunting use of LSD will have the inevitable result of increasing the number of marginal "psychoses" attributable to LSD. The social anxiety caused by illegalization will enter the environmental setting and influence LSD experimenters to greater traumatic disorientation than normal under LSD influence. The answer to marginal dangers of experimentation would be for Bellevue or some other place to serve its purpose as a temporary comfortable reassuring haven where people with LSD-consciousness anxiety could come to be protected and encouraged to healthy reintegration of their self-awareness, and not labeled "psychotic."

There are no real figures on LSD taking, it might be anywhere from 1,000 to 10,000 in 12 months in New York City according to Dr. Donald B. Louria of the New York Medical Society, probably a great deal more. Above figures average perhaps one breakdown in a thousand users; it is a speculative, uncontrolled survey by New York County Medical Society. The incidence of semipermanent breakdown may be lower than liquor-drinking, auto-driving, and marriage, much less war-making, or any business activity where a healthy amount of stress is encountered.

Footnote 2. Here are some more authoritative statements on LSD breakdown:

Cohen, Sidney, M.D.: *The Beyond Within.* Atheneum, New York, 1964, pages 210–211 says:

> Major or prolonged psychological complications were almost never described in the group of experimental subjects who had been selected for their freedom from mental disturbances ... When patients were given these drugs for therapeutic purposes, however, the untoward reactions were somewhat more frequent. Prolonged psychotic states occurred in 1 out of every 550 individuals. These breakdowns happened to individuals who were already emotionally ill: some had sustained schizophrenic breaks in the past.

Digest of Cohen's giant survey in R. E. O. Masters and Jean Houston book, called *Varieties of Psychedelic Experience,* Holt, New York, 1966, note 23, page 319 says:

Cohen, S., "Lysergic Acid Diethylamide: Side Effects and Complications," *Journal of Nervous and Mental Disorders,* 130: 30, 1960. Cohen's report is based on 5,000 LSD and mescaline subjects who received the drugs 25,000 times, LSD dosages. In other words, some of them have high dosages, that are mythologically reputed to be absolutely damaging, though they are not actually. Among experimental subjects there were no suicide attempts and psychotic reactions lasting longer than 48 hours were met with in only 0.8/1000 of the cases. In patients undergoing therapy the rates were, attempted suicide: 1.2/1000, completed suicide: 0.4/1000; psychotic reaction over 48 hours: 1.8/1000.

Then we have another statement which I saw in the *New Republic* magazine, May 14, 1966, by one who I presume is authoritative. He works for the investigational drug branch of the Food and Drug Administration, Dr. Lescek Ochota, M.D., D.S.C.:

> The suicide rate (in investigational group) has been reported as 0.1 percent, a remarkably low rate considering that LSD has been usually given to the rather severely ill patients including chronic alcoholics, neurotics, psychopaths, drug addicts, et cetera.

Even after reviewing 1,000 medical publications, surveying all of the literature and there is an immense mass of literature already accumulated, the author was unable to confirm reports that a psychosis can develop in a hitherto mentally healthy individual several months after his last LSD intake.

Questions then I propose to the committee for its thought and for research by the government: What is the suicide rate among the mentally ill who don't try LSD? What is the suicide rate of the average population? Does LSD significantly affect these rates in fact?

Or may it possibly turn out, and I have no idea, this is something I think we could begin thinking about, is it possible that the suicide rate for mentally ill people who have taken LSD is lower than the suicide rates for mentally ill people who have not taken LSD?

Is it ecstasy or is it bunk, the reports of the LSD consciousness state? It plainly shows a lack of friendly commonsense for the head of an agency charged with responsibility for licensing experiments with LSD to dismiss reports of its startling religious, or if we want to use the word peak experience, or another word, transcendental, or another word, esthetic effects as "pure bunk." I saw that in the *New York Times* yesterday, a government official whose work I respect incidentally, but who I feel has not read sufficiently the literature or spoken perhaps to people who have had experience with LSD said that he thought that reports of visionary or religious experience were pure bunk, and I believe that that was repeated before one of the congressional committees.

I repeat, I recommend that those responsible for legislation and administration consider the myriad documents that have accumulated since Havelock Ellis and William James researched in the last century.

Here follows a summary of recent surveys in the book by Masters and Houston, *Varieties of Psychedelic Experience,* which came out this year [1966]:

Taken altogether these findings must be regarded as remarkable in the five studies just cited between 32 and 75 percent of psychedelic subjects will report religious-type experiences if the setting is supportive, that means friendly, and in a setting providing religious stimuli, from 75 to 90 percent report experiences of a religious or even mystical nature.

The studies cited were—I have listed a series of very legitimate proper studies, one done for the Rand Corp.; one done by Timothy Leary. That may be questionable scientifically if anybody continues to insist on questioning Leary's experience, which is considerable in the matter, but also there are studies that were printed in the *Journal of Nervous and Mental Disease,* and a paper delivered at a meeting of the American Psychiatric Association in St. Louis. I have got these listed for your reference.

Exhibit No. 76
Suggested Aspects of Creative Research on LSD

Informal conversations with two dozen MD's who had done clinical experimental and exploratory work with LSD and other psychedelic chemicals have articulated the following suggestions for formal research. Some were characterized as logical research needs, others as likely areas for study according to classical traditions of normal intelligent scientific curiosity. The language here used to characterize these possible aspects of creative research is informal, the points made are not fixed points but suggestions for consideration.

(1) A giant voluntary study of all persons who have taken LSD, with no shadow of punitive anxiety attached to the research: scientific inquiry into the statistics, subjective reports of the experience, post-experience intelligence and psychological testings to be compared with pre-experience school testing data commonly available, comparative evaluations of statistics on "bad" trips and "good" trips, inquiry into the quality of the trip matched with circumstantial environment, detailed surveys of indifferent or "good" trips matching already heavily empha-sized analyses of "bad" trips, etc. It is generally claimed that non-medi-cal (and medical) usefulness of LSD is neither "proved" or "unproved"; statistics and data should therefore be gathered from the massive num-bers of people who have experimented with LSD in the last decades.

(2) Enlarged systematic research on efficacy of LSD with dying patients.

(3) Enlarged systematic research on efficacy of LSD against alco-holism.

(4) Research on LSD effects on psychosomatic ills.

(5) Research on LSD influence on problems of obesity.

(6) Research on usefulness of LSD to break up depression states.

(7) Research on usefulness of LSD with autistic children.

(8) Research on usefulness of LSD against opiate addiction and other psychochemical addictions.

(9) Massive research on efficacy of LSD use with neurotics in psy-chotherapeutic situations (which research on the part of individual MD's is now effectively forbidden).

(10) Research on efficacy or non-efficacy of LSD use with neurotics in non-psychotherapeutic situations.

(11) Research into classification of personality types, mental illnesses and other human characteristics in terms of LSD drug reactions.

(12) Research on LSD influence on problems of homosexuality in psychotherapeutic circumstances.

(13) Research on usefulness of LSD experience in preventing psychic crises leading to hospitalization (i.e. how many who *had* been in hospi-tals took LSD and then did *not* go back to hospitals?).

(14) Depth evaluation of recorded LSD breakdown statistics by case to determine—

      (a) Was total experience positive and creative or negative and destructive in actual context? and by hindsight?

(b) To what extent was hospitalization during or after LSD stress the "elegant" acting out of prior wish for psychotherapeutic help? (The word "elegant" here used was suggested by the head of a hospital in Long Island.)

(15) Research on statistics of "breakdown" where LSD is taken freely and legally compared to circumstances where its use is illegal: i.e. research on the imagery, sensations, and psychic effects caused by illegalization of LSD.

(16) Massive research on social conditions, tradition, ritual, terminology, effects, medical data, etc. of American Indians in their use of psychedelic cactus peyote; and projections of possibilities for adapting Indian traditional forms to other American subcultures. In other words, research into safe forms of social-institutional use of psychedelics.

(17) Research into chemistry, metabolic changes and subjective phenomenology of LSD experience as compared with experience of weightlessness, sensory deprivation, space-travel, dance, chanting, yoga, religious ritual practice, drowning visions, progressive relaxation, hypnosis, starvation states, Amerindian vision-questing, sleeplessness, and stroboscope stimulation of alpha-rhythms, etc.

(18) Research into the practicality or non-practicality, value or valuelessness, of such Utopian LSD communities (aside from Amerindian) already come into being as available models for study: Neo-American Church, Ken Kesey's Merry Pranksters Community, Dr. T. Leary's Millbrook Research Center, and the mutual help communities already evolved informally in Midwest campuses, etc.

(19) Depth research and evaluation of commonly observed LSD effect of "impairment of socially learned behavior." Is this due to changed *motive*, and is this change of motive creatively valid or not? Are we, in effect, in regulating LSD actually regulating value judgments? What are the consequences (as far as social scientists and psychotherapists can determine) of authoritative regulation of value judgments?

(20) Comparative study and correlation of language and attitudes used by various social groups according to their roles in reacting to LSD experience directly and indirectly: legislators, police, psychoanalysts with experimental experience, psychoanalysts without experimental experience, anthropologists, artists, newsmen, theologians, Marxists (re Dr. Jiri Roubichek's language in Prague, "LSD inhibits conditioned reactions"), college administrators, FDA chiefs, Indians, culture morpholo-

gists, musicians, painters, cinéasts. Correlation would be useful in determining whether terminology used by different groups coincided in any respect, and in what respects differ, from categorization of the event under survey, namely the effect of LSD.

(21) Straight research and gathering of data in how to handle LSD panic, stress or crisis reaction: "We need research to know what to do when people come in sick, doctors need to be able to work with it to get experience—otherwise it's hush hush like VD and public and professional ignorance spreads"—a lady doctor, head of a midtown Manhattan hospital research section.

Thank you for listening to my paper, which has been very long.

TESTIMONY GIVEN: June 14, 1966

FIRST PUBLISHED: *Congressional Record* (June 14, 1966).

A National Hallucination

The dope fiend menace in America is a national hallucination. Heroin addicts' status (somewhat as Jews in Nazi society) as monster criminals is a glaring example of an extraordinary viciousness inherent in our post-McCarthyite society. All legislation about junk hangs around one ideological/scientific dispute: can a junk habit or opiate habit be stabilized so that junkies can be given to doctors for ambulatory maintenance and lead otherwise normal lives? Administrative legal men who have formulated the actual language of 1966 legislation, somehow have got it into their heads that junk habits cannot be stabilized. Most professionals i.e. junkies and doctors with personal knowledge agree, in general, probably with some hedging, with some rule of thumb, that, with some common sense, all kinds of opiate habits can be stabilized except one—*mainline* heroin. There is dispute on this last point but very little "institutional" "documented" "scientific" "medical" "reliable" studies are available—or proposed by anybody at all to figure out the answer. My own guess is that the criminal instability of supply and total anxiety of social circumstance is the primary factor in hoggishness on the part of mainline junkies. It is a minor medical problem, a tranquil problem, not insoluble with common sense, helpfulness and goodwill towards sick junkies yet this single point is the fulcrum on which the whole junk problem balances.

"Enlightened" liberals are hoping that methadone or other synthetic ambulatory supply experiments will offer "clinical" data someday that habits can be stabilized and the addiction problem finally balanced out. Goodwill is the key historically lacking on the subject mainly due to Narcotics Bureau monster propaganda. Behind that lies a moral barrier: IF junk habits could be stabilized, IF junkies can get their supplies from doctors, IF the black market in junk were removed from the streets where it infects newcomers, IF junkies could be pensioned off with jobs, IF due process were restored to New York and California courts, IF court calendars were relieved of narcotics cases and burglaries associated with getting enough money to score for black market expensive junk, IF police officers and narcotics agents no longer were conditioned to bribery entrapment use of stool pigeons and plea-copping deals with informers, IF states could abolish stop and frisk and no-knock invasions of privacy—would "enlightened" bureaucrats be willing to accept the lesser evil of 50,000 American junkies retiring to their little apartments in a state of relative vegetable calm? Our Puritan heritage balks at the idea of leaving junkies in their state of "sin." Aside from a general sexual depression most junkies could go on to some kind of existence no more abnormal and much more *tranquil* than America's vast pool of alcoholic newspapermen.

Marijuana and LSD

The 1937 Marijuana Tax Act was engineered by Anslinger (Narcotics Bureau Commish, 1930–1962) personally with official claims that "The Narcotics Section recognizes the great danger of marijuana due to its definite impairment of the mentality and the fact that its continuous use leads direct to the insane asylum" unquote Opium Report 1938. Systematic propaganda linking marijuana with violence, killing, shame and tragedy "including murder and rape" was passed through media networks. Seventy years of institutional documentation indicate that this vision was a big American fib: latest such document New York County

Medical Society Narcotics Sub-Committee Report May 5, 1966, "There is no evidence that marijuana use is associated with crimes of violence in the United States . . . marijuana is not a narcotic nor is it addicting . . . New York State should take the lead in attempting to mitigate the stringent federal laws in regard to marijuana possession." Well, everybody knew that 10 years ago.

House Marijuana Hearings, Ways and Means Committee 1937, page 24, Rep. John Dingall: "I'm just wondering whether the marijuana addict [sic] graduates into a heroin, an opium or a cocaine user?" Anslinger: "No sir. I have not heard of a case of that kind. I think it's an entirely different class. The marijuana addict does not go in that direction." Nowadays the Narcotics Bureau propagandizes the idea that marijuana leads direct to heroin which is obviously silly as millions of college boys can inform their parents. But the Narcotics Bureau has raised such an unscientific scream on this point that nothing will suffice to prove the obvious except a giant survey of comparative statistics showing that millions of pot smokers are not junkies. When such documents are at hand, timid but sympathetic medical authorities in key places have declared themselves ready to move toward legislation, licensing or reduction of punishment for marijuana possession to the status of a parking violation.

The mysterious LSD experience has never been clearly explained to those closed off from the experience by the door of choice. It is not *that* mysterious. Here it is: like Wordsworth's descriptions of natural unity, like the breakdown to complete personal self during sexual communion, like Tolstoi's dying soldier looking past Napoleon at the sky, like the strange world appearing after first loss of virginity, or like seeing a whole lifetime flash before drowning. These experiences natural to man we have all glimpsed and pushed to the back of the mind. LSD brings this area of consciousness in front of us where we see it for eight continuous hours. Such deep realization may be rejected by our mechanical society sometimes with terror, but very few *individuals* are really unprepared to weather the stress of such deep self-knowledge. Therein lies the social riddle proposed by LSD. It can only be solved with tender legislation. Any tendency to bring police anxiety onto the scene will literally cause more traumatic damage to LSD users than the LSD itself. Models for sensible integration of psychedelic experience into the community are provided by American Indian peyote rituals. It will be 1984 science fiction space-age nightmare unless the riddle is answered gently by all concerned. *Gently.*

WRITTEN: June 1966

FIRST PUBLISHED: *Washington Bulletin,* vol. 19, no. 50 (Aug. 8, 1966) pp. 241–242.

Preface and a Trip [LSD]

The following text was written October 1977 on LSD, taken mid morning in St. Paul Minnesota. I ingested several tiny tablets I had saved, then did Buddhist meditation practices from 10 A.M. to noon while the elixir took effect, was driven on a car tour of Minneapolis building structures and freeways downtown, spent an hour at the Walker Art Gallery admiring some large-scale sculptures of imaginary cities which were on display that month, and was delivered to the airport in good time for my plane. I was flying to the West Coast to attend the Santa Cruz Conference on "LSD: A Decade Later" assembling next day. The trip was pleasant, I engaged in conversation with a veteran of the late Gen. Douglas MacArthur's army now flying to the Pacific for an old soldier's reunion, who quoted thru planeroar an ironic comment by one member of a generation younger than ourselves: "It's alright, I'm willing to perish with the System!" I wrote my thoughts down on the airplane, and present them here exactly as written, with the exception of a few marginal comments and footnotes; and two phrases added parenthesized to clarify an otherwise enigmatic clause.

Some exemplary informal remarks by Dr. Hoffman at the Santa Cruz conference should be published. Asked how often he had taken LSD, he said seven times, the last with the Swiss poet Ernest Juenger in 1970. What philosophy had he derived from his experiences? That there were many realities. Why had he not gone back for more? He replied that having had the experience, there was no need to repeat the same experience. Did he practice any meditation? He often walked in the woods near his house. Was the official explanation true, that the CIA had begun LSD experiments only after the Russians had ordered 50,000,000 doses from Sandoz? "No," he said unequivocally, it was not true: he himself had supervised all orders and shipments of Sandoz LSD in that era and the Russians neither ordered nor received any. Thus from the horse's mouth, this CIA alibi for fifties LSD mind-control experiments proves to be a hoax. At dinner, Dr. Hoffman said to the family of psychedelic veterans present that he felt not like "Godfather" but "more like a Grandfather."

My own conclusion parallel to Dr. Hoffman's is that LSD is OK because it teaches one not to cling to anything, including LSD. "I've always known the truth," one thinks high; that notion, dismissed for later recollection, emerges later as a guide-thought for most experimenters who like myself come to accept ordinary mind as working basis for infrequent later acid trips, charming as they are.

My experience has been that prolonged meditation practice, Buddhist style (centering on mindfulness of ongoing breath exhalation thru nostrils—*Samantha* practice or similar *zazen*) provides clarity of awareness that encompasses the LSD experience and eliminates, or makes transparent, any tendency toward fantasy or projection of thought-forms. Such meditation practice has the in-built advantage of continually "letting go" of thought-forms instead of clinging to them or solidifying them; thus hope and fear are dissolved. Intelligence is a "Sword of Non-Discrimination."

"If you see anything horrible, don't cling to it; if you see anything beautiful, don't cling to it," was advice given by Dudjom Rinpoche (Tibetan Buddhist Nyingmapa lineage meditation master) for my acid qualms of 1963.

Concentration on more advanced meditative visualization practice is not impeded; at least that was my experience in this case as a beginner in Vajrayana studies and amateur experimenter with LSD.

I recommend such traditional non-theistic *Samantha-vipassana* (mindfulness-insight) meditative training in advance for anyone inclined to experiment with psychedelic substances. In most cases that would provide a reliable "set," insuring tranquillity, spaciousness and open attitude: anxiety-insurance so to speak. Through instruction from an experienced practitioner one may correlate one's own notion of meditation with others' experience. This is a very light task, certainly less forbidding than an egocentric side-trip down Anxiety Alley.

Lest the trip recorded seem to contradict the above light-hearted advice, dealing as it does with a perplexing condition of psychopolitical paranoia (to label it dourly), I would plead in advance, to the thoughtful reader, that the idea-succession is articulated quite playfully; the subject, of "serious" national importance, is treated with transparent humor. The composition, happily written on LSD, examples a direct aesthetic action influenced by a psychedelic drug, and provides a glimpse of some social history of LSD.

WRITTEN: June 29, 1978 as a preface to
"The Great Marijuana Hoax"

Unpublished

The Great Marijuana Hoax

First Manifesto to End the Bringdown

The first half of the essay was written while the author was smoking marijuana.
7:38 P.M. Nov. 13, 1965
San Francisco, California, USA, Kosmos

How much to be revealed about marijuana especially in this time and nation for the *general* public! for the actual experience of the smoked herb has been completely clouded by a fog of dirty language by the diminishing crowd of fakers who have not had the experience and yet insist on being centers of propaganda about the experience. And the key, the paradoxical key to this bizarre impasse of awareness is precisely that the marijuana consciousness is one that, ever so gently, shifts the center of attention *from* habitual shallow purely verbal guidelines and repetitive secondhand ideological interpretations of experience to more direct, slower, absorbing, occasionally microscopically minute engagement with sensing phenomena during the high moments or hours after one has smoked.

One who has the experience needs no explanations in the world of explanatory language, which is, after all, a limited charming part of the whole phenomenal show of life. A few people don't *like* the experience and report back to the language world that it's a drag and make propaganda against this particular area of nonverbal awareness. But the vast majority all over the world, who have smoked the several breaths necessary to feel the effect, adjust to the strangely familiar sensation of time slow-down, and explore this new space thru natural curiosity, report that it's a useful area of mind-consciousness to be familiar with, a creative show of the silly side of an awful big army of senseless but habitual thought-formations risen out of the elements of a language world: a metaphysical herb less habituating than tobacco, whose smoke is no more disruptive than insight—in short, for those who have made the only objective test, a vast majority of satisfied smokers.

This essay in explanation, conceived by a mature middle-aged gentleman, the holder at present of a Guggenheim Fellowship for creative writing, a traveler on many continents with experience of customs and modes of different cultures, is dedicated in the author's right mind (i.e., not high) to those who have *not* smoked marijuana, as an attempt to bridge the conceptual gap, or cultural gap as may be, to explain the misunderstanding that has too long existed between those who know what pot is by experience and those who don't know exactly what it is but have been influenced by sloppy, or secondhand, or unscientific, or (as in the case of drug-control bureaucracies) definitely self-interested language used to describe the marijuana high pejoratively. I offer the pleasant suggestion that a negative approach to the whole issue (as presently pertains to what are aptly called "square" circles in the USA) is not necessarily the best, and that it is time to shift to a more positive attitude toward this specific experience.[1] If one is not inclined to have the experience oneself, this is a free country and no one is obliged to have an experience merely because a great number of one's friends, family, or business acquaintances have had it and report themselves pleased. On the other hand, an equal respect and courtesy is required for the sensibilities of one's familiars for whom the experience has not been closed off by the door of choice.

The main negative mythic images of the marijuana state that the general public is familiar with emanate from one particular source: the U.S. Treasury Department Narcotics Bureau.[2] If the tendency (a return to common sense) to leave the opiate problem with qualified MD's prevails, the main function of this large bureau will shift to the persecution of marijuana. Otherwise, the bureau will have no function except as a minor tax office for which it was originally purposed, under the aegis of Secretary of the Treasury. Following Parkinson's Law that a bureaucracy will attempt to find work for itself, or following a simpler line of thought, that the agents of this bureau have a business interest in perpetuating the idea of a marijuana "menace" lest they lose their employment, it is not unreasonable to suppose that a great deal of the violence, hysteria and energy of the antimarijuana language propaganda emanating from this source has as its motive a rather obnoxious self-interest, all the more objectionable for its tone of moralistic evangelism.[3] This hypocrisy is recognizable to anybody who has firsthand experience of the so-called narcotic; which, as the reader may have noticed, I have termed an herb, which it is—a leaf or blossom—in order to switch away from negative terminology and inaccurate language.

A marvelous project for a sociologist, and one which I am sure will be in preparation before my generation grows old, will be a close examination of the actual history and tactics of the Narcotics Bureau and its former chief power, Harry J. Anslinger, in planting the seed of the marijuana "menace" in the public mind and carefully nurturing its growth in the course of a few decades until the unsuspecting public was forced to accept an outright lie.[4] I am not a thorough patient sociologist and this is not my task here, so I will limit myself to telling a few stories from personal experience, or relating stories that have been told me.

I must begin by explaining something that I have already said in public for many years: that I occasionally use marijuana in preference to alcohol, and have for several decades. I say occasionally and mean it quite literally; I have spent about as many hours high as I have spent in movie theaters—sometimes 3 hours a week, sometimes 12 or 20 or more, as at a film festival—with about the same degree of alteration of my normal awareness.

To continue, I therefore do know the subjective possibilities of marijuana and therein take evidence of my own senses between my own awareness of the mysterious ghastly universe of joy, pain, discovery, birth and death, the emptiness and awesomeness of its forms and consciousness described in the *Prajnaparamita Sutra* central to a Buddhist or even Christian or Hindu view of Kosmos which I sometimes experience while high, as for the last two paragraphs, and the cheap abstract inexperienced version of exactly the same thing one may have read in the newspapers, written by reporters (who smoke pot themselves occasionally nowadays) taking the main part of their poorly written squibs of misinformation from the texts and mouths of Chiefs of Narcotics Bureaus, Municipal or Federal—or an occasional doctor notorious for his ungracious stupidity and insulting manners.

One doctor, facing me across a microphone in a radio broadcasting booth on a six o'clock chat show, pre-recorded, opened our conversation reading aloud a paragraph of *Kaddish* (a poem I had written in memory of my mother, and a tribute to her which made my own father weep; a text widely read, set to music or anthologized in portions, translations of which had met with some critical approval in various languages—Spanish, French, Italian and German, by now some Bengali or Hebrew; a text which I submitted as among my major poems in applying for monies from great foundations; a text applauded in recitation before academies; a text recorded for a large commercial business establishment's circulation; a text which I'd spent months daily transcribing as a movie scenario—in short a straightforward piece of communication integrating the subjective and objective, private and public, and what is common between them)—disapproving and confused— declared firmly that the dashes used as this—indicated that the broken measures of phrase—moment-to-moment consciousness during which syntax and meaning and direction of the—pauses for thought—were a sign of marijuana intoxication and were incomprehensible. He could not follow the thought. He said, as I remember—marijuana retains associations and goes from one thought to another if verbalized—that I was, in fact, quite mad.

Such a notion I thought quite mad on his part; my mother had been that. They were both quite insistent in their obsessions, or opinions, and sometimes harsh and premature in their judgments. This doctor and my mother did not differ so much from myself; the announcer was sympathetic to both of us. After the show I got quite angry with the doctor—it seemed quite a self-righteous remark; but I suppose I could not match his Power by any other means at the moment and felt that frankness and a show of emotion might shake his composure—alas, I yelled Fascist in his face, and had to be reprimanded by my companion Mr. Orlovsky for losing my temper with the doctor. I have a most excellent reason in such cases and so calmed myself, but I did believe that he was a quack-mind of sorts and a sort of negative judger with professional credentials. I had as friends many psychiatrists who treated me as interesting and no madder than themselves; and had in fact graduated from 8 months in a psychiatric institute to be told smilingly by a doctor that I was not schizophrenic but in fact a bearable neurotic, like many other people—but this was years earlier when I was a poet with a tie and an obsession with eternity. True, I had changed much in the intervening 13 years, I had pursued my thoughts to India and was now satisfied with my self and bodily existence, and a little more in harmony with desire for life, I had begun singing mantras daily—Hindu practice of *japa* and *kirtan*—and I had smoked a lot of marijuana in those years; but I had not, despite my odd little biography in *Who's Who*, maintained so much confusion over my identity as to forget to end a sentence, if I wished to, tying together simultaneous association and language and memory with correct punctuation and obvious thought for the reader (to make it obvious, I am doing it now): I had not so much changed and broken away from communication from my fellow selves on earth that anyone should judge me mad. His remark (on the radio) only made me feel slightly paranoid; and I suppose it is no cure to try to make the other fellow feel paranoid, so perhaps I misunderstood the doctor and must take a charitable position and assume that I am Mad (or Not-Mad) but that the doctor also misunderstood my syntax; and judged too abruptly before the revelations possible thru pot had been deciphered . . . In any case I had *not* been high on marijuana when *Kaddish* was composed. The original mss. were bought by New York University library and are clearly labeled as written primarily under the influence of amphetamines, more popularly known as Benzedrine or Dexedrine, familiar to many a truck driver, doctor, student, housewife, and harried business executive and soldier in battle—a common experience not generally termed mad.

The mind does wander and that's another way around; to give by example a manifestation of the precise record of the effects of marijuana during composition on the subject itself, showing the area of reality traversed, so that the reader may see that it is a harmless gentle shift to a "more direct, slower, absorbing, occasionally microscopically minute, engagement with sensing phenomena"—in *this* case the phenomenon of transmuting to written language a model of the marijuana experience, which can be understood and related to in some mode by those who have not yet met the experience but who are willing to slow their thought and judgment and decipher the syntax clause by clause; not necessarily as slowly as composed, so the affect will differ; and of course two bodies cannot, they say, occupy the same place in space. Yet in another light, they say we are one being of thought and to that common being—perceived in whatever mode one perceives—I address this syntax.[5]

Returning to the mundane world of order,[6] may I compare the mental phenomena of the preceding anecdote with the criminal view of it as presented by the Narcotics Department for years in cheap sex magazines and government reports—reports uninfluenced by the Narco Department take a contrasting view[7]—base paranoia close to murder, frothing at the mouth of Egyptian dogs, sex orgies in cheap dives, debilitation and terror and physiological or mysterious psychic addiction. An essentially grotesque image, a thought-hallucination magnified myriad thru mass media, a by-product of fear—something quite fiendish—"Dope Fiend," the old language, a language abandoned in the early sixties when enough of the general public had sufficient personal experience to reject such palpable poppycock and the bureaucratic line shifted to defense of its own existence with the following reason[8]: necessary to control marijuana because smoking leads to search for thrill kicks; this leads to next step, the monster heroin. And a terrible fate.[9]

In sound good health I smoked legal *ganja* (as marijuana is termed in India where it is traditionally used in preference to alcohol), bought from government tax shops in Calcutta, in a circle of devotees, yogis, and hymn-singing pious *Shivaist* worshippers in the burning ground at Nimtallah ghat in Calcutta, where it was the custom of these respected gentlemen to meet on Tuesday and Saturday nights, smoke before an improvised altar of blossoms, sacramental milk-candy and perhaps a fire taken from the burning wooden bed on which lay a newly dead body, of some friend perhaps, likely a stranger if a corpse is a stranger, pass out the candy as God's gift to friend and stranger, and sing holy songs all night, with great strength and emotion, addressed to different images of the Divine Spirit. *Ganja* was there considered a beginning of *sadhana*[10] by some; others consider the ascetic yogi Shiva himself to have smoked marijuana; on His birthday marijuana is mixed as a paste with almond milk by the grandmothers of pious families and imbibed as sacrament by this polytheistic nation, considered by some a holy society. The professors of English at Benares University brought me a bottle for the traditional night of *Shivaratri*, birthday of the Creator and Destroyer who is the patron god of this oldest continuously inhabited city on earth. "*Bom Bom*

Mahadev!" (Boom Boom Great God!) is the mantra yogis' cry as they raise the *ganja* pipe to their brows before inhaling.

All India is familiar with *ganja,* and so is all Africa, and so is all the Arab world; and so were Paris and London in smaller measure in high-minded but respectable 19th-century circles; and so on a larger scale is America even now. Young and old, millions perhaps smoke marijuana and see no harm. And we have not measured the Latin-American world, Mexico particularly, who gave the local herb its familiar name. In some respects we may then see its prohibition as an arbitrary cultural taboo.

There has been a tendency toward its suppression in the Arab world with the too hasty adoption of Western rationality and the enlarged activity of the American fanatic Mr. Anslinger as US representative to the UN World Health Organization Single Narcotics Commission—a position from which he circulates hysterical notices and warnings, manufactured in Washington's Treasury Department, to the police forces of the cities of the world—so I was told by a police official in Tel Aviv, an old school chum who laughed about the latest release, a grim warning against the dangers of *khat,* a traditional energizing leaf chewed by Bedouins of Arabia and businessmen and princes in Ethiopia, as well as a few traditional Yemenite Jews.

There seems to be a liaison between Anslinger and some policemen in Egypt, which has now formally outlawed its hashish or *kif* form of marijuana (even though masses of nondrinking faithful Muslims prefer a contemplative pipe of *kif* to the dangers of violent alcohol forbidden by the Koran). We find government bureaucrats with the well-to-do (as in India) taking knowing delight in alcohol as a more sophisticated and *daring* preference; and stories of mad dogs frothing at the mouth and asylums full of people driven mad by some unheard-of brand of hashish (would god it were imported to America like some fine brand of Scotch or pernod) circulated from the police information bureaus of Egypt—or perhaps some single cranky Egyptian Dr. Baird—thru the Treasury Department Narcotics Bureau and thence by interview and press release to the mass media of America and an inexperienced public (encouraged to drink intoxicating beer by millions of dollars' worth of advertisement). The Egyptian evidence has been quoted for years, most recently by the present head of the Narcotics Bureau, a Mr. Giordano, one of Mr. Anslinger's former intimates in the department.

Professor Lindesmith has already objected in public print to the

Department's manipulation and attempted quashing of various medical-juridical reports; a Canadian documentary film on the drug subject has been blocked from being shown in this country thru activity of the Treasury Department—perhaps an import license was refused; the impartial LaGuardia Report was rudely attacked by Anslinger; a President's Judicial Advisory Council Policy Statement (1964) has characterized the activities of the Bureau as exceeding legal rightfulness in "criminalizing" by executive fiat and administrative dictum those addicted to addicting drugs who for decades have been prevented from going to a doctor for treatment unless it was under the aegis of Lexington jail and thru police channels. Memory of the British East India Hemp Commission report, the largest in history, done in the 1880s, which concluded that marijuana was *not* a problem, has been ignored,[11] memories of our own Panama Canal military reports giving marijuana a clean bill of health have been unavailing in consideration of the Bureau,[12] doctors have complained of being harassed and framed by one or another police agency; sick junkies have died in jail; thousands of intelligent citizens have been put in prison for uncounted years for possession or sale of marijuana,[13] even if they grew it themselves and only smoked in private; youths have been entrapped into selling small or large quantities of grass to police agents and consequently found themselves faced with all the venomous bullshit that an arbitrary law can create from the terrors of arrest to the horror of years in jail; the author receives letters of complaint and appeals for help from many US cities, from acquaintances, fellow litterateurs, even scholarly investigators of the subject writing books about it, as well as from one energetic poet founding a fine project for an Artist's Workshop (John Sinclair in Detroit, sentenced to 6 months for letting an agent buy marijuana for the second time)—one becomes awed by the enormity of the imposition.[14]

It is not a healthy activity for the State to be annoying so many of its citizens thusly; it creates a climate of topsy-turvy law and begets disrespect for the law and the society that tolerates execution of such barbarous law,[15] and a climate of fear and hatred for the administrators of the law. Such a law is a threat to the existence of the State itself, for it sickens and debilitates its most adventurous and sensitive citizens. Such a law, in fact, can drive people mad.

It is no wonder then that most people who have smoked marijuana in

America often experience a state of anxiety, of threat, of paranoia in fact, which may lead to trembling or hysteria, at the microscopic awareness that they are breaking a law, that thousands of investigators all over the country are trained and paid to smoke them out and jail them, that thousands of their community are in jail, that inevitably a few friends are "busted" with all the hypocrisy and expense and anxiety of that trial and perhaps punishment—jail and victimage by the bureaucracy that made, propagandized, administers, and profits from such a monstrous law.

From my own experience and the experience of others I have concluded that most of the horrific affects and disorders described as characteristic of marijuana "intoxication" by the US Federal Treasury Department's Bureau of Narcotics are, quite the reverse, precisely traceable back to the effects on consciousness not of the narcotic but of the law and the threatening activities of the US Bureau of Narcotics itself. Thus, as the Buddha said to a lady who offered him a curse, the gift is returned to the giver when it is not accepted.

I myself experience this form of paranoia when I smoke marijuana, and for that reason smoke it in America more rarely than I did in countries where it is legal. I noticed a profound difference of affect in my case. The anxiety was directly traceable to fear of being apprehended and treated as a deviant criminal and put thru the hassle of social disapproval, ignominious Kafkian tremblings in vast court buildings coming to be judged, the helplessness of being overwhelmed by force or threat of deadly force and put in brick and iron cell.

This apprehension deepened when on returning this year from Europe I was stopped, stripped, and searched at customs. The dust of my pockets was examined with magnifying glass for traces of weed. I had publicly spoken in defense of marijuana and attacked the conduct of the Bureau, and now my name was down on a letter dossier at which I secretly peeked, on the customs search-room desk. I quote the first sentence, referring to myself and Orlovsky: "These persons are reported to be smuggling (or importing) narcotics . . ."

On a later occasion, when I was advised by several friends and near-acquaintances that Federal Narcotics personnel in New York City had asked them to "set me up" for an arrest, I became incensed enough to write a letter of complaint to my Congressman. He replied that he thought I was being humorless about the reason for my being on a list for customs investigation, since it was natural (I had talked about the dread subject so much in public); anyway, not Kafkian as I characterized it. As for my complaint about being set up—that, with my letter, was forwarded to the Treasury Department in Washington for consideration and reply.[16] I had schemed writing some essay such as this in addition to a letter of reminder to my Representative, for it would be to my safety to publish.

I had had the earlier experience after a nationwide TV discussion show, during which the moderator, John Crosby, the anthropologist Ashley Montagu, and celebrated fellow-writer Norman Mailer all concluded—perhaps for the first time over a nationally publicized medium of communication in the last three decades—that as far as we knew there was nothing wrong with marijuana—of learning that the Treasury Department, true to its obsession, had forced its opinion back on the medium thru a seven-minute video-taped refutation (including an incredible rehash of the Egyptian mad dogs), and placed it on the air against the wishes of Mr. Crosby on the insistence of his network, which had received a communication from the Narco Bureau, possibly thru intervention of FCC. Years later I read an account of the incident by Mr. Crosby in his syndicated column, formally complaining about the affair.[17]

At that time, looking forward to the occasion of this essay, a difficult one, I made a preliminary epistle on the subject to Anslinger himself, a ten-page composition saying I thought he was a dangerous fraud, responsible for untold death and suffering, and that some day soon, those who had experience of the matter would band together with reasoning and documentation—such as one may find in this book—to come out in the open to explain the actual horror of the US Treasury Department Federal Narcotic Bureau to an already suspecting public.

Allen Ginsberg
2 A.M. Nov. 14, 1965

II

Rather than alter the preceding composition—let it remain, for the reader who has not smoked marijuana, a manifestation of marijuana-high thought structure in a mode which intersects our mutual consciousness, namely language—the author wishes to add here a few thoughts.

The author has spent half a year in Morocco, smoking *kif* often: old gentlemen and peaceable youths sit amiably, in cafés or under shade trees in outdoor gardens drinking mint tea, passing the tiny *kif* pipe, and looking quietly at the sea. This is the true picture of the use of *kif* in North Africa, exactly the opposite of the lurid stereotype of mad-dog human beings deliberately spread by our Treasury Department police branch. And I set this model of tranquil sensibility beside the tableau of aggravated New York executives sipping whiskey before a 1966 TV set's imagery of drunken American violence covering the world from the highways to Berkeley all the way to the dirt roads of Vietnam.

No one has yet remarked that the suppression of Negro rights, culture, and sensibility in America has been complicated by the marijuana laws. African sects have used pot for divine worship (much as I have described its sacred use in India). And to the extent that jazz has been an adaptation of an African religious form to American context (and will have been in no small measure the salvation of America, if America survives the decades of coming change), marijuana has been closely associated with the development of this indigenous American form of chant and prayer. Use of marijuana has always been widespread among the Negro population in this country, and suppression of its use, with constant friction and bludgeoning of the law, has been one of the major unconscious, or unmentionable, methods of suppression of Negro rights. The mortal sufferings of our most celebrated heroic Negro musicians, from Billie Holiday thru Thelonious Monk, at the hands of police over the drug issue are well known. Such sadistic persecutions have outraged the heart of America for decades. I mean the cultural and spiritual heart—US music.

Although most scientific authors who present their reputable evidence for the harmlessness of marijuana make no claim for its surprising *usefulness*, I do make that claim:

Marijuana is a useful catalyst for specific optical and aural aesthetic perceptions. I apprehended the structure of certain pieces of jazz and classical music in a new manner under the influence of marijuana, and these apprehensions have remained valid in years of normal consciousness. I first discovered how to see Klee's *Magic Squares* as the painter intended them (as optically 3-dimensional space structures) while high on marijuana. I perceived ("dug") for the first time Cézanne's "petit sensation" of space achieved on a 2-dimensional canvas (by means of advancing and receding colors, organization of triangles, cubes, etc. as the painter describes in his letters) while looking at *The Bathers* high on marijuana. And I saw anew many of nature's panoramas and landscapes that I'd stared at blindly without even noticing before; thru the use of marijuana, awe and detail were made conscious. These perceptions are permanent—any deep aesthetic experience leaves a trace, and an idea of what to look for that can be checked back later. I developed a taste for Crivelli's symmetry; and saw Rembrandt's *Polish Rider* as a sublime youth on a deathly horse for the first time—saw myself in the rider's face, one might say—while walking around the Frick Museum high on pot. These are not "hallucinations"; these are deepened perceptions that one might have catalyzed not by pot but by some *other* natural event (as natural as pot) that changes the mind, such as an intense love, a death in the family, a sudden clear dusk after rain, or the sight of the neon spectral reality of Times Square one sometimes has after leaving a strange movie. So it's all *natural.*

At this point it should be announced that most of the major (best and most famous too) poets, painters, musicians, cinéasts, sculptors, actors, singers and publishers in America and England have been smoking marijuana for years and years. I have gotten high with the majority of the dozens of contributors to the Don Allen *Anthology of New American Poetry 1945–1960*; and in years subsequent to its publication have sat down to coffee and a marijuana cigarette with not a few of the more academic poets of the rival Hall-Pack-Simpson anthology. No art opening in Paris, London, New York, or Wichita at which one may not sniff the incense-fumes of marijuana issuing from the ladies' room. Up and down Madison Avenue it is charming old inside knowledge; in the clacketing vast city rooms of newspapers on both coasts, copyboys and reporters smoke somewhat less marijuana than they take tranquilizers or Benzedrine, but pot begins to rival liquor as a non-medicinal delight in conversation. Already 8 years ago I smoked marijuana with a couple of Narcotics Department plainclothesmen who were trustworthy enough to invite to a literary reception. A full-page paid advertisement in the *New York Times*, quoting authoritative medical evidence of the harmlessness of marijuana, and signed by a thousand of its most famous smokers, would once and for all break the cultural ice and end once and for all the tyranny of the Treasury Department Narcotics Bureau. For it would only manifest in public what everybody sane in the centers of communication in America knows anyway, an enormous open secret—that it is time to end Prohibition again. And with it put an end to the gangsterism, police mania, hypocrisy, anxiety, and national stupidity generated by administrative abuse of the Marijuana Tax Act of 1937.

It should be understood once and for all that in this area we have been undergoing police-state conditions in America, with characteristic mass brainwashing of the public, persecution and deaths in jails, elaborate systems of plainclothes police and police spies and stool pigeons, abuse of constitutional guarantees of privacy of home and person (even *mode of consciousness*) from improper search and seizure. The police prohibition of marijuana (accompanied with the even more obnoxious persecution of sick heroin addicts who all along should have been seeing the doctor) has directly created vast black markets, crime syndicates, crime waves in the cities, and a breakdown of law and order in the State itself. For the courts of large cities are clogged with so-called narcotic crimes and behind schedule, and new laws (such as the recent NY Rockefeller Stop and Frisk and No-Knock) spring up against the citizen to cope with the massive unpopularity of prohibition.

Not only do I propose end of prohibition of marijuana, and total shift of treatment of actually addictive drugs to the hands of the medical profession, but I propose a total dismantling of the whole cancerous bureaucracy that has perpetrated this historic fuck-up on the United States. And not only is it necessary that the Bureau of Narcotics be dismantled and consigned to the wax-museum of history, where it belongs, but it is also about time that a full-scale Congressional investigation, utilizing all the resources of the embattled medical, legal and sociological authorities, who for years have been complaining in vain, should be undertaken to fix the precise responsibility for this vast swindle on the administrative, business and mass-media shoulders where it belongs. What was the motive and method in perpetrating this insane hoax on public consciousness? Have any laws of malfeasance in public office been violated?

Not only an investigation of how it all happened but some positive remuneration is required for those poor citizens, many of them defenseless against beatings, sickness, and anxiety for years—a minority directly and physically persecuted by the police of every city and state and by agents of the nation; a minority often railroaded to jail by uncomprehending judges for months, for years, for decades; a minority battling idiotic laws, and even then without adequate legal representation for the slim trickery available to the rich to evade such laws. Pension must be made obviously for the cornered junkies. But for the inoffensive charming smokers of marijuana who have undergone disgraceful jailings, money is due as compensation. This goes back decades for thousands and thousands of people who, I would guess, are among the most sensitive citizens of the nation; and their social place and special honor of character should be rewarded by a society which urgently needs this kind of sensibility where it can be seen in public.

I have long felt that there were certain political implications to the suppression of marijuana, beyond the obvious revelation (which Burroughs pointed out in *Naked Lunch*) of the cancerous nature of the marijuana-suppression bureaucracy. When the citizens of this country see that such an old-time, taken-for-granted, flag-waving, reactionary truism of police, press, and law as the "reefer menace" is in fact a creepy hoax, a scarecrow, a national hallucination emanating from the perverted brain of one single man (perhaps) such as Anslinger, what will they begin to think of the whole of taken-for-granted public REALITY?

What of other issues filled with the same threatening hysteria? The spectre of Communism? Respect for the police and courts? Respect for the Treasury Department? If marijuana is a hoax, what is Money? What is the War in Vietnam? What are the Mass Media?

As I declared at the beginning of this essay, marijuana consciousness shifts attention from stereotyped verbal symbols to "more direct, slower, absorbing, occasionally microscopically minute engagement with sensing phenomena during the high . . ." Already millions of people have got high and looked at the images of their Presidents and governors and representatives on television and seen that all were betraying signs of false character. Or heard the impersonal robot tones of radio newscasters announcing mass deaths in Asia.

It is no wonder that for years the great centers of Puritanism of consciousness, blackout and persecution of the subtle vibrations of personal consciousness catalyzed by marijuana have been precisely Moscow and Washington, the centers of the human power war. Fanatical rigid mentality pursuing abstract ideological obsessions make decisions in the right-wing mind of America, pursuing a hateful war against a mirror-image of the same "sectarian, dogmatic" ideological mentality in the Communist camp. It is part of the same pattern that both centers of power have the most rigid laws against marijuana. And that marijuana and versions of the African ritual music (rock 'n' roll) are slowly catalyzing anti-ideological consciousness of the new generations on both sides of the Iron-Time curtain.

I believe that future generations will have to rely on new faculties of awareness, rather than on new versions of old idea-systems, to cope with the increasing godlike complexity of our planetary civilization, with its overpopulation, its threat of atomic annihilation, its centralized network of abstract word-image communication, its power to leave the earth. A new consciousness, or new awareness, will evolve to meet a changed ecological environment. It has already begun evolving in younger generations from Prague to Calcutta; part of the process is a re-examination of certain heretofore discarded "primitive" devices of communication with Self and Selves. Negro worship rituals have invaded the West via New Orleans and Liverpool, in altered but still recognizably functional form. The consciousness-expanding drugs (psychedelics) occupy attention in the highest intellectual circles of the West, as well as among a great mass of youth. The odd perceptions of Zen, Tibetan yoga, mantra yoga, and indigenous American Shamanism affect the consciousness of a universal generation, children who can recognize each other by hairstyle, tone of voice, attitude to nature, and attitude to Civilization. The airwaves are filled with songs of hitherto unheard-of frankness and beauty.

These then are some of the political or social implications of the legalization of marijuana as a catalyst to self-awareness. The generalizations I have made may also apply to the deeper affects and deeper social changes that may be catalyzed thru the already massive use of psychedelic drugs.

And it is significant that, as marijuana was once monopolized by a small rabid bureaucracy in the Treasury Department, the psychedelic drugs have this year in America been officially monopolized by the Pure Food and Drug Administration—within months a large amateur police force has mushroomed. I've heard it rumored that the precise group of citizens *least* equipped for "responsibility" in this area—the *least* "mature" pressure-group in the States—already acts in an advisory capacity on licensing. This group is the Chemical Warfare Division of the Pentagon.

A Little Anthology of Marijuana
Footnotes

[1] Editorial in the English journal of medicine *The Lancet*, November 9, 1963.

... At most of the recent conferences the question was raised whether the marijuana problem might be abolished by removing the substance from the list of dangerous drugs where it was placed in 1951, and giving it the same social status as alcohol by legalizing its import and consumption.

This suggestion is worth considering. Besides the undoubted attraction of reducing, for once, the number of crimes that a member of our society can commit, and of allowing the wider spread of something that can give pleasure, a greater revenue would certainly come to the State from taxation than from fines. Additional gains might be the reduction of interracial tension, as well as that between generations; for 'pot' spread from South America to Britain via the United States and the West Indies. Here it has been taken up by the younger members of a society in which alcohol is the inheritance of the more elderly.

[2] Anslinger, Harry J., and Oursler, W. C.: *The Murderers,* Farrar, Straus and Cudahy, 1961 (p. 38).

Much of the irrational juvenile violence and killing that has written a new chapter of shame and tragedy is traceable directly to this hemp intoxication ...

As the Marijuana situation grew worse, I knew action had to be taken to get proper control legislation passed. By 1937, under my direction, the Bureau launched two important steps: First, a legislative plan to seek from congress a new law that would place Marijuana and its distribution directly under federal control. Second, on radio and at major forums, such as that presented annually by the New York Herald Tribune, I told the story of this evil weed of the fields and river beds and roadsides. I wrote articles for magazines; our agents gave hundreds of lectures to parents, educators, social and civic leaders. In network broadcasts I reported on the growing list of crimes, including murder and rape. I described the nature of Marijuana and its close kinship to hashish. I continued to hammer at the facts.

I believe we did a thorough job, for the public was alerted, and the laws to protect them were passed, both nationally and at the state level.

³H. J. Anslinger, Commissioner of Narcotics, Correspondence, *JAMA*, Jan. 16, 1943 (p. 212).

> . . . information in our possession . . . that marijuana precipitates in certain persons psychoses and unstable and disorganized personality . . . may be an important contributory cause to crime . . . by relaxing inhibitions may permit antisocial tendencies . . .
>
> Of course, the primary interest of the Bureau of Narcotics is in the enforcement aspect. From that point of view it is very unfortunate that Drs. Allentuck and Bowman should have stated so unqualifiedly that use of marijuana does not lead to physical, mental, or moral degeneration and that no permanent deleterious effects from its continued use were observed.

⁴"Traffic in Opium and Other Dangerous Drugs," Report by the Government of the United States of America for the Year Ended December 31st, 1938, by Hon. H. J. Anslinger, Commissioner of Narcotics (p. 7). "The Narcotics Section recognizes the great danger of marijuana due to its definite impairment of the mentality and the fact that its continuous use leads direct to the insane asylum."

⁵As stated in the text, which stands almost completely unrevised from first composition, the author smoked one marijuana cigarette at the beginning of the fourth paragraph.

⁶ The author is still high to the end of Section I.

⁷ *The Pharmacological Basis of Therapeutics*, Goodman and Gillman, 1956 ed., (p. 20). "The federal narcotic regulations and a number of supplementary laws include drugs such as papaverine and marijuana which do not produce narcosis."

(pp. 170–177). "There are no lasting ill effects from the acute use of marijuana, and fatalities have not been known to occur.

"Careful and complete medical and neuropsychiatric examinations of habitués reveal no pathological conditions or disorders of cerebral functions attributable to the drug.

"Although habituation occurs, psychic dependence is not as prominent or compelling as in the case of morphine, alcohol, or perhaps even tobacco habituation."

[8] Hearings before the Committee on Ways and Means, U.S. House of Representatives, 75th Congress, 1st session April and May 1937: House Marijuana Hearings (p. 24).

Rep. John Dingall: "I am just wondering whether the marijuana addict graduates into a heroin, an opium, or a cocaine user?"

Anslinger: "No, sir. I have not heard of a case of that kind. I think it is an entirely different class. The marijuana addict does not go in that direction."

[9] In historical context this recent excuse for repression of marijuana seemed to the author so irrational that it was unnecessary to analyze. Yet public confusion may warrant some precise analysis.

A) There are no legitimate sociological/medical study documents warranting the Narcotics Department's assertion of causal relation between use of marijuana and graduation to opiates.

B) There never had been any hint of such association before the two classes of drugs were forcibly juxtaposed in black market by said department; Anslinger testified to that in 1937 (see footnote 8).

C) A greater number of opiate users started with bananas, cigarettes and alcohol than started with marijuana—no causal relationship is indicated in any case.

D) The number of millions of respectable Americans who smoke marijuana have obviously not proceeded to opiates.

E) In test sociological cases, i.e., societies such as Morocco and India where marijuana use is universal, there is very small use of opiates and no social association or juxtaposition between the two classes of drugs. What juxtaposition there is in America has been created and encouraged by the propaganda and repression tactics of the Narcotics Bureau.

[10] Saddhana: yogic path or discipline.

[11] Report of the Indian Hemp Drugs Commission, 1893–94, Ch. XIII (pp. 263–264, par. 552).

Summary of conclusions regarding effects. The Commission have now examined all the evidence before them regarding the effects attributed to hemp drugs. It will be well to summarize briefly the conclusions to which they come. It has been clearly established that the occasional use of hemp in moderate doses may be beneficial; but this use may be regarded as medicinal in character. It is rather to the popular and common use of the drugs that the Commission will now confine their attention. It is convenient to consider the effects separately as affecting the physical, mental or moral nature. In regard to the physical effects, the Commission have come to the conclusion that the moderate use of hemp drugs is practically attended by no evil results at all. There may be exceptional cases in which, owing to idiosyncrasies of constitution, the drugs in even moderate use may be injurious. There is probably nothing the use of which may not possibly be injurious in cases of exceptional intolerance . . .

In respect to the alleged mental effects of the drugs, the Commission have come to the conclusion that the moderate use of hemp drugs produces no injurious effects on the mind . . .

In regard to the moral effects of the drugs, the Commission are of opinion that their moderate use produces no moral injury whatever. There is no adequate ground for believing that it injuriously affects the character of the consumer . . . for all practical purposes it may be laid down that there is little or no connection between the use of hemp drugs and crime.

Viewing the subject generally, it may be added that the moderate use of these drugs is the rule, and that the excessive use is comparatively exceptional.

[12] Panama Canal Zone Governor's Committee, Apr.–Dec. 1925: *The Military Surgeon,* Journal of the Association of Military Surgeons of the United States, Nov. 1933, p. 274.

After an investigation extending from April 1 to December 1925, the Committee reached the following conclusions:
There is no evidence that marijuana as grown here is a "habit-

forming" drug in the sense in which the term is applied to alcohol, opium, cocaine, etc., or that it has any appreciably deleterious influence on the individual using it.

Panama Canal Zone Governor's Committee, June 1931 (vide supra, p. 278):

Delinquencies due to marijuana smoking which result in trial by military court are negligible in number when compared with delinquencies resulting from the use of alcoholic drinks which also may be classed as stimulants and intoxicants.

[13]12,229 convictions for marijuana in 1963 and 1964 reported from California alone, according to Prof. Lindesmith. The whole scene is so shrouded in bureaucratic mystery that there are no national figures available *anywhere*.

[14] By March 1966 Dr. Timothy Leary faced a minimum of 5 years in jail and A.P. reported that the celebrated novelist Ken Kesey was a refugee in Mexico threatened with extradition by the FBI to face marijuana charges in California.

[15]Proceedings White House Conference on Narcotic and Drug Abuse, Sept. 27–28, 1962, State Department Auditorium, Washington, D.C. (p. 286).

It is the opinion of the Panel that the hazards of Marijuana per se have been exaggerated and that long criminal sentences imposed on an occasional user or possessor of the drug are in poor social perspective. Although Marijuana has long held the reputation of inciting individuals to commit sexual offenses and other antisocial acts, the evidence is inadequate to substantiate this. Tolerance and physical dependence do not develop and withdrawal does not produce an abstinence syndrome.

[16]Reply received December 22, 1965:

"I would advise you that I have been in touch with the Bureau of Narcotics and am of the opinion that nothing has been done in your case that is illegal or inconsistent with law enforcement practices designed to enforce the narcotics laws." In this case it was police request to arrested friends that they carry marijuana to *my* apartment and to that of the novelist William S. Burroughs.

[17] *New York Herald Tribune,* Nov. 22, 1963.

FIRST PUBLISHED: *Atlantic,* vol. 218, no. 5 (Nov. 1966) pp. 104, 107–112. Enlarged and reprinted: David Solomon, ed., *The Marihuana Papers* (Indianapolis: Bobbs-Merrill, 1966).

Ginsberg Talks about Speed

Let's issue a general declaration to the underground community, contra speedamos ex cathedra. Speed is anti-social, paranoid making, it's a drag, bad for your body, bad for your mind, generally speaking, in the long run uncreative and it's a plague in the whole dope industry. All the nice dope fiends are getting screwed up by the real horror monster Frankenstein Speedfreaks who are going around stealing and bad-mouthing everybody.

I've used speed, briefly, like for a day for writing, but the use of speed over two days tends to lead to irritability and inconsistency and a kind of Hitlerian fascist mentality, which may be the byproducts of real perceptions of interest. But generally, the interpretations are over-forced, with too much will power and insistence, so they're always leaning on everyone else around them, trying to force everybody else into their universe. It's not a common universe that is the problem, it's one everyone can participate in—the speed-crystal universe. Speed was originally invented by the Germans for use by the pilots in bombing England, so it's originally a kind of totalitarian synthetic.

The physiological problem is that if you stay up three or four or five days, you tend not to eat well enough to nourish your body, and pretty soon there comes to be a metaphysic of despising your body out of that crystal universe. Since you don't sleep, you don't get your 45 necessary minutes of dreaming each night, and so after a while the unconscious dream life begins to erupt during waking, walking around consciousness and you begin to act out your dream life and mistaking hallucinations from the unconscious as being manifest sensory realities that other people can pick up on, which is not true, so there's disjunction of realities. Or there's the insistence on your reality being the only reality, if you're on the speedfreak, which is undemocratic, and that's where it's totalitarian.

Since 1958, it's been a plague around my house. People that I liked or who were good artists, have gotten all screwed up on it, and come around burning down the door, stealing. All the stuff I brought back from India was stolen by speedfreaks.

The junk problem's an easy problem to handle compared to the speed problem. With speed you don't have a physiological addiction, but you do have a psychic addiction, which is strong and is followed by a long depression that lasts during this time. Apparently getting off speed requires a great deal of attention and care and love and nature. But the speed addict has generally so offended everybody by the time he wants to get off that he's created a social void for himself.

FIRST PUBLISHED: *Nickel Review*, vol. 4, no. 18 (Jan. 9, 1970) p. 5.

Prefatory Remarks Concerning Leary's Politics of Ecstasy

By the late '40s of this memory century the people I knew best and loved most had already broken thru the crust of old reasons and were dowsing for some supreme reality, "Christmas on Earth" Rimbaud said, "Second Religiousness" according to Spengler's outline of civilization declining through proliferation of non-human therefore boring technology; Blake had called "O Earth O Earth return!" centuries before, echoing the ancient gnostic prophecy that Whitman spelled out for America specifically demanding that the steam-engine "be confronted and met by at least an equally subtle and tremendous force-infusion for purposes of spiritualization, for the pure conscience, for genuine aesthetics, and for absolute and primal manliness and womanliness . . ." Ezra Pound's mind jumped to diagnose the dimming of the world's third eye: "With Usura the line grows thick."

One scholar who transmitted Blake's kabbala, S. Foster Damon, could remember his sudden vision of tiny flowers carpeting Harvard Yard violet before World War One, an image that lingered over 60 years in mind since his fellow student Virgil Thomson gave him the cactus peyote to eat. Damon concluded that rare beings like Blake are born with physiologic gift of such vision, continuous or intermittent. William James, whose pragmatic magic probably called the peyote god to Harvard in the first place, had included shamanistic chemical visions among the many authentic "Varieties of Religious Experience." His student Gertrude Stein experimented in alteration of consciousness through mindfulness of language by twentieth century had made language the dominant vehicle of civilized consciousness; her companion Alice B. Toklas contributed a cookbook recipe for hashish brownies to enlighten those persons over-talkative in drawing rooms unaware that "the medium is the message."

This synchronism is exquisite: William S. Burroughs also once of Harvard shared Miss Stein's mindfulness of the hypnotic drug-like power of language, and collaborated on cut-up rearrangement of stereotyped language forms with friend Brion Gysin, who recounts that he had originally given Miss Toklas the recipe for her famous brownies. Burroughs among others had begun experiments with drug-shamanism after World War Two—for the author of *Naked Lunch* it was a pragmatic extension of his Cambridge interest in linguistic anthropology. That same gnostic impulse broke through to clear consciousness simultaneously in many American cities: Gary Snyder realized the entire universe was "alive" one daybreak 1948 in Portland when a flight of birds rose out of the tree stillness in a gully by the city river, a natural vision—The masters of the Berkeley Renaissance read Gertrude Stein aloud and practiced poetic kabbala (charming synchronism that psychologist Timothy Leary met poets Jack Spicer and Robert Duncan in that same 1948 student scene)—Neal Cassady drove Jack Kerouac to Mexico in a prophetic automobile to see the physical body of America, the same Denver Cassady that one decade later drove Ken Kesey's Kosmos-patterned schoolbus on a Kafka-circus tour over the roads of the awakening nation—And that wakening began, some say, with the first saxophone cry of the new mode of black music which shook the walls of white city mind when Charles Parker lifted his birdflightnoted horn and announced a new rhythm of thinking, an extended breathing of the body in music and speech, a new consciousness. For as Plato had said, "When the mode of the music changes, the walls of the city shake."

The new consciousness born in these States can be traced back through old gnostic texts, visions, artists and shamans; it is the consciousness of our ground nature suppressed and desecrated. It was always the secret tale of the tribe in America, this great scandal of the closing of the doors of perception on nature's naked human form divine. It began with the white murder of Indian inhabitants of the ground, the theft and later usurious exploitation of their land, it continued with an assault on all races and species of Mother Nature herself and concludes today with total disruption of the ecology of the entire planet. No wonder black slaves kept for non-human use into this century in tear-gassed ghettos of megalopolis were the first aliens to sound the horn of change, the first strangers to call the great call through Basilides' many heavens. Amazing synchronism again, that Mr. Frank Takes Gun, Native American Church Amerindian Peyote Chief, invited the brilliantly talkative silver-haired psychiatrist who directed a Saskatchewan mental hospital in the early '50s to participate in a peyote ritual, and that the same Dr. Humphry Osmond having recognized a wonder of consciousness thus experienced passed on the catalyst in mescaline synthetic form to Aldous Huxley; and that Huxley's 1954 essay on the chemical opening of the doors of perception found its way to the tables of Bickford's Cafeteria Times Square New York and the couches of Reed College and Berkeley, where artist persons, having heard the great call of the blacks, already initiated themselves en masse to subtle gradations of their own consciousness experienced while puffing on the same Afric hemp smoked by Lester Young, Charles Parker, Thelonious Monk and Dizzy Gillespie.

Dr. Timothy Leary takes up his part of the tale of the tribe in a Mexican hut and brings his discovery to Harvard harmoniously—and there begins the political battle, black and white magic become publicly visible for a generation. Dr. Leary is a hero of American consciousness. He began as a sophisticated academician, he encountered discoveries in his field which confounded him and his own technology, he pursued his studies where attention commanded, he arrived beyond the boundaries of public knowledge. One might hesitate to say, like Socrates, like Galileo?—poor Dr. Leary, poor earth! yet here we are in science fiction history, in the age of hydrogen bomb apocalypse, the very *kali yuga* wherein man's stupidity so overwhelms the planet that ecological catastrophe begins to rehearse old tribe-tales of *karmic* retribution, fire and flood and Armageddon impending.

It would be natural (in fact *déjà vu*) that the very technology stereotyping our consciousness and desensitizing our perceptions should throw up its own antidote, an antidote synthetic such as LSD synchronous with mythic tribal Soma and peyote. Given such historic comedy, who could emerge from Harvard technology but one and only Dr. Leary, a respectable human being, a worldly man faced with the task of a Messiah. Inevitable! Not merely because the whole field of mental psychology as a "science" had arrived at biochemistry anyway. It was inevitable because the whole professional civilized world, like Dr. Leary, was already faced with the Messianic task of accelerated evolution (i.e., psychosocial revolution) including an alteration of human consciousness leading to the rapid mutation of social and economic forms. This staggering realization, psychedelic, i.e., consciousness expanding and mind-manifesting in itself, without the use of chemical catalysts, is now forced on all of us by images of our own unconscious rising from the streets of Chicago, where city teargas was dumped on Christ's very Cross in Lincoln Park AD 1968. The drains are backing up in the cities, smog noise and physiologic poison in food turns us to insect acts, overpopulation crazes the planet, our lakes corrupt, old riverways become dank fens, tanks enter Prague and Chicago streets simultaneous, police state arrives in every major city, starvation wastes African provinces, Chinese genocide in Tibet mirrors American genocide in Vietnam, Alarm! Alarm! howls deep as any Biblic prophecy.

Ourselves caught in the giant machine are conditioned to its terms, only holy vision or technological catastrophe or revolution break "the mind-forg'd manacles." Given one by-product of the technology that might, as it were by feed-back, correct the berserk machine and liberate the inventor's mind from captivity by robot hypnosis, Dr. Leary had in LSD an invaluable civilized elixir. For, as Dr. Jiri Roubichek observed early in Prague ("Artificial Psychosis," 1958), "LSD inhibits conditioned reflexes," and this single phrase, for rational men, might be the key to the whole gnostic mystery of LSD and Dr. Leary's role as unique, alas solitary, courageous, human and frank public democratic *bodhisattva*-teacher of the uses of LSD in America. For he took on himself the noble task of announcing the evidence of his senses despite the scary contumely of fellow academicians, the dispraising timorous irony of scientific "professionals," the stupidity meanness self-serving cowardice and hollow vanity of bureaucratic personnel from Harvard Yard to Mexico City to Washington, from the ignorant Sheriff's office in Dutchess County NY to the inner greedy Gordon-Liddy-haunted sanctums of the US Treasury Department in D.C., our whole "establishment" of civilization that defends us from knowledge of our own unconscious by means of policemen's clubs, and would resist the liberation of our minds and bodies by any brutish means available including teargas, napalm and the hydrogen bomb.

Dr. Leary conducted himself fairly and equitably, given the extraordinary nature of his knowledge; it took an innocent courage to explore his own unconditioned consciousness, to take LSD and other chemicals often enough to balance praxis with explanation, and to attempt to wed the enormity of his experience to reason. An heroic attempt to communicate clearly and openly through civilized technologic media to his fellow citizens, despite centuries of identity brainwash accelerated now to mass neurosis and Cold War apocalypse paranoia, required of Dr. Leary the proverbial wisdom of serpent and harmlessness of dove . . .

Dr. Leary was jailed for theory and practice of research on LSD and cannabis. He took the burden of giving honest public report of LSD and cannabis in terms more accurate and harmless than the faked science of the government party hacks and therefore his imprisonment was an act of insult to science, liberty, common sense, freedom, academy, philosophy, medicine, psychology as an art, and poetry as a tradition of human mind-vision.

WRITTEN: Sept. 12, 1968. Revised: 1968, 1970, 1985

FIRST PUBLISHED: *Village Voice* (Dec. 12, 1968) pp. 5–6, 8.

Declaration of Independence for Dr. Timothy Leary

From San Francisco Bay Area Prose Poets' Phalanx: to whomever concerned with liberty of expression in letters and speech, concerning immediate action to relieve the burden of imprisonment from the shoulders of Dr. Timothy Leary, who because of his philosophy, science and art practiced in the form of letters and speech has long suffered persecution, arrest, denunciation, numerous and prolonged jailings, bail denial, flight, and exile from the United States.

At time of writing, this Doctor of Philosophy without country, arrested in Switzerland, is held without charges awaiting extradition by California for the State's Department of Correction. This aggressive prolongation of the boring scandal of Dr. Leary's persecution by state bureaucracies, and present denial of his personal freedom by the Swiss state is an unnecessary injustice resolvable as follows:

Bay Area Prose Poets' Phalanx petitions the Swiss government, in faithfulness to the best of Western free-thinking tradition, to grant Dr. Leary status as permanent respected exile. We recommend that International P.E.N. Club request its Swiss chapter to intervene directly to Swiss authorities and propose the following information on behalf of Dr. Leary's request for freedom and privacy as a literary refugee persecuted by government for his thoughts and writings:

1. That federal prosecutors and judges proceeded against him and jailed him without bail for 30 years for the minor offense of carrying a tiny amount of marijuana, with the motive that because of his "publicized activities," namely, essays and speeches on drug usage theory, Dr. Leary "is regarded as a menace to the community so long as he is at large."

2. That although this original conviction of Dr. Leary was overthrown by the U.S. Supreme Court, the Federal police bureaucracy in America indicated its continued hostility to his "publicized activities" (namely, essays and speeches on drug usage theory) by trying him again for the same minor event, and by such abuse of language succeeded in having Dr. Leary sentenced to a 10-year jail term.

3. That California state prosecutors and judges escalated this legal abuse of philosophy by duplicating prosecution for possession of another tiny amount of marijuana, adding the enormity of another 10-year sentence and persecutive denial of bail, and super-added insult to injury by proclaiming in court openly that Dr. Leary, on the basis of the following essays: "Deal for Real," in

East Village Other, vol. 4, no. 3 (Sept. 24, 1969) and *Los Angeles Free Press;* "Episode and Postscript," in *Playboy,* vol. 16, no. 12 (Dec. 1969); was "an insidious and detrimental influence on society . . . a pleasure-seeking, irresponsible Madison Avenue advocate of the free use of LSD and marijuana." The Judge McMillan who pronounced these words held above his bench a copy of *Playboy* in justification for his language denying bail and sentencing Dr. Leary to the second 10-year imprisonment from which the author of:

Jail Notes (New York: Douglas Book Corp., 1970) surprisingly escaped on September 12, 1970, and took troubled refuge abroad.

Whatever one's opinions, or natural or national preferences amongst intoxicants, letters, religions, and political or ecological theory, the Bay Area Prose Poets' Phalanx hereby affirms that Dr. Leary must certainly have the right to publish his own theories; that at stake in this case, once and for all, is Dr. Leary's freedom to manifest his thoughts in the form of poems, psychological commentaries, dialogues, and essays of literary nature before a public whose younger generations, by themselves credibly experienced with the machines, politics and drugs that are the subject of Dr. Leary's writings, include a large minority (perhaps a majority in his native land) who wish Dr. Leary well, and pray for his security, peace and protection from persecution by government police bureaucracies everywhere.

It is in fact remarkable to note that Dr. Leary is, for a modern intellectual, a solitary splendid example of a Man Without a Country. Refused entry by most governments, he cannot visit other countries lest he be extradited to face the cruel and unusual punishment of now more than 20 years' jail if forcibly carried back to America's shores. Bay Area Prose Poets' Phalanx takes note that this proposed imprisonment of Dr. Leary rises merely from differences of opinion on public philosophy involving drug use, a scientific matter now being debated in professional circles (psychology, art, religion, poetry, neurochemistry).

We take note that a previous domestic appeal against American persecution of Dr. Timothy Leary issued early in the history of this government's war on him was published on May 10, 1966, and signed by: Howard S. Becker, Ph.D., Arnold Beichman, Eric Bentley, George

Bowering, Joe Brainard, Harvey Brown, Robert Creeley, Robert S. de Ropp, Ph.D., Diane di Prima, Jason Epstein, Jules Feiffer, Leslie Fiedler, Peter Fonda, Joel Fort, M.D., Jack Gelber, Nat Hentoff, Laura Huxley, Kenneth Koch, Stephen Koch, Irving Kristol, Lawrence Lipton, Robert Lowell, Norman Mailer, Jonas Mekas, Anaïs Nin, Charles Olson, Norman Podhoretz, Ned Polsky, Ad Reinhart, Rabbi Zalman Schachter, Richard Seaver, Robert Silvers, Gary Snyder, Susan Sontag, Alan Watts, D.D., Philip Whalen, and many others. The statement of that date stated:

1. "The infringement of constitutional rights of privacy, interference with religious and scientific practice, excessive enforcement and public anxiety have grown to the crisis stage— through the application of irrational marijuana statutes.
2. The long imprisonment given to the psychological researcher Dr. Timothy Leary, for the possession of one-half ounce of marijuana, illustrates the irrationality of present marijuana laws, and is a cruel and unjust punishment in violation of the Constitution of the United States."

Bay Area Prose Poets' Phalanx also takes note of the very police bureaucracy in the U.S. that has hounded Dr. Leary for his professional opinions is the same Narcotics Bureau that in its historic "war on physicians"* including suppression of documents and prohibition of medical research, has helped create a major "national plague" of heroin addiction. Personnel of these Narcotics Bureaus are themselves involved in narcotics traffic.

Bay Area Prose Poets' Phalanx also takes note of recent accusations implicating the U.S. C.I.A. and other military and intelligence organizations in an historic role of subsidizing major traffickers in Indo-Chinese opium (namely, Gen. Ouane Rathikoune of Laos, Marshall Ky of South Vietnam, KMT armies presently in northern Thailand).

Given vast confusions of modern technology and now the much-publicized credibility gap between American government and public, as well as previously much-publicized difficulties of generation gap, the request of California (U.S.) Dept. of Correction through the American State

---

*As well as the undersigned poets, essayists, and novelists.

Dept. to the Swiss Government for criminal extradition of Dr. Leary from the mandarin anonymity of his short life of letters in Switzerland, seems to the under-signed poets, essayists and novelists an unseemly and intolerable continuing and exasperating literary vendetta against a specific gifted individual. Dr. Leary is certainly a "High Priest" within his area of specialized scholarship as against the questionable authority of any state in this scientific controversy.

The case of Dr. Leary is outright a case of persecution of ideas and texts—the persecution of his philosophy. Though arrested for grass, he was sentenced for philosophy. Jailed for grass, he was long prisoned for opinion. Denied bail for grass possession, he was detained behind barbed wire for ideological heresy.

Bay Area Poets' Phalanx hereby petitions U.S. officials concerned to re-think hostile attitudes and adopt behavior more tolerant of natural controversy and common opinion: to recognize that in exercise of arbitrary authority over Dr. Leary they are engaging in unfortunate "State Policy."

Bay Area Prose Poets' Phalanx takes note of the public viability of the formulation proposed by the late poet Charles Olson, friend of Dr. Leary, that now "Private is public, and public is how we behave." We affirm that Dr. Leary has the literary right to make his private opinions known publicly, and to engage unpunished in public literary activity. Poet Olson, 1961 Cambridge, addressing Professor Leary: "When the police come after you, you can stay in my house."

Bay Area Prose Poets' Phalanx specifically requests the American State Dept. to waste no more time, money or passion in this case, and to take no further steps to make a physical prize of Dr. Leary's person. No move is a good move for the American government in this case. We hereby request the Swiss government to accept Dr. Leary as an archetype of the traditional political, cultural, literary, or philosophic refugee and grant him personal asylum.

As fellow writers, we recommend that Dr. Leary be considered, by all countries, advanced or underdeveloped on both sides of the so-called Cold War, a distinguished refugee from persecution by an International Police Bureaucracy whose executive and philosophic center in this case is long-corrupted American Narcotics Bureau and its propaganda lobby, the International Narcotics Enforcement Officers Association (INEOA, Albany, N.Y., Honorary President Harry Anslinger, former chief of the U.S. Narcotics Bureau).

Bay Area Prose Poets' Phalanx takes note that the above bureaucracy has arrested and persecuted artist-persons and "underground" newspapers in many countries on pretexts of possession of small amounts of hemp grass for motives ranging from political hostility to culture shock; and has attempted to frame a number of celebrated writers, including William Burroughs, Allen Ginsberg, some defendants in the Chicago Conspiracy Trial, and black and white political intellectuals, such as the presently-jailed Martin Sostre and John Sinclair, on charges similar to those used to entrap Dr. Timothy Leary for almost a decade now in a web of legal complications, a threatening bureaucratic maya created for him by financially-compromised officious members of as anti-intellectual, criminally-associated and professionally-corrupt a bureaucracy as U.S. Narcotics Bureaus—federal, state and local—have proved in recent history.

Finally, the undersigned take note of Dr. Leary's influence on "students and others of immature judgment or tender years" for which he "is regarded as a menace to the community so long as he is at large," in the eyes of his government prosecutors by their own word. We take note of Dr. Leary's public essays in opposition to the American government's war in Vietnam, and his dialogues such as that published widely with Eldridge Cleaver in Algiers touching the same subject. We understand that Dr. Leary's request for Swiss asylum will be based upon his opposition to the war in Vietnam, and that in context of this disastrous war's crises his plea is a legitimate statement of his situation.

In sum, Bay Area Prose Poets' Phalanx and associate friends urge the Swiss government to release Dr. Timothy Leary from provisional extraditional arrest, not cooperate in extraditing Dr. Leary to America. We recommend to Swiss and all other governments that they grant our fellow author philosopher safe political asylum to complete his work— exploration of his consciousness, vocal literary expression of that unique individual person whose presence is held sacred in all humane and gnostic democratic nations, and ever enshrined in their literary monuments, witness Whitman and Thoreau for America.

WRITTEN: July 4, 1971

FIRST PUBLISHED: *Declaration of Independence for Dr. Timothy Leary, July 4, 1971,* San Francisco, privately printed flyer.

Om Ah Hum: 43 Temporary Questions on Dr. Leary

1. Trust. (Should we stop trusting our friends like in a hotel room in Moscow?)
2. Is he a Russian-model prisoner brought into courtroom news conference blinking in daylight after years in jails and months incommunicado in solitary cells with nobody to talk to but thought-control police interrogators?
3. Is his head upside down?
4. Will he indulge in cannibalism, eating his mind?
5. Isn't it common sense to turn the other cheek to his forced confessions?
6. What advice give young on LSD? (Try it with healthy body mind and speech!)
7. No LSD cactus mushroom teachers needed now in cities, isn't Lady Psychedelia big enough to teach by herself with all her granny-wisdom?
8. Is it *déjà vu,* Leary's forced confession so outrageous—are all my serious prefaces to his books and imperious anti–thought-control declarations reduced to rubbish?
9. "Flow along with the natural errors of things." Old Chinese wisdom and sense of humor. Will this be harder for those caught in Leary's new truthfulness and new lying?
10. Isn't his new truthfulness a lie to please the police to let him go?
11. Is he like Zabbathi Zvi the False Messiah, accepted by millions of Jews centuries ago, who left Europe for the Holy Land, was captured by the Turks on his way, told he'd have his head cut off unless he converted to Islam, and so accepted Allah? Didn't his followers split into sects, some claiming it was a wise decision?
12. Isn't there an element of humor in Leary's new twist?
13. Doesn't he recently hear of voices from outer space, does he want to leave earth like a used-up eggshell? Has he given up on the planet?
14. Is he finally manifesting an alchemical transformation of consciousness?
15. Is there more police space henceforth, no opposition allowed?
16. Are not the police, especially drug police, corrupt and scandal-ridden, Watergate person like Liddy and Mardian connected

with his long persecution, with urban narcs stealing and
peddling heroin?

17. Is Leary on his way to outer space in Space Ship Terra II still?

18. What of the rumors and messages heard last spring that brain
    conditioner experiment drugs were to be administered to Leary
    in Vacaville prison, where such experiments were rumored
    common?

19. Isn't it clear that no friend has spoken with Leary personally
    recently, he's been shifted prison to prison, his lawyers can't
    reach him, he's been incommunicado sequestered for
    "confession" surrounded by government agents and informers,
    no one else hears from him?

20. Is Joanna Harcourt Smith his one contact-spokes-agent a sex spy,
    agent provocateuse, double-agent, CIA hysteric, jealous tigress
    or what?

21. What was Joanna's role, isolating him from decade-old
    supporters and friends, using up all his crucial legal defense
    money? Remember when I suggested to Leary that she might be
    some sort of police agent he turned to her asking, "What do you
    say?" She looked at him and answered, "He hates women."
    Folsom Prison Spring 1973.

22. Shouldn't police give up their case as preposterous and
    remember that 410,000 other Americans were busted for pot in
    1973?

23. Wasn't Leary trusted by many people who contributed to his
    legal defense funds, wrote declarations, lectured and sang
    moneyraising in defense of his professional and constitutional
    rights as psychologist experimenting new research field?

24. Didn't he turn in his own lawyer for bringing him pot in jail, is
    that a light matter like 50 dollar fine, or jail and disbarment?

25. Is Leary exaggerating and lying to build such confused cases and
    conspiracies that the authorities will lose all the trials he
    witnesses, and he'll be let go in the confusion?

26. Where has Leary's humor gone? Did he ever claim to be priest
    except to escape obnoxious law? Is he messianic? Can his word
    be trusted in court? Can President Ford's? Or the entire
    Government's?

27. Will it end that all the victims of his song are his lawyers?

28. Will there be more political trials like those of Spock, Berrigan, Chicago 7, Ellsberg, collapsible conspiracy entrapments of bohemian left by right-wing government fanatics left over from Watergate conspiracy? More domestic police violence against non-alcoholic teaheads? Government prosecutors who have Leary by the balls for smoking pot, like Guy Goodwin, do they drink cocktails?

29. Does Leary see himself spiritual President like Nixon, and is he trying to clean the *karma* blackboard by creating a hippie Watergate? Will he be pardoned by the next guru?

30. Is the Government-announced change on Leary's part rational, objective, free and calm—or angry fearful suffering jail too long?

31. Will Leary's documentary confession film be seen by friends in theater or court room?

32. Speaking of acid capitalism, Leary was too broke to fund his very solid legal appeals, thousands of people including myself contributed too little to see it to successful conclusion, so who makes money on acid and grass, men in jail, or their jailers and prosecutors? How many million dollars have the police spent entrapping Leary?

33. Prosecutors like Goodwin to whom Leary sings, have conducted witch-hunts with false witness before, is it not?

34. Did anybody ever hear of the need to hide Leary incommunicado to protect him from his old friends who might harm him, except from police mouths? Is it not police mind naiveté that imagines "contracts" on his body?

35. Would the Government agree to public symposium (such as this) and Leary free to present his new thoughts to old friends in press conference in calm many-sided discussion, to clear the air of false and forced confession? Must his changes be announced by remote control from secret rooms through selected media contacts, or via videotape screens behind which no friend can look?

36. Wasn't it amazing to begin with, prophetic mix of Liddy and Leary at Millbrook in mid-sixties, and Liddy's dozens of illegal raids?

37. Are there any police here at the press conference?

38. America, must I re-examine my conscience?
39. In the gas-petroleum ballgame are the police winning a metaphysical victory?
40. Will more citizens be arrested and taken to jail as was Leary?
41. What will Kissinger say? Will he also be arrested for conspiring "more than 8 million dollars" Chile subversion lying and Allende killed?
42. Will citizens be arrested indicted taken to jail for Leary's freedom?
43. Doesn't the old cry "Free Tim Leary!" apply now urgent as ever?

WRITTEN: March 18, 1974

FIRST PUBLISHED: *Berkeley Barb* (Sept. 20–26, 1974) p. 1.

PART 3
Mindfulness and Spirituality

PERSONAL CONSCIOUSNESS

Public Solitude

EDITOR'S NOTE: This address was delivered at the Arlington Street Church, Boston, on the occasion of the First Convocation of the Unitarian-Universalist Layman's League Center for Research and Development.

I am speaking from this pulpit conscious of history, of my role as poet, of the addresses and essays in public consciousness by my transcendental predecessors in this city, with all the awesome prophecies about these states pronounced by Thoreau and Emerson, and elsewhere the more naked Whitman: prophecies that have now come true.

—I say of all this tremendous and dominant play of solely materialistic bearings upon current life in the United States, with the results already seen, accumulating, and reaching far into the future, that they must either be confronted and met by at least an equally subtle force-infusion for purposes of spiritualization, for the pure conscience, for genuine esthetics, and for absolute and primal manliness and womanliness—or else our modern civilization, with all its improvements, is in vain, and we are on the road to a destiny, a status, equivalent, in its real world, to that of the fabled damned.

—[Walt Whitman] *Democratic Vistas*

Because our governors and politicos have failed to perceive the obvious I wish to make some political suggestions to this community; make them as poet, and claim powers of prophecy as did the good gray bards before me in this country, because one who looks in his heart and speaks frankly can claim to prophecy. And what is prophecy? I can not propose right and wrong, or objective future event such as purple balloons on

125

Jupiter in 1984: but I can have the confidence to trust my own fantasy and express my own private thought. All have this gift of prophecy; who dare assume it though?

The present condition of life for American person is one of deathly public solitude. We've built a technological Tower of Babel around ourselves, and are literally (as in Gemini) reaching into heaven to escape the planet. Now giant overpopulation depends on a vast metallic superstructure to feed and transport all the bodies here together. The stupendous machinery surrounding us conditions our "thoughts feelings and apparent sensory impressions," and reinforces our mental slavery to the material universe we've invested in.

Yet according to Chuang Tzu 2,500 years ago, "The understanding of the men of ancient times went a long way. How far did it go? To the point where some of them believed that things have never existed—so far, to the end, where nothing can be added . . . Words like these will be labeled the Supreme Swindle. Yet, after ten thousand generations, a great sage may appear who will know their meaning, and it will still be as though he appeared with astonishing speed." Yeats appearing in Ireland in this century declared:

> This preposterous pig of a world, its farrow that so solid seem
> Must vanish on an instant, did the mind but change its theme.

How can we Americans make our minds change theme? For unless the theme changes—encrustation of the planet with machinery, inorganic metal smog violent outrage and mass murder will take place. We witness these horrors already.

Abruptly then, I will make a first proposal: on one level symbolic, but to be taken as literally as possible, it may shock some and delight others—that everybody who hears my voice, directly or indirectly, try the chemical LSD at least once; every man woman and child American in good health over the age of 14—that, if necessary, we have a mass emotional nervous breakdown in these States once and for all; that we see bankers laughing in their revolving doors with strange staring eyes. May everybody in America turn on, whatever the transient law—because individual soul development (as once declared by a poet in jail in this city) is our law transcending the illusions of the political state. Soul also transcends LSD, may I add, to reassure those like myself who would fear a chemical dictatorship. I propose, then, that everybody including the President and his and our vast hordes of generals, executives, judges and legislators of these States go to nature, find a kindly teacher or Indian peyote chief or guru guide, and assay their consciousness with LSD.

Then, I prophecy, we will all have seen some ray of glory or vastness beyond our conditioned social selves, beyond our government, beyond America even, that will unite us into a peaceable community.

The LSD I am proposing is literal. I hope it will be understood as not the solution, but a typical and spiritually revolutionary catalyst, where many varieties of spiritual revolution are necessary to transcend specifically the political COLD WAR we are all involved in.

Anger and control of anger is our problem. Already we have enough insight into politics to be aware of one very simple thing: that we can judge all politics and all public speech and ideology by perceiving the measure of anger manifested therein. All present political parties propose violence to resolve our confusions, as in Vietnam. We might look for a third party, specifically named a Peace Party—referring to individual subjective peaceableness (such as we have not seen in our populace or our leaders) as well as consequent public peaceableness; a party founded on psychology not ideology. We obviously need to feed China and India not ignore, manipulate, or threaten to destroy them. The earth is yet to be saved from our aggression, and living organic life like unto our own nature be replaced on its surface which has been overgrown with cancerous inanimate matter, metal and asphalt. And though many mammal species have been made extinct in this century there are many we can yet save including ourselves.

Driving out of New York or into Boston at night we see the transparent apparitional glitter of buildings walling the horizon, and we know that these are transient specters. In cold daylight we believe in their finality. But it is that half-dreaming insight of normal consciousness that may provide the direction for our imagination to manifest itself in the material world.

What can the young do with themselves faced with this American version of the planet? The most sensitive and among the "best minds" do drop out. They wander over the body of the nation looking into the faces of their elders, they wear long Adamic hair and form Keristan[1] communities in the slums, they pilgrimage to Big Sur and live naked in forests seeking natural vision and meditation, they dwell in the Lower East Side as if it were a hermetic forest. And they assemble thousands together as they have done this year in Golden Gate Park San Francisco or Tompkins Park in New York to manifest their peaceableness in demonstrations of fantasy that transcend protest against—or for—the hostilities of Vietnam. Young men and women in speckled clothes, minstrel's garb, jester's robes, carrying balloons, signs "President Johnson we are praying for you," gathered chanting Hindu and Buddhist mantras to calm their fellow citizens who are otherwise entrapped in a planetary barroom brawl.

But there has been no recognition of this insight on the part of the fathers and teachers (Father Zossima's famous cry!) of these young. What's lacking in the great institutions of learning? The specific wisdom discipline that that young propose: search into inner space.

Children drop out of schools because there are no, or very few, gurus. Those elders concerned with this practical problem might consider that there is an easy practical solution: the establishment within centers of learning of facilities for wisdom search which the ancients proposed as the true function of education in the first place: academies of self-awareness, classes in spiritual teaching, *darshan*[2] with holymen of disciplined mind-consciousness. One might well, in fact, employ the drop-out beatniks as instructors in this department, and thereby officially recognize and proclaim the social validity of exploration of inner space. Tibetan monks, swamis, *yogins* and *yoginis*, psychedelic guides, Amerindian peyote chiefs, even a few finished Zen Roshis and many profound poets are already present and available in our cities for such work, though at present they battle immigration bureaucracies and scholarly heads of departments of Oriental Religion.

What I am proposing as policy, for us elders, for what community we have, is self-examination as Official Politics; an Official Politics of Control of Anger. With state propaganda reversed in that direction, church and university teaching and research in that direction, and request to the government for vast sums of money equal to the outerspace program; and consequent billboards on the highways "Control Your Anger—Be Aware of Yourself."

There is a change of consciousness among the younger generations, in a direction always latent to Elder America, toward the most complete public frankness possible. As the Gloucester poet Charles Olson formulated it, "Private is public, and public is how we behave." This means revision of standards of public behavior to include indications of private manners heretofore excluded from public consciousness.

Thus, new social standards, more equivalent to private desire—as there is increased sexual illumination, new social codes may be found acceptable to rid ourselves of fear of our own nakedness, rejection of our own bodies.

Likely an enlarged family unit will emerge for many citizens; possibly, as the Zen Buddhist anarchist anthropologist Gary Snyder observed, with matrilineal descent as courtesy to those *dakinis*[3] whose *saddhana* or holy path is the sexual liberation and teaching of *dharma* to many frightened males (including myself) at once. Children may be held in common, with the orgy an acceptable community sacrament—one that brings all people closer together. Certainly one might seduce the Birch Society to partake in naked orgy, and the police with their wives, together with LeRoi Jones the brilliantly angry poet. America's political need is orgies in the parks, on Boston Common and in the Public Gardens, with naked bacchantes[4] in our national forests.

I am not proposing idealistic fancies, I am acknowledging what is already happening among the young in fact and fantasy, and proposing official blessing for these breakthroughs of community spirit. Among the young we find a new breed of White Indians in California communing with illuminated desert redskins; we find our teenagers dancing Nigerian Yoruba dances and entering trance states to the electric vibration of the Beatles who have borrowed shamanism from Afric sources. We find communal religious use of *ganja,* the hemp sacred to Mahadev (Great Lord) Shiva. There's now heard the spread of mantra chanting in private and such public manifestations as peace marches, and soon we will have Mantra Rock over the airwaves. All the available traditions of U.S. Indian vision-quest, peyote ritual, mask dancing, Oriental *pranayama,*[5] east Indian ear music are becoming available to the U.S. unconscious through the spiritual search of the young. Simultaneously there is a new Diaspora of Tibetan Lamaist initiates; texts such as the *Book of the Dead* and *I Ching* have found fair-cheeked and dark-browed Kansas devotees. And rumor from the West Coast this season brings the legendary Hevajra Tantra—a document central to Vajrayana Buddhism's Lightningbolt Illumination—into public light as a source book for tantric community rules. LSD structured by ancient disciplines for meditation and community regulation.

Ideas I have dwelled on are mixed: there is some prescription for public utopia thru education in inner space. There is more prescription here for the individual: as always, the old command to free ourselves from social conditioning, laws and traditional mores.

And discover the guru in our own hearts. —And set forth within the new wilderness of machine America to explore open spaces of consciousness in self and fellow selves. If there be the necessary revolution in America it will come that way. It's up to us older hairs who still have relation with some of the joy of youth to encourage this revolutionary individual search.

But how can peaceful psychological politics succeed when $50 billion a year is spent on busy participation in armed conflict? "Vietnam War Brings Prosperity"—headline *Lincoln Nebraska Star*, February 1966. Certainly the awareness itself of this condition will help some of us: as did Ike's warning against the military-industrial complex running the mind of the nation.

As a side note: there *are* specific methods for combating the mental dictatorship over "thoughts feelings and apparent sensory impressions" imposed on us by military-industrial control of language and imagery in public media. W. S. Burroughs has provided a whole armamentarium of counter-brainwash techniques: cut-up of newspapers and ads, collage of political entertainment news to reveal the secret intention of the senders, observation of TV imagery with sound off and simultaneous apperception of voices on the radio or street. These methods are effective in jolting the soft machine of the brain out of its conditioned hypnosis.

Cutting out, or dropping out, of the culture will not lead to a chaos of individuality: what it will mean, for the young, is training in meditation and art (and perhaps Neolithic lore), and responsibility of a new order, to the community of the heart, not to our heart-less society wherein we have read the headline in the *Omaha World Herald*: "Rusk Says Toughness Essential For Peace."

The "oversoul" to be discovered is a pragmatic reality. We can all tell signs of an illuminated man in business of the church—one who is open-hearted, non-judging, empathetic, compassionate to the rejected and condemned. The tolerant one, the observer, the aware. And we see that these souls do influence action.

Finally, detachment comes naturally: we all know the war is camp, hate is camp, murder is camp, even love is camp, the universe is a grand camp according to Chuang Tzu and the *Prajnaparamita Sutra*. This detachment is salvation. We have an international youth society of solitary children—stilyagi, provo, beat, mufada, nadaista, energumeno, mod and rocker—all aghast at the space age horror world they are born to, not habituated to—and now questioning the nature of the universe itself *as is proper* in the space age.

There are many contradictions here, especially between proposed communal sex orgy and contemplative choiceless awareness (as the sage Krishnamurti articulated it this Fall in New York). Whitman noticed that too: "Do I contradict myself? Very well, I contradict myself." A dialogue between these contradictions is a good healthy way of life, one correcting the other. Indulgence in sexuality and sensational ecstasy may well lead to contemplative awareness of desire and cessation of desire.

I know although when looks meet
I tremble to the bone,
The more I leave the door unlatched
The sooner love is gone.

What satisfaction is now possible for the young? Only the satisfaction of their desire—love, the body, and orgy: the satisfaction of a peaceful natural community where they can circulate and explore persons, cities, and the nature of the planet—the satisfaction of encouraged self-awareness, and the satiety and cessation of desire, anger, grasping and craving.

Respect for the old? Yea when the old are tranquil and not nervous and respect the sport of the young. Holymen do inspire respect. One conservative Vaishnavite Swami Bhaktivedanta moved into the Lower East Side this year and immediately dozens of young LSD freak-outs flocked to sing the Hare Krishna Maha mantra with him—chant for the preservation of the planet.

But a nation of elders convinced that spiritual search is immaturity, and that national war and metallic communication is maturity, cannot ask for respect from the young. For the present conduct of the elders in America is a reflection of lack of self-respect.

I am in effect setting up moral codes and standards which include drugs, orgy, music and primitive magic as worship rituals—educational tools which are supposedly contrary to our cultural mores; and I am proposing these standards to you respectable ministers, once and for all, that you endorse publicly the private desire and knowledge of mankind in America, so to inspire the young.

It may appear from this address that I find myself increasingly alienated from the feeling-tone, ideology and conduct of the supposed majority of my fellow citizens: thus the title public solitude. But I do not feel myself alienated from all our inmost private desire, which the prophet Walt Whitman articulated in his second preface to his life work 90 years ago, still passionately expressive of our hearts in space-age America:

> Something more may be added—for, while I am about it, I would make a full confession. I also sent out "Leaves of Grass" to arouse and set flowing in man's and women's hearts, young and old, endless streams of living, pulsating love and friendship, directly from them to myself, now and ever. To this terrible, irrepressible yearning (surely more or less down underneath in most human souls)—this never-satisfied appetite for sympathy, and this boundless offering of sympathy—this universal democratic comradeship—this old, eternal, yet ever-new interchange of adhesiveness, so fitly emblematic of America—I have given in that book, undisguisedly, declaredly, the openest expression. Besides, important as they are in my purpose as "Calamus" cluster of Leaves of Grass (and more or less running through the book, and cropping out in Drum-Taps) mainly resides in its political significance. In my opinion, it is by a fervent, accepted development of comradeship, the beautiful and sane affection of man for man, latent in all the young fellows, north and south, east and west,—it is by this, I say, and by what goes directly and indirectly along with it, that the United States of the future (I cannot too often repeat,) are to be most effectually welded together, intercalated, anneal'd into a living union.

Footnote to Public Solitude Essay, Boston 1966

Our life consciousness is increasingly conditioned by the massive material structure we have erected around ourselves to sustain the innumerable population born of technological meditation. A circular feedback: the more thought for these bodies, the more bodies, and the more need for thought for the care sustenance and prolongation of body life. These thoughts have led us to escape the physical limit of the planet. So we find ourselves preparing to spread our seed throughout a physical universe, and all our thought consciousness trapped in this particular universe; and conditioning to this area of consciousness continually reinforced on threat of pain starvation death by the Tower of Babel we are building.

That is one thought, that passes through our minds often. Another thought we all have entertained is that "this preposterous pragmatic pig of a world, its farrow that so solid seem, would vanish on the instant, did the mind but change its theme." We have Buddhist meditation documents to prove this experience; we also have a technological chemistry to precipitate this sensation. We have texts such as the *Tibetan Book of the Dead*, that link the two traditions of transcendentalism, ancient and modern. Ancient documents, presently unearthed or translated, reveal a certain secret about the ordinary world we inhabit. Chuang Tzu's yatter, "I'm going to try speaking some reckless words and I want you to listen to them recklessly . . . The understanding of the men of ancient times went a long way. How far did it go? To the point where some of them believed that things have never existed—" And Highest Perfect Wisdom Heart Sutra hints the same. Thus we are in the nightmarish condition of beings existing in a dream universe wherein our politics have led us to expand our claims to that dream stuff unto its physical limits. And we have a dream chemistry that like a few puffs of DMT can make the "apparent sensory impression" of Maya disappear instantly in a radiant explosion of wave vibrations that look like Einstein's platonic eyeball and just as real as the First National Bank.

WRITTEN: Nov. 12, 1966

FIRST PUBLISHED: *East Village Other* (Dec. 15, 1966-Jan. 1967) pp. 6–7.

Everybody Should Get High for the Next Ten Years

Makes very little difference what happens, the next ten years, because the main thing in the universe isn't at all affected by these little shifts of anthills, musics, nations, marriages. The main thing's nameless, so I'll call it beauty—the King and Lord of the Cosmos, a perfect being who sits on a throne made of vanishing ink. It has a face so radiant that once you've seen it, or guessed at it, you know that this creature has always been here and will be around as long as it wants, and won't be touched by men's atomic claws or the scary dust of the Apocalypse.

Beauty is so perfect that it doesn't depend on anything happening in this world that we see with our feet and brains. We've all seen beauty face to face, one time or other—and said "oh, my god, *of course*, so that's what it's all about, no wonder I was born and had all those secret weird feelings!" Maybe it was a moment of instantaneous perfect stillness in some cowpatch in the Catskills when the trees suddenly came alive like a Van Gogh painting or a Wordsworth poem. Or a minute listening to, say, Wagner on the phonograph when the music sounded as if it was getting nightmarishly sexy and alive awful, like an elephant calling far away in the moonlight.

At that moment you either kill your soul and go out and make money, or you pick up on the fact for good that there's something ALIVE behind the universe that nobody, but nobody, has ever had the guts to meet. Or said much about it if they did, except in strange art or mathematic forms. Meeting the invisible elephant and looking in his eye means the end of you, and the eternal return of the old God that everyone at once knows and that never dies.

Beauty is beauty, that's all there is to it. If you are interested in *you,* then you're stuck with you and you're stuck with your death. But if you get interested in beauty, then you've latched on to something mysterious inside your soul that grows and grows like a secret insane thought, and takes over completely when you die, and you're IT.

A shuddery situation—it's hard to let go your selfhood and have a good time with beauty—we're brought up to scheme and battle to make it here and now with gold, lovers, power, clothes, and face that anyone from our mother to the next door neighbor cop can see and respect. But in the long run we're all going to have to give up and drop dead and enter beauty—in fact beauty is what kills us, beauty is the great murderer.

Get used to it early and it'll save us all from a life of phony nightmare.

Life is a nightmare for most people, who want something else, not what life offers freely. People want a lesser fake of beauty, something transient and faulty, a hot-dog that's doomed to disappear in the blink of an eye—any old grandmother will tell you.

This is a lot of nutty raving, but it needs to be said, if people want to hassle about the fate of the next 10 years. What'll happen is that we'll all grow older, get nearer to death, bear children, write poems, buy cars, see Paris or Moscow, mow the lawn, goof under trees in springtime.

And some of us will realize that our fate is old age, sickness and death, as the oriental sages say.

Now it's weird enough to be in this human form so temporarily, without huge gangs of people, whole societies, trying to pretend that their temporary bread and breasts are the be-all and end-all of the soul's fate, and enforcing this ridiculous opinion with big rules of thought and conduct, bureaucracies to control the soul, FBI's, television, wars, politics, boring religions.

So what'll we do in the next ten years? Blow up the universe? Probably not. But let's blow up America—a false America's been getting in the way of realization of beauty—let's all get high on the soul.

WRITTEN: Nov. 4, 1959

Unpublished.

Prose Contribution to Cuban Revolution

I have been sitting in lovely club-bar across the street where Greek boys congregate, they are friendly and they make love between men like in Plato, the whole classic love scene preserved intact with no faggotry involved, a huge relief to find it's really true and good as an ideal, but for real. Though I find myself now shy and so except for a few not so satisfactory flings with boys I dug for cock but not really in love with, have not been very promiscuous or don't get too deep involved, but dig watching the scene and being in presence of men who are open, that is, where my feelings are not *queer* but something out of old human love story.

This will have to be long junk letter so might as well relax and get to the point that's bothering me, you maybe right now, jump in, what to do about politics, Cuba, human history, what I should do, what you are doing. I didn't know I was your monster that much, meaning in your respect and conscience, though that's what I've tried to be for a lot of people, that's the image I had of myself as poet-prophet friend on side of love and the Wild Good. That's the karma I wanted, to be saint. That's what I told Van Doren anyway and dreamed of myself; although wanting to get into heaven without paying ugly prices as of yore. Prophesy without death as a consequence, giggle into paradise, that was the dream Peter and I had together; that was the ideal mellow feeling I had respecting Kerouac and other heroes for me, Neal, Bill, including Huncke; and anybody that dug that scene with us. Already it's an exclusive club; and my measure at the time was the sense of personal genius and acceptance of all strangeness in people as their nobility; staying *out* of conflict and politics, staying with sort of Dostoyevskian-Shakespearean *know*, ken, of things as mortal, tearful, transient, sacred—not to join one side or other for an idea, however serious, realizing the relativity and limitation of all judgments and discriminations, relying on the angel of wide consciousness in us to always sympathize or empathize with anybody, even Hitler, because that's natural as in Whitman it's natural to be everybody at once, as it is in Dostoyevsky to understand the weirdness of everybody, even if it seems to conflict or lead to conflicts; wanting to stay sympathetic, even to Trilling, as to thieves or suicides or murderers. All this in the free atmosphere of US and appropriate to it, where we are not directly faced with threat of starve or extermination; except private deaths suicides faced and touched and for me shied away from. Now Bill and Jack were my monsters in that, that is they were the broad funny minds in which I recognized this sense of life, thru whose eyes I saw; Jack always telling me I was a "hairy loss," chiding my attempts to be vain, control moralities thru my mind, seeing in me vanities of wanting to Howl on stages and be hero, be famous, or be a leader or intellectual, be superior thru mind-intelligence, criticize, get involved in politics, which in his-my eyes is always vanity trying to have power and impress other people which finally leads to big decisions and executions and unkindnesses and loss of the mortal empathy, i.e. if you take sides you make others enemies and can't see them any more; and you become like them, a limited identity. Well all this very simpatico and true in its way, except I did have this desire to be labor leader people's hero, that is, with my Jewish left wing atheist Russian background I even made a vow (not ever to be broken) on the ferryboat when I went to take entrance exam at Columbia, vow forever that if I succeeded in the scholarship test and got a chance I would never betray the ideal—to help the masses in their misery. At the time I was very political and just recovering from Spanish Civil War which obsessed me in Jersey age 11 or 13. First upset of this idealism I had, entering to study law as per plan of becoming pure Debs, was being mocked and shamed at my idea structure of the time by Lu. C. [Lucien Carr] in workman's cafeteria on 125 Street, where as a trembling Columbia intellectual, hardly "one of the roughs," I found I was actually so self-conscious and mental I was scared of the workmen in the cafeteria— that having to do with my complete inexperience of life and also sensitive homosexual virginity and general naiveté—scared that is, in sense of feeling strange, an outsider, superior-inferior, I couldn't have a conversation with any of the soup eaters—I was obviously too gauche to fit in any way, and yet I had this image of myself as a *leader* of these imaginary masses. So then my direction turned to getting experience, working on ships and as welder and kicked out of school and hanging around lumpen and Times Square scene and dishwashing and mopping up cafeterias and all that till some rough external edges were smoothed out and I could at least fade into the landscape of the common world, so that by 20 I took pride in this wholly or part imaginary accomplishment of, though being a Columbia genteel type, at least being able to get along with non-intellectuals and poor people and knowing the argot of jazz and Times Square and varying my social experience more than is usually, or was, varied in most law students—not realizing partly that most people were not as crazy as myself and didn't make it all a big problem like I did, not being homosexual virgins like myself. Meanwhile developing with Jack a sense of poesy as mellow as could be, reading Rimbaud, and with Burroughs, a sense of Spenglerian history and respect for the "irrational" or unconscious properties of the soul and disrespect for all law. Something broader than formalistic anarchism, that is, that you can make a law as good as you want and it can be, but that still doesn't cover what you will feel when someone's trapped in your law. So a distrust of mental decisions, generalizations, sociology, a hip sense; plus then experience with love and with drugs actually causing telepathic and what were to me "mystic" experiences, i.e. feelings

outside of anything I ever felt before. Meanwhile for a sense of the right-
ness of life I trusted people most, that is friendship and the recognition of
the light in people's eyes and from then on I pursued and idealized friendship and especially in poesy which was the manifestation of this light of
friendship secret in all man, open in some few.

Then as I've said but never fully described nor in context of development, came a time when college days were o'er and I had to depend on
myself, and Jack and Bill went their ways in the world—though I felt
bound to them by sacramental mellow lifelong-to-be ties—and the one
idealistic love affair I had with Neal came to end because it was impracti-
cal and he was married and not really the same thing I was after—which
was lifelong sex-soul union—he was willing but not to the extreme all out
homo desire I had—anyway I realized I was alone and not ever to be loved
as I wanted to be loved—though I'd had with him some great pathos love-
bed scenes which surpassed in tenderness anything I'd ever be handed on
earth—so that the loss was even more utterly felt, as a kind of permanent
doom of my desires as I knew them since childhood—I want somebody to
love me, want somebody to carry me Hoagy tenderness—and at that point
living alone eating vegetables, taking care of Huncke who was too beat to
live elsewhere—I opened my book of Blake (as I've said before, it's like the
Ancient Mariner repeating his obsessional futile tale to every guest he can
lay his hand on) and had a classical hallucinatory-mystical experience, i.e.
heard his voice commanding and prophesying to me from eternity, felt
my soul open completely wide all its doors and windows and the cosmos
flowed thru me, and *experienced* a state of altered apparently total consciousness so fantastic and science-fictional I even got scared later, at having stumbled on a secret door in the universe all alone. Meanwhile
immediately made vow No. 2 that henceforth, no matter what happened
in later decades, always to be faithful to that Absolute Eternal X I had thru
destiny seen face to face—several times that week. As per usual it made my
social behavior frantic, but I saw I was in danger of being considered
mad—and possibly (what horror) was mad—so I kept cool enough to continue somewhat normal life. However the crash came within the visions
themselves, as, one time, when I summoned the Great Spirit, this Great
Spirit did appear but with a sense of doom and death so universal, vast and
living that it felt to me as if the universe itself had come alive and was a hostile entity in which I was trapped and by which I would be eaten consciously alive.

So these are the deepest sense experiences I have had, and the only things I can know. I can't get around them any way yet, and they are in some form or other my own destiny, any move I make I always meet that depth in new guise. At the same time afraid of meeting eternity face to face, lie tempted and fearful, like hound of heaven or moth to flame. Later somewhat similar experiences though weaker, and approximations of almost equal intensity with peyote, mescaline, ayahuasca, lysergic acid, hashish concentrates, and psylocybin mushrooms and stroboscopic lights; also at intervals of tranquillity or changes of life and personal crises, all open out to the same vastnesses of consciousness in which all I know and plan is annihilated by awareness of hidden being-ness.

For that reason then, all loves, poetries and politics and intellectual life and literary scenes and all travels or stay-home years, are by me pursued as much spontaneously, without plan, without restrictive regulation of rules and rights and wrongs and final judgments, without fixed ideas—as much as possible; and I do get into ruts that lead to habit that thin my consciousness, being actually always careful to keep myself together and pursue poesy and have a forwarding address.

However various basic rules have evolved, as far as my instincts and feelings, which is that all creation and poesy as transmission of the message of eternity is sacred and must be free of any rational restrictiveness; because consciousness has no limitations. And this led to experiments with new kinds of writings and literary renaissances and new energies and compositional techniques—most of which I got from Kerouac who all along let himself go to ball with his spontaneous art, to tell the secrets of his memory. And I expected that, given this widening of belief and tolerance and empathy, some touch of natural basic consciousness would emanate from poesy and my activities and serve to remind others outside me of human original wide nature, and thus affecting their consciousness little though it be, serve the general uplift of man and the purpose of vow No. 1, to aid the masses in their suffering. But if that end were approached directly, I always felt it would become a surface idea and get tangled in limited sometimes mistaken front-brain judgments, such as Kerouac warns about when he laments my being what seems to him involved in politics; and that way he makes sense.

Another basic generalization that emerged was to finally trust my natural love feelings and that led to now almost decade alliance with Peter whom I thought a saint of lovely tolerance and joy—for me, strange tender ambulance driver, is what I wrote Jack announcing his presence in our company; Jack later pronounced him to be the guard at gate of heaven, "but he's so goofy he lets everybody in."

And so, on poesy and Peter and all described before, I began to get a fixed identity and creational life, with sort of basic sentiments and some ideas, which, as far as public "pronouncements" I kept to just urging freedom, of meter and technique in poesy, to follow the shape of the mind, and laws (narcotic) to follow thru to wider consciousness, and love, to follow natural desire.

However, taking drugs, and in solitude, I still was faced with omnivorous oblivion, chills of isolation and sterility not having met the woman half of the universe and progenied new babes, natural dissatisfactions with the incompleteness of the comes we could have together being men, and it made me vomit to realize the whole identity now built around me, poetry, Peter, me, visions, consciousness, all my life, were destined by dissolution of time (a la Buddha) to be separated from me and I would later if not willingly sooner be faced with having it all taken away with my corpse.

In fact in Peru with witch doctors taking ayahuasca one night I came face to face with what appeared to be the Image of Death come to warn me again as 12 years before in Harlem, that all this me-ness of mine was mere idea vanity and hollow and fleeting as the mosquitoes I was killing in the tropic night. In fact, though I'd made a principle of non-identity, I was scared to have my identity taken away, scared to die—clinging to the self-doomed (transient by nature) pleasures of dependable love, sex, income, cigarettes, poesy, fame, face and cock—clinging, frightened, to *stay in* this identity, this body, vomiting as it was—and seeing its doom as a living monster *outside* of me that would someday EAT ME ALIVE.

Thus faced with human limitation I turned back from eternity again and wanted to stay the Allen I was and am.

At this point frightened, seeing my basic saint-desire might be death and madness, I wrote Burroughs long letter from Peru asking for advice—Burroughs who had kicked junk habit and thus in very real way kicked his own identity habit, as can be seen in *Naked Lunch* hints.

His answer, go right ahead, into space, outside of Logos, outside of time, outside of concepts of eternity and god and faith and love I'd built up as an identity—Cancel all your messages, said he, and I also cancel mine.

Then thinking of wandering East with Peter and Gregory we looked into Bill in Tangier this year, and I met *someone I didn't know*, who rejected me, as far as Allen and Bill were concerned and all previous relationships they built up. And if I don't know Bill I sure don't know myself, because he was my rock of tolerance and friendship and true art. And what was he doing with his art? He was cutting it up with a razor as if it weren't no sacred texts at all, just as he was cutting up all known human feelings between us, and cutting up the newspapers, and cutting up Cuba and Russia and America and making collages; he was cutting up his own consciousness and escaping as far as I can tell outside of anything I could recognize as his previous identity. And that somewhat changed my identity since that had been something built I had thought and permanently shared with him. And Peter and I suddenly broke thru the automaton love-faith habit we were junked-up and comfortable in, and looked in each other's eyes—and nobody was there but a couple robots talking words and fucking. So he left for Istanbul and I stayed in Tangier and vomited off the roof.

Now the serious technical point that Burroughs was making by his cut-ups, which I resisted and resented since it threatened everything I depend on—I could stand the loss of Peter but not the loss of hope and love; and could maybe even stand the loss of them, whatever they are, if poesy were left, for me to go on being something I wanted, sacred poet however desolate; but poesy itself became a block to further awareness. For further awareness lay in dropping every fixed concept of self, identity, role, ideal, habit and pleasure. It meant dropping language itself, *words*, as medium of consciousness. It meant literally altering consciousness outside of what was already the fixed habit of language-inner-thought-monologue-abstraction-mental-image-symbol-mathematical abstraction. It meant exercising unknown and unused areas of the physical brain. Electronics, science fiction, drugs, stroboscopes, breathing exercises, exercises in thinking in music, colors, no thinks, entering and believing hallucinations, altering the neurologically fixated habit pattern reality. But that's what I thought poetry was doing all along! *but* the poetry I'd been practicing depended on living inside the structure of language, depended on words as the medium of consciousness and therefore the medium of conscious being.

Since then I've been wandering in doldrums, still keeping habit up with literature but uncertain if there is enough Me left to continue as some kind of Ginsberg. I can't write, except journals and dreams down; as the next step if any for poetry, I can't image—Perhaps we've reached point in human or unhuman evolution where art of words is oldhat dinosaur futile, and must be left behind. I also stopped reading newspapers two months ago. Also the paranoid fear that I'm degenerate robot under the mind-control of the mad spectre of Burroughs. Except that it finally seems (after dreams of killing him) that he has only taken the steps, or begun to take steps, toward actual practice of expanded consciousness that were in the cards for me anyhoo, since the first days of mind break-up with Blake, and of which I was repeatedly reminded in drug trances.

A side effect of loss of dependence on words is the final break-up of my previously monotheistic memory-conception of one holy eternity, one God. Because all that conceptualization depends on the railroad track of language. And actual experience of consciousness is not name-able as One. I suppose this is all in sophisticated form in Wittgenstein.

Meanwhile I am carrying for the last few months a dose of mushroom pills which I have been too fearful to take. Waiting for a day to look into that, or *be* that, THING, again. And operating still on language, thus this letter.

What to do about Cuba? Can the world reality (as we know it through consciousness controlled by the cortex part of the brain) be improved? Or, with expanded population and increasing need for social organization and control and centralization and standardization and socialization and removal of hidden power controllers (capitalism), will we in the long run doom man to life within a fixed and universal monopoly on reality (on materialist level) by a unison of cortex-controlled consciousness that will regulate our being's evolution? Will it not direct that evolution toward stasis of preservation of its own reality, its idea of reality, its own identity, its Logos? But this is not the problem of socialism, this is the problem of Man. Can any good society be founded, as all have been before and failed, on the basis of old-style human consciousness? Can a vast human-teeming world "democratically" regulate itself at all in future with the kind of communications mechanism this present known and used consciousness has available? How escape rigidification and stasis of consciousness when man's mind is only words and these words and their images are flashed on every brain continuously by the interconnected networks of radio television newspapers wire services speeches decrees laws telephone books manuscripts? How escape centralized control of reality of the masses by the few who want and can take power, when this network is now so interconnected, and the decision over the network? Democracy as previously sentimentally conceived now perhaps impossible (as proved in U.S.) since a vast feed-back mechanism, mass media, inescapably orients every individual, especially on subliminal levels. Same problem for Russia, China, Cuba.

I have no notion of future state or government possible for man, I don't know if continuance of machine civilization is even possible or desirable. Perhaps science may have to dismantle itself (or kill the race)—this is parallel to individual intellectual experience of cycles of reasoning leading back to non-intellectual "natural" life. However I assume (for no good reason yet) the latest cycle of human evolution is irreversible except by atomic apocalypse, so I suppose science is here to stay in one form or other, and civilizations too. I think the possible direction of development, then, to solve problems created by vast population and centralized network control, is toward increasing the efficiency and area of brain use, i.e. widening the area of consciousness in all directions feasible. For example, telepathy might annihilate mass media power centers of control. In any case the old sense of identity of human consciousness, the sense of separate identity, self and its limited language, may alter. Individuals may have to step into hitherto unrecognizable areas of awareness, which means, for practical purposes, unrecognizable or undiscovered areas of BEING.

The change may be so far out as to be unimaginable to present-day two-dimensional poet's consciousness. I may have to (willingly) give up say being me, being Poet A.G., (or unwillingly depending on how fixed my cravings for security and the old life are). The social changes I can't even guess. It may be that we find the material reality we take for granted was literally an illusion all along. We may not *have* bodies. Nothing can be assumed, everything is UNKNOWN.

Space exploration is secondary and only triumphant in limited areas of consciousness; whereas an evolution or scientific exploration of consciousness itself (the brain and nervous system) is the inevitable route for man to take.

I see no reason why no government on earth is really alive in this evolutionary direction. All governments including the Cuban are still operating within the rules of identity forced on them by already outmoded means of consciousness. I say outmoded since it has brought all governments to edge of world destruction. No government, not even the most Marxian revolutionary and well-intended like Cuba presumably, is guiltless in the general world mess, no one can afford to be righteous any more. Righteous and right and wrong are still fakes of the old suicidal identity.

Now the Cuban Revolutionary government as far as I can tell is basically occupied by immediate practical problems and proud of that, heroic resistances, drama, uplift, reading and teaching language, and totally unoccupied as yet with psychic exploration in terms which I described above. When I talked with Franqui of *Revolucion* in NY he parroted the U.S. Imperialist line against marijuana and added, "It should be easier for a poet to understand a revolution than for a revolution to understand poetry." Poetry here meaning my contention that poet had right to use marijuana. He gave me all sorts of rationalistic arguments against social use of marijuana—though he added liberally that he himself was not personally opposed to it. And also I see that there has been no evidence of real technical revolution in poesy or language in recent Cuban poetry—it still is old hat mechanistic syntax and techniques. So that it is obvious that any, meaning ANY, mediocre bureaucratic attempt to censor language, diction or direction of psychic exploration is the same old mistake made in all the idiot academies of Russia and America. Arguments about immediate practical necessities are as far as I can tell from afar strictly the same old con of uninspired people who don't know what the writing problem is, and don't have any idea of the consciousness problems I'm talking about.

Re censorship of language. I wrote an article for *Show Business Illustrated* on the Cannes film festival which they accepted and paid $450 for, using the word shit (describing use of it in *The Connection*); now they want to chicken out on the single use of Shit in one sentence. I wrote back no, same day I got your letter, thus pledging myself to repay them 450 dollars I've already spent—over one little Shit. Censorship of language is direct censorship of consciousness; and if I don't fit in I can't change the shape of my mind. No. No revolution can succeed if it continues the puritanical censorship of consciousness imposed on the world by Russia and America. Succeed in what? Succeed in liberating the masses from domination by secret monopolists of communication.

I'm NOT down on the Cubans or anti their revolution, it's just that it's important to make clear *in advance, in front,* what I feel about life. Big statements saying Viva Fidel are/would be meaningless and just two-dimensional politics.

Publish as much of this letter as interests you, as prose contribution to Cuban Revolution.

WRITTEN: Oct. 16, 1961

FIRST PUBLISHED: *Pa'Lante,* vol. 1, no. 1 (May 19, 1962) pp. 61–73.

Letter to *Wall Street Journal*

Every American wants MORE MORE of the world and why not, you only live once. But the mistake made in America is persons accumulate more more dead matter, machinery, possessions and rugs and fact information at the expense of what really counts as more: feeling, good feeling, sex feeling, tenderness feeling, mutual feeling. You own twice as much rug if you're twice as *aware* of the rug. Possessing more means being *aware* of more: and that "awareness" is banked in areas we call feeling. Bodily feeling sense or sensual feeling. You can own an elephant or bank or power thereof but if there's no personal breast bliss all you own is a lot of dead atoms and ideas. Well our business tendency has been to mechanize and literally suppress feeling, it doesn't fit the machine. People flowing in and out of buildings on time slave to the inanimate machine that houses them. The media's become cannibalistic of person. Well if you want to live in a dead universe, an impersonal universe, that's an option—which most people choose or are forced to, they think. Finally they get to think there's no option everything's really dead. Total distrust in every direction and naturally the end product of that is exclusively H Bomb hypnosis and the kind of China policy we've been stuck with—paranoia and no lively way out.

We're all born Person—babies need personal meat contact or they die. That's our nature—tender—infant or at menopause. But the culture—and the system, the capitalist system itself as practiced thru competition rather than free cooperation—simply enforce impersonal reactions. "Decisions" and even physical postures that cut out 9/10 of the feeling world. So you wind up with less less not more more. Even if you own not merely First National even if you could own the whole planet. The kind of relationship you have, if you monopolize matter, is a dead feeling one. Or like amphetamine, a false electric nervous thrill without the whole organism involved in communication—in communion with the outside.

"Success" as such, by U.S. standards, is just a big loss of our real existence: which is *personal feeling.* You get less, you don't get your more. Most people seem to be hung up in this dead matter like junkies. Their habits get bigger and bigger like junkies too. Burroughs pointed it out in *Naked Lunch.* Naturally comes ulcers, loss of identity, witty role playing. Christ noticed it long ago, so did Whitman in America, it's a *real* loss.

The drugs come in here, at right historic moment. LSD cuts thru the whole illusion of dead matter; unconscious realization of person and feeling and sensory awareness is restored temporarily. It seems like a cosmic vision, only because we've been literally *cut off* from our maximum organic awareness so long. Someone stuck in a dead universe all his life suddenly wakes up and sees the whole universe alive, including himself. It could be nerve wracking if you've invested your whole life in the wrong universe, which most everybody has by now.

But this is the space age, Buck Rogers already come true, just like old radio storybook. Overpopulation, electronic communication networks worldwide, planetary death threat with bombs, escalation of irrational hostilities, moment of leaving the planet in space-ships—and opening up of chemistries that alter consciousness and take all this into account with total awe. So it's no wonder that it seems strange for the older folks. History's accelerating like technology's accelerated. Can't go back. We can blow the whole show up. Or we can calm fear, see the world is really changing, like a dream, and go explore and help each other through. It's all safe because as Einstein and the Buddhists secretly tipped everybody off long ago: the whole show is a harmless wave-illusion. That may be hard to take but it's better than going mad and seeing devils in every corner in typical pre-space-age American style.

I've used hard American business terminology here to intersect with familiar spiritual thought patterns. Only to indicate there are other *modes of consciousness* they may not have explored yet. May have glimpsed, but dismissed as not, like, real. So shut selves off from exploring and owning the *whole* world.

Delight in the human universe—personal relations—will probably function in future to balance the gigantic extension of our possession of outer space properties. It better or we'll be murdering each other on Mars.

WRITTEN: June 1966

Unpublished.

Anger Advice

At root of intolerance is anger. The medicine for anger is awareness of anger: "Anger doesn't like to be reminded of fits," said poet Jack Kerouac. If we make a practice of noticing our thoughts, to "catch yourself thinking" (as the phrase goes in idiomatic Americanese), we have a better chance of making our own irritations and fits of anger more transparent, airing out the "hot air" of emotion—as Tibetan Buddhist Lamas say, that dissolves 80 percent of the anger.

If all mankind can't practice this kind of meditation—sitting, standing or lying down—at least the elite and the "leaders," Premiers, Presidents, Dictators, and Senators can do so—I do as best I can.

WRITTEN: Undated

Unpublished.

MEDITATION AND EASTERN INFLUENCES

Reflections on the Mantra

Mantram (singular), *mantra* (plural) is a short verbal formula like Rolling Stones' "I'm going home" or Gertrude Stein's "A rose is a rose is a rose," which is repeated as a form of prayer meditation over and over until the original thin-conscious association with meaning disappears and the words become pure physical sounds uttered in a frankly physical universe; the word or sound or utterance then takes on a new density as a kind of magic language or magic spell and becomes a solid object introduced into the science fiction space-time place where the worshiper finds himself, surrounded by jutting mountain crags or city buildings.

After several minutes of devoted repetition—such as Alfred Lord Tennyson practiced with his own name (a form of worship of a form of the self categorized by one Hindu as *Atma Darshan*. Self-communion translated—one might garland one's own photo with flowers and kneel to worship that particular manifest image of divinity)—it is possible that the awesome physical sound reverberating out of the body into the air might serve as a vehicle for the expression of nonconceptual sensations of the worshiper. That is to say, the magic formula pronunciation can be loaded with affects—feelings, emotions—(*Bhakti* or devotion is the Hindu term) passing through the body of the devotee. Feelings which arise spontaneously all the time, but rarely have suitable channels for direct expression. So that longer stretches of mantra chanting may become the opportunity for realization of certain blissful or horrific feelings which are latent and hitherto unrealized—tears may arise of which the devotee was not aware earlier. Or gaieties, or Hebraic solemnities. Thus the *mantram* may serve as an instrument for widening the area of immediate self-awareness of the singer; much as an intense conversation with psychoanalyst or lover, or priest or connection may bring out emotional news; singing (from olden times) deepens the soul of the singer.

By deepens the soul, I mean not that the soul is added to like brick by brick, but that what's already there becomes visible or audible. Well, we all know that about singing. I'm just explaining these simplicities to dispel mysterious notions or provincial resentments against the use of oriental tricks.

Negro spirituals which involve deepening of the expression of a repeated refrain function like mantra. So lovers' cries in moments of crisis like "Oh I'm coming, coming. I'm coming. I'm coming. I'm coming, etc." Singing in the bathroom or on lonesome bridges may have some general function of providing situations where full force of feeling is slowly developed and outwardly expressed in solitude. From Yoruba drum-dance-and-shout worship rituals to electronic folk-rock we have developed Western situations to manifest our fugitive ethereal consciousness.

The Indian practice of mantra-chanting is ancient and useful to know; but I don't know enough about it technically to be the right guru. I wish to explain what I do know through gossip and practice, and hope that scholarly holymen will make allowances for my ignorance.

One Oriental idea is suggestive: that the mantra in itself has magic or practical power irrespective of the sincerity or propriety of its pronunciation in a given situation; and that mere pronunciation of the mantra is a meritorious and mysterious art. On this assumption I take liberty to chant and explain *mantram* publicly.

The name of Shiva pronounced accidentally by a dying man asking for a glass of water was, on one occasion of legend, cause for his immediate release from bondage to rebirth and suffering, thus I've heard.

Why is that? Because, according to theory, the names of the Gods used in the mantra are *identical* with the Gods (or powers invoked) themselves. So that one who sings Shiva's name becomes Shiva (Creator and Destroyer) himself. The subjective experience of repeated singing of Shiva's name confirms this theory, as far as I have been able to tell. Obviously it is a subjective experience, not an "objective" one. Subjective sensation is what I'm interested in recovering contact with; and here interpret "objectivity" as a retreat from feelable phenomena.

The *mantram* is generally given by a teacher to pupil, and most often is to be kept secret, and recited aloud when alone, or silently with lips or only mentally; and recited continually, until the mind's activities become fixed around the *mantram.* That way a continuum is begun that deepens till maybe deathbed. Fixing the mind on one point, focusing and deepening in one spot is a classical method of yoga meditation.

Some mantra are all-Indian common property, and are universal, public. The late Swami Shivananda (may his self bless us all!) of Rishikesh recommended Hare Krishna as the Maha Mantra—Great Mantra—for this age, infallible publicly and privately for everyone. He as a large souled man, "Vishnu Himself" as one beautiful yogi, Prem Varni, explained in a hermitage across the river from Shivananda's Ashram. Shivananda was the first "accredited" guru I encountered; a year later at the confluence of Yamuna and Ganges rivers called Trivondrum in Allahabad at a great fair of half a million holymen and ladies, I passed by a larger wooden Nepalese structure where a lady saint supposed to be some Northern princess sat enthroned, with her attendants and worshipers gathered to one side around a harmonium (hand portative organ) and heard her smiling enrapt singing of the same Hare Krishna Hare Krishna Krishna Krishna Hare Hare Hare Rama Hare Rama Rama Rama Hare Hare. Her face had an inner smile reflected, eyes half closed, the song had a lilt of tenderness and odd inevitable sweet rhythm, and though I did not notice it at the time, the song was impressed on my own memory. It came back after many adventures. I never knew her name.

WRITTEN: Aug. 1, 1966

FIRST PUBLISHED: *Back to Godhead,* vol. 1, no. 3 (Dec. 1966) pp. 5–9.

CBC Broadcast on Mantra

"HARE KRISHNA HARE RAMA." That's called *mantra* chanting. *Mantra* is like a short magical formula prayer, which is chanted or sung, which is an appeal to an aspect of the self. The practice is Hindu in this case, or Buddhist in other cases; there are Buddhist *mantras,* and Sufi *mantras* for Moslems; and there are also in the Jewish tradition rabbinical songs, rabbi songs, which are generally without words, which are used at the end of the year after the Jews read the Torah through—Simchas Torah, the Day of Celebration of Torah. They go in the synagogue, drinking a little wine. The rabbi sets forth a little tune like "la la la la la la . . ." So. All the scholars sing, dance, jump around all night. So this is like universal in Neolithic religions like American Indians, Africans, all the others, that basic body rhythm chant, which has been lost to a great extent in our own civilization, except for what we get out of the Beatles these days: "All we are saying / Give peace a chance . . ." Since there is so much fragmentation of my mind and everybody else's mind, I'm finding the body vibrations projected or articulated by soulful yogic devotional tearful chanting to be a communication that sometimes surpasses argumentative language, especially in public political circumstances like mass meetings, because that kind of chanting articulates the mutuality of soul and feeling of unison and feeling of community tenderness and hope that much of the angry political speechmaking or the angry official police politician electronic yakking did not touch on.

But, at any rate, I was trying to explain why I got concerned with music as an extension of body, of voice, of the body's voice. And then I went from there—actually quite literally, after the Chicago convention of last year [1968 Democratic National Convention], when I returned home, I had about two weeks completely free in which I began setting Blake's *Songs of Innocence and Experience* to music [because] they seemed the nearest thing to holy *mantra* or holy prayer poetry that I could find in my own consciousness, and also because, seeing that rock 'n' roll—the Stones, the Beatles, Dylan, even Donovan, even the Birds, the Band, the Grateful Dead, the Fugs, Jefferson Airplane, all the lovely youthful bands that have been wakening the conscience of the world, really, were approaching high poetry and cosmic consciousness in their content, so I was interested in seeing if Blake's highest poetry could be vocalized, tuned, and sung in the context of the Beatles "I am the Walrus" or "Day in the Life of" or in the context of "Sad-eyed Lady of the Lowland" or "John Wesley Harding" by Dylan. Also Dylan said that he didn't like Blake, so I thought this would be an interesting way of laying Blake on him. So when I got home from the convention I began tuning *Songs of Innocence and Experience* by William Blake, finding out also in the process that Blake himself used to sing *Songs of Innocence and Experience*. He'd go to his friends' houses and chant unaccompanied.

Piping down the valleys wild
How sweet is the shepherd's sweet lot!

So those are the first two songs in Blake's "Innocence and Experience." And I went on to learn chords, which turned out to be interesting. So at the age of 43 I learn how to make a major and minor chord. It's so simple, you know . . . It's so simple that it amazes me that it took me 43 years to find that out. So then I got most of Blake's "Innocence and Experience" into music, and I made an album out of it, working with some black musicians, jazz musicians, and some rock musicians and some country-western musicians. The nicest of the songs is when I began learning how to make chord changes. This seemed appropriate particularly when friend poet Kerouac died; this song kept running through my mind:

When the voices of children are heard on the green
And whisp'rings are in the dale . . .

WRITTEN: late 1969

Broadcast on Canadian Broadcasting Corporation in late 1969.

Meditation and Poetics

Spiritus means breath, etymologically, and breath spirit is the
    vehicle for poetry and song as well as the air horse
the Mind rides during meditation practice. Sit down and relax
    with straight spine and pass into space with your air.
People followed their outbreath in Tibet. So did Poets in the
    west, filling their body-wind with vowels and tones of Voice.
Sometimes you forget you're breathing and the mind
    daydreams poems of past history future furniture present
    erotic bliss
Old shameful conversations but a fly buzzing when you died
    like Emily Dickinson brings you back mindful to the room
    where
you sit and keep breathing aware of the walls around you and
    the endless blue sky above your mind
The daydreams isolated recollected as objects can be poetry
    stormy epics or flashy haikus.

A thought like a poem begins you can't tell where then it gets
   big in the mind's eye an imaginary universe and then
Disappears like a white elephant into the blue or "as a bird
   leaves the imprint of its flight in the sky"
So thought ends you can't tell where, except it disappears into
   thin air like Shakespeare's plays.
Shakespeare left his breath for us to hear his Cadence, so did
   Shelley and William Carlos Williams and Kerouac.
"The breath whose might I have invoked in song Descends on
   me; my spirit's bark is driven, far from the shore . . . "
One Thursday in 1919 William Carlos Williams stood in his
   shoes and remembered the breath coming in and out at his
   nose,
right at the end of World War I. It's almost World War III and
   we're still breathing.

WRITTEN: March 9, 1980

FIRST PUBLISHED: *New Wilderness Letter*, no. 9 (1980) p. 1.

A Collage of Haiku,
Kerouac's Spontaneous Writ,
Zengakuren Couplets,
Tibetan Mind-Training Slogans,
And Blake's Auguries

—with brief explanations

A wild sea!
And stretching across to the Island of Sado
The Galaxy.

—Basho
(*Haiku*, Volume I, Eastern Culture:
Tuttle Co., R. H. Blyth; p. 377)

Coming out of the box
This pair of dolls,—
How could I forget their faces?

—Buson
(Blyth's *Haiku*; p. 378)

A bowel-freezing night;
The sound of the oar striking the wave,—
Tears.

—Kikaku
(Blyth's *Haiku*; p. 374)

On a withered branch
A crow is perched;
An autumn evening.

—Kikaku
(Blyth's *Haiku*; p. 374)

In the beginning of Kerouac's *Desolation Angels* there's a whole series of haikus. They're done in classical style, yet it was self-invented. He knew the tradition but he adapted it to the novel; the tradition being a travel journal, prose, economical paragraphs, giving a setting and suddenly the flash thought:

> the wind, the wind, and there's my poor endeavoring human desk at which I sit so often during the day facing South, the papers and pencils and the coffee cups with sprigs of alpine fir and a weird orchid of the heights wiltable in one day—My Beechnut gum, my tobacco pouch, dusts, pitiful magazines I have read, view south to all those snowy majesties—The waiting is long.

He ends the paragraph in three lines:
On starvation ridge . . .
little sticks
Are trying to grow
(Part One: Desolation in Solitude #4)
then came the long daydream of what I do when I get out of there, that mountain top trap. Just to drift down the road, on 99, fast, mebbe a filet mignon on hot coals in a riverbottom some

night, with good wine, and on in the morning—to Sacramento,
Berkeley, go up to Ben Fagan's cottage and say first off this Haiku:

Hitch hiked a thousand
         miles and brought
You wind

(Part One: Desolation in Solitude #13)

hiss, hiss says the wind bringing dust and lightning nearer—
Tick, says the lightning rod receiving a strand of electricity from
the strike on Skagit Peak. Great power silently and unobtrusively
slithers through my protective rods and cable: and vanishes into
the earth of desolation—No thunderbolts, only death-Hiss, tick,
and in my bed I feel the earth move—Fifteen miles to the south just
east of Ruby mountain and somewhere near Panther Creek I'd
guess a large fire rages, huge orange spot at 10 o'clock electricity
which is attracted to heat—hits it again and it flares up disastrously,
a distant disaster that makes me say "Oo wow"—Who burns eyes
crying there?

Thunder in the mountains
         the iron
Of my mother's love

                              (Part One: Desolation in Solitude #28)

Where'd he get his mother's love? It just came up out of his head,
unborn.

The days go—
         they can't stay—
I don't realize

(ibid.)

The fog in Japan is the same fog in Northwest Washington, the
sensing being is the same and Buddha is just as old and true anywhere you go. The sun sets dully on Bombay and Hong Kong like it
sets dully on Chumsford, Mass. I called Hanshen into the fog and
there was no answer. The sound of silence is all the instruction you'll
get. Whatever happens to me down that trail (gulp) the world is all
right because I'm God and I'm doing it all myself. Who else?

While meditating
         I am Buddha—
Who else?

                              (Part Two: Desolation in the World #49)

Those are the best of what I saw in *Desolation Angels*. There are a couple of others:

Neons, Chinese restaurants
    coming on—
Girls come by in shades

                      (ibid., #65)

Eat your eggs
    and
Shut up

                      (ibid., #69)

Sit in fool and be fool,
    that's all

                      (ibid., #72)

These are more abstracted. Although they're just thoughts that come naturally. Gregory Corso had one: "In Mexico City Zoo there are ordinary American cows." That was the American traveler's flash.

Here are some similar in form from *Zengakuren:*

To be able to trample upon the Great Void,
The iron cow must sweat.
Meeting, the two friends laugh aloud:
In the grove, fallen leaves are many.
In the vast inane there is no back or front;
The path of the bird annihilates East and West.

                (Blyth's *Haiku:* p. 13, 14, 16)

William Blake has a series of two-line poems like these which verge on the Vajrayana insight in Buddhism. In other words, turning things inside out, taking accident and mishap and learning from it. So any broken leg is an opening to experience of empty space, i.e., There's no place to stand on. This is from Blake's "Auguries of Innocence":

To see a world in a Grain of Sand
And Heaven in a Wild Flower,
Hold Infinity in the palm of your hand
And Eternity in an hour.
A Robin Red breast in a Cage
Puts all Heaven in a Rage . . .

It's like the two-line Zen poem: "A cow eats in Kyushu, a horse's belly bloats in Boston."

. . . A dove house fill'd with doves and Pigeons
Shudders Hell thru all its regions.
A dog starv'ed at his Master's Gate
Predicts the ruin of the State
A Horse misus'd upon the Road
Calls to Heaven for Human blood.
Each outcry of the hunted Hare
A fibre from the brain does tear . . .

This is absolutely literal: "Each outcry of a hunted Hare," particularly if unexpected, could give you that shudder-shock, a little electrical short-circuit in the brain. There's a literality to these that's really uncanny. It looks like they're opposites, impossibilities, but Blake's intelligence has filled it in, or has found or seen the relations, or guessed the relations without thinking. If you read some of these lines, for example, "The cut worm forgives the plow," it will stick in your brain for years until you understand it—like a Zen koan. Every atom bumps into every other atom sooner or later. "A dog starved at his Master's Gate / Predicts the ruin of the State." The cruelty that would literally starve the dog, the quality of emotion that would starve the dog if prevalent in the state, would ruin the state. The insight needn't mystify us, so to speak. It's more simple.

A truth that's told with bad intent
Beats all the Lies you can invent.
It is right and should be so;
Man was made for Joy and Woe;
And when this we rightly know
Thro' the World we safely go

Actually, that's the First Noble Truth: Man was made for joy and woe—existence contains suffering. It's not so much suffering and woe, it's "the suffering of suffering," the echo of suffering, the clinging to suffering; the cultivation of it, the addiction to it in the sense of resentment of it, that hurts most. Rather than letting the thought of it drop to allow another Haiku:

> Man was made for Joy and Woe;
> And when this we rightly know
> Thro' the World we safely go,
> Joy and Woe are woven fine,
> A clothing for the soul divine:
> Under every grief and pine
> Runs a joy with silken twine . . .
> The Bleat, the Bark, Bellow and Roar
> Are Waves that Beat on Heaven's Shore.
> The Babe that weeps the Rod beneath
> Writes Revenge in realms of death.
> The Beggar's Rags, fluttering in Air,
> Does to Rags the Heavens tear.

"The Beggar's rags, fluttering in air,"—you just see the leprous beggar lying down on the ground with rags fluttering in the air. Actually, it's a very funny sort of space shot there. But how does it tear the heavens to rags? Quite literally, we see through the beggar's rags, into the air, into the firmament itself; the Dome of Heaven has become split with excessive suffering, blocked by rags to the eye.

> One Mite wrung from the Labrer's hands
> Shall buy and sell the Miser's Lands:
> Or, if protected from on high,
> Does that whole Nation sell and buy

Now how can the unjust taxation, or the strong-arm robbery of a little tiny mite of money from a beggar, or from a laborer, buy and sell the land? Obviously, the government's completely askew if it's wringing a mite from the actual laborer's hands, and so, in that sense that mite can buy and sell the whole nation. It's like "The dog starv'ed at his Master's

Gate / Predicts the ruin of the State." He's showing the gap, or connection between mightily magnificent, and tiny—just like:

for want of a nail, a horse was lost
for want of a horse, the battle was lost
for want of a battle, the war was lost

He who mocks the Infant's Faith
Shall be mock'd in Age and Death

So watch out for ageism or babeism—

He who shall teach the Child to Doubt
The rotting Grave shall ne'er get out.
He who respects the Infant's faith
Triumphs over Hell and Death.
The Child's Toys and the Old Man's Reasons
Are the Fruits of the Two Seasons.

Sensible, "negative capability."[6] In other words two separated, completely separated, conceptions are simply natural perceptions of differing brains.

The Questioner, who sits so sly,
Shall never know how to Reply.

I keep seeing that every day at big lectures. Slyness itself is a funny kind of aggressive falsity; so obviously, when presented with something open or empty, the falsity becomes dumb.

He who replies to words of Doubt
Doth put the Light of Knowledge out.
The Strongest Poison ever known
Came from Caesar's Laurel Crown.

He means the poison of power.

Nought can deform the Human Race
Like to the Armour's iron brace

When Gold and Gems adorn the Plow
to peaceful Arts shall Envy Bow

That's a classic. Pound repeated it over and over, and Robert Duncan pointed it out also; that in the Inca Empire, Cuzco, there was a garden full of flowers and trees made of gold. Gold was used for art and artisanship rather than as a means of usury or commercial manipulation.

A Riddle of the Cricket's Cry
Is to Doubt a fit Reply

Now he's talking about problems with conceptualization and over-rationalization. The cry cuts through conceptualization.

An Emmet's Inch and Eagle's Mile
Make Lame Philosophy to smile

That's Einstein's theory of relativity.

He who Doubts from what he sees
Will ne'er Believe, do what you Please.
If the Sun and Moon should doubt,
They'd immediately Go out

And . . .

To be in Passion you Good may do,
But no good if a Passion is in you.

That's the whole key to the Vajrayana practice in Buddhism: participation in passion. Passion is real, thought is real, emotion is real, the microphone is real. If you are attached to your passion, then it so fills up your brain that you forget the space where the passion takes place. It's a very clear thing, and I chose that out of English literature for an arrow of direction. It's a clear arrow of direction, very similar to a Tibetan text, Jamgon Kongtrul's *A Direct Path to Enlightenment* (Kagu Kunkhyab, Chuling, Vancouver, B.C., trans. Ken McLeod), composed in the fifth or sixth century A.D.

This text presents mind-training by slogans; one-line slogans for directing the mind in training, *Mahayana*, like:

Think that all phenomena are like dreams.

Examine the nature of unborn awareness. Awareness that is simply there, without traceable rational conceptual underpinnings, simply there like we are.

Regarding mindfulness: *Let even the remedy go free on its own.* If you solidify mindfulness, or if you solidify the notion of breathing, of following breath, or meditation, the difficulty there is that you can get addicted to meditation as a conceptual solidification. In other words, using meditation for your own passion, aggression, ignorance, pride, vanity; allowing the *idea* of meditation to displace the actual disappearance of conception in the breath. When you're meditating you have to forget you're meditating. Which is to say, finally, at the most literal level; let the breath go free on its own and dissolve.

Drive all blame into one. Where there is "the great stinky ball of blame," take it—because it's empty to begin with—take it on yourself, because at that point you can get on with your business of clear lucidity, in open space. Otherwise you are blocked (i.e., "Well you're to blame, it's all your fault"). Having tried to project the fault outward, on to something else, you never get to adjust the perceiver, or adjust the perception of the perceiver, or adjust the faulty perception.

Be grateful to everyone . . . Always rely on a happy frame of mind. That's a nice one.

Do not discuss defects. In other words, accentuate the positive, work towards that which is workable, rather than be attached to what is unworkable, and constantly complain and resent.

Don't be consistent. That's sort of the beginning of Vajrayana. It's actually an old American saying, "A foolish consistency is the hob-goblin of little minds." (Emerson)

It's interesting to note that Ezra Pound's idea of poetry was also a few "don'ts"—for images and imagists. His essay on poetics is simply a few "don'ts" (i.e., Don't say, "The dim misty lands of peace." Don't use reference instead of presentation).

These are interesting metaphors, they aren't rules. In the course of inserting one of these slogans into your nervous system, you have to figure out what the language means. They're more like metaphorical guidelines, born in four or five hundred A.D., the Boy Scout rules for mind training. Long-needed rules in the state of confusion, they are good reference points for what you do, or what you don't do, warnings against getting into mind traps. Although we only know them in relatively unsettled English translation, they're really interesting. "Drive all blame into one" is a classic worthy of Blake.

And so, back to William Blake's "Auguries of Innocence."

> To be in a Passion you Good may do,
> But no Good if a Passion is in you.
> The whore and Gambler, by the state
> Licens'd, build that Nation's Fate.

That's interesting: consider the modern licensing of gambling in New Jersey, and you *can* see the Mafia taking over.

> The Harlot's cry from Street to Street
> Shall weave Old England's winding Sheet.
> The Winner's Shout, the Loser's Curse,
> Dance before dead England's Hearse.
> Every Night and Every Morn
> Some to Misery are Born.
> Every Morn and Every Night
> Some are Born to sweet delight.
> Some are Born to sweet delight.
> Some are Born to endless Night.

That's Vajrayana, "unobstructed play of the mind."

> We are led to Believe a Lie
> When we see not Thro' the Eye

Actually, that's good instruction on how to compose your eyes during meditation: to see through the eye from the back of the head, into space through the window of the eyeball, realizing the particular perception which you will get if you're actually attentive to the optical phenomena. By attentive I mean resting within the eyeball, not trying to rationalize, but simply seeing physically through the front surface of the eye into space. Otherwise, staring hard at a wall, you get a solidified external universe which looks real, and you are led to believe a lie. Whereas, if you are actually sitting in a resting position, with your eyeball relaxed, aware of the space at the surface of the eye and all the dust-motes floating in it, you see that there's a certain transparency. "We are led to Believe a Lie / When we see not Thro' the Eye." That's simply an Einsteinian notion; that the measuring instrument determines the shape of the external thing measured—and as the measuring instrument changes, the shape of the universe of phenomena changes. In "The Mental Traveler," Blake says, "For the Eye altering alters all." (Anybody who has taken acid knows what that slogan means.)

An earlier version in Blake's hand clarifies his intention:

We are led to believe a Lie
When we see not Thro' the Eye
Which was born in a Night to perish in Night
When the Soul Slept in Beams of Light.

That's kind of mysterious. It sounds sometimes to me that he's signifying. He's not referring to the night before birth and the night after death; he's referring to *this* as night, the vegetable world. Then he goes on:

God appears and God is Light
To those poor Souls who dwell in Night

He really reverses it, you know:

But does a Human Form Display
To those who dwell in Realms of Day

This is more Vajrayana. It's really an innocent angel voice singing: da-da-da-da-da-da-da-da.

We might look at "The Mental Traveler." William Butler Yeats thought it was one of Blake's greatest poems. He said, however, that it was impenetrable, that nobody could understand it. Yet I think it's the obvious scheme of an eternal return, or cycle of what comes and goes back, a snake eating its own tail and it has a number of great slogans within it.

There is an interpretation of it by Foster Damon. His contention is that the two characters are youth and age, youth giving in to age. Youth or the Babe is revolution, political revolution as well as psychic—in that it is only born from death, or revolution is only born from cutting through the present status quo, or is born from the death of the status quo. However, as revolution ages, it becomes more and more encrusted, solidified, conceptualized, and so becomes an old woman. You could apply that to the Cuban or Russian Revolution. He's writing about the French Revolution, a revolution betrayed by Napoleon, in the sense that Napoleon finally had himself crowned King after being a republican all along. It's also a parable of alternations of mental states—in other words, the uncreation of a solidified identity, and the opening up to open space and then slow solidification again. So it's a cycle of solidification of conceptual thought forms, and then de-solidification of them ... "The Mental Traveler," it's a terrific title. Imagine writing anything like that.

WRITTEN: Nov. 8, 1978

FIRST PUBLISHED: *Zero,* vol. 3 (1979) pp. 158–170.

PART 4

Censorship and Sex Laws

Letter to Ralph Ginzberg

Inspired by a visit to a local Chinese opium den, I collected the following general comments on sex laws.

Are there really federal government laws regulating so ineffably personal a tickle as sex? Can it be possible that state governments (mostly full of everybody knows self-seeking politicians) have been dictating where and when we can sleep with our friends? Conceivable that local townships and city supervisors supervise people's ejaculations of semen? Now this is really a bit thick.

The simple fact is we're victims of a presumptuous vulgar persecution, our own private skin and genitals don't belong to us. Power groups going under the respectable name of "government" have the brazen chutzpah to tell us who can be intimate with whom, whom we can play with, what position and if we may move our bodies this way and that, as if our bodies were not our own PRIVATE PROPERTY. Where does any politician get off controlling other men's penises? How can a bunch of hair dressers, ambitious lawyers and used car dealers that call themselves municipal government GET OFF telling women to whom they haven't even been introduced what these women can do with their vaginas?

Are our stalwart statesmen going to make us stand in the corner and repeat one thousand times I WILL NOT HAVE AN UNAUTHORIZED ORGASM?

The plain fact is this bunch of shrewd SEX FIENDS intrude their hands underneath our pants and bloomers, and these filthy hands (one set of politicians' after another) have been touching us without invitation in our private parts as far back as we can remember. And that is MASS RAPE, the vilest kind of sexual perversion practiced on this planet. Done in the name of Virtuous Social Order to make it sound respectable inevitable natural only a matter of course absolutely necessary dearies quite proper for you harrumph.

Not only mass sexual rape but also mass brainwash, you being unconscious that some other power outside you has taken off with your sex life, it's the law, and they got cops and revolvers to prove it. Law 69 says you can't legally sleep with your boyfriend girlfriend, law 169 forbids fun among friends of the same sex, 269 says without a license your ejaculation is punishable by fine or imprisonment, 369 says don't play with yourself in front of the mirror, 469 tells you at what age you can make love ten years late (interpreted by some sheriffs as defining skin color too), 569 prevents tantric sex practices in large companies of mutually agreeable friends, 669 gives you the exact position you can use once you get their license to do it at all, 769 forbids your appearance naked in public as if that were a public nuisance instead of the charming thing it is in India for instance among the Jaina saints and naked yogins. In India the citizenry throws flowers in their path, in America they're dragged off by the fuzz. These are counted crimes only because someone has TOLD us it's all criminal behavior.

Prepubescent boys and girls don't have to be protected from big hairy you and me, they'll get used to our lovemaking in 2 days provided the controlling adults will stop making those hysterical NOISES that make everything sexy sound like rape. RAPE is the only obnoxious love, which we all want to discourage naturally, so you can call up the cops for that. If you still need sex-cops when nobody steals what they can get for free. Yes there'll always be a few irreducibly unattractive eccentrics, to be sure, grabbing unpleasantly as long as there are little girls coming home from school. One barely needs a bit of law to deal with them, and that law a law against violence, not really a sex law. Also need a couple of tantric cops or mescaline detectives, men of a certain delicacy to pacify the violent.

Laws governing indirect sexual activity in poetry prose movies comic books TV radio are altogether silly. Who cares if people want to copulate in public on TV? Why not? The controllers can always turn off the screen if it doesn't please them, or find another station where they're showing murder. But no, control powers can't look the other way they want to make a federal case a state case a local case any kind of case that's the way they get their rocks off.

It is a fact that the last Postmaster General (a politician named Summerfield notorious for his preoccupation with postal sex) underlined the dirty words *in red* in a copy of *Lady Chatterley's Lover* and put the book open on the desk of our last President Eisenhower. And Eisenhower took a look and said "Dreadful . . . we can't allow this!" This disgusting scene was reported straight-faced verbatim in *Newsweek*. It's like two big monstrous Laurel and Hardys were running the country, no wonder we wound up in the middle of the atomic cold war.

Extra thoughts: A.D. 1962 sex has nothing to do with procreation, an historical fact invented by rubbers. Now God knows what future evolution the hairy dinosaur snudges toward.

> Meanwhile all sex laws are themselves sex rape on the Q.T.
> Which anybody with the least chicken brain can see.
> Even shy shockable so-called liberals should agree (if only
>   theoretically)
> And poor earnest young conservative collegeboys especially
> Should defend themselves against this creepy invasion of their
>   private property:
> When government controls your sex it's just a Communistic
>   hex
> Against grass root enterprise and rugged individualism.
> (read Reich's *The Mass Psychology of Fascism*):
> For once they got you by the balls you got to stand for their
>   roll-calls,
> They clip you in your private parts to weaken all your public
>   arts
> and this is the true and secret cause the pow'rs that be love
>   their sex laws.

Words to the Wise: Everybody knows indiscriminate sex is not good for you if you're studying yoga, practicing ascetic mysticism and/or raising the *kundalini*, that is the serpent power. This is strictly a private matter for seekers to experiment with. No pious purpose whatever is served by government sex regulation, it only encourages superficial lip service to the gods. Furthermore government supervised sex famine prevents man from getting enough satisfaction to be satiated and disillusioned by experience, that he pass on to higher state of freedom. Through liberation from all craving and desire, as suggested by the Buddha. All these pious sex laws only hinder the process of enlightenment, thus Blake and Yeats also warned the public.

WRITTEN: Calcutta, July 1962

FIRST PUBLISHED: *Eros,* vol. 1, no. 4 (Winter 1962) p. 24.

AUTHOR'S NOTE: The dedicatee, then editing *Eros,* sent a letter 1962 received in a rooftop blockhouse room Hotel Amjadia, Choudui Chowh, Calcutta—asking for essay on sex laws—then under discussion was *Naked Lunch* text won freedom in courts that year. Bold thought then reconsidered the whole notion of sex laws, and this boldness led to further breakthroughs—underground movie lib, overground movie liberation, gay lib, women's lib, heterosexual, men's lib. One would have thought that "conservatives" (i.e. [William F.] Buckley et al) who wanted lib from government (Get the government off our backs) would have been consistent in getting the government off our backs sexually. But no, they were just sex coward hypocrites—Closet queens some of them in fact.

The tone is lighthearted, the subject heavy. But I took liberty of saying what I really thought at moment of composition (small typewriter and airgramme unrevised) sent off without delay.

Thoughts on NAMBLA[1]

"Always be ready to speak your mind, and a base man will avoid you."
—William Blake

I became a member of NAMBLA a decade ago as a matter of civil liberties. In the early 1980s, the FBI had conducted a campaign of entrapment and "dirty tricks" against NAMBLA members just as they had against black and anti-war leaders in previous decades. In the January 17, 1983, issue *Time* magazine, following the FBI disinformation campaign, attacked NAMBLA as a group involved in the "systematic exploitation of the weak and immature by the powerful and disturbed." That struck me as a fitting description of *Time* magazine itself. NAMBLA's a forum for reform of those laws on youthful sexuality which members deem oppressive, a discussion society not a sex club. I joined NAMBLA in defense of free speech.

Historically, societies have taken different views of this issue and the political heat that surrounds the subject is unnatural. Demagogic reaction to NAMBLA demeans the subject as a political football. At present European nations do not share current US public sexual hysteria. Various cultures and states offer widely varying definitions of age of consent—age 15 in Czechoslovakia and some US states, 14 in Hawaii. There's no universal consensus on "consent." It's a fit subject for discussion, NAMBLA provides a forum.

Most people like myself do not make carnal love to hairless boys and girls. Yet such erotic inclinations or fantasies are average and are commonly sublimated into courtly sociability. An afternoon's walk through the Vatican Museum will attest centuries of honorific appreciation of nude youths, an acceptable pleasure in the quasi erotic contemplation of the "naked human form divine." From Rome's Vatican to Florence's Uffizi galleries to New York's Metropolitan Museum of Art, we see statues of prepubescent Eros, pubescent Bacchus, male ephebes (naked bodies 12 to 18), the adolescent goddess Kore, nymphs, naiads, young fauns and satyrs in abundance, Laocoon and his boys with pubes exposed, wrinkled old Neptune's loins, old hags with undraped withers and dugs, Olympian Zeus and kid Ganymede. Western Civilization prides itself on its foundation in classical Greek culture, wherein intergenerational love was a social practice praised by philosophers.

A dash of humor, common sense humanity and historical perspective would help discussion of NAMBLA's role. Further, libertarians or anarchists may remember Blake's warning, "One Law for the Lion and the Ox is Oppression."

These considerations shouldn't be distorted to apologize for rape and mental or physical violation of children. I respect those who want to fix a general law to prevent abuse of minors. This is a real problem though less politically demagogic than advertised by some aggressive therapists, politically correct thought police, and the obsessive senator Jesse Helms. It is NAMBLA's mission to raise the subject, explore it, and provide a platform for debate.

Child abuse laws have been abused, especially since the Reagan-Meese commission's predictably incompetent linkage of pornography and violence. Subsequent formation of a Justice Department child porn bureaucracy sent federal squads roaming the states teaching local police to practice prurient snooping, invasion of privacy and lawless entrapment. Often police intrusion into consensual intergenerational affections and affairs results in abuse of both parties. Police authority also has made use of mind rape of the younger person, forcing unwilling youths to fink on close friends with threats of jail or beatings. One important function of NAMBLA is to keep track of bureaucratic manipulations of adolescents by police, FBI, media, and other agencies who handle such delicate issues with a meat ax. *A Witch Hunt Foiled: The FBI vs. NAMBLA*[2] provides an impressive volume of information on these outrageous police practices.

WRITTEN: July 13, 1994

Unpublished.

Big Table Support Testimony

In my opinion the writers Jack Kerouac and William S. Burroughs are the most important prose geniuses to have emerged in America since the last war. In the case of Kerouac, this is not only my own opinion, but also the opinion of many critics and journalists. He is considered in France and Germany as one of the most exciting manifestations of U.S. literary temperament. Many articles, in almost all countries of Europe and South America, have been devoted to a description of his writing. Mr. Burroughs' work is less well known, since very little of it has been published. In fact, the section of *Naked Lunch* published in this issue of *Big Table* is the first sizable chunk of his prose printed in the last 8 years. I think it is the most significant piece of social criticism that has been published in America in this century and will ultimately rank, in both content and prose style, with the work of Dean Swift, author of *Gulliver's Travels* and *A Modest Proposal.*

The question under discussion is whether the works *Old Angel Midnight* and *Naked Lunch* are too obscene to send thru the mail. I have made the above paragraph of generalization about their literary work in order to emphasize that a censorship of their work will not be greeted with indifference by literary figures here or abroad.

In my opinion the works are not obscene at all. Both are in their mood and conscious intention religious testaments. Both are concerned with an illumination of consciousness wherein the divinity of the soul is revealed. The method of composition of both works is similar: a transcription of the inmost and deepest fantasies and insights of the authors, without care for anything but the truth of the reporting. This is an attempt of great value and could only be attempted by writers of great human virtue. It is in the tradition of great democratic documents, statements of individual realities, confessions and insights, that includes the work of Thoreau and Whitman. This literary tradition is the very life-blood of the individualistic spirit in this country and any attempt to suppress it by the present government or any of its agencies would be a sign of degeneracy of the soul of this nation that has taken place since its founders first agreed that individuals should be encouraged to explore the divinity within themselves. One must re-read Thoreau, Emerson and Whitman to understand that they felt that this was exactly the ideal purpose of America. It is a virtue that has been much overlooked in recent times, and may even now seem absurd to the materialistic modern mind.

The specific works in question, *Old Angel Midnight* and *Naked Lunch*, are the most advanced pieces of prose composition that the two authors have penned.

In Kerouac's case the principle of spontaneous unrevised composition (similar to experiments in prose by James Joyce and Gertrude Stein) has been carried out to its necessary and logical conclusion. Each section of the work—(49 sections are published here)—is the result of a short session of writing, in which the author puts down on the page all the actual thoughts in his mind, uncensored and in the rhythm in which they naturally come. This is an experiment in truthful meditation. It is a sample of a man's actual mind. If the actual truthful mind of a man cannot be printed in America, as set forth after years of competent craftsmanship and practiced art, then it speaks less for the official laws of the land than for the natural laws of the mind. If a man cannot communicate his mind thru the mail then perhaps it ought to be the mail that is to be stopped, rather than the mind.

The grievance of censorship here is made more unendurable by the realization of the religious nature of Kerouac's meditations. The prose is primarily an exposition of the fact that an examination of the contents of his mind leads him to an understanding of a divinity, an enlightened one, underneath his consciousness. This is not in the province of the officials of this government to censor nor would they presumably censor it if they understood what he was getting at. The officials would probably rejoice and be happy to grant second class mailing privileges and deliver the magazine with joy. Kerouac's piece is called *Old Angel Midnight,* and that's what it's about, an angel in the midnight of the meditative mind.

I should add that I consider it his most advanced piece of writing *technically,* i.e. it most closely realizes his desire for a *science* of prose to transcribe the most minute variations of inner thought. This is a contribution to American prose which later writers will come to value and learn from. It is a sample of an important prose method. Its value is, from this point of view, too great to even think of worrying about its obscenity.

We have very similar considerations to take into account when examining W. S. Burroughs' *Naked Lunch.* It is his *Word* (the title of one section)—his revelation of his own actual mind. He is a man who is well educated, who has traveled much, and suffered much, and in his advancing years (he is over 40) he has come to understand certain things about himself and society which he wishes to express. Thus the title *Naked Lunch.* The truth, his truth, is here naked. One of the main insights of this portion of the manuscript is into the nature of the mass brainwash of individuality that has come about in our century thru scientific technique. That a prose exposition on this subject of brainwash should itself be censored by an arm of the government is to me proof of the urgency of his message, and the advisability of its being left free to be disseminated to the public thru the mails. What we have in question here, to my mind, is none other than the subtle spread of a mental dictatorship in America which inhibits free individualistic expression of insight into its nature. To censor *Naked Lunch* in the mail will be an act of political censorship in its significance.

Burroughs' main prose technique is what might be called a "Routine"—a section of fantasy wherein he takes an idea and carries it out to illogical dreamlike limits. In the course of such mental freedom he often arrives at very useful and entertaining insights. Thus he has described imaginary political parties, brainwash technicians, presidents with obscene dope habits, a whole class of spiritual police, exaggerated nightmare rock 'n' roll riots, etc. etc. These all seem to be valid artistic paraphrases of our present human situation. He speaks at length of junk, or heroin, both literally and as a *symbol* of habitual dependence on materialistic ideas of selfhood, or false worldly ego. Thus it is quite appropriate for him to extend this fantasy to describe an unnamed symbolic president as a man hung up on symbolic junk, with all appropriate psychological and sexual abnormalities. I see no reason why an author need hesitate to examine the possibility of a government and its officials being hung up or addicted to false psychological and spiritual conceptions of the world. For that is what that passage means. And censorship of that passage would be treason to democracy.

The whole book *Naked Lunch,* and the passages printed in *Big Table,* are very fine, perceptive, dry, comic, nightmarish prose. The writing sometimes approaches a kind of prose-poetry which is found in 20th Century French writing—notably St. John Perse. To this extent it is also an innovation in American style. It is high class literature, and shouldn't be classed with girlie magazine worries by the Post Office Department. Why it was ever called into question at all I cannot imagine, except it be the literary incompetence of those officials of the P.O. Dept. to judge such matters. It should certainly be taken out of the hands of people who would censor it; they should be told to leave true art alone. The artist has enough trouble without having to battle the government.

WRITTEN: ca. 1960

Unpublished.

Open Letter Re: *New York Review of Sex and Politics*

To the Public, and the Legal Community:

The *New York Review of Sex and Politics* presents material to public consciousness that has hitherto been ritually suppressed in its form (i.e. public newspaper). Its reportage covers that portion of the spectrum of our intellectual, emotional, aesthetic, visual and political consciousness which though universal in private awareness is presented in "official" public information as nonexistent, not to be recognized, like mainland China's government, or unmentionable and unfit to represent in public.

There is what is known as "honest difference of opinion" as to whether or not the suppression of public examination of sexual imagery and language news is part of a larger network of culture-biased suppression of the democratic person. A main stream of American thought embodied in our national poet Walt Whitman maintains that complete freedom of expression in this area of sexual imagery is essential to the development of our social and political system as a free-personed democracy.

Suppression of the *New York Review of Sex* is therefore suppression of this tradition of political and social philosophy in this nation.

It may aid one's perspective in this case to remember that strict Puritanism of public imagery is characteristic of authoritarian police bureaucracy in Czechoslovakia and Russia at the present time. The sense of humor and public independence of feeling and the primacy of person above state manifested in "libertine" imagery is considered politically and ideologically inopportune by those who direct Iron Curtain social-police-state bureaucracies. As I have found in conversation with such bureaucrats in Havana, Moscow, Prague and Warsaw, there is a tendency to equate their rigid social systems with a state of interpersonal normalcy. The same may be said of any police bureaucracy or legal bureaucracy or media bureaucracy in our own country: the humorless and rigidly authoritarian tendency of any bureaucracy anywhere tends to equate its own politics, emotions, manners and imagery with interpersonal normalcy. For that reason in our own country as well as behind the Iron Curtain the rhetoric of suppression of freedom includes the argument that public exposure of sexual imagery degenerates the moral fiber of the nation, is immoral, is antisocial, is unnatural, may tend to enfeeble the resolution of the public in regard to military aggressiveness, is not conducive to respect for authority, and is prohibited by highest moral authorities including Stalin and the head of the Federal Bureau of Investigation or whatever police force supervises the moral fiber of the citizenry.

As we have gone to the moon it is imperative that we go to our own bodies and into our own hearts and minds and sex to find out who we are. We will not find out who we are if exchange of public information as to our sexual identity, such as it is, is suppressed.

What is under discussion is quite literally the *New York Review of Sex and Politics*. In the twentieth century sex is politics. To acknowledge this statement as a fact is merely to acknowledge living in the twentieth century and reading the last twenty-nine words. If we are to maintain even the illusion of free contest of opinion and argument and information in the public arena as vital for maintenance of traditional, basic republican and democratic value in this nation, agents of the State will have to cease prosecuting newspapers such as the *New York Review of Sex and Politics.*

WRITTEN: July 27, 1969

Unpublished.

Statement [On Censorship]

My poetry has been broadcast uncensored for thirty years, particularly the poems *Howl, Sunflower Sutra, America, Kaddish, Kral Majales,* and *Birdbrain.* In the last two decades all these poems have been recorded on disk by Atlantic, Fantasy and Island Records, issued commercially and been broadcast by university, public educational and listener supported stations, such as the Pacifica stations.

Most of these poems have been republished in standard anthologies used for college and high school English courses throughout America. *Howl* alone has been translated into 24 languages, even recently published in hitherto forbidden Iron Curtain countries from Poland to China.

Translations and publications into Polish, Hungarian, Czechoslovakian, Chinese, Macedonian, Serbo-Croatian, Lithuanian and Romanian have been part and parcel of the *glasnost* or freedom of speech and literature accumulated in the last half-decade in those countries. In a recent article by Bill Holm on teaching literature (including D. H. Lawrence) to students in China titled "In China, Loving Lady Chatterley" (*New York Times Book Review,* February 18, 1990, pages 1, 30–31), we read: "Orwell's description of Big Brother's attempts to destroy and pervert sexual life is exactly and literally true. Change the names and it describes any institution like China, name your own preferred church or government." Fundamentalists, mass media hucksters, Senator Jesse Helms, and the Heritage Foundation are attempting to enforce in U.S.A. this Orwellian doublethink in destroying and perverting representation of sexual life in our art and literature.

What is their motive? Professor Holm states it precisely: "My Chinese students existed in a state of sexual suspended animation and yet underneath this mad repression, I sensed that many Chinese are hopeless romantics, doors waiting to be opened. Real sexual energy is a genuine threat to political authority. The moral Stalinists are not wrong."

I remember the insistent language of Moscow Writers Union bureaucrat Mr. Sagatelian at a Soviet American literary conference November 1985 in Vilnius just before the announcement of *glasnost.* I complained of political and erotic censorship; he replied "Henry Miller will never be published in the Soviet Union."

Broadcast censorship of my poetry and the work of my peers is a direct violation of our freedom of expression. I am a citizen. I pay my taxes and I want the opinions, the political and social ideas and emotions of my art to be free from government censorship. I petition for my right to exercise liberty of speech guaranteed me by the Constitution. I reject the insolence of self-righteous moralistic fundraising politicians or politically ambitious priests in using my poetry as a political football for their quasi-religious agendas. I have my own agenda for emotional and intellectual and political liberty in U.S.A. and behind the Iron Curtain. This is expressed in my poetry.

The poems named above were part of a large-scale domestic cultural and political liberalization that began with ending print and broadcast censorship of literary works 1957–1962. A series of legal trials, beginning with my poem *Howl,* liberated celebrated works including books by Henry Miller, Jean Genet, D. H. Lawrence, William Burroughs, and other classic writings.

Much of my poetry is specifically aimed to rouse the sense of liberty of thought and political social expression of that thought in young adolescents. This is the very age group which the Heritage Foundation and Senator [Jesse] Helms' legislation and FCC regulations have attempted to prohibit me from reaching with vocal communication of my texts over the air. It is in the body, speech and mind of these young people that the state of our nation rests and I believe I am conducting spiritual war for liberation of their souls from the mass homogenization of greedy materialistic commerce and emotional desensitization. Since Walt Whitman, who foresaw this situation, many generations have suffered alienation of feeling and sympathy with their own bodies and hearts and with the bodies and hearts of all those in America and other continents that do not fit into a commercially or politically stereotyped convention of color, sex, religion, political allegiance, or personal sense of self.

Pseudo-religious legal interference with my speech amounts to setting up a state religion much in the mode of intolerant Ayatollah or a Stalinoid bureaucratic party line.

In this situation neo-conservative and religious ideologues have taken the weapons of their old communist enemies: party line, censorship, Catch-22 evasion of authority of their own solidified thought police religious and ethical systems. How dare I compare these so-called patriotic citizens to communist bureaucrats? In the words of William Blake: "They became what they beheld."

These censors would abridge my rights of artistic and political freedom of speech just as communist countries did in censoring my work in 1957–1985.

Here an aesthetic consideration enters the argument. A major characteristic of my poetry, at least for its wide circulation, has been its quality of American speech, idiomatic and vernacular, a diction drawn from living language and clarity of vocalization. My ideal is a poetry of majestic and dignified proclamation. I've tried to practice unobstructed vocalizations of sometimes inspired verse, the human voice sounded with its various rhythms and emotional tones, a poetry spoken from head, throat and heart centers; as reading out loud has been my study and my art. This practice has affected many poets in many countries and is part of a long American tradition from the day of Walt Whitman through William Carlos Williams to the lyricist Bob Dylan. Proposed FCC regulation could forbid broadcast of *Howl* (a critique of nuclear hypertechnology), *King of May* (a denunciation of both "communist and capitalist assholes"), *Sunflower Sutra* (panegyric to individual self-empowerment), *America* (a parody of cold-war stereotypes), *Birdbrain* (a satire on Eastern and Western ecological stupidities), and *Kaddish* (a pouring forth of real grief and love for my mother). How can this speech be censored from broadcast without violating our U.S. Constitution?

Censors may fulminate all they wish over the word "indecency," which is never precisely defined, but those who want to extend the Helms amendment to ban this mystific "indecency" on the air 24 hours a day cannot deny they are trying to censor art and socially relevant speech. In the case of the texts specified above, the position of neo-conservatives is quite parallel to that of Nazi book burners of "degenerate works," Chinese dictators who launch attacks on "spiritual pollution," and old Stalinists forbidding erotic texts. The purpose of such censorship is to concentrate all emotional authority in the State, and eliminate all ideological and emotional competition. Conservatives proclaim their ideology to be "get the government off our backs." I petition these so-called "neo-conservative" authoritarians to get off my back.

Walt Whitman called specifically for candor of poets and orators to follow him. Despite the unconstitutional bans that have been put on my poetry, I repeat that call and affirm that I have fulfilled the Good Gray Poet's prescription for a patriotic, candid, totally American art.

WRITTEN: Feb. 19, 1990

FIRST PUBLISHED: *Exit Zero,* no. 1 (1990) pp. 100–101.

Noticing What Is Vivid

The suppression of poetry in America can't be mistaken for unpopularity. Poetry is not as popular as it might be because you can't broadcast it in our main marketplace of ideas: television and radio.

The mass media is controlled by the government, which bans poetry from the air from 6:00am to 8:00pm. Regulations forbid broadcasting most of the standard anthologies and texts that kids study in school, according to various laws put in by Sen. Jesse Helms and others. Important poetry can't get on the air as a great deal of writing, my own included, won't pass the censor's eye.

Much poetry is in Jesse Helms' view "indecent" language. Helms wanted—and Ronald Reagan signed—a 24-hour ban that the courts later found unconstitutional.

There is no "free market" for poetry, since poetry that criticizes gasoline, petrochemical, fossil fuel, lumber and agribusiness industries and the automobile industry wouldn't be sponsored. Poetry on the public education networks immediately gets attacked by the right wing as liberal and un-American. Little real poetry gets on the air.

Yet Jesse Helms, who sets himself up as a moral arbiter, is the main licit killer drug pusher in America, the lobbyist for killer weed, coffin nails, cigarettes.

But Jesse Helms is only a front man, an instrument of Joe Coors, the alcohol and tobacco industries, and of fundamentalist evangelists like Pat Robertson and Donald Wildmen. It's a big, big, big network organized like the old Communist party.

Conservative religious fundamentalists already control the airwaves, on which I can't recite my poetry. If they take control of the grass roots school boards, they'll kick my work out of school libraries as they have [J. D.] Salinger's wherever they can. Check your local library to see what books have been banned and under what pressure.

Fundamentalists who took control of the Texas school board made the big New York textbook companies include scientific creationism and soft peddle the theory of evolution and a lot of American history, black, Indian and colonial, changing the cast, just like in Russia.

Fundamentalists in New York City now prevent schools from teaching about AIDS. To believe the fundamentalist assertion that AIDS is an act of retribution by God against deviant lifestyles, you have to believe in their God, and I have no idea who that is. Should there be a God, how can we be sure that the fundamentalists speak for Him? The last thing we'd want is a bunch of ignorant loudmouths claiming to have His authority. Many non-Western religions, Buddhism and Confucianism, for example, have nothing like the Western conception of God, and certainly no sexual intelligence agency in Heaven.

Much of the political pressure is based on the Meese Commission on pornography, which Reagan appointed under Ed Meese, a sleaze to begin with. A bunch of homophobes on the commission stated unscientifically that pornography led to violence and rape, including the worst of them, Father [Bruce] Ritter, head of Phoenix House, who was recently busted for playing with boys. The other puritanical fundamentalist maniac on it, Charles Keating, head of the Lincoln Savings and Loan, just went to prison for robbing $2.5 billion from the public. His Citizens for Decency in Literature, which became Citizens for Decency Through Law because it sounded too much like censorship, set the stage for the arrest of a Cincinnati museum director for showing [Robert] Mapplethorpe.

When I was young I did believe that there was a God, but as I grew up I found that the belief had no ground, and it was a desire to see God that made it impossible to see what was in front of me on earth.

As a poet I seek to maintain awareness, mindfulness, of what goes on in my head, to notice what is vivid, to summon the energy and overcome the inertia to write it down on the spot, whether in bed in the middle of the night or driving in a car, seeing a Marlboro ad covered with the United States flag as a means of propaganda.

Ordinary thoughts in an ordinary mind, aware of what seems to be vivid in my eyesight in the external world, that is, the world outside of my skull. My poetry recollects a vivid moment after it happens rather than inventing or cogitating anything or trying to cook anything up. I am a stenographer for my own mind, writing what comes naturally.

My method of writing follows my mentors, Jack Kerouac and William Carlos Williams, who wrote in spoken American-ese, in living speech. When I first heard William Carlos Williams at the Museum of Modern Art in 1948, he was just talking as one talks in Paterson or East Rutherford, New Jersey, rather than recycling other poets' literary styles.

I am especially satisfied when I break through to writing candidly about real things in my own life in a way that others recognize, and so wakening recollections of their own hidden life, serving as a mirror for those afraid to articulate their inner-most thoughts.

The spoken aspect of poetry was submerged for many years in America after the restraint of Eliotic New Critics, and the exuberance of spoken American-ese was discouraged. But where it had play in blues, lyrics, or Woody Guthrie, or the Rolling Stones, poetry emerged and dominated an element of consciousness in America and spread around the world as part of a huge political revolution. In fact, poetry is revered and memorized by practically everybody in America in the form of song, whether Bob Dylan, the Beatles, the Sugar Cubes, Sonic Youth, Dinosaur, or Lou Reed. Lyric poetry, including Rap, is extremely popular.

Poetry defined only as poetry that is read, but not spoken or sung, is naturally of less interest, less noticed and less memorized. But in a couple of hundred years when they make anthologies, Dylan will, I think, be the dominant poet of this half of the century.

Centers like the St. Mark's Poetry Project in New York are hot spots for poetry. There is the ongoing tradition of Buddhist Beat combination with the Jack Kerouac School of Disembodied Poetics. All over the country there are mushrooming poetry slams, readings and poetry cafes, and even a resurgence of interest in San Francisco Renaissance and Beat poetry, to a point that it has become commercialized. Rip-off imagery is being used to sell *Gap* jeans and *Pepsi Cola.*

But whether published in expensive little magazines or spoken at poetry slams, whether stand-up in cities or sit-down in the provinces with high class reviews, more activity produces more mulch and compost, and the soil for poetry will become richer.

"Good poetry" is either visual clarity, melodic rondure, or language play that is exuberant and amusing, plus some sense of grounded seriousness and emotion, which usually is manifested in the sight, sound or intellect of the work, and ultimately the sense that the author is purposing to relieve the mass of human suffering.

I write in a little school notebook, mostly in bed, but when I get up in the middle of the night or in the morning I carry a pocket notebook around for ephemera. While I write, when I begin a sentence, I try to include in the sentence anything that rises in my mind related to the sentence, balancing it syntactically like a tightrope walker till I get to the end of the original thought that began the sentence. I try to register thoughts that rise in between the main thought while my hand is moving on the page.

If one were writing about one's girlfriend, for example, thoughts would rise while writing and be either postponed till later or integrated in the sentences being written at that moment. I try to integrate the thoughts that rise *during* the time of writing, even though they may seem disparate or miscellaneous, into the same sentence or paragraph.

FIRST PUBLISHED: *Northern Centinel,* vol. 205, no. 4 (Fall 1993) pp. 8–9.

Political Correctness

"Political Correctness" a Marxist term was used in US by the left as a joke on old style Marxist criticism, then seized by right wing as a serious club of baloney to attack all the left—blacks, women, gays. Middle-class extremist Zionists of yester-decade were exempted ("It's bad for the Jews to criticize Israeli censorship").

In actual fact, "political correctness" as an excuse for censorship was initiated by neo-conservative right wing pundits and televangelist theopoliticians as far back as 1982's Heritage Foundation's Policy Review's two-part attack on N.E.A. grants for poetry to myself and other avant-garde poets. Their argument was the same as the old Stalinist party line that the poems were elitist individualist subjectivist scribblings that had dirty words the tax payers shouldn't have to fund. This version of political correctness was taken up by Sen. Jesse Helms an old windbag who swore it wasn't "censorship" but only populist anger at abuse of public funding for arts, with the [Robert] Mapplethorpe photo shows as his example. He waved homosexual photos around in the senate cloak room, himself obsessed with gay images. This was followed by his October 1988 legislation (framed for him by Heritage Foundation) directing F.C.C. to prohibit all so-called "indecent" language off radio and television, our main market place of ideas. This affected listener supported and college stations *not* funded by government. This major censorship which has bumped my major anthology poems and other literature off private airwaves during daytime study hours over the last 6 years is the most colossal (and most invisible) example of "political correctness" that's taken over and suppressed public discourse in this last decade.

WRITTEN: Oct. 4, 1994

Unpublished.

C.O.P. Statement on Lenny Bruce

ARTS, EDUCATIONAL LEADERS PROTEST USE OF NEW YORK OBSCENITY LAW IN HARASSMENT OF CONTROVERSIAL SOCIAL SATIRIST LENNY BRUCE

SEVERAL SCORES OF PROMINENT AMERICAN UNIVERSITY PROFESSORS, PUBLISHERS, EDITORS, NOVELISTS, PLAYWRIGHTS,

POETS, ARTISTS, CRITICS, COLUMNISTS, SOCIOLOGISTS, CAR-
TOONISTS, ACTORS, MUSICIANS, DIRECTORS—INCLUDING
MANY NON-FANS—JOINED TODAY IN ISSUING A STRONGLY-
WORDED PROTEST AGAINST THE APPLICATION OF STATE LAWS
TO HALT PERFORMANCES OF COMEDIAN LENNY BRUCE BEFORE
THE NEW YORK CITY PUBLIC.

Theologian Reinhold Niebuhr, Columbia University Professor Lionel
Trilling, critic Dwight Macdonald, novelists Norman Mailer, James Jones
and James Baldwin, psychoanalyst Theodor Reik, singer Rudy Vallee,
actor Paul Newman and columnist Max Lerner headed a list of persons
demanding today that the New York City Police Department cease "censorship and harassment" of this "popular and controversial" nightclub
personality.

Bruce, who was taken into police custody from the stage of a New York
City supper club on April 3 and again on April 7 at the instigation of the
New York District Attorney's office and booked on charges of "indecent
performance," has worked in New York with an act in the same vein for
the past four years. Assistant District Attorney Richard Kuh, who initiated action without a citizen's complaint, agreed to postpone hearings
until June 16 only if Bruce would agree not to perform publicly anywhere in New York City pending the outcome of the court case.

Bruce's attorney, Ephraim London, who helped fight a successful battle against censorship of Henry Miller's novel *Tropic of Cancer* in Boston,
maintained in N.Y. Criminal Court that the Lenny Bruce case will be far-
reaching in effect and become "a precedent regulating freedom of
expression in all theaters and places of entertainment in New York."

London held that the social and educational value of Bruce's work
guarantee him freedom to perform under the First and Fourteenth
Amendments to the Constitution—those assuring freedom of speech
and due process of law.

Those signing the petition granted that Bruce uses four-letter
words—described in the petition as "vernacular"—in his monologues,
but they maintained that Bruce is a vital modern representative of the
satirical tradition of Swift, Rabelais and Twain.

Bruce has been saluted by critics from *Cue* magazine ("A preacher
without portfolio; a monologist on morality") to British commentator
Kenneth Tynan ("The most original, free-speaking, wild-thinking gym-

nast of language"). Critic Albert Goldman in the American intellectual magazine *Commentary* compared Bruce to a witch-doctor "who makes both visible and public the systems of symbolic fantasy that are present in the psyche of every adult member of society."

Bruce, who has been prosecuted at various times in other American cities on the same allegations as those in New York, won his most recent victory in mid-May in Los Angeles, where he was acquitted of obscenity charges for the second time. Another such charge is on appeal in Chicago.

The 38-year-old New York-born comedian was arrested in New York State under Penal Law 1140-A. His New York performances included an erudite discussion of laws defining obscenity.

WRITTEN: June 13, 1964

FIRST PUBLISHED: as a press release.

AUTHOR'S NOTE: The document reproduced here is a formal press release. Sonnet, sestina, Sapphic, press release; some sense of logic, condensation, elegance, maximum amount of information in minimum number of syllables, "hooks" or signal words to beguile the minds of various types of readers, are common properties features characteristics of all such forms. I tried to treat the press release as a sort of prose poem, assuming sublimity of the theme (defense of liberty of expression): the surprising historicity of the occasion (the ambiguous genius of Lenny Bruce); the classic villainy of the accusers—District Attorney Richard Kuh acting role of the obsessed avenger Inspector Javert pursuing the noble ex-criminal Jean Valjean in Victor Hugo's *Les Misérables*—same Richard Kuh who unsuccessfully (temporarily) prosecuted Jack Smith's *Flaming Creatures* underground movie driving that film-maker to distraction as the only victim of censorship in an era when underground film cases finally exploded Hollywood film code of self-censorship.

Readers contemporary of 1980s may not remember or realize that from 1959–62 an heroic campaign for freedom of speech in literature was waged by Grove Press to free such classic authors as Henry Miller, D. H. Lawrence, Jean Genet from prohibition.

Burroughs' 1962 *Naked Lunch* decision seems to have broken the back of censorship of print. City Lights' 1957 victory with my own *Howl* text had been an early skirmish; the *Chicago Review-Big Table* magazine battle for liberation of the first chapters of *Naked Lunch* (as well as major Corso poems and Kerouac's Joycean *Old Angel Midnight*) followed, simultaneous with Grove Press prose liberation.

At the time (1964) [New York] City bureaucracies attempted to impose cabaret licensing on coffeehouses wherein the renewed vogue of poetry reading was practiced. That meant fire inspections, costly architectural alterations, city control. Background history: Lester Young, Billie Holiday, Charlie Parker, and Thelonious Monk had been prohibited from performing in N.Y. in the earlier '50s at a time when classic jazz artists themselves had to get "cabaret" licenses. Those who had prior narcotic arrest records were denied license—including Lady Day, Bird and Monk.

Though these laws may now seem medieval—in light of common day—some form of Devil Worship did take place which involved persecution of Lenny Bruce in 1964.

Sensing a rising tide of resistance to libertarian speech poets, I formed a spiritual police force, C.O.P., or Committee on Poetry, to circulate classic petition for Bruce's defense concurrent with the Bruce obscenity trial. Only a decade and half removed from Columbia College peer network now matured and respectable, and with volunteer help of two friends from that era—Helen Eliot and Helen Weaver, both with publishing experience—we cast as wide a net as possible for support, including a liberal who'd attacked Kerouac one time or another, Robert Brustein, Norman Podhoretz—as well as CIA associates Irwin Kristol and Arnold Beichman, the latter Chairman Board of Directors, American Committee for Cultural Freedom then a supposedly secret front funded by "the Agency." More elegant literatees conservative aesthetically but open-minded—F. W. Dupee, John Hollander, Richard Howard from Columbia. Middle echelon publishers and thinkers and old American classic figures—Malcolm Cowley, Lillian Hellman, Granville Hicks, James Jones, Alfred Kazin, Robert Lowell, Dwight MacDonald, Henry Miller, Reinhold Niebuhr, Lionel Trilling, Louis Untermeyer, even Rudy Vallee (by then I believe a secret acid head in any case).

Most exquisitely the list included a number of avant-garde geniuses—Corso, Dylan, Robert Frank, Frank O'Hara, Merce Cunningham.

The list's interesting literary politics.

Given the intellectual weight of signatories one might have thought the ambition of the District Attorney Richard Kuh'd been moved to acknowledge a dignity affronted. His response was to threaten to subpoena the aged theologian Niebuhr—who'd signed less out of familiarity with Bruce than to keep company with peers whose wisdom he trusted—to come down to court to be examined on the subject. A "smart move" if you're a cultural cutthroat, a singularly vulgar piece of aggression if you're an old bohemian gnostic onlooker, used to the age old contest between genius and philistinism.

I got so mad I cut my beard and mailed it in an envelope to the district attorney.

By 1978 Mr. Kuh ran for Congress, his old Karma haunted him; controversy on his old role as over-zealous aggressor in censorship matters. He washed his hands of the matter saying "It was just my job, the law said so." All cases ultimately went against his judgment and an interesting aspect (as with the inventor of Napalm for Dow Chemicals) is that bureaucrats explain they "had" to act as they did, and be objective. However such choices are only subjective projections. Maybe they do think "they have to" but they didn't, the courts decided, did they really "have to"? What egoic motifs and political pressures on their rear end does this rationale "have to" mystify with subjective abstraction?

In other words he didn't have to, and his front was, he had to. He wanted to. He needed to prosecute. His whole life Karma's haunted by that. He's still alive as of this writing. Is he liberated yet? What a way to take revenge, a generation later. What'll his children think reading this and looking back?

For the "Press Release" project I consulted professional news men, wire service editors and on their advice designed our ideal form, to fit into their current print media. Elements:

1. include time and date of release to occur (in this case) in proper time for Sunday newspapers

2. a prefabricated headline
3. a sort of sub head explaining the whole story in newspaper telegraphese for thickheaded, impatient, or harried editors
4. a head paragraph, who when where why what
5. sub paragraph with historical information
6. sub sub paragraph with philosophic rationale and more history by lawyer
7. 4th paragraph rationale of signatories
8. 5th paragraph quotes from respectable critics (*Cue* and *Commentary*)
9. 6th paragraph prior legal vindication of Bruce
10. specifics on Bruce's arrest and law and his actual performance
11. text of petition signed
12. list of signatories alphabetized with identification of their careers.

I had not occasion before to be so polished in attempts to communicate via media—I once went to *Times* or *Mademoiselle* to speak my piece—But I thought here to play the "game" "within the system," make as "serious" formal and polished a petition as possible and appeal to the better nature and intelligent judgment of prosecutors, judges media—the community concerned called "society." This despite what seemed to me the vulgar mugging of every literary cause I was familiar with from *On the Road* to San Francisco Poetry Renaissance ("Beatniks").

Reaction was odd. The DA redoubled his efforts, won his case temporarily, helped drive Bruce further up the wall. Given the historical weight of the case as understood by anybody literate, and affirmed by the phalanx of signatories I thought the press would've responded in defense of liberty.

This was the pattern to be found later in many cases—a failure of the press of the day to take seriously attacks on liberty. Betrayal by conservatives of their major commitment to get government off our backs. Timidity of civil libertarian liberty oriented media like *Times* and then Jewish *NY Post*. Obscurantist venom and blockheadedness by bureaucracy in this case Richard Kuh and Courts. Later cases of unjust government persecution of U.S. artists and dissidents repeat the pattern: LeRoi Jones set up for bust Newark Riots 1966; Leary

persecuted unconstitutionally at psychedelic experimental commune Millbrook by later-to-become-felon Watergate burglar G.
Gordon Liddy; persecution of John Sinclair, and chain of events that
led to persecution of John Lennon—FBI persecution of underground press; further persecution of Jack Smith film-maker; FBI
surveillance of myself and myriad other activist artists.

Committee on Poetry Charter Statement

This group is formed to gather money from those who have it in
amounts excess to their needs and disburse it among poets and philosophers who lack personal finance or wherewithal to accomplish small
material projects in the society at large. The committee's money will be
used to sustain artists and their projects in times of stress; promote freedom of expression where such expression is threatened by social prejudice or outside force; publish works of art which have no immediate
commercial vehicles for publicity; aid sick, wounded or nervous creative
souls who might otherwise be financially isolated; participate in projects
for altering the consciousness of the nation toward a more humane
spirit of adhesiveness prophesied by Whitman; give joy to writers and
artists who wish to escape unpleasant circumstances and travel or meditate; help unlucky poets and painters avoid confinement in jails and
madhouses or ease their return to freedom; and otherwise aid in spiritual emergencies.

WRITTEN: March 26, 1966

Unpublished.

PART 5
Autobiographical Fragments

Autobiographic Precis

Grammar High School Paterson New Jersey, B.A. Columbia College 1948; associations with Jack Kerouac, William S. Burroughs, Herbert Huncke and Neal Cassady begun 1945 NYC and next decade after with Gregory Corso, Peter Orlovsky companion 1954 and poets Michael McClure, Philip Lamantia, Gary Snyder and Philip Whalen in San Francisco became known 1955 on as "Beat Generation" and/or "San Francisco Renaissance" literary phases; acquaintance with William Carlos Williams 1948 and study of his relative-footed American speech prosody led to *Empty Mirror* early poems with William Carlos Williams preface, as later Williams introduced *Howl*.

Illuminative audition of William Blake's voice simultaneous with eternity-vision 1948 and underground bust-culture Apocalypse realization conduced to eight-month stay NY State Psychiatric Institute and later preoccupation with gnostic-mystic poetics and politics, residence in India and Vietnam, Japan visit 1962–63, mantra chanting beginning with Hare Krishna Maha mantra and Buddhist *Prajnaparamita* (Highest Perfect Wisdom) *Sutra* same years, and experiment with poetic effects of psychedelic drugs beginning 1952 and continuing with Dr. Timothy Leary through Cambridge experiments 1961: certain texts "Howl Part II" (1955) and "Wales Visitation" (1967) were written during effects of peyote and LSD respectively.

Travel began early 1950s half year Mayan Mexico, several voyages years Tangier-Europe late 50s on, earlier merchant marine sea trips to Africa and Arctic, half year Chile Bolivia and Peru Amazon 1960, half year Cuba Russia Poland Czechoslovakia culminating May Day 1965 election as King of May (Kral Majales) by 100,000 Prague citizens.

Literary Awards: obscenity trial with "Howl" text declared legal by court San Francisco 1957, Guggenheim Fellowship 1963–64, National Institute of Arts and Letters grant for poetry 1969. Contributing Editor: *Black Mountain Review* #7 edited by Robert Creeley; Advisory Guru: *The*

Marijuana Review, writing published variously in *Yugen, Floating Bear* mimeo, *Kulchur, Big Table, City Lights Journal, "C," Evergreen Review, Fuck You/A Magazine of the Arts, Atlantic Monthly, Life, New Yorker, Look, N.Y. Times, Izvestia, Rolling Stone,* Underground Press Syndicate, etc.

Participated in college poetry readings and NY literary scene 1958–61 with LeRoi Jones and Frank O'Hara; poets' *Pull My Daisy*, Robert Frank film 1959; early trips festivals with Ken Kesey Neal Cassady and Merry Pranksters mid-'60s; Vancouver '63 and Berkeley '65 Poetry Conventions with Olson, Duncan, Creeley, Snyder, Dorn and other poet friends; Albert Hall Poetry Incarnation, readings with Voznesensky in London, and anti-Vietnam War early Flower Power marches in Berkeley 1965.

Attended mantra-chanting at first Human Be-in San Francisco 1967; conferred at Dialectics of Liberation in London and gave poetry readings with poet father Louis Ginsberg there and in NY; testified U.S. Senate hearings for legalization of psychedelics; arrested with Dr. Benjamin Spock blocking Whitehall Draft Board steps war protest NY same year. Tear gassed chanting "OM" at Lincoln Park Yippie Life-Festival Chicago 1968 Presidential convention, then accompanied Jean Genet and William Burroughs on front line peace "conspiracy" march led by Dave Dellinger.

Mantric poetics and passing acquaintance with poet-singers Ezra Pound, Bob Dylan, Ed Sanders and Mick Jagger led to music study for tunes to *Blake's Songs of Innocence and Experience.* This homage to visionary poet-guru William Blake, occasioned by visit to West Coast to touch a satin bag of body-ashes the late much-loved Neal Cassady, was composed one week on return from police-state shock in Chicago and recorded summer 1969. Chanted "OM" to judge and jury December 1969 Anti-War Conspiracy Trial Chicago; thereafter interrupted by Miami police on reading poetry exorcising police bureaucracy Prague and Pentagon, rapid Federal Court Mandatory Injunction declared texts constitutionally protected from police censorship. Pallbore funerals late Kerouac and Olson, last few '60s winters spent outside cities learning music, milking cows and goats.

WRITTEN: February, 1970

Chronological Addenda

1971—Began daily hour sub-vocal mantra heart meditation, Swami Muktananda Paramahamsa teacher; brief journey Bengal Jessore Road Calcutta to E. Pakistan refugee camps and revisited Benares. Jamming at home and recording studios w/Dylan and Happy Traum learned blues forms. *Kaddish* play mounted N.Y. Chelsea Theater. Researched and publicized CIA subsidization Indochinese opium traffic; assembled 16 phono albums *Collected Poems Vocalized 1946–71* from decades' tape archives. Completed second album Blake songs.

1972—Began study *Kagyü* lineage Tibetan Buddhist meditation; Chögyam Trungpa, Rinpoche teacher; took Refuge and *bodhisattva* vows; extended poetic practice to public improvisation on blues chords with political *dharma* themes. Adelaide and Central Australia meeting with Aboriginal song-men, Darwin Land travel with Russian poet Andrei Voznesensky. Jailed with hundreds of peace protesters, Miami Presidential Convention; essays in defense of Tim Leary, Abbie Hoffman, John Lennon, etc., from Federal Narcotics Bureau entrapment, as member of P.E.N. Freedom to Read Committee.

1973—Poetry International London and Rotterdam; meetings with Basil Bunting and Hugh MacDiarmid, tour Scotland/Inner Hebrides. Taught poetics Naropa Seminary; all autumn retreat Buddhist study including month's 10-hour daily sitting practice.

1974—Inducted member American Academy of Arts and Letters. National Book Award for *Fall of America*; apprenticed rough carpentry wooden cottage neighboring Gary Snyder's Sierra land; with Anne Waldman founded Jack Kerouac School of Disembodied Poetics, Naropa Institute, Boulder Colorado, co-director teaching subsequent summers.

1975—Poetics school solidified; poet-percussionist on Bob Dylan's Rolling Thunder Review tour; *First Blues* with lead sheet music notation published.

1976—Reading Academie Der Kunste, Berlin with William Burroughs; *First Blues* recordings produced by John Hammond Sr.; several months fall seminary retreat with Chögyam Trungpa, Rinpoche.

1977—Read through Blake's entire works, wrote "Contest of Bards," narrated TV-N.E.T. film *Kaddish*, presented poetry/music Nightclub Troubadour L.A. under Buddhist auspices, thereafter N.Y. Other End and Boston Passim folk clubs. *Journals Early '50s, Early '60s,* Grove Press, N.Y. ed. Gordon Ball. Read with Robert Lowell St. Mark's Poetry Project N.Y.; taught Blake's "Urizen" Naropa Institute spring, summer discoursed on "Literary History Beat Generation 1940s." Attended University of California Santa Cruz LSD Conference with Dr. Albert Hoffman, visited Kauai.

1978—*Mind Breaths, Poems 1972–77,* City Lights, S.F. *As Ever: Correspondence A.G. and Neal Cassady 1948–68,* Creative Arts, Berkeley; *Poems All Over the Place,* Cherry Valley Ed., N.Y.; *Mostly Sitting Haiku,* From Here Press, Paterson, N.J. Naropa Summer Discourse on "Meditation and Poetics"; composed music for Blake's "Tyger" to trochaic heart-beat meters; acted "The Father," danced, sang Blake and visited Kerouac's grave with Dylan in *Renaldo and Clara* film. Composed "Plutonian Ode" and arrested twice at Rocky Flats Colorado nuclear facility with Orlovsky and Daniel Ellsberg practicing sitting meditation on railroad tracks blocking train bearing Plutonium/fissile materials: conviction appealed. Month's fall meditation retreat at Bedrock Mortar Hermitage in California Sierras.

1979—Taught Blake's Lambeth Prophetic books to "Four Zoas" at Naropa and poetry workshop at Brooklyn College, spring: video film with Alan Kaprow by Nam June Paik; attended gay rights mass meet Washington Monument; several European tours accompanying Corso, Orlovsky and Living Theatre with Steven Taylor musician, visited Blake's Cottage Felpham, read and sang at Oxford, Heidelberg, Tübingen and International Poetry convocations Cambridge, Rotterdam and Amsterdam, Paris, Genoa, Rome.

1980—*Composed on the Tongue* (Literary Conversations 1967–77) Don Allen, Grey Fox Press, Bolinas. Winter, spring, summer teaching basic poetics at Naropa Institute. Gay Sunshine Press edition of *Straight Hearts' Delight,* 25 years' letters and poems done with Peter Orlovsky. National Endowment for the Arts Fellowship and New York State Arts Council grants; Rome International Poetry Festival, fall trip to Yugoslavia, Hungary poetry readings and rock 'n' roll movie concerts, Switzerland, Austria, Germany, Holland tour. *Gaté* song disc produced by Loft Munich. "Capitol Air," New Wave lyric composed on Frankfurt-New York plane December.

1981—Recorded "Capitol Air" Z.B.S. Studios, for John Hammond Records; Naropa Spring Discourse, "Literary History Beat Generation

1950–53"; Summer Discourse "Twentieth Century International Heroic Expansive Poetics: An Anthology." Mexico City International Poetry Conference with Voznesensky, Borgés, Grass, Merwin, Paz, Popa; *Kaddish* play Toronto; readings and singing Piazza della Signoria, Florence and San Carlo Opera House, Naples with Amiri Baraka; attended *Dharma* Art Festival San Francisco and sang with The Job New Wave Band; Columbia University McMillin Theater 25th Anniversary "Howl" reading; lectured with William S. Burroughs at Institute for Policy Studies, D.C.; recorded "Birdbrain" with Gluons Denver New Wave band; prepared manuscript *Plutonian Ode: Poems 1977–80* for City Lights; MLA convention discourse on "Journals." Poetry reading N.Y. YMCA with Jim Carroll. *First Blues* recorded 1974 in Chelsea Hotel by Harry Smith issued by Folkways. Recorded on "Combat Rock" album and sang live with Clash at Bond's rock club.

1982—Attended Poetry Festival Managua, composed "Declaration of Three" with Ernesto Cardinal and Yevtuchenko requesting non-interference in Nicaraguan evolution; completed *Unamerican Activities*, P.E.N. Club report on FBI harassment, underground press '60s–'70s published by City Lights; recorded two rock songs with Bob Dylan Santa Monica. Continued "Literary History Beat Generation" Spring Discourse Naropa Institute, where collaborated five poem-paint canvases with Karel Appel; sang "Capitol Air" with various New Wave bands including Still Life Denver, Black Hole Milwaukee and national TV Dave Letterman broadcast. Hosted Naropa *On the Road* 25th Anniversary National Celebration with Burroughs, Corso, Orlovsky, Creeley, Ferlinghetti, McClure, di Prima, Kesey, Berrigan, Carl Solomon, Ray Bremser, Jack Micheline, Robert Frank, Herbert Huncke, Dave Amram, Anne Waldman, Abbie Hoffman, Timothy Leary, Jan Kerouac, and others; Taos anti-nuke readings with Ram Dass. Mexican Tarahumara Sierras train trip with Corso and Orlovsky; visited Maezumi and Eido Roshi LA and NY; participated first meeting P.R.C. Peking Writers' Union Delegation at U.C.L.A. with Vonnegut, Arthur Miller and Gary Snyder; Naropa Fall Discourse, "Beat Literary History, 1957–60"; *Plutonian Ode* awarded *LA Times* poetry book prize; December Paris U.N.E.S.C.O. "War Against War" International Poetry reading with Voznesensky and friends; began tour Northern Europe and Scandinavia.

1983—Completed Copenhagen Stockholm Oslo Helsinki, East and West German tours, video record *Back to Wuppertal.* Residence Naropa

Institute, Boulder, Colorado; William Carlos Williams Centennial Conferences, National Poetry Foundation, University of Maine, Orono, and Rutherford, New Jersey. Visits with Berenice Abbot, Maine and New York. Karme Chöling seminar "*Dharma* and Poetics"; double album, *First Blues* (1971–1981) issued by John Hammond Records. *Poetry in Motion* filmed; workshop "Meditation and Poetics," Folger Shakespeare Library, Washington, D.C. Following ten-year co-directorship, now emeritus Naropa Kerouac Poetics School.

1984—New Year's Day sang "Do the Meditation Rock" with Peter Orlovsky and Steven Taylor in Nam June Paik's "Good Morning Mr. Orwell" Satellite TV performance with Cage, Cunningham, and Laurie Anderson. One World Poetry Brussels visit; Liverpool; poetry reunion Albert Hall, London, with Basil Bunting, Tom Pickard, Gregory Corso. "White Shroud" text *New York Times Magazine*, also Basel edition illustrated by Francesco Clemente. Awards Committee, American Academy of Arts and Letters; Freedom to Write Committee, P.E.N. Club. Teaching collaboration, poetry music video with Elvin Jones and Robert Frank, Florida Atlantic Center for Arts; 30 years' photograph archives indexed and new printed, advised by Robert Frank. Readings with Nicanor Parra; "Father Death Blues" poetry video, Out There Productions. American Academy Arts and Letters China delegation with Gary Snyder, Francine du Plessix Grey, Harrison Salisbury; Beijing encounter with Liu Binyan and poet Bai Dao; then two month China travel teaching poetry—readings Foreign Language Institute, School for Foreign Languages, Beijing, Canton, Baoding Hebei, Shanghai Fudan U., Suchow and Kunming after Yangtze three gorges river trip. Harper and Row, *Collected Poems, 1947–1980.*

1985—First photographic exhibits "Hideous Human Angels" at Holly Solomon NYC and "Memory Gardens," Middendorf Gallery, Washington. Pound Conference with Robert Creeley, Olga Rudge and Hugh Kenner at National Poetry Foundation, Maine, and Berenice Abbot visit with Creeley; Yiddish Poetry Conference with Zalman Schachter and Stanley Kunitz, Reconstructionist Rabbinical College, Philadelphia; readings Vancouver and London; "Sacramental Snapshots," discourse with photographs, *Aperture* #101; other photos *Vanity Fair, People Magazine.* "One World Poetry" Conference, summer Naropa Institute, Southampton Gay Rights Benefit, Willem de Kooning visit, sat Alex Katz portraits. Harry Smith painter, filmmaker, sound archivist and occult bibliophile, roommate for bulk of year. Interview with China poems "Reading Bai Juyi" U.P.I. newsfeature wireserviced. First delegation U.S.-Soviet Writers meet Vilnius Minsk Leningrad Moscow with Gass, Gaddis, Miller, Cousins, Auchincloss; visits with Bela Achmadulina, and poets S. Kushner, Y. Rein. Visa denied then granted for solitary visit Tbilisi encounter with filmmaker S. Parajanov; Moscow performance A. Kozloff birthday jazz concert and poetry reading Lomonosov University, Yevtuchenko and Sergiev translators. Chinese "Howl" published Hefei, P.R.C. Poetry Press.

1986—Drafted controversial widely-endorsed delegates' statement against American intervention in Nicaragua with Arthur Miller and Gunther Grass for P.E.N. International Conference NYC; Vice President, American chapter. Second visit Rubén Darío Poetry Festival, Nicaragua, meetings with poets Jose Coronel Urtecho, Pablo A. Cuadra, Ernesto Cardinal, Carlos Martinez Rivas. Host India Poetry Festival, MOMA; Harvard Advocate AIDS Benefit. "Airplane Blues" and Blake's "Nurses Song" recorded Paris Records, Dallas. Group photo show Forum Stadtpark, Graz; Inaugural Program Naropa Halifax Meditation-poetics seminar. Sixtieth Birthday Festschrift, *Best Minds A Tribute to Allen Ginsberg*, edited Bill Morgan and Bob Rosenthal, contributors Burroughs, Cage, Creeley, Genet, etc. Forward to John Wieners *Selected Poems: 1958–1984*, Black Sparrow Press. Middleurope visit, recorded Poetry Rock LP, Hobo Blues Band, Budapest; Golden Wreath prize, Evenings of Poetry, Struga, Yugoslavia; Krakow and Warsaw Solidarity readings. Poetry Society of America Gold Medal Award; appointment Distinguished Professor, Brooklyn College, Twentieth Century Expansive Heroic Verse seminar. Accreditation Naropa Institute by Western College Association; summer poetics program with Creeley, Burroughs, et al; "White Shroud" string quartet conducted by Steven Taylor. *White Shroud Poems 1980–85* published, Harper and Row; also edition *Howl Annotated* w/facsimile manuscript. "Howl" 30th anniversary panel and gala reading MLA Convention, New York. WNYC-Moscow radio hook-up chainpoem conversation with Bela Achmadulina, year end.

1987—Photograph exhibits Books and Books Miami; Dallas Museum of Art; Watari Gallery Tokyo; Århus Denmark; Lawrence Kansas; Graz Austria. Brooklyn College spring discourse Literary History of Beat Generation, tandem reading series with H. Huncke, R. Creeley, P. Whalen, Ray Bremser, Carl Solomon, P. Orlovsky, M. McClure, W. S. Burroughs. Etching collaboration Francesco Clemente "Improvisation in Beijing"; premiere William Carlos Williams film portrait w/A.G. commentary. Spring Seminars Naropa Boulder and Halifax, last visit the late Vidyadhara, Chögyam Trungpa in hospital; encounters and readings N.Y. with Bitov, Akhmadulina, Yevtuchenko, Voznesensky, Nicanor Parra. NEA Creative Writing Fellowship Grant; Wallace Stevens Award Timothy Dwight College Yale visit w/Voznesensky. Mississippi Delta trip Oxford "Ole Miss" Southern Folklore Center Blues Archive and Clarksdale with Harry Smith, thence Jackson and Mobile Alabama. Twentieth anniversary St. Mark's Poetry Project, reading and panels with Robert Creeley, K. Koch, A. Waldman, E. Sanders, J. Rothenberg. Modern Language Association of America honorary membership; summer discourse: objectivist poetics, Naropa Institute. *Lion For Real* spoken poetry/music album recorded, Hal Willner producer. Attended Kalapa Assembly at Rocky Mt. Dharma Center; "Howl" reading at Burroughs' River City Reunion, Lawrence, Kansas; attended weeklong Family Service and Therapy Program, Hazelden Hospital, Minneapolis. Francophone Kerouac Convention, Quebec. Addressed Buddhist Psychotherapy Conference, N.Y.; organized consortium P.E.N. American Center, ACLU with Pacifica Radio to oppose F.C.C. censorship of arts broadcasting.

1988—Israel readings, with Natan Zach at Tel Aviv Haifa Universities and Jerusalem Cinemathique, meeting with Palestinian moderates Mubarak Awad and Hanna Senoria, addressed 60,000 Peace Now Rally, taught Camera Obscura School "Photographic Poetics" with Robert Frank. Organized P.E.N. American Center protest Israeli censorship of minority Palestinian literature and media. Collaboration with Philip Glass "Wichita Vortex Sutra," Lincoln Center premiere. Eye and Ear Theater *Kaddish* play revival, music Steven Taylor, sets Eric Fischl. Hamburg State Opera House *Cosmopolitan Greetings*, director Robert Wilson, music George Gruntz, opera libretto Allen Ginsberg. Japan Tour: readings Tokyo with Kazuko Shiraishi, American Literature Society of Japan, Osaka Anti-Nuke Rally, Seika and Kyoto Universities with Nanao Sakaki to protect Okinawan Shiraho Blue Coral Reef. Reunion with Georgian film director Sergei Parajanoff, N.Y. Readings: Museum of Modern Art with Bei Dao, Gong Liu "Poets from the People's Republic of China"; Home Aid Benefit with Ram Das and rock/movie stars, N.Y. cathedral St. John the Divine 6,000 congregation; Smithsonian Institute; new Student Action Union, Rutgers; with

Burroughs Marquette University; Kerouac Commemorative Park, Lowell; S.F. Jewish Community Center; U.C. Davis with Gary Snyder; New Mexico Sanctuary Defense Committee Benefit. Olson Lectures, S.U.N.Y. Buffalo; Zen Mountain Monastery N.Y. Seminar "Snapshot Poetics"; Orono National Poetry Foundation, discourse "Romantic Poets and the Absolute"; Conference Barnard College reunion with translators Andrei Sergeiev, Fernanda Pivano, Carl Weissner. Photo shows: Tokyo, Krakow, Warsaw, and Stadttheater, Tübingen, Germany; also Whistler House Lowell, Fogg Museum Cambridge; Vision Gallery Boston; Tilton Gallery New York.

1989—Keynote poetry reading with Fugs rock group Associated Writing Programs' Convention, Philadelphia; various high school and college poetry readings Utah, Amherst, Albion, Duke, Bates, etc. Fundraising readings inaugurating Albert Hoffman Memorial Library Los Angeles, other various benefits: NYC Homesteaders, Squatters, Hanuman Books, WNYC, Gay Pride rallies, AIDS Prevention, NAMBLA Convention, St. Mark's Bookshop, Abbie Hoffman Foundation celebrations New York and Pennsylvania, P.E.N. Club Salman Rushdie event, Stalin Victims Memorial, Gelek Rinpoche's Jewel Heart with Philip Glass and Naropa *dharma* centers. Co-instructor Brooklyn College course: African American Poetic Genius Ma Rainey to Gwendolyn Brooks with Prof. Marie Buncomb, hosting teacher poets Quincey Troupe, David Henderson, Jayne Cortez, Lorenzo Thomas, June Jordan, Audre Lorde, Alice Childress, Sonia Sanchez, Michael Harper and Gwendolyn Brooks. Contemplative poetics: "Mind Forms / Poetic Forms" discourses Boulder and Canada Naropa, Karma Chöling Meditation Centers. Assisted CCNY Langston Hughes Award presentation to Amiri Baraka; *Paris Review* interview and poetry; music performances with Baraka at New York 92nd St. YMHA and Village Gate. Also performances with False Prophets punk band Pyramid Club and Continental Divide New York; chaired Alumni Day Brooklyn College with Tuli Kupferberg, Carl Solomon, and Jackson MacLow; hosted Poets and Writers fundraiser New York; Poetry Project Spring Symposium with Marjorie Perloff, Hugh Kenner; California Harmonium Mundi Conference with Dalai Lama; Vancouver reading with Gregory Corso; San Francisco National Poetry Association Week Award for Distinguished Service to poetry art; Knitting Factory Kerouac *Mexico City Blues* marathon; Eye and Ear Company revival *Kaddish* Rapp Theater New York. Photo exhibitions in Los

Angeles, Chicago, Austria, Poland and Germany. *Reality Sandwiches,* Nishen/Germany (photography book). *The Lion For Real* record cassette and CD Great Jones/Island Records produced Hal Willner. Biography: *Ginsberg,* Barry Miles, Simon and Schuster. Won Federal DC Court Appeal against FCC all broadcast day ban on "indecent" language, chilling anthologized poetry off air. Manhattan Borough President Dinkens' award for Arts Excellence 1989.

1990—Keynote speaker, Gay and Lesbian Writers Conference, San Francisco; lecture/performance—Blake's *Songs of Innocence and Experience,* accompanied by Steven Taylor, St. Mark's Poetry Project, New York; lecture, "Photography and Poetics," School of the Arts, Rutgers University; host, PEN Gala Dinner as Vice President of the American PEN Center, New York; speaker, Earth Day Rally, Philadelphia; first return to Prague since 1965, received by Mayor Koran and President Havel. Recrowned King of May after 25 years. Concert, President Havel in attendance. Lectures on American poetry, Charles and Olomuc Universities, Czechoslovakia; interview, Lewis Hyde, Radio Program Series, *Poetry* magazine, Chicago; Premiere *Hydrogen Jukebox* opera with Philip Glass, Spoleto festivals, Charleston, South Carolina and Spoleto, Italy; readings, Royal Festival Hall, London and Centre George Pompidou, Paris; Co-Director Emeritus, Naropa Institute Summer Poetics Program, Boulder, Colorado; American delegate, 12th World Congress of Poets, Seoul, South Korea; lecture, "Censored Writings," Boston Museum of Fine Art; inauguration of traveling photo show, FNAC Galerie, France; lecture, "Chemical Substances and Poetics," Pharmacy School, SUNY, Albany; reading, National Academy of Sciences, for Junior Academy members, New York; Lifetime Achievement Award, Before Columbus Foundation, Miami, Florida.

1991—Week-long resident lecturer, Virginia Military Institute, Lexington, Virginia; lecture, "Performance" with Gary Snyder, Pitzer College, Claremont, CA; taught master class at Poetry Project Symposium, NYC; public talk "Shambhala Poetics in the Western Tradition—Working with Spontaneous Poetry," Shambhala Training Center, NYC; master class at the Walt Whitman Birthplace Association, Long Island, NY; symposium on Tiananmen Square with Feng Lizhi, New York Academy of Sciences, NY; keynote speaker, Buddhist Psychology Conference, Karma Triyana Monastery, Woodstock, NY; symposium with Lewis Hyde, "Art and Politics," Kenyon College, OH;

keynote lecture, Great Falls Preservation and Development Corporation 200th Anniversary, Paterson, NJ; MLA Special Session on *Kaddish*, chair Gordon Ball with Helen Vendler, San Francisco, CA; Harriet Monroe Poetry Award, University of Chicago, IL; photo book: *Allen Ginsberg Photographs,* Twelvetrees Press, Santa Monica; reading Jack Kerouac's *Dharma Bums* and Jacob Rabinowitz's *Translations of Catullus,* Spring Audio Cassettes, New York.

1992—Lecture/demonstration International Center for Photography, NY; William Carlos Williams Conference, "Paterson: The Poem and the City," Great Falls Preservation and Development Corporation, Paterson, NJ; Jewel Heart Benefit readings with Anne Waldman and Gelek Rinpoche, Netherlands; week residence National Poetry Foundation, University of Maine, ME; three lectures on poetics: Santa Monica Writers Conference with Annie Dillard; lectures/addresses Walt Whitman Centenary celebrations: Brooklyn College, CUNY Graduate Center with Galway Kinnell, SUNY, Purchase, Teachers and Writers at St. Mark's Poetry Project with Kenneth Koch, St. John the Divine Cathedral with Lucille Clifton and Galway Kinnell, Brooklyn Historical Society, Manhattanville College, The Garrison Keillor Show with Robert Bly, Charlie Rose PBS with Kinnell and Sharon Olds; "Chevalier de l'Ordre des Artes et des Lettres" presented by Jacques Lang, French Minister of Culture, Paris; elected Fellow of the American Academy of Arts and Sciences, Boston, MA; "Exorcising Burroughs": colloquy with William Burroughs, *London Observer Sunday Magazine;* individual volumes of poetry published in China, Czechoslovakia and Bulgaria; *Indian Journals,* paperback, Viking Penguin, India; essay "Whitman's Influence: A Mountain Too Vast To Be Seen," *The Teachers and Writers Guide to Walt Whitman,* New York; Preface, Kerouac's *Pomes All Sizes,* City Lights, San Francisco; *Louis Ginsberg, Collected Poems,* Northern Lights, Orono, ME; essay: "Negative Capability: Kerouac's Buddhist Ethic," *Tricycle, The Buddhist Review,* Fall; biography *Dharma Lion,* Michael Schumacher, St Martin's Press, NY.

1993—National Writer's Voice Project tour of American heartland, Boise, St. Louis, Billings, Phoenix, Lexington. Tibet House benefit with Philip Glass, Laurie Anderson, and chanting Gyuto monks. Jewel Heart Lincoln, Nebraska benefit for Gelek Rinpoche. FAIR Benefit screening *Damned in the USA.* Performances at McCabes, Santa Monica, and Iron Horse, Amherst. Colleges: Chapman, Stonehill, University of Oklahoma, Earlham College. High school curriculum teaching at Dalton prep school. Collaboration with dancer Cyndi Lee. Readings with Galway Kinnell at St. Mark's, David Cope in Grand Rapids. 50th High School Class Reunion at Eastside HS in New Jersey. Jewish-Buddhism conference with Rabbi Zalman Schachter and Gelek Rinpoche. "Neglected Whitman" reading with Sam Abrams. John Jay Distinguished Alumnus Award Columbia. Introduced Brooklyn College Rainbow series: Joe Bruchac, Pat Hampl, Andy Clausen, Sharon Olds, Galway Kinnell, Lucille Clifton and Simon Ortiz. Orono, Maine conference on 1930s poets. July at Naropa Institute for annual writing program, August Jewel Heart Retreat with Gelek Rinpoche. Four month European tour in the fall during Brooklyn College Sabbatical: ten days teaching with Anne Waldman at Vienna Poetry School, travel to Budapest; Belgrade; Bydgoszcz, Krakow, Lodz, and Warsaw in Poland; Cheltenham Festival England. First visit to Ireland reading in Dublin and Belfast, TV collaboration with Bono at U2 studio, Dublin; readings in Norway, Munich, with premieres of Jerry Aronson's film *The Life and Times of Allen Ginsberg* in Paris, Berlin, Prague, Barcelona, Madrid, Cordoba, Athens. Visited with Alan Ansen in Greece, final stop Tangier visit with Paul Bowles and revisitation of old room habited with Peter O. and Jack Kerouac (c. 1957 and 1961). Home January for Vajrayogini Buddhist retreat with Gelek Rinpoche, Michigan.

1994—Early January Buddhist retreat, Ann Arbor; read "Howl" with Kronos Quartet, at Unterman and Savinar Residence, SF, Jan. 14 and at Carnegie Hall, Jan 20; Visiting Adjunct Prof. NYU, Craft of Poetry Course; reading, St. Mary's College of Maryland, Jan. 28; benefit reading for Jewel Heart, Hill Auditorium, Feb. 4; visit with William Burroughs, Lawrence KS, 80th birthday celebration; benefit reading for Tibet House with Philip Glass, Paul Simon, Richie Havens, Natalie Merchant, Spaulding Grey; reading with Quincy Troupe, Gwen Fowler Museum of Contemporary Art, San Diego, Feb. 17; weekend workshop, Pacifica Graduate Institute, Lambert, CA Feb. 19; reading UC Santa Barbara, Feb. 24; reading and weekend workshop, Zen Mountain Monastery, Mt. Tremper, NY, March 11 and 12; reading and talk, Concordia University, Montreal, March 18; benefit reading for Coffee House Press, Minneapolis, March 19; shot poetry video for *United States of Poetry,* Mark Pellington director, April 16; reading Columbia Green College, NY April 22; reading Portland, ME March 29; panel with Ed Sanders, Bernadette Mayer, David Henderson, "Investigative Poetics," Poetry Project

Symposium, May 7; reading and lecture for NYU Beat Conference May 18–21; book tour for *Cosmopolitan Greetings Poems* sign and read in New York, Hartford, San Diego, Los Angeles, Ventura, San Francisco, Boston, Chicago, Seattle, Portland; Harvard Phi Beta Kappa Poet, June 7; workshop with Gelek Rinpoche, Omega Institute; Naropa Institute, Boulder, CO lecture and reading month of July; lecture Skowhegan School, Skowhegan, ME, Aug. 5; spent week with editor Gordon Ball, final edits for *Journals Mid-Fifties* Aug. 15; reading at "The Real Woodstock Festival" with Ed Sanders, Country Joe McDonald, Woodstock; benefit reading for "Doctors without Borders," Lincoln Center, NYC; Buddhist retreat with Gelek Rinpoche Aug. 29; reading McCabes Guitar Shop, Santa Monica, Sept. 9; benefit reading for Albert Hoffman Foundation at Living Planet, Long Beach CA, Sept. 10; reading, Viper Room, Santa Monica, Sept. 12; benefit reading for Maitri Hospice, SF; reading Solo Mio Festival, SF Sept. 19; reading with Robert Creeley, John Wieners, U Mass Sept. 23; read and roundtable for Annual Kerouac Fest, Lowell, MA Sept. 24; reading with Kamau Braithwaite, New School, Tischman Auditorium, NYC, Oct. 6; benefit reading for Black Mountain Museum, Asheville, NC Oct. 13; benefit reading and workshop, Karme Chöling, Barnett, VT, Oct. 21; read and lecture Swarthmore College, Oct. 31; lecture and read Penn University, Oct. 1–3; reading Hot Springs, Arkansas, Oct. 5; reading Kent State, Nov. 6; guest of *Nouvel Observateur,* Paris for roundtable Nov. 22-Dec. 2; read and sign booktour for *Cosmopolitan Greetings* London, Dec. 3–9.

1995—Panel with Carl Rakosi, and reading Stanford University, Feb. 10; reading benefit for Jewel Heart, Hill Auditorium, Ann Arbor Feb. 16; reading benefit at Village Vanguard with Ray Bremser, Feb. 23; reading benefit for Tibet House, Carnegie Hall NY, with Philip Glass, Natalie Merchant, Paul Simon, Edie Brickel, Feb. 28, 1995; benefit reading with Philip Glass and Gelek Rinpoche for Jewel Heart, Cleveland; reading, United Kingdom Year of Literature and Writing Festival, Swansea, Wales, April 7; reading with Andrei Voznesensky, Galway Arts Center, Galway, Ireland, introduced by U2's Bono, April 1; panel with Camille Paglia, Leslie Fiedler, Ishmael Reed, SUNY Buffalo, April 29–30; reading benefit, Halifax Nova Scotia, in conjunction with Tibetan Buddhist Sakyong Enthronement May 19; readings at the Knitting Factory, 5 nights successive, complete *Selected Poems 1947–1995* before manuscript, over May 4–11; Hungarian-Russian documentary on Lower East Side with Gregory

Corso, George Condo, Philip Glass, Francesco Clemente, Peter Orlovsky, June 2–4; symposium and exhibition, with Hiro Yamagata, Venice Biennial, June 9; reading tribute to Fernanda Pivano, Conegliano, Italy, June 10; teaching and performance, two weeks at Naropa Institute, Boulder Colorado, July 1–15; interview and photography week long with William Burroughs, Lawrence, KS July 16–22; reading benefit for Mumia Abu-Jamal with Amiri Baraka, Marc Ribot and other musicians, at The Cooler, N.Y. Aug. 8; reading benefit for ABC No Rio, Rivington St. N.Y., Aug. 11; Buddhist retreat Ann Arbor Michigan, Jewel Heart Center, and performance with Philip Glass Aug. 28-September 6; reading with Anne Waldman, Tom Pickard, Alice Notley et al. the Royal Albert Hall, London, October 16.

1996—January: residence L.A., Gemini GEL Lithography press; readings at McCabes Guitar Shop, Santa Monica; Feb. 12–27: Eberhard L. Faber Fellow Princeton University, lectures & reading: Carnegie Hall performance with Philip Glass, Tibet House benefit; collaborated with Ornette Coleman poetry-jazz telecast, European Canal Plus, Paris; March tour: Paris, Prague, photo show Milan & reading w/Philip Glass in France & Czech Republic; translations of *Cosmopolitan Greetings,* Paris & Milan; April: Jewel Heart Benefit, with Patti Smith, Ann Arbor, National Portrait Gallery photo show & poetry readings "Rebel Poets & Painters of the 1950s" Washington, DC; May: publication of *Illuminated Poems* illustrated by Eric Drooker, Four Walls Eight Windows, NY; recorded *The Ballad of the Skeletons* with Paul McCartney, Philip Glass, Marc Ribot, Lenny Kaye, Mercury Records, released Oct. '96; June-July: poetry taught at Naropa Institute; poetry reading Los Angeles County Museum of Art for William Burroughs painting exhibition; residence July L.A., Gemini GEL Lithography press, completed portfolio of 6 images; 10 day residence with William Burroughs, Lawrence, KS to take photos, record interview, edit his essay on "Bureaucracy & Drugs"; Aug: vocalist for "Sunflower Sutra," string orchestra, music Philip Glass conducted by Yehudi Menhuin, Avery Fisher Hall, Lincoln Center, NY; Sept-Oct: week's Buddhist Summer study retreat; publication *Selected Poems 1947–95*, HarperCollins, N.Y.: music video directed by Gus Van Sant *Ballad of the Skeletons*; poetry reading De Young Museum, SF, accompanying Whitney Museum traveling Beat Generation exhibit; St. Mark's Church Poetry Project benefit *Selected Poems* & record party musicale with twelve-musician accompaniment including members of Sonic Youth band produced by Hal Willner; "Beginner's Blake" class, Brooklyn College; Dec. awarded National Jewish Book Council Lifetime Award; SF Cow Palace 14,000 attendance for Live 105 radio Green Christmas Ball, performed three poems with Ralph Carney & band, in company with Orbital, Lemonheads, Beck; ten day Buddhist Winter study retreat with Gelek Rinpoche, Camp Copneconic, Michigan.

1997—Continued Buddhist Winter study with Gelek Rinpoche; February: Carnegie Hall Tibet House benefit performance with Philip Glass, Michael Stipe, Natalie Merchant, Patti Smith, et al, short appearance group poetry slam NYU Loeb Center; [late February ordered leave of absence from teaching after diagnosed with terminal liver cancer; April 2 returned home from Beth Israel Hospital and began hospice; April 4 suffered stroke early AM resulting in coma; died at home April 5 early AM in presence of close friends and teacher Gelek Rinpoche].

Published in various forms as press releases over the years.

Chamberlain's Nakeds

EDITOR'S NOTE: Written for an art exhibition that included pictures of a naked Allen Ginsberg by his friend artist Wynn Chamberlain.

Why am I interested in seeing myself naked? Because for years I thought I was ugly, I still do, but I no longer look at myself through my own eyes, I look out—my eyes look outward—at my desire, and I reach out to touch the bodies I love without fear that I'll be rejected because I'm ugly. Because I don't feel ugly now, I feel me, I feel sexy—more than that, I feel desirous, longing, lost, mad with impatience like fantastic old bearded Whitman to clasp my body to the bodies I adore. So I'm interested in nakedness, no I love my own nakedness, I love my old love's nakedness, I love anyone's nakedness that expresses their acceptance of being born in this body in this flesh on this planet that will die. This flesh is only an episode, what will we do, reject it because of liver complaints? Some people misinterpret Eastern texts to say the body is shit, Blake and Whitman interpret gnostic texts to say the body is the only body in eternity, better live in it while it exists. The feelings that play in the body are its spirit, and without the body there's no place to play. Not in the head, you couldn't feel anything if the head were cut off from the body. Desire is felt in the lower abdomen. So Chamberlain has painted every body naked—modern Joves, Ganymedes, Aphrodites, etc., if you want a tradition—modern friends as they really are to themselves, with their naked babies, lifted in poetic triumph on Bacchic friend's shoulders, stepping forth from the picture toward society happy, victorious, still alive, photographic, fleshy, truthful to their own birth without clothes.

WRITTEN: Christmas 1964

FIRST PUBLISHED: exhibition flyer, Fischbach Gallery, New York, Feb. 2, 1965.

[Early Influences]

The single most soul-manifesting book I stumbled on in the Paterson Public Library was *The Idiot* (I was attracted by the title) by Dostoyevsky— I was 14 years old then and read it through and continued with other Dos. and other Russians including The Golovlyov Family. The next great poetic magic I encountered was Rimbaud's *A Season in Hell*. When I was 18, in college, and talking with Burroughs, he gave me Yeats' *Vision*, Spengler's *The Decline of the West* and Blake's poems to read, as well as Shakespeare's lines. Before I was 20, I read through Korzybski's *Science and Sanity* as best I could so discovered the difference between words and the 'things' they're supposed to represent, not substitute for. Hart Crane's *Atlantis* also hypnotized me with its mighty rhyme. For history, I had read *Genesis of the World War* by a revisionist historian—who?— Barnes?—which struck me down ideologically.

FIRST PUBLISHED: Evelyn B. Byrne and Otto M. Penzler, eds. *Attacks of Taste* (New York: Gotham Book Mart, 1971).

What Six Nice People Found in the Government's Drawers

EDITOR'S NOTE: This is a report on what was contained in secret government files obtained by Allen Ginsberg under the provisions of the Freedom of Information Act.

My DEA [Drug Enforcement Administration] file begins in 1961 when Norman Mailer and myself and Ashley Montagu had a discussion of marijuana on John Crosby's television show, and we recommended legalization. On that occasion, the Treasury Department Narcotics Bureau began a file on me, and most of my file has to do with my opposition to the laws and the behavior of the drug agency.

Then there are many reports on the LeMar organization, which has been trying to legalize marijuana through public demonstrations since 1965.

Around that time, there was an attempt to set me up for a drug bust, which was noted in the *New York Times* and mentioned in a public trial. The file has nothing on that. Nothing on the attempt to set me up for a bust, as reported in the *Times*. I complained to my Congressman Charles Jolson of Paterson, about that, and from that point on, the file gets very thick. There are letters from me to my Congressman—which he sent them—and an interoffice memorandum trying to figure out how to answer him. The memorandum of August 23, 1965, by a narcotics agent whose name is crossed out, is four solid pages of discussion on how to answer Jolson's letter, most of which is blacked out. But at the very end, as part of preparing ammunition to discredit me to Congressman Jolson, there are a number of quotations from a Czechoslovakian Communist youth newspaper accusing me of "homosexuality, narcomania, alcoholism, posing and a social extremism verging on orgies."

Then there's a DEA report made in New York, September 28, 1967, by a narcotics agent whose name is deleted: "Subject of this memorandum: Photograph of Allen Ginsberg. Recommendation. Pending. On this date, I received a photograph of Allen Ginsberg where he is pictured in an indecent pose. For possible future use, the photograph has been placed in a locked sealed envelope marked 'photograph of Allen Ginsberg—General File: Allen Ginsberg.' The locked sealed envelope has been placed in the vault of this office for safekeeping." The signatures of the narcotics agent and the district supervisor have been obliterated. Now the covering letter from the DEA of April 10, 1975, signed by John Bartels, who resigned under pressure, says: "In one DEA document that will be released to you, reference is made to an obscene photograph of Mr. Ginsberg contained in DEA's New York Regional Office. A search has been made in the New York Regional Office and it has been determined that the referred-to photograph was destroyed seven years ago."

In other words, in 1967 they had what they thought was an obscene photo, which may have been the cover of *Evergreen Review*—a photo of me and Peter Orlovsky by Richard Avedon—or they might have had a secret drug agent/informer photographing me through his asshole, I don't know. In any case, they felt they had something there. Then they claim that they destroyed the photograph, though I think they're probably lying.

The Customs Bureau sent me a funny thing in 1965, it sent around a memorandum placing me on a suspect list—suspected of international trafficking in opium. The reasons for placing me on it were "travel abroad which appeared on Interpol files, planned and applied for passport validation for Cuba trip," and my association with LeMar. That led, a half year later, to my being stopped, stripped and searched by New York Customs when I came back from Prague.

Customs has a note, from February 1970, that they had caught me with pictures of "nude women in suggestive poses" in my suitcase. That was a copy of a Canadian underground newspaper in which I had some poetry.

In 1972, the Secret Service had a photograph of me that was apparently a blow-up of a newspaper photograph of me walking around in the snow. Remember the POT IS FUN poster? Well, they had a cutout of it, just my face, looking very ghostly because it was blown up. That was their identification photo.

The CIA file has a copy of a handwritten letter that I sent to Richard Helms. I met him at a party, and I'd asked him about opium dealing and gotten into a big, funny argument with him. I made a bet with him: If I was right that the CIA was dealing, he had to sit down and meditate for one hour a day for the rest of his life. So it's a letter of June 28, 1972, checking back with him, saying, "Are you convinced yet?"

There was one very funny literary biography of me done by the FBI in 1965. The subject was internal security regarding Cuba, because I had applied to go to Cuba. Agents had read a long article I wrote about consciousness revolution and Cuban revolution. They wrote: "Allen Ginsberg admits using narcotics, having homosexual experiences and homosexual love affairs. He describes himself as a person who decided to be a laboring people's hero. He describes his background as Jewish, left wing, atheist, Russian . . . [and] refers to various individuals such as Van Doren, Kerouac, Neal, Bill, Humphrey, Peter, Trilling. An editor's note identifies these individuals as Mark Van Doren, a Columbia University professor, American writers Peter Orlovsky, Neal Cassady, William Burroughs, Hubert Humphrey [sic] and Columbia University professor Lionel Trilling."

In 1965, I had written a very brief letter in *Jewish Currents* defending LeRoi Jones, saying that LeRoi Jones was a good guy and he once kissed me. So there was a three-page document saying that *Jewish Currents,* formerly known as *Jewish Life,* is a Communist-front organization and that it was cited to be one in 1946.

The CIA has nothing, hardly anything, in the files about my accusations that the CIA was involved with opium, nor does the FBI, nor does the DEA.

WRITTEN: 1976

FIRST PUBLISHED: *Oui,* vol. 6, no. 2 (Feb. 1977) pp. 116–117.

Contemplation on Publications

I did not exactly plan a large persona though it was within literary bounds set by Walt Whitman and other sympathetic precursors. My original ideal was actually spare and brilliant: to publish nothing but purest gemwork like Rimbaud, with no dross left over prosaic vulnerable quotidian un-eternal tendentious to bore the eager youthful reader seeking visionary diamond. Rimbaud-Whitman, mad sanity, was my ideal.

Kerouac's teaching of the sacramental quality of spontaneous utterance, later interpreted as a practice of bodhisattvic open-ness, led me to a plethora of letters in all dimensions. An early impulse to treat scholars, newsmen, agents, reporters, interviewers and inquirers as sentient beings equal in Buddha-nature to fellow poets turned me on to answer questions as frankly as possible. All situations from Queen Elizabeth Hall, London, to Rocky Flats' Rockwell Corporation Plutonium Plant railroad tracks, to the classrooms of the Jack Kerouac School of Disembodied Poetics at Naropa Institute thus become *Dharma*-Gates. "*Dharma*-gates are endless, I vow to enter all."

Diabolic egoism? Unthinkable to presume in advance that this path might lead to a hell of media self-hood replicated vulgar, obnoxious Ginsberghoods troublemaking throughout America with spiteful lecherous loudmouth hypocritic trips, projecting cowardly errors of spirit, chemistry, and aesthetic form o'er the world, in Ossianic yawps.

The presumption was of prophecy, part Blakean inspiration, part ordinary mind from Whitman—that is to say, the poet who speaks from his frank heart in public speaks for all hearts. "Who touches this book touches a man." . . . "One touch of nature makes the whole world kin." . . . "What oft was thought but ne'er so well expressed."

Another presumption that runs thru these letters is the Grand Conspiracy of governments, that the state is a lie as Kenneth Rexroth said. Thus many poems and interviews touching on corruption of the U.S. narcotics bureaucracy, CIA involvement with Indochinese opium trafficking, surveillance-state censorship, war psychosis, alterations of national consciousness involving grass and LSD, physical assassination and character overheard by public and secret police mind all along, taking part in mental fight for America's "soul." A secret war: most citizens were careless or indifferent to details of massive brainwash perpetrated on themselves by their armies, industries, police agencies and public media interconnected by alcohol, nicotine and money to the powers that be. So all "statements" make an attempt to break thru to public consciousness with some detail of personal life at variance from the establishment cover story. I was conscious that my gossip would go into the inner ear of media government bureaucracies, somewhere to be recorded, have its effects, alter an official brain cell here or there, waken a provincial genius in Iowa, liberate a professor at midnite in Wichita, trouble the head of the CIA some sleepless dawn wondering should he learn to meditate or not, flash in a rock star brainpan rousing mortal consciousness, comfort an anonymous old lady in the Bronx with repetition of her grief sympathetic powerful unobstructed compassionate, seduce a youth to meditative blues in New Jersey.

Certain errors of judgment emerge by hindsight: advocacy of LSD legalization would now be accompanied by prescription for meditation practice to qualify its use. I would extend my self-hood less widely in sympathy with "movement" contemporaries whose subconscious belief in confrontation, conflict or violence encouraged public confusion and enabled police agents to infiltrate and provoke further violence and greater confusion. We were finding "new reasons for spitefulness," Kerouac complained. Experience with Buddhist sitting practice since 1971 has left me more open to such criticism. We need greater space, it is vanity not to include our errors in the universe. My practice of mantra chanting and Hindu theistic public ceremony now seems relatively naive to me, that is to say inexperienced and unlearned, inefficient for its time, leading to spiritual delusion of Godhood rather than breakthru of common awareness. On the other hand that's too narrow a judgment, too humorless, of total "Hippie" effect, in the American war scene. I wish I knew then (1969) what I know now: how to sit silent following the breath—traditional nontheistic mindfulness.

My intention was to leave a record, in some Akashic Heaven if not on contemporary earth. I did have in mind that everything said, written or aesthetically imaged would be accounted in later decades by scholars who might uncover behind the police-state commercial version of Beat Poetics another version composed by poets alone, single handed, or with company of friends, working for a *sangha*[1] in new consciousness beyond the reach of public illusion—a version of late twentieth century America as a gnostic story, full of humor and public double entendre such as the expansion of poetic consciousness to vivify the police and their Capitalist-Communist wars, and the confident adventure of visionary seekers to encompass ordinary mind: self and its fabulous trips into politics, nonself discovering eternal geography, newspaper-headlined egolessness, strophic ego confession, cosmic war conspiracies, empty loves and deaths, city meditations, country crazy wisdom studies that occupied body, speech and mind of this poet for decade.

WRITTEN: September 13, 1978

FIRST PUBLISHED: Michelle P. Kraus, *Allen Ginsberg: An Annotated Bibliography, 1969–1977* (Metuchen, NJ: Scarecrow Press, 1980).

Notes on Stanford Literary Acquisition of My Archives

The literary and social revolutions manifested in 1940–50s generation and San Francisco Renaissance and ripening '40s to '90s counterculture seemed to be a continuation of the earlier century modernist movement. I archived all I could of this new consciousness and saved every literary piece of paper that passed through my hands. As a record of spiritual war for liberation of form and content of poetry (bearing in mind that "When the mode of music changes, the walls of the city shake") as against police state censorship and close-down of consciousness, for future scholars and youngsters who'll have to revive historic memory. University archivists in late '60s requested me to save everything (including laundry lists). So this collection cross-references various schools of poetry New York Black Mountain Beat SF Northwest and Boulder Kerouac School, wars on drugs and intersection between Mafia CIA and FBI in government drug dealing and other illegal practices, waves of literary censorship, growth of American Buddhism as literary influence, family affairs, manuscripts of rare but unrecognized poets like Ray Bremser, Antler and others mixed with unique manuscripts of Wm. Burroughs and John Wieners. The center is literary, the spokes to periphery include radical social movements versus plastic police state mind control. I intended a treasure trove "to be rediscovered when the dove descended"—including thousands of hours of taped poetry readings by a galaxy of open form, beat and minority poets. Heavy documents and manuscripts cover half century 1944s to 1994s.

WRITTEN: 1994

Unpublished.

———————

Confrontation with Louis Ginsberg's Poems

Living a generation with lyrics wrought by my father, some stanzas settle in memory as perfected. "In this mode perfection is basic," William Carlos Williams wrote, excusing himself for rejecting my own idealized iambic rhymes sent him for inspection. The genre itself seems imperfect on the twentieth century page: a heavy leather Webster's International Dictionary published the same decade Louis Ginsberg (October 1, 1895) was born defines *lyric* as "1. Of or pertaining to a lyre or harp. 2. Fitted to be sung to the lyre; hence, also appropriate for a song;—"

Few lyres sounded aloud in Newark, New Jersey, in the 1920s, although in first editions of the then standard popular *Modern American Poetry*[2] edited by Louis Untermeyer most of the poems anthologized still "rely greatly on the steady pace of iambics," including "A Quiet Street After Rain":

> . . . While every front yard lawn is seen
> Twinkling a myriad tongues of green.
> Marvelous too, it is to see
> A rose-bud dipped in deity!
> Nearby a spider has begun
> Upon a fence to thread the sun.

Continuing his attempts to perfect this form, Louis Ginsberg received the anthologist's later praise: "You have the lyric touch. You know how to make words sing something as well as say something." Yet no literal music was intended. Originally these forms were fitted to music by Waller and Campion, Blake sang his *Songs of Innocence and Experience* with his own voice unaccompanied; even Yeats wrote "with a chune in his head" we were told by Ezra Pound who consistently remembered the musical body of which these lyric forms were skeletons.

Though lyric words had parted company from music a century or centuries before, the standard educational system anthologies are bulked with rhymed and metered stanza forms (including those of E. Dickinson) that look like the lyrics of short songs, that echo in the head with old tune fragments, that might be put to melody had students world enough and time, but which were written out of language symmetry rules adapted and patched together from differing ancient traditions and then labeled "traditional" in schoolbooks for a few decades in the early twentieth century. English measures of stress drawn from Greek and Latin nomenclature originally definitive of pitch and quantity (vowel-length) of sound were applied to bold accent and weak; foursquare stanzas abstracted from song still chimed with parallel sounds at the end of parallel-cadenced lines prescribed as standard—such forms were read less and less aloud and more solely in the universe of the eye-page or silent mind and never sung from the lung. Since that mode of poetry lost track of music, its very rules confused the measures and weights of American speech, as William Carlos Williams pointed out at the time. One collection[3] of "representative American poems for boys and girls" of 1923 "planned to meet the requirements of the College Entrance Board" with the following illustration of *Iambic Tetrameter:*

Thou too / sail on, / O Ship / of State. /

Nearly half a century later the student may have sufficiently wakened from the rhythmical hypnosis proposed above to notice that the only way to make affective spoken sense of *Thou, sail* and especially *O* is to pronounce them (contrary to schoolbook instructions) with expressive emphasis equal to the syllables *too* and *on* and *Ship. Iambic Trimeter* was illustrated in a manner that completely distorted the pronounceable sense of an exampled line:

Whose heart / -strings are / a lute. /

In this case the stress indications for "strings are" literally reverses sensible emphasis and obliterates significance. Awareness of this fault of ear caused by rote degenerate lyric meter was Ezra Pound's contribution to U.S. prosody after the turn of the century.

Thus from Whitman's time thru Williams and Pound to Kerouac and Olson, Horace Trabel to Gregory Corso, early Eliot on to Ted Berrigan a new tradition of poets improvised prosodies echoing our actual speech our stutters our jazz our blue bop our body chant the tone leading of our vowels or whatever mystic zap-talk that came natural. "I'll kick yuh eye," William Carlos Williams quoted from New Jersey town streets, as an example of musical phrasing which did not fit the metric system described in 1923 by the Secretary of the New England Association of Teachers of English as "particularly well adapted to the needs of English poetry . . . definite rules, which have been carefully observed by all great poets from Homer to Tennyson and Longfellow."

Ironically, a self-enclosed academy rose to follow such "definite rules" (No playing tennis without nets! Frost rebuked prosodic anarchists) and an intellectually frosty accentual prosody, non-physical or meta-physical and only remotely musical in nature, became the manner of versification professionalized at best from the later Eliot through John Crowe Ransom to the earlier Robert Lowell in the fourth and fifth decades of this century, and such stingy rhythm was for a while the dominant mode of poetics in the giant universities of cold-war megalopola till the ampler-bodied and more naked breath'd tradition began to sound freely prophetic a return to common sense in the robotic market places and electric media of apocalyptic planetary and pre-lunar-voyage times.

Ezra Pound's scholarly intuitions came true after the mid-century when a third generation of minstrel poets including Bob Dylan *sang* their poems aloud in contemplative rooms black alleyways or bardic halls thru microphones and a new consciousness that had broken thru the crust of old lyric forms like my father's evolved back to the same forms refreshed with new emotions and new subtleties of accent and vowel articulated in consequence of deep breath'd song.

II

Latent in the unsung written lyric form, songs are suggested, echoed or new-jived, whole melodies buried their voices resonant in the unconscious never sounded aloud—in a sort of timeless eternal imaginary place where poets' minds dwell after the death of their bodies, and this is the subject of much of this mode of poetry. All poets from Shelley to Housman knew that melancholy immortality, their body impulses, sensations, consciousness and feelings embedded like flies in amber verse. I have resisted this mode as an anachronism in my own time—the anachronism of my own father writing the outworn verse of previous century voices, reechoing the jaded music and faded affect or sentiment of that music in a dream-life of his own side-street under dying phantom elms of Paterson, New Jersey—at the very time that Paterson itself was (having been articulated to its very rock-strata foundations and aboriginal waterfall voice in William Carlos Williams' epic) degenerating into a twentieth century mafia-police-bureaucracy-race-war-nightmare-tv-squawk suburb.

Yet if this nightmare world explodes it will all have been a dream with latencies, symbols, daydreams clairvoyant, and tiny perfect poems, archaic stanzas full of intuition and unconscious prophecy, faithful craft in outworn arts, triumphs of the meek and unmodish, forlorn ideals redeemed thru fatal changes, bankruptcy of all right and wrong, reasons and prosodies confounded, vision and prophecy confounded, mortality and immortality confounded—beauty as truth a last remaining tearful smile at dream's end.

Confronting my father's poems at the end of his life, I weep at his meekness and his reasons, at his wise entrance into his own mortality and his silent recognition of that pitiful immensity he records of his own life's time, his father's life time, and the same mercy his art accords to my own person his son.

I won't quarrel with his forms here anymore: by faithful love he's made them his own, and by many years practice arrived at sufficient condensation of idea, freedom of fancy, phrase modernity, depth of death-vision, and clarity of particular contemporary attention to transform the old "lyric" form from an inverted fantasy to the deepest actualization of his peaceful mortal voice.

This last book of poesy begins with a contemporary prophetic glimmer of the planetary catastrophe—

When bombs on Barcelona burst,
I was a thousand miles away—

that a third of a century ago established the permanent authoritarian bureaucratic police state so familiar to later generations in almost every country of the world. "Remembering Ruined Cities" follows with its house rubble *déjà vu* superimposed on 416 East 34 Street, Paterson, New Jersey. The warning deepens "After the Blast"; next "Our Age's" hallucination crowds downtown Paterson Central High School "Repeaters' Class" with phantom-identity victims, till the poet himself is included with "Mr. Anonymous" among those "Lost in the Twentieth Century."

The ancient recollection of cosmic identity breaks through one [in] "Morning in Spring" and "After the Rain." Here the clearest, surest, oldest personal vision commonly recognizable to all human generations, squares and acidheads alike, is set forth as "Testament of Wonder." These eternal generalizations are located perfectly in an "Autumn on a Pool" which, compared to Cleopatra's barge, displays in short magical verses an Emily Dickinson vision. "Night in Silver" sets forth artful lines plated with silent rhymes near to some pure tune imaginable while pictures flash on the mind:

And with a shining crystal,
  All shingled is the shed;
Each icicle shows in it
  A moon is tenanted.

Following thereon, "Morning in Ice" beacons from the abode of Shelleyan realization of Platonic personality where

Trees are archangels thinking light.

This spectral gold radiance, seen through suburb-man's eyes as also through pastoral Wordsworth's in meadow buttercup, again manifests clearly around city houses:

. . . I could see
The street was like a long ravine of light.

Therefore "At the Zoo" the poet sees sacred monsters, and looking twice out through "Zoo" bars sees his own bestial person. A solitary humor among all this multiple identity frees the poet's imagination to exchange impressions with a caterpillar, comparing their visions and feet and doubts until

The caterpillar crept away
In hurried ripples to a tree.

Time as the impression of "Something Timeless" recurs over and over in these three decades of poetry:

The autos, the buses,
  The traffic all,
Like pageant, stream to
  A festival.

That awareness clarifies all phenomenal perceptions even "Scents and Smells" to

The crisp fresh mint of violets tinct with chill;

and when specified to "My Love" the humor of world-identity ends sensationally when

In her thighs,
Africa sighs.

But the deepest tones are measured for death's woe and here at "Burial" in

The cemetery drugged with light

a single man's voice is heard slow word by word unalterable in eternity:

Through blur of years, I saw you go,
  From Time at last now moving free;

pronouncing farewell to "Olden Days"

We used to welcome Summers in
  With children by the shore,
But now how long the time has been
  We journey there no more.
For now our sons are tall and grown
  And summers come and pass
So that I never leave alone
  Without you under grass.
The Summers move above your mound;
  The shore is full as then.
Long will you sleep beneath the ground
  Before I go again.

One by one all relations are resigned to oblivion, self, love, wife, mother,

And if sometimes spring up the tears
  That kennel loss of days we knew,
Be sure, my father, that the years
  Keep leading me more close to you.
In vain my striving to decode
  Some message as of hope and trust
Which Truth has cached in that abode,
  That synagogue of silent dust.
For, with myself less busy now,
  I hear more clear your tender tones.
Mercy is flowing from your brow,
  Forgiveness streams up from your bones.

This agnostic compassion emotionally dense as any deity-faith completes a cycle of generations and is transmitted through myself in *Kaddish* as a litany in praise of oblivion that buries mortal grief. A rational image of the mystery of life perpetuating life enclosed inside itself is presented as in a "Chinese Box," with its very last question self-answered in terse rhymes terminating thought—

And what do the years
  Finally stow
In a box of wood,
  Narrow and low?

Is this the end? Yes, stoic, agnostic and melancholy as the nineteenth century-styled closure must sound, "Conversation with My Skeleton" suspends further speculation:

"One short rhyme, when I am gone,
Time may break his teeth upon."
.. . .
Silent grinned my skeleton.

This art is a last grim remnant of the transcendental flash that life was, the consciousness of consciousness vanishing: "Suddenly I remembered that I was dead." As in "Loneliness," concealed in an anonymously formal sonnet, all human poets are

Lackeyed at last by fevers to the grave,
Where we sink cold, as is, above, the stone,
Unfriended, unaccompanied, alone.

It is the same absolute darkness and endless void that shades mortal
appearance so tenderly spectral, that surrounds the commonplace "City
Twilight" with conscious glory fading in god's shadowy eye:

And with a softness as of petals,
  Like fringe of lights about some boats,
As on a lake where darkness settles,
  So, lamp by lamp, the city floats.

Would that all sons' fathers were poets! for the poem and the world
are the same, place imagined by consciousness, and the squared
exact forms of these poems are tiny models of Hebrew-Buddhist
universes rhyming together in imagination, as if art were the one
activity in the flux of time wherein place becomes completely self-
conscious, "Terse"

So I
Shall try
To hammer
My stammer
And beat
It neat
Exact,
Compact—

identical with itself aeon to aeon, climaxed immortal. This imaginary
place remarked earlier is precisely the subjective matter of this mode of
lyric, an evanescent eternity as weird as any invented by Poe (or mapped
in the Zohar or unhexed after Avelokiteshvara's *Prajnaparamita Sutra*), to
which this poet returns obsessively again and again in poem-trances even
at "Morning in Spring"

    . . . until I knew
I was the world I wandered through.

The same self of our odd universe recurs everywhere—observing a "Dragonfly," upside down in a "Lake in the Park," glancing at a lion's "shaggy, uncle-bearded face" "At the Zoo," or watching "At the Burial of My Mother"

> . . . the casket,
>   With one who gave me birth,
> Take a curious leisure
>   To sink to earth,

—feeling a familiar little sensation named "Correspondences" by Baudelaire and recalled in the "page of Baudelaire" framed by "Snow at Midnight."

Buried in anthologies unvocalized and lack-harp, hundreds of lyrics in this mode by generations of poets whisper eternal secrets of their place. A frenzied feverish reader with third-eye open for a month may discover their reality and pathos—perhaps in a more leisure-populaced afterworld to our present apocalyptic place such verses will be sounded aloud, Lizette Woodworth Reese herself syllable by syllable tuned to electronic lyres. Living a generation with lyrics wrought in this mode by my father, some stanzas reflecting this eternal place settle in memory as perfected.

WRITTEN: Aug. 18–Sept. 13, 1969

FIRST PUBLISHED: Louis Ginsberg, *Morning in Spring and Other Poems* (New York: William Morrow and Co., 1970).

Brother Poet
[For Eugene Brooks]

EDITOR'S NOTE: Eugene Brooks is quite literally Allen Ginsberg's brother and a poet as well.

One's brother's secret sorrow—the vast intelligence of anyone, democratic perception unexpressed beneath the commercial and family surface of America—is not only the sadness of time passing by, but clear knowledge and foresight into the ruin of our civilized lives: the fall of America, the great robot bent over weeping in sorrow for ourselves. After all the human heart's the center of our nation, not the computer in the bank tower. So this poetry realizes mortal feeling, and that amounts to a vision, because it's not in the papers or on T.V.

Thus the insight's universal, applicable to Aborigines though writ by Long Island lawyer. Is it done openly with full saintly clarity? Well the poetry is still awkward, "too many words" as Basil Bunting told Eugene Brooks' brother Allen regarding his own texts: and public mannerisms excuse or hide many real feelings—still, the humane knowledge breaks through clearly, shocking—as once returned from the wars the soldier-author sat in family dining-foyer in Bronx surrounded by maternal aunts and uncles and wept like Christ at table, inconsolable returned to our poor relative city transient life doom.

A few early youth poems are here in inevitable classic iambic familiar mode, one or two or more 'classic' lines as in "Battle Dead"

> now immortality
> like a great lighted room, is all around

But as fellow Jerseyite poet William Carlos Williams wrote to brother Allen several decades back in regard to similar derivative rhymed texts, "In this mode perfection is basic." So that admonition's repeated here, with acknowledgement that within these flawed forms brother Brooks wrote a number of perfect lines.

The consciousness slowly learns, both style and realism of subject. Take early romantic sonnet for dead in war, "Soldier Choice"—place this in context of Viet Nam, as elegy for civilian or soldier, Arvin or NLF? War's now (and was) really so degraded that such romantic elegies depending on sense of stable national community with human-sounding values no longer fit. Seen even in public newspapers now, the sonnet would be taken as an emotional delusion. Compare that text to "Arlington's Filled," still wordy but it gets to the point as does Melville's bitter blank verse in "The House Top": the worldly wise snarl of a solid citizen who's begun to understand America's tragic truth; an angry poetic voice rises, speaks up!

The citizen is always on the verge of Apocalyptic perception as in

"Book of Old Masters"; the poet surpasses the citizen in "Duchamp" with a totally witty moment, "Not yet so ravaged by the world's beauty as to leave the page blank, I'm tempted to stammer of . . ."

"It's Really Lucky" he's a poet of Russian origin, a Russian poet in translation with Slavic ironic devices, as Voznesensky takes a simple thought like a nose and builds a political poem, so here's an idea like "How Lucky" we are our feeling wishes don't come true lest the world wind up smothered in rosy gas bombs.

Poem after poem the perceptions are ecologically or meta-atomistically accurate, historically there's solid critique of the citizen-poet's culture—where the citizen dominates, it's too wordy, not trusting the poet's facts, trying to *make* poetry of the already tragic materials at hand: too Roman a style in "Stones In Washington" frames the poet's brilliant funny list of history's victims. But both citizen and poet are occasionally wiped out by a person, grim as some kind of demon reality, who wanders through "Memphis '72" as through neon *samsara* muttering "Man will always be evil." Wow! heavy statement.

Thus "Emancipation" gets serious, as mature statement, of an eternal psychological order governing what seems to be a necessary renunciation of human desires (cutting of attachments as gnostic Buddhists would say). "Heritage" poem continues that truth exemplified in *déjà vu,* so we have real speech here, tho' paradise seems lost, at least paradise rhetoric drops away. What shall we do with the griefs of our families, defeats and depressions of our brothers? "Having Nothing" answers that—the procession of one self's selves over Williamsburg Bridge articulates humane visionary consciousness within nature available to all citizens, traditional as Whitman's self democracy, government of unbroken knowledge.

There always was great sweetness of intention, witness the poem to myself the citizen poet's brother. And there always was inner realism rarely expressed, witness "Metronome's" flash of memories, a fast photo of great time-gap bare to facts, accurate close to home, with almost no poetic distortion of home speech.

Given realistic psychological and dictional basis, it's possible as in "Houses Gnashed Teeth" for writing to get "poetic" again—subject matters loosen'd up world-fantasy so this poem's remarkable for baroque inventions of temporarily free imagination. The relaxed tone first lines of "$E=MC^2$" continues the relief. Still the poetry doesn't often enough break out of classical "mortal" perception (as *idée fixe*) to completely independent funny invention, "direct presentation" of

the churning of lawn mowers

Yet at rare times the poet's ideas about life become identical (as in "Reality") with palpable forms of experience, and the philosophic bias mind of the poems comes through with strength and attention pointed to

... Legions
of slugs, lions, battalions
of lizards, regiments of birds and grassblades,
amoeba armadas fording lymph estuaries ...

"Outcry" sounds a gnostic leap of imagination—the citizen (lawyer in fact) poet finally makes use of his vocational language in combination with scientific temperament and poetic inspiration to state his mortal case to the supreme judge. *Om ah hum.*

WRITTEN: July 27, 1972

FIRST PUBLISHED: Eugene Brooks, *Rites of Passage* (New York: privately printed, 1973).

PART 6
Literary Technique
and
the Beat Generation

Notes Written on Finally Recording *Howl*

By 1955 I wrote poetry adapted from prose seeds, journals, scratchings, arranged by phrasing or breath groups into little short-line patterns according to ideas of measure of American speech I'd picked up from William Carlos Williams' imagist preoccupations. I suddenly turned aside in San Francisco, unemployment compensation leisure, to follow my romantic inspiration—Hebraic-Melvillean bardic breath. I thought I wouldn't write a *poem,* but just write what I wanted to without fear, let my imagination go, open secrecy, and scribble magic lines from my real mind—sum up my life—something I wouldn't be able to show anybody, writ for my own soul's ear and a few other golden ears. So the first line of *Howl,* "I saw the best minds etc.," the whole first section typed out madly in one afternoon, a tragic custard-pie comedy of wild phrasing, meaningless images for the beauty of abstract poetry of mind running along making awkward combinations like Charlie Chaplin's walk, long saxophone-like chorus lines I knew Kerouac would hear *sound* of—taking off from his own inspired prose line really a new poetry.

I depended on the word "who" to keep the beat, a base to keep measure, return to and take off from again onto another streak of invention: "who lit cigarettes in boxcars boxcars boxcars," continuing to prophesy what I really knew despite the drear consciousness of the world: "who were visionary Indian angels." Have I really been attacked for this sort of joy? So the poem got awesome, I went on to what my imagination believed true to eternity (for I'd had a beatific illumination years before during which I'd heard Blake's ancient voice and saw the universe unfold in my brain), and what my memory could reconstitute of the data of celestial experiences.

But how sustain a long line in poetry (lest it lapse into prosaic)? It's natural inspiration of the moment that keeps it moving, disparate thinks put down together, shorthand notations of visual imagery, juxtapositions of hydrogen jukebox—abstract *haikus* sustain the mystery and put iron poetry back into the line: the last line of *Sunflower Sutra* is the extreme, one stream of single word associations, summing up. Mind is shapely, art is shapely. Meaning mind practiced in spontaneity invents forms in its own image and gets to last thoughts. Loose ghosts wailing for body try to invade the bodies of living men. I hear ghostly academies in limbo screeching about form.

Ideally each line of *Howl* is a single breath unit. My breath is long—that's the measure, one physical-mental inspiration of thought contained in the elastic of a breath. It probably bugs Williams now, but it's a natural consequence, my own heightened conversation, not cooler average-daily-talk short breath. I get to mouth more madly this way.

So these poems are a series of experiments with the formal organization of the long line. Explanations follow. I realized at the time that Whitman's form had rarely been further explored (improved on even) in the U.S.—Whitman always a mountain too vast to be seen. Everybody assumes (with Pound?) (except [Robinson] Jeffers) that his line is a big freakish uncontrollable necessary prosaic goof. No attempt's been made to use it in the light of early twentieth century organization of new speech-rhythm prosody to *build up* large organic structures.

I had an apartment on Nob Hill, got high on peyote, and saw an image of the robot skullface of Moloch in the upper stories of a big hotel glaring into my window; got high weeks later again, the visage was still there in red smoky downtown metropolis, I wandered down Powell street muttering, "Moloch Moloch" all night and wrote *Howl II* nearly intact in cafeteria at foot of Drake Hotel, deep in the hellish vale. Here the long line is used as a stanza form broken into exclamatory units punctuated by a base repetition, Moloch.

The rhythmic paradigm for Part III was conceived and half-written same day as the beginning of *Howl*, I went back later and filled it out. Part I, a lament for the Lamb in America with instances of remarkable lamb-like youths; Part II names the monster of mental consciousness that preys on the Lamb; Part III a litany of affirmation of the Lamb in its glory: "O starry spangled shock of Mercy." The structure of Part III, pyramidal, with a graduated longer response to the fixed base.

I remembered the archetypal rhythm of Holy Holy Holy weeping in a bus on Kearny Street, and wrote most of it down in notebook there. That exhausted this set of experiments with a fixed base. I set it as *Footnote to Howl* because it was an extra variation of the form of Part II. (Several variations on these forms, including stanzas of graduated litanies followed by fugues, will be seen in *Kaddish*.)

A lot of these forms developed out of an extreme rhapsodic wail I once heard in a madhouse. Later I wondered if short quiet lyrical poems could be written using the long line. *A Strange New Cottage in Berkeley* and *A Supermarket in California* (written same day) fell in place later that year. Not purposely, I simply followed my angel in the course of compositions.

What if I just simply wrote, in long units and broken short lines, spontaneously noting prosaic realities mixed with emotional upsurges, solitaries? *Transcription of Organ Music* (sensual data), strange writing which passes from prose to poetry and back, like the mind.

What about poem with rhythmic buildup power equal to *Howl* without use of repetitive base to sustain it? *The Sunflower Sutra* (composition time 20 minutes, me at desk scribbling, Kerouac at cottage door waiting for me to finish so we could go off somewhere party) did that, it surprised me, one long who.

Next what happens if you mix long and short lines, single breath remaining the rule of measure? I didn't trust free flight yet, so went back to fixed base to sustain the flow, *America*. After that, a regular formal type long poem in parts, short and long breaths mixed at random, no fixed base, sum of earlier experiments—*In the Baggage Room at Greyhound*. *In Back of the Real* shows what I was doing with short lines (see sentence above) before I accidentally wrote *Howl*.

Later I tried for a strong rhythm built up using free short syncopated lines, *Europe! Europe!* a prophecy written in Paris.

Last, the Proem to *Kaddish* (NY 1959 work)—finally, completely free composition, the long line breaking up within itself into short staccato breath units—notations of one spontaneous phrase after another linked within the line by dashes mostly: the long line now perhaps a variable stanzaic unit, measuring groups of related ideas, grouping them—a method of notation. Ending with a hymn in rhythm similar to the synagogue death lament. Passing into dactylic? says Williams? Perhaps not: at least the ear hears itself in Promethean natural measure, not in mechanical count of accent.

All these poems are recorded now as best I can, though with scared love, imperfect to an angelic trumpet in mind. I have quit reading in front of live audiences for a while. I began in obscurity to communicate a live poetry, it's become more a trap and duty than the spontaneous ball it was first.

A word on the Academies: poetry has been attacked by an ignorant and frightened bunch of bores who don't understand how it's made, and the trouble with these creeps is they wouldn't know poetry if it came up and buggered them in broad daylight.

A word on the Politicians: my poetry is angelic ravings, and has nothing to do with dull materialistic vagaries about who should shoot who. The secrets of individual imagination—which are transconceptual and non-verbal—I mean unconditioned spirit—are not for sale to this consciousness, are no use to this world, except perhaps to make it shut its trap and listen to the music of the spheres. Who denies the music of the spheres denies poetry, denies man, and spits on Blake, Shelley, Christ, and Buddha. Meanwhile have a ball. The universe is a new flower. America will be discovered. Who wants a war against roses will have it. Fate tells big lies, and the gay creator dances on his own body in eternity.

WRITTEN: July 4, 1959

FIRST PUBLISHED: *Evergreen Review,* vol. 3, no. 10 (Nov./Dec. 1959) pp. 132–135.

AUTHOR'S NOTE: Need comment on end—This provocative even inflammatory peroration seems to have offended a number of straight poets, and was oft quoted, a declaration of absolute poetic purpose that the critic Richard Howard still remembered decades later, taking exception to my insistence of "unconditioned Spirit." This aggression may have exacerbated the Battle of Anthologies between Open Form and Closed Form poets. An incendiary tract, aimed at both Marxist and CIA Capitalist (*Encounter*) Critics, as well as bourgeois judgmental sociologists, Norman Podhoretz probably in mind.

How *Kaddish* Happened

First writing on *Kaddish* was in Paris '58, several pages of part IV which set forth a new variation on the litany form used earlier in *Howl*—a graduated lengthening of the response lines, so that the *Howl* litany looks like a big pyramid on the page. *Kaddish* IV looks like three little pyramids sitting one on top of another, plus an upside-down pyramid mirror—reflected at the bottom of the series. Considered as breath, it means the vocal reader has to build up the feeling-utterance three times to climax, and then, as coda, diminish the utterance to shorter and shorter sob. The first mess of composition had all these elements, I later cut it down to look neat and exact. (Further extension of this form, litany, can be found in poem 4 years later, "The Change.")

Sometime a year later in New York I sat up all night with a friend who played me Ray Charles' genius classics—I'd been in Europe two winters and not heard attentively before—also we chippied a little M and some then new-to-me meta-amphetamine—friend showed me his old barmitzvah book of Hebrew ritual and read me central Kaddish passages—I walked out in early blue dawn on to 7th Avenue and across town to my Lower East Side apartment—New York before sunrise has its own celebrated hallucinatory unreality. In the country getting up with the cows and birds hath Blakean charm, in the megalopolis the same nature's hour is a science-fiction hell vision, even if you're a milkman. Phantom factories, unpopulated streets out of Poe, familiar nightclubs bookstores groceries dead.

I got home and sat at desk with desire to write—a kind of visionary urge that's catalyzed by all the strange chemicals of the city—but had no idea what Prophecy was at hand—poetry I figured. I began quite literally assembling recollection data taken from the last hours—"Strange now to think of you gone without corsets and eyes while I walk etc." I wrote on several pages till I'd reached a climax, covering fragmentary recollections of key scenes with my mother ending with a death-prayer imitating the rhythms of the Hebrew Kaddish—"Magnificent, Mourned no more, etc."

But then I realized that I hadn't gone back and told the whole secret family-self tale—my own one-and-only eternal child-youth memories which no one else could know—in all its eccentric detail. I realized that it would seem odd to others, but *family* odd, that is to say, familiar—everybody has crazy cousins and aunts and brothers.

So I started over again into narrative—"This is release of particulars"—and went back chronologically sketching in broken paragraphs all the first recollections that rose in my heart—details I'd thought of once, twice often before—embarrassing scenes I'd half amnesiaized—

hackle-raising scenes of the long black beard around the vagina—images that were central of scars on my mother's plump belly—all archetypes.

Possibly subjective archetypes, but archetype is archetype, and properly articulated subjective archetype is universal.

I sat at same desk from six AM Saturday to ten PM Sunday night writing on without moving my mind from theme except for trips to the bathroom, cups of coffee and boiled egg handed into my room by Peter Orlovsky (Peter the nurse watching over his beloved madman) and a few Dexedrine tablets to renew impulse. After the twentieth hour attention wandered, the writing became more diffuse, dissociations more difficult to cohere, the unworldly messianic spurts more awkward, but I persevered till completing the chronological task. I got the last detail recorded including my mother's death-telegram. I could go back later and clean it up.

I didn't look at the handwritten pages for a week—slept several days—and when I re-read the mass I was defeated, it seemed impossible to clean up and revise, the continuous impulse was there messy as it was, it was a patient scholar's task to figure how it could be more shapely.

Standing on a streetcorner one dusk another variation of the litany form came to me—alternation of Lord Lord and Caw Caw ending with a line of pure Lord Lord Lord Caw Caw Caw—pure emotive sound—and I went home and filled in that form with associational data. The last three lines are among the best in the poem—the *most* dissociated, on the surface, but, given all the detail of the poem, quite coherent—I mean it's a very great jump from the broken shoe to the last highschool caw caw—and in that gap's the whole Maya-Dream-Suchness of existence glimpsed.

It took me a year—trip to South America half that time—to have the patience to type poem up so I could read it. I delayed depressed with the mess, not sure it was a poem. Much less interesting to anyone else. Defeat like that is good for poetry—you go so far out you don't know what you're doing, you lose touch with what's been done before by anyone, you wind up creating a new poetry-universe. "Make it new" saith Pound. "Invention," said William Carlos Williams. That's the "Tradition"—a complete fuck-up so you're on your own.

The poem was typed, I had to cut down and stitch together the last sections of narrative—didn't have to change the expression, but did have to fit it together where it lapsed into abstract bathos or got mixed in time or changed track too often. It was retyped by Elise Cowen, a girl I'd known for years and had fitful lovers' relations with. When she gave me the copy she said, "You still haven't finished with your mother." Elise herself had been reading the Bible and heard voices saying her own mind was controlled by outside agent-machinery and several years later she died by jumping off her family apartment or roof.

By 1963 looking back on woman and on the poem for new City Lights edition I tried to make Amen: in the midst of the broken consciousness of mid twentieth century suffering anguish of separation from my own body and its natural infinity of feeling its own self one with all self, I instinctively seeking to reconstitute that blissful union which I experienced so rarely I took it to be supernatural and gave it holy name thus made it hymn laments of longing and litanies of triumphancy of self over the mind-illusion mechano-universe of un-feeling time in which I saw my self my own mother and my very nation trapped desolate our worlds of consciousness homeless and at war except for the original trembling of bliss in breast and belly of every body that nakedness rejected in suits of fear that familiar defenseless living hurt self which is myself same as all others abandoned scared to own our unchanging desire for each other. These poems almost un-conscious to confess the beatific human fact, the language intuitively chosen as in trance and dream, the rhythms rising thru breath from belly to breast, the hymn completed in tears, the movement of the physical poetry demanding and receiving decades of life while chanting Kaddish the names of Death in many mind-worlds the self seeking the key to life found at last in our self.

I've read this huge poem aloud only three times in front of an audience—I used to read the Proem and last sections in the early '60s, and a recording of that time is on Fantasy Record 7006: the *Big Table* Chicago reading. The first reading of the complete text was for the *Catholic Worker* when they opened a new salvation center near the Bowery in 1960. I didn't read the whole poem aloud (except once to Kerouac in my kitchen) in public again till occasion of the recording at Brandeis University Nov. 24, 1964. I had read at Harvard several times the previous week, we'd had trouble with the administration there—kicked out of Lowell house after a poesy reading in fact—Orlovsky reading his sex experiments after our chanting Buddhist prayers had been too confusing to the Academy—the audience at the Jewish university was sympathetic and encouraging—I'd drunk a little wine—as can be heard by slowed down pace of the reading and occasionally slurred language—so for self-dramatic historic reasons I decided to open up my soul and read *Kaddish* complete. I've done it only once since then a year later in Morden Tower, Newcastle, England for a small group of longhaired kids in the presence of the greatest living British poet Basil Bunting. I was afraid that reading it over and over, except where there was spiritual reason, would put the scene into the realm of performance, an act, rather than a spontaneous poetic event, happening, in time.

WRITTEN: March 20, 1966

FIRST PUBLISHED: liner notes, *Allen Ginsberg Reads Kaddish* (Atlantic Recording Corp., 1966).

A Definition of the Beat Generation

The phrase "beat generation" rose out of a specific conversation with Jack Kerouac and John Clellon Holmes around '50–'51 when, discussing the nature of generations recollecting the glamour of the lost generation, Kerouac said, Ah, this is nothing but a beat generation. They discussed whether it was a "Found" generation, which Kerouac sometimes referred to, or "Angelic" generation, and/or various other epithets. But, Kerouac waved away the question and said, "beat generation" not meaning to name the generation but to un-name it.

John Clellon Holmes' celebrated article in late '52 in the *New York Times* magazine section carried the headline title "This Is the Beat Generation"; that caught public eye. Then Kerouac published anonymously a fragment of *On the Road* in *New American Writing*, a paperback anthology of the '50s, called "Jazz of the Beat Generation," and that reinforced the curiously poetic phrase. So that's the early history of the term "Beat Generation" itself.

Herbert Huncke, author of *The Evening Sun Turned Crimson* and friend of Kerouac, Burroughs and others of that literary circle from the '40s, introduced them to what was then known as "hip language." In that context the word "beat" is a carnival "subterranean" (subcultural) term, a term much used in Times Square in the '40s. "Man, I'm beat . . ." meaning without money and without a place to stay. Could also refer to those "who walked all night with shoes full of blood on the snowbank docks waiting for a door in the East River to open to a room full of steam heat and opium" (*Howl*). Or, as in a conversation, "Would you like to go to the Bronx Zoo?" "Nah, man, I'm too *beat,* I was up all night." So, the original street usage meant exhausted, at the bottom of the world, looking up or out, sleepless, wide-eyed, perceptive, rejected by society, on your own, streetwise. Or, as it was once implied, finished, undone, completed, in the dark night of the soul or in the cloud of unknowing. "Open," as in Whitmanic sense of "openness," equivalent to humility, and so it *was* interpreted in various circles to mean emptied out, exhausted, and at the same time wide-open—perceptive and receptive to a vision.

A third meaning of the term, beatific, was articulated in 1959 by Kerouac, counteracting abuse of the term in media (the term being interpreted as being beaten completely, a "loser" without the aspect of humble intelligence, or "Beat" as "the beat of the drums" and "the beat goes on": varying mistakes of interpretation or etymology). Kerouac did try to indicate the correct sense of the word by pointing out the root— beat—as in beatitude, or beatific (various interviews and lectures). In his essay "Origins of the Beat Generation," Kerouac defined it so. This is a definition made early within the popular culture (circa late-fifties) though it was already a basic understanding of the subculture (circa mid-forties): he clarified his intention, "beat" as beatific, the necessary beatness or darkness that precedes opening up to the light, egolessness, giving room for religious illumination.

A fourth meaning accumulated, that of the "beat generation literary movement." This was a group of friends who had worked together on poetry, prose and cultural conscience from the mid-forties until the term became popular nationally in the late fifties. The group consisting of Kerouac and his prototype hero of *On the Road*—Neal Cassady, William Burroughs, author of *Naked Lunch* and other books, Herbert Huncke, John Clellon Holmes, author of *Go, The Horn* and other books, Allen Ginsberg, myself; we met Carl Solomon and Philip Lamantia in '48; encountered Gregory Corso in 1950, and we first saw Peter Orlovsky in 1954.

By the mid-fifties this smaller circle, through natural affinity of modes of thought or literary style or planetary perspective, was augmented in friendship and literary endeavor by a number of writers in San Francisco, including Michael McClure, Gary Snyder, Philip Whalen and a number of other powerful but lesser-known poets such as Jack Micheline, Ray Bremser, or the better-known black poet LeRoi Jones— all of whom accepted the term at one time or another, humorously or seriously, but sympathetically, and were included in a survey of beat general manners, morals, and literature by *Life* magazine in a lead article in the late '50s by one Paul O'Neill, and by the journalist Alfred Aronowitz in a large series on the Beat Generation in the *New York Post*. Neal Cassady, who was interviewed in both surveys, was writing at the time: his works were published posthumously.

By the mid-fifties a sense of some mutual trust and interest was developed with Frank O'Hara and Kenneth Koch, as well as with Robert Creeley and other alumni of Black Mountain. Of that literary circle, Kerouac, Whalen, Snyder, poet Lew Welch, Orlovsky as well as Ginsberg and others were interested in meditation and Buddhism. Relationship between Buddhism and its friends in the "beat generation" can be found in a recent scholarly survey of the evolution of Buddhism in America, *How the Swans Came to the Lake,* by Rick Fields.

The fifth meaning of the phrase "Beat Generation" is the influence of the literary and artistic activities of poets, filmmakers, painters, writers and novelists who were working in concert in anthologies, publishing houses, independent filmmaking, and other media. Some effects of the aforementioned groups refreshed the bohemian culture which was already a long tradition (in film and still photography, Robert Frank and Alfred Leslie; in music, David Amram; in painting, Larry Rivers; in poetry publishing, Don Allen, Barney Rosset, and Lawrence Ferlinghetti) extended to fellow artists, such as Susan Sontag and Norman Mailer, and to the youth movement of that day, which was also growing; and was absorbed by the mass and middle class culture of the late '50s and early '60s. These effects can be characterized in the following terms:

- Spiritual Liberation; Sexual "Revolution" or "Liberation," i.e. Gay Liberation, Black Liberation, Women's Liberation, Grey Panther activism, etc.,
- Liberation of the Word from censorship,

- Demystification and/or decriminalization of some laws against marijuana and other drugs,
- The evolution of rhythm and blues into rock 'n' roll into high art form, as evidenced by the Beatles, Bob Dylan, and other popular musicians influenced in the late 1950s and '60s by beat generation poets' and writers' works,
- The spread of ecological consciousness, emphasized early by Gary Snyder and Michael McClure; notion of a "Fresh Planet,"
- Opposition to the military-industrial machine civilization, as emphasized in the works of Burroughs, Huncke, Ginsberg, and Kerouac,
- Attention to what Kerouac called, after Spengler, "Second Religiousness" developing within an advanced civilization,
- Return to appreciation of idiosyncrasy as against state regimentation, and
- Respect for land and indigenous peoples and creatures as proclaimed by Kerouac in his slogan from *On the Road,* "The Earth Is An Indian Thing."

The essence of the phrase "beat generation" can be found in *On the Road* in another celebrated phrase, "Everything belongs to me because I am poor."

WRITTEN: 1981

FIRST PUBLISHED: *Friction,* vol. 1, no. 2/3 (Winter 1982) pp. 50–52.

The Six Gallery Reading

In the fall of 1955 a group of six unknown poets in San Francisco, in a moment of drunken enthusiasm, decided to defy the system of academic poetry, official reviews, New York publishing machinery, national sobriety and generally accepted standards to good taste, by giving a free reading of their poetry in a run down second rate experimental art gallery in the Negro section of San Francisco. They sent out a hundred postcards, put up signs in North Beach (Latin Quarter) bars, bought a lot of wine to get the audience drunk, and invited the well known Frisco Anarchist resident poet Kenneth Rexroth to act as Master of Ceremonies. Their approach was purely amateur and goofy, but it should be noted that they represented a remarkable lineup of experience and character—it was an assemblage of really good poets who knew what they were writing and didn't care about anything else. They got drunk, the audience got drunk, all that was missing was the orgy. This was no ordinary poetry reading. Indeed, it resembled anything but a poetry reading. The reading was such a violent and beautiful expression of their revolutionary individuality (a quality bypassed in American poetry since the formulations of Whitman), conducted with such surprising abandon and delight by the poets themselves, and presenting such a high mass of beautiful unanticipated poetry, that the audience, expecting some Bohemian stupidity, was left stunned, and the poets were left with the realization that they were fated to make a permanent change in the literary firmament of the States.

The poets participating were a curious group. First, Philip Lamantia, a surrealist blood poet, former member of San Francisco Anarchist group, who at the age of 13 had in imitation of Rimbaud written surrealist poetry, come to New York, consulted Breton and other surrealists, renounced surrealism, lived with Indians and priests in Mexico, took drugs, underwent visions, became Catholic, became silent, and reappeared at age of 28 in native town to take part in the reading.

The second poet, the youngest, was representative of the Black Mountain School—which derives in influence from Pound and William Carlos Williams. He, Michael McClure, read some of his own work, and some of theirs. He writes relatively sober mystical poetry.

The next poet, Philip Whalen, a strange fat young man from Oregon—in appearance a Zen Buddhist *bodhisattva*—read a series of very personal relaxed, learned mystical-anarchic poems. His obvious carelessness for his reputation as a poet, his delicacy and strange American sanctity is evident in his poetry, written in rare post-Poundian assemblages of blocks of hard images set in juxtapositions, like haikus.

The most brilliant shock of the evening was the declamation of the now-famous rhapsody, *Howl*, by Allen Ginsberg. The poem initiates a new style in composition in the U.S., returning to the bardic-strophic tradition of Apollinaire, Whitman, Artaud, Lorca, Mayakovsky, 'til now neglected in the U.S.—and improving on the tradition to the extent of combining the long lines and coherence of Whitman, with the cubist imagery of the French and Spanish traditions, and adding to that a fantastic rhythmic structure which begins on a relatively flat base of repetition, and builds up to the rhythmic crisis of a Bach fugue, and ends on a high peak of ecstatic elongation of the line structure.

The poem is built like a pyramid, in three parts, and ends in fantastic merciful tears—the protest against the dehumanizing mechanization of American culture, and an affirmation of individual particular compassion in the midst of a great chant.

The reading was delivered by the poet, rather surprised at his own power, drunk on the platform, becoming increasingly sober as he read, driving forward with a strange ecstatic intensity, delivering a spiritual confession to an astounded audience—ending in tears which restored to American poetry the prophetic consciousness it had lost since the conclusion of Hart Crane's *The Bridge,* another celebrated mystical work.

But this was not all! The last poet to appear on the platform was perhaps more remarkable than any of the others. Gary Snyder, a bearded youth of 26, also from the Northwest, formerly a lumberjack and seaman, student of literature and anthropology who had lived with American Indians and taken the religious drug peyote with them, and who is now occupied in the study of Chinese and Japanese preparatory for the drunken silence of a Zen monastery in Japan. He read parts of a hundred page poem he had been composing for 5 years, *Myths and Texts*—composition of fragments of all his experiences forming an anarchic and mystical pattern of individual revelation.

Perhaps the most strange poet in the room was not on the platform— he sat on the edge of it, back to the poets, eyes closed, nodding at good lines, swigging a bottle of California red wine—at times shouting encouragement or responding with spontaneous images—jazz style—to the long zig-zag rhythms chanted in *Howl.* This was Jack Kerouac, then unknown also, now perhaps the most celebrated novelist in America. Mr. Kerouac is also a superb poet, his poems are automatic, pure, brilliant, awesome, gentle, and unpublished as of yet.

I should, at this point, remark that William Carlos Williams, of all the great older poets, has remained in closest touch with these young poets, and he, if anyone, supplies the line with the democratic experimental tradition of the poet. Mention should also be given Mr. Lawrence

Ferlinghetti, publisher of Mr. Ginsberg's *Howl,* and himself poet of a book of verse, *Pictures of the Gone World.* Ferlinghetti is the most advanced publisher in America in that he publishes 'suspect' literature, literature usually rejected by other publishing houses because of its wild neo-bop prosody, non-commercial value, extreme expression of soul, and the pure adventure of publishing it. For his pains Mr. Ferlinghetti is now on trial in the American courts for having published Mr. Ginsberg.

This article should properly end with the announcement of the completion of *Naked Lunch,* a long epic prose-poem by William Seward Burroughs. Burroughs is the shadowy unknown genius behind the more publicized figures of Kerouac and Ginsberg, and the completion and editing of his work was the occasion of a transatlantic reunion of the three earlier this year in Tangier. The book seems destined to have great difficulties in finding a publisher—its style, almost surrealistic, its structure, its automatism, its theme, the desecration of the unity, the human image desecrated by a mad society, its images, sex, drugs, dreams, riots, hangings, secret narcotic phantasmal police—in short, *Naked Lunch* is a prose-poetic novel in the tradition of Rimbaud, Artaud, Genet, but the treatment of the work is too *naked* to be admitted into American consciousness past the barrier of commercial publishing, customs inspection, and legal censorship of its 'obscenity.'

In America, apart from the Little Rock stagnant sign of doom, apart from moneywild cultureless majority of humans that inhabit it, apart from the wealth and woe and fear and sorrow and false joy and guilt, there is, out of all this, in America, a new forceful stir of young poets, and they have taken it upon themselves, with angelic clarions in hand, to announce their discontent, their demands, their hope, their final wondrous unimaginable dream.

Excerpts from "The Literary Revolution in America."
FIRST PUBLISHED: Gregory Corso [and AG], *Litterair Paspoort,* no. 110 (Nov. 1957) pp. 193–196.

EDITOR'S NOTE: The above prose is the part of the uncredited collaboration written by Allen Ginsberg and Gregory Corso.

Abstraction in Poetry

I said in the preface to Corso's *Gasoline:* "he gets pure abstract poetry, the inside sound of language itself." I didn't realize at the time that lots of things in Gregory's poetry which I took for sheer, flaming verbal construction—with no practical meaning—were really extremely complicated and poetic statements of real ideas—as for instance the ultimate lines of "Ode To Coit Tower": *hay-like universe / golden heap on a wall of fire / sprinting toward the gauzy eradication of / Swindleresque Ink*—which now strikes me, after the laughing gas experience, as one of the most perfect statements I've seen of the sensation of the self-elimination or disappearance of the universe and all being with the disappearance of the mind: when the mind is eliminated into unconsciousness either by yogic withdrawal or artificial knockout or possibly death.

No matter how crazy Corso sounds he usually makes great sense to me after a year or so. I have to catch up with his advanced methods of composition. I've seen him start a line on a typewriter—"I pump him full of"—(of what? he says to himself, having no idea in the world)—"of lost"—(lost what? his fingers circling magically over the keyboard, waiting for some incongruous inspiration which will alter the meaning of the whole sentence gone before)—"lost watches"—or fried shoes, or radiator soup, or flying owl cheese, or how to bring the dead back to life: carrots dipped in Kangarooian Weep for certain corpses. He has a whole poem made like that. He gets to "In ran the moonlight and grabbed the prunes," but all these are built on some kind of later explainable ellipse—the mind instinctively attracted to images coming from opposite ends of itself which, juxtaposed, present consciousness in all its irrational, un-figure-outable-in-advance completeness.

Kerouac has several examples of what might be called abstract prose. In *Visions of Cody*—after writing several hundred pages of sketch and narrative and copying actual recorded tape conversations of his hero and then imitating it in ideal dream-conversation prose—his mind breaks down during the book's composition (in which he has followed the rhythmic zigzag flow of his thinks thru all their a-syntactic forms) and for the next forty or fifty pages the book plunges into an organic prose bebop babble. The rhythm is continued, though, long, beautiful sentences, with variable base rhythms, an endless sound. The book slowly picks up from there, emerges from the mud of real prose and with the same endless rhythm (and slowly beginning to make sense again) into narrative, chronological accounts of a last voyage thru America. In a later example of his work, *Old Angel Midnight*, there is a sort of Joycean babble flow—a mixture of American sounds and styles predicated on the basic spontaneous rhythm that Kerouac has discovered in his speech, his mind, in other friends' speech, perhaps drunk old friends' explanatory bar room conversation. "All the sounds of the universe coming in through the window" at once—Kerouac hears that because he meditates a lot in silence. I find that he and Corso are usually right and make sense—which I miss at first, but catch later.

Without meaning to oppose abstraction to the making of sense, there are several other elements which might be considered (what is abstract in poetry?). Perhaps pure sound: Schwitters, Isou, etc.—though perhaps they too make sense in context, Artaud's "*tara bulla / rara bulla / ra para hutin . . .*" is, in context, a pure crucifixion cry. Certain elements can be abstracted—rhythm, as in Kerouac, or elliptical phraseology, as in Corso—carrying these out to logical conclusion (where the circle meets itself) they make common sense also.

Another interesting example of recent abstract composition—so might it be called—is W. S. Burroughs' *Word*. This consists of a sort of visual free-association abstract summary of all the images—linked together and passing into one another—that the author has conceived in the writing of the previous seven years. Burroughs has habituated himself (thru natural inclination and many years' addiction to opiates) to thinking visually rather than verbally, so that this was a noncommittal transcription into words of a succession of visual images passing in front of his mental eye. If a poet is concentrating on one specific thing—say, direct, spontaneous flow—anything he says is appreciable and makes sense once you know what he is doing. All you have to do is listen to what comes next if you are interested in the man's mind or in a general theory of actual mind.

Frank O'Hara (*Second Avenue*) and Kenneth Koch (*When the Sun Tries to Go On*) both wrote at the same time long meaningless poems to see what would happen—well maybe not meaningless, but they were just composing, bulling along page after page. The result, I guess, is that they learned how to write, learned the extent of their own imagination, learned how far out they could go, learned freedom of composition, and turned up some beautiful lines. Koch did many strange things. I heard a poem which I understood was composed of purely fixed (abstract) elements—each line to contain, I think I remember, the name of a city, a cold drink, an animal, maybe three other tough categories, and the word "bathtub." It sounded like an abstract Bach fugue; I came when I heard the phrase "mosquitoes squirting buttermilk, into (was it?) Wounded Knee bathtubs." That area of experiment is what attracted me—the freedom of composition and the sense it finally comes to—the final revelation of the irrational nonsense of Being.

WRITTEN: 1961

FIRST PUBLISHED: *Nomad,* no. 10/11 (Autumn 1962) pp. 50–51.

AUTHOR'S NOTE: Requested by art critic Emmanuel Maneretta, 1959, part of a large exchange of sociability between Black Mountain New York Beat Poets and the painters' community. At the time O'Hara's *Second Avenue,* Koch's *When the Sun Tries to Go On* and Ashbery's *Skaters* were new novel and logical works to me, so I tried to find reason and common sense in the thickness of the associative compositions. I was already notified of that dissociation of sensibility of prose pursued by Kerouac 1952 *Visions of Cody* (pure sound in parts and parody of earnest speech in heaven) and Burroughs' tendency to "cut-up" then developing Tangier to Paris. This is attempt to bridge spontaneous composition methods of NY School Poets trained in abstraction so to speak by the painters and Kerouac, trained to improvisatory far-out-ness ("abstraction") by Bop sound.

June 10, 1985

Retrospect on Beat Generation

Meditating, still thinking of Kerouac's role as *dharma bodhisattva* bringer or messenger in *Mexico City Blues,* and after conversation with William Burroughs at 4:00 PM inquiring Jack's catalytic effect in encouraging Bill to write—also having inspected Charter's Viking Portable Library 1992 *Beat Reader*,[1] ruminated—:

That the quality most pure in Kerouac was his grasp that life is really a dream ("a dream already ended" he wrote) as well as being real, both real *and* dream, both once at the same time—a deep insight that cut through knots of artificial intellect, extremism, totalitarian rationality, "new reasons for spitefulness"—cut through all the basic vanity, resentment, and wrongheadedness that cursed most twentieth century political and literary movements—or weakened them with impermanent grounding or stained them with the fog of misdirection. That realization of dream as the suchness of this universe pervaded all the spiritual intelligence of Beat writers on differing levels, whether Burroughs' suspicion of all "apparent sensory phenomenon"; Herbert Huncke's "setting sun turned crimson"; Corso's paradoxical wit (viz.: "Death hiding beneath the kitchen sink: 'I'm not real' it cried, 'I'm just a rumor spread by Life,'" a late paradox, or his earlier "Dirty Ears aims a knife at me / I pump him full of lost watches"); or Orlovsky's compassionate view of Minnerbia: "Her teeth-brush dream is the one she loves best"; or Snyder's meditations in mind wilderness, or Sensei Whalen's pith aphorisms, "Poetry is a graph of the mind moving"; or McClure's insight into the gnat, "Nature abhors a vacuum" or Lamantia's *Ecstasis* prophecy "I long for the, / it is nameless that I long for"; or even John Wieners' heavy woe's the work of conscious dreamer "Particles of light / worshipped in the pitches of the night."

But the doctrine of consciousness of *sunyata*, emptiness, with all its transcendental wisdom including panoramic awareness, oceanic city vastness, a humoresque appreciation of minute details of the big dream, especially "character in the bleak inhuman aloneness" in "Memorial cello time" is most clearly and consistently set forth in the body of Kerouac's prose, poetry, and essays.

This basic metaphysical understanding of the eternal nature of dream, more or less clearly perceived by the various "Beat" authors according to their individual temperaments, served as common ground and saved their essential work from the decay of time—because the "message" was permanent, as "change" and "emptiness" are a permanent gnosis from Heraclitus' time to now. As beauty itself is the realization of simultaneous "emptiness and form," the co-emergent wisdom of *Buddhadharma*.

"Come back and tell me in a hundred years" Kerouac commanded, his koan.

"What was the face you had before you were born?"—that question was always at the heart of Beat poetry. It could be called the "Golden Ash" school, as Kerouac qualified existence. Thus, Beat: "a dream already ended . . ." Thus beatific, "the Golden Ash" of dream. One could call this Heart Failure a big success.

WRITTEN: Jan. 8, 1991; revised March 13, 1992

Unpublished.

"When the Mode of the Music Changes, the Walls of the City Shake"

Trouble with conventional form (fixed line count and stanza form) is, it's too symmetrical, geometrical, numbered and pre-fixed—unlike to my own mind which has no beginning and end, nor fixed measure of thought (or speech—or writing) other than its own cornerless mystery—to transcribe the latter in a form most nearly representing its actual "occurrence" is my "method"—which requires the skill of freedom of composition—and which will lead poetry to the expression of the highest moments of the mindbody—mystical illumination—and its deepest emotion (through tears—love's all)—in the forms nearest to what it actually looks like (data of mystical imagery) and feels like (rhythm of actual speech and rhythm prompted by direct transcription of visual and other mental data)—plus not to forget the sudden genius-like imagination or fabulation of unreal and out of this world verbal constructions which express the true gaiety and excess of freedom—(and also by their nature express the first cause of the world) by means of spontaneous irrational juxtaposition of sublimely related fact, by the dentist drill singing against the piano music; or pure construction of imaginaries, hydrogen jukeboxes, in perhaps abstract images (made by putting together two things verbally concrete but disparate to begin with)—always bearing in mind, that one must verge on the unknown, write toward the truth hitherto unrecognizable of one's own sincerity, including the avoidable beauty of doom, shame and embarrassment, that very area of personal self-recognition (detailed individual is universal remember) which formal conventions, internalized, keep us from discovering in ourselves and others—For if we write with an eye to what the poem should be (has been), and do not get lost in it, we will never discover anything new about ourselves in the process of actually writing on the table, and we lose the chance to live in our works, and make habitable the new world which every man may discover in himself, if he lives—which is life itself, past present and future.

Thus the mind must be trained, i.e. let loose, freed—to deal with itself as it actually is, and not to impose on itself, or its poetic artifacts, an arbitrarily preconceived pattern (formal or subject)—and *all* patterns, unless discovered in the moment of composition—all remembered and *applied* patterns are by their very nature arbitrarily preconceived—no matter how wise and traditional—no matter what sum of inherited experience they represent—The only pattern of value or interest in poetry is the solitary, individual pattern peculiar to the poet's moment and the poem *discovered* in the mind and in the process of writing it out on the page, as notes, transcriptions,—reproduced in the fittest accurate form, at the time of composition. ("Time is the essence" says Kerouac). It is this personal discovery which is of value to the poet and to the reader—and it is of course more, not less, communicable of actuality than a pattern chosen in advance, with matter poured into it arbitrarily to fit, which of course distorts and blurs the matter . . . Mind is shapely, art is shapely.

II

The amount of blather and built-in misunderstanding we've encountered—usually in the name of good taste, moral virtue or (at most presumptuous) civilized value—has been a revelation to me of the absolute bankruptcy of the academy in America today, or that which has set itself up as an academy for the conservation of literature. For the academy has been the enemy and Philistine host itself. For my works will be taught in the schools in 20 years, or sooner—it is already being taught for that matter—after the first screams of disgruntled mediocrity, screams which lasted 3 years before subsiding into a raped moan.

They should treat us, the poets, on whom they make their livings, more kindly while we're around to enjoy it. After all we are poets and novelists, not Martians in disguise trying to poison man's mind with anti-earth propaganda. Though to the more conformist of the lot this beat and Buddhist and mystic and poetic exploration may seem just that. And perhaps it is: "Any man who does not labor to make himself obsolete is not worth his salt."—Burroughs.

People take us too seriously and not seriously enough—nobody interested in what *we* mean—just a lot of bad journalism about beatniks parading itself as highclass criticism in what are taken by the mob to be the great journals of the intellect.

And the ignorance of the technical accomplishment and spiritual interests is disgusting. How often have I seen my own work related to Fearing and Sandburg, proletarian literature, the 1930s—by people who don't *connect* my long line with my own obvious reading: Crane's *Atlantis,* Lorca's *Poet in NY,* Biblical structures, psalms and lamentations, Shelley's high buildups, Apollinaire, Artaud, Mayakovsky, Pound, Williams and the American metrical tradition, the new tradition of measure. And Christopher Smart's *Rejoice in the Lamb.* And Melville's prose-poem *Pierre.* And finally the spirit and illumination of Rimbaud. Do I have to be stuck with Fearing (who's alright too) by phony critics whose only encounter with a long line has been anthology pieces in collections by Oscar Williams? By intellectual bastards and snobs and vulgarians and hypocrites who have never read Artaud's *Pour En Finir Avec Le Jugement de Dieu* and therefore wouldn't begin to know that this masterpiece which in 30 years will be as famous as *Anabasis* is the actual model of tone for my earlier writing? This is nothing but a raving back at the false Jews from Columbia who have lost memory of the *Shekinah* and are passing for middle class. Must I be attacked and condemned by these people, I who have heard Blake's own ancient voice recite me the "Sunflower" a decade ago in Harlem? and who say I don't know about "poetic tradition"?

The only poetic tradition is the voice out of the burning bush. The rest is trash, and will be consumed.

If anybody wants a statement of values—it is this, that I am ready to die for poetry and for the truth that inspires poetry—and will do so in any case—as all men, whether they like it or no—. I believe in the American Church of Poetry.

And men who wish to die for anything less or are unwilling to die for anything except their own temporary skins are foolish and bemused by illusion and had better shut their mouths and break their pens until they are taught better by death—and I am sick to death of prophesying to a nation that hath no ears to hear the thunder of the wrath and joy to come—among the "fabled damned" of nations—and the money voices of ignoramuses.

We are in American poetry and prose still continuing the venerable tradition of compositional self exploration and I would say the time has not come, historically, for any effort but the first sincere attempts at discovering those natural structures of which we have been dreaming and speaking. Generalizations about these natural patterns may yet be made—time for the academies to consider this in all technical detail—the data, the poetry and prose, the classics of original form, have already been written or are about to be—there is much to learn from them and there may be generalizations possible which, for the uninitiated, the non-poets, may be reduced to "rules and instructions" (to guide attention to what is being done)—but the path to freedom of composition goes through the eternal gateless gate which if it has "form" has an indescribable one—images of which are however innumerable.

There is nothing to agree or disagree with in Kerouac's method—there is a statement of fact (1953) of the method, the conditions of experiment, which he was pursuing, what he thought about it, how he went about it. He actually did extend composition in that mode, the results are apparent, he's learned a great deal from it and so has America. As a proposed method of experiment, as a completed accomplishment, there is nothing to agree or disagree with, it is a fact—that's what he was interested in doing, that's what he did—he's only describing his interest (his passion) for the curious craftsman or critic or friend—so be it. Why get mad and say he's in "error"? There's no more error here than someone learning how to build a unicorn table by building one. He's found out (rare for a writer) *how* he really wants to write and he is writing that way, courteously explaining his way.

Most criticism is semantically confused on this point—should and shouldn't and art is and isn't—trying to tell people to do something other than that which they basically and intelligently want to do, when they are experimenting with something new to them (and actually in this case to U.S. literature).

I've had trouble with this myself, everybody telling me or implying that I shouldn't really write the way I do. What do they want, that I should write some other way I'm not interested in? Which is the very thing which doesn't interest me in their prose and poetry and makes it a long confused bore?—all arty and by inherited rule and no surprises no new invention—corresponding inevitably to their own dreary characters—because anyway most of them have no character and are big draggy minds that don't *know* and just argue from abstract shallow moral principles in the void? These people are all too abstract, when it comes down to the poetry facts of poetry,—and I have learned in the past 2 years that argument, explanation, letters, expostulation are all vain—nobody listens anyway (not only to what I say, to what I *mean*) they all have their own mental ax to grind. I've explained the prosodic structure of *Howl* as best I can, often, and I still read criticism, even favorable, that assumes that I am not interested in, have no, form—they just don't recognize any form but what they have heard about before and expect and what they want (they, most of them, being people who don't write poetry even and so have no idea what it involves and what beauty they're violating).—And it is also tiresome and annoying to hear Kerouac or myself or others "Beat" described because of our art as incoherent, we are anything but. After all.

But so far we have refused to make arbitrary abstract generalizations to satisfy a peculiar popular greed for banality. I perhaps lose some of this ground with this writing. I occasionally scream with exasperation (or giggles); this is usually an attempt to communicate with a blockhead. And Kerouac sometimes says "Wow" for joy. All this can hardly be called incoherence except by ototverbal madmen who depend on longwinded defenses of their own bad prose for a livelihood.

The literary problems I wrote of above are explained at length in Dr. Suzuki's essay "Aspects of Japanese Culture" (*Evergreen Review*) and placed in their proper aesthetic context. Why should the art of spontaneity in the void be so, seem so, strange when applied in the U.S. prose-poetry context? Obviously a lack of intuitive spirit and/or classical experience on the part of these provincial frauds who have set themselves up as conservators of tradition and attack our work.

A sort of philistine brainwashing of the public has taken place. How long the actual sense of the new poetry will take to filter down, thru the actual writing and unprejudiced sympathetic reading of it, is beyond my power to guess and at this point beyond my immediate hope. More people take their ideas from reviews, newspapers and silly scholarly magazines than they do from the actual texts.

The worst I fear, considering the shallowness of opinion, is that some of the poetry and prose may be taken too familiarly, and the ideas accepted in some dopey sociological platitudinous form—as perfectly natural ideas and perceptions which they are—and be given the same shallow treatment, this time sympathetic, as, until recently, they were given shallow unsympathy. That would be the very we of fame. The problem has been to communicate the very spark of life, and not some opinion about that spark. Most negative criticism so far has been fearful overanxious obnoxious opinionation about this spark—and most later "criticism" will equally dully concern itself with favorable opinions about that spark. And that's not art, that's not even criticism, that's just more dreary sparkless blah blah blah—enough to turn a poet's guts. A sort of cancer of the mind that assails people whose loves are eaten by their opinions, whose tongues are incapable of wild lovely thought, which is poetry.

The brainwashing will continue, though the work be found acceptable, and people will talk as emptily about the void, hipness, the drug high, tenderness, comradeship, spontaneous creativity, beat spiritual individuality and sacramentalism, as they have been talking about man's "moral destiny" (usually meaning a good job and full stomach and no guts and the necessity of heartless conformity and putting down your brother because of the inserviceability of love as against the legal discipline of tradition because of the unavailability of God's purity of vision and consequent souls angels—or anything else worthwhile). That these horrible monsters who do nothing but talk, teach, write crap and get in the way of poetry, have been accusing us, poets, of lack of "values" as they call it is enough to make me vow solemnly (for the second time) that pretty soon I'm going to stop even trying to communicate coherently to the majority of the academic, journalistic, mass media and publishing trade and leave them stew in their own juice of ridiculous messy ideas. SQUARES SHUT UP and LEARN OR GO HOME. But alas the square world will never and has never stopt bugging the hip muse.

That we have begun a revolution of literature in America, again, without meaning to, merely by the actual practice of poetry—this would be inevitable. No doubt we knew what we were doing.

WRITTEN: 1961

FIRST PUBLISHED: *Second Coming Magazine,* vol. 1, no. 2 (July 1961) pp. 2, 40–42.

AUTHOR'S NOTE: At this time my own poetry, Kerouac's prose and poetry, and Burroughs' work were subject to amazing attack—not openly critical denunciation by younger friends and older writers who might have been expected to show interested sympathy (Hollander, Podhoretz, Kazin, Hentoff, Rexroth, Simpson and Spender stick in memory, aside from *Time* and *Life* mags)—but also legal attack. Various censorships of Corso Kerouac Burroughs and myself and our works in *Chicago Review* and *Big Table,* as well as *Howl* and *Naked Lunch* trials, and New Directions' fear of publishing complete text of Kerouac's *Visions of Cody.*

I felt at the time the poetics would be triumphant, the texts permanent, my complaints exemplary—to set example to future generations what depression and inertia and hostility we had to plough thru instruct, cajole, admonish, plead with for possession of America's heart. Why? So as to leave a record of combat against native fascist militarization of U.S. soul. It seemed to me that the poetic critics, in so disowning the new open poetics and the freedom of mind, desire, imagination, were setting the mental stage for repression of political liberty in the long run—a political liberty that could only be defended by undaunted, free, bold humorous imagination, open field mentality, open field poetics, open field democracy. The closed forms of the older poetry, it seemed to me, were ostrich-head-in-sand-like. It seemed to me the breakthroughs of new poetry were social breakthroughs, that is, political in the long run.

I thought and still think that the bulwark of libertarian-anarchist-sexualized individual poems and prose created from that era to this day—under so much middle-class critical attack—were the mental bombs that would still explode in new kid generations even if censorship and authoritarian (moral majority) fundamentalist militarily-hierarchical "New Order" neoconservative fascistoid creep Reaganomics-type philistinism ever took over the nation. Which it nearly has. Thus the title—Poetics and Politics, out of Plato out of Pythagoras—continuation of gnostic—secret and politically suppressed—liberty of consciousness and art—old bohemian—tradition—thru the existence of exquisite paperbacks too many in print to be burned. The clock could never be turned back.

Poetics: Mind Is Shapely, Art Is Shapely

I really don't know what I'm doing when I sit down to write. I figure it out as I go along (and revise as little as possible). I see the writing is interesting if there are a lot of awkward poetic ideas made up by accident in the course of rapid notation of thoughts. It's usually a subject I've wondered about before, so it's a matter of transcription in visual shorthand of whatever is there on my mind, plus spontaneous improvisation and excitement when I realize I'm suddenly talking about something I never did before.

But my attention is weak, so I put down all I can in one single mental breath or thought at a time, one after another, long lines, they have their own rhythm. Lately I notice my attention is weaker, I leave the notation of thought within the line to natural staccato phrase-links.

While writing, my feeling for the subject can deepen, I begin to improvise and build up a rhythm. I cry if I write something beautiful. Sometimes this appears to be divine inspiration—I get the feeling, it's an ecstatic lucidity, that the world can be entered and prophesied to by a single soul, alone.

WRITTEN: April 1959

FIRST PUBLISHED: flyer, San Francisco Poetry Center, 1959.

AUTHOR'S NOTE: Written at request of Ruth Witt Diamant for reading April 29, 1959 on return to San Francisco from several years' absence including crucial stay in Tangier, Venice, Amsterdam and long residence at 9 Rue Git Le Coeur, Paris, with Orlovsky Corso Burroughs and others, at time of composition of *Naked Lunch,* by William S. Burroughs, Corso's *Bomb,* and Orlovsky's *Frist Poem.* I had written Proem and Parts III, IV and V of *Kaddish,* and so read these poems at the reading one of an important series sponsored by R. W. Diamant, a series of historically crucial poetic presentation. During *Kaddish* Robert Duncan walked out (I thought disapproving, he later explained he was drunk and sick). The reading itself seemed disappointment to audience, accustomed to my reputation as author of *Howl,* not the new work *Kaddish;* I went home depressed. This statement on poetics writ in advance applies particularly to recent composition of *Kaddish.*

What Way I Write

Once, chancing to read Blake and dwelling on the words of "Ah! Sunflower," I heard his voice and looked out of the window, realizing that *this* universe was the sunflower seeking eternity. The experience led me to know art as a time-machine to carry the secret revelation and transmit it unbroken from mind to mind.

Cézanne speaks of his "petit sensation," a feeling he derived from the observation of nature, and at the end of his life refers to it in his letters as none other than "Pater Omnipotens Aeterna Deus." His art became an attempt to "reconstitute" on canvas an abstract (by means of planes, cubes, etc.) of the spacetime data fed to his senses by Mount St. Victoire.

Pound turned to the Chinese written character as a medium for poetry seeing that data can be juxtaposed (like planes, cubes, etc.) in clear word-pictures (visual images) on the page. Elliptical flashes of "sensation" in the reader's mind connect these polar images.

With this as the basic form of the poem, certain practical effects develop. There can be no interruption of the poem for mechanical measure, outside of the data presented. The images by their very nature are the design of the poem as in William Carlos Williams or the later American School of Haiku. The purest shape of the image on the page is the true measure.

This seems to work out in practice, since, when the natural-tongue words that compose these images are pronounced aloud, many curious rhythms are heard. These are rhythms heard in day-to-day speech, hitherto unnoticed. Practically speaking, classical systems of prosody are not workable in dealing with these natural rhythms.

It's premature to expect classification of sounds only recently noticed, but as they become familiar they will become subject to stereotype and classification perhaps.

Some methods of handling these rhythms consciously have become evident in the practice of various poets. Short lines in William Carlos Williams are balanced mainly by relative weight of phrasing—speech-size, special emphasis, weight as mental imagery, silences indicated, etc. In Olson[2] the lines may be said to bear equal weight in that each is a unitary particle of energy in spontaneous composition. In Creeley,[3] discrete short rhythmic entities are separated by breathstop to form new type couplets.

However, the mind is more than the tongue, as many writers have noticed recently. We are aware of events in other parts of the psyche besides that part which thinks in words. At certain times all diverse simultaneous impressions and events focus together to make a new, almost a mutant, consciousness.

It is necessary to resort to some very crude and rapid method of notation to sketch some fleeting sensory detail of this process of myriad sensations running thru the being.

I have adapted, for myself, the single breath-unit as the measure of how much material I can handle-notate-compose at one continuous stroke. I learned much from Kerouac.[4]

The rhythm of this transcription becomes in this case the guiding rhythm of the poem when read aloud.

This means that I generally compose in long lines, depending on how falls my attempt to become conscious of my thought, look aside and notate it. I focus on the verbal transaction level, then my mind goes blank and I'm left only with words. So I must go on with the next thought. I do not know what I do. On what multitudes of levels do I operate? I get lost. I tell lies. I follow what comes in my mind next. Often short lines come in because I'm afraid I'll miss notating some particularly striking recurrent realization flashed thru the mind. The tricks of notation are many and varied. Just how do we think? and how can we watch ourselves think and notate that? I'm not sure what happens; generally I pause at the beginning of a new line, having short circuited my visual processes by the constant stop to notate. Unless the impulse-rhythm of the last speeds me forward; then I may stop in midline to invent a continuation of what I had forgotten after I began writing it down—or move on with a dash. I get some very strangely unexpected verbal and imagual connections this way, illogical recognitions that I cry as they are poetry. In the course of this notation I finally get out beyond what I'd anticipated and discover what it is that's underlying my whole mind and soul at the moment—and find the course of that discovery now transcribed in the composition just finished. So that it is good to be able to say that I never in advance really know what I'm going to write, if the writing is to become anywhere near sublime. That's that.

FIRST PUBLISHED: *Writer's Digest,* vol. 40, no. 10 (Oct. 1960) pp. 35, 75–76.

AUTHOR'S NOTE: Some intelligent editor of middlebrow digest, impressed by my transitory notoriety of late '50s, invited me to contribute a statement of "How I Write." I enjoyed the opportunity to explain the startling (?) freedom possible in really professional writing to this commercial trade journal. I had to talk down and explain myself from my high horse, and thus assumed a relative modesty and moderation in explanation to presumably junior high school teachers in a class of scriveners. Explaining to multitudes was the focus.

Poet's "Voice"

In 1948 I had a vision and heard William Blake's voice reciting "Ah! Sunflower": deep, earthen, tender, suffused with the feeling of the ancient of days. After that experience I imagined a "Voice of Rock" as the sound of prophesy.

Subsequent composition, following the prosodic precepts of William Carlos Williams based on breath-measure and the fresh swift naturalness of thought-voice in Kerouac's poetry and prose, circa 1955, brought me to my native New Jersey voice issuing from throat and breast and mind.

Subsequent experience in Benares with mantra chanting (short magic formulae sung or repeated aloud as invocation to inner divinity) and in Kyoto with Zen belly-breathing delivered my accustomed voice (and center of self) from upper chest and throat to solar plexus and lower abdomen. The timbre, range and feeling-quality of the physical voice was thus physiologically deepened, till it actually approximated what I'd youthfully imagined to be the voice of rock.

Feeling, and rhythm, which is concomitant bodily potential of feeling, take place in the *whole* body, not just the larynx. The voice cometh from the whole body, when the voice is full, when feeling is full. (Poesy may be seen as a rhythmic articulation of feeling.)

Practice chanting and reciting aloud before other souls has confirmed my pleasure in this unexpected occurrence of voice.

Ideological consequences follow naturally—revolution and eternity and death.

WRITTEN: July 11, 1965

FIRST PUBLISHED: William J. Martz, ed., *The Distinctive Voice* (Glenview, IL: Scott, Foresman and Co., 1966).

Some Metamorphoses of Personal Prosody

Much early training in versification and time sense modeled after pages of Wyatt resulted in overwritten coy stanzas permuting abstract concepts derived secondhand from Silver Poets, which carefulness managed to suppress almost all traces of native sensibility diction concrete fact and personal breath in my own vers de college. "In this mode perfection is basic," William Carlos Williams reproved me correctly; simultaneously he responded with enthusiasm to short fragments of personal notation drawn from diaries and rearranged in lines emphasizing crude breath-stop syncopations. Later practice in this mode (Kerouac urging to "speak now or ever hold thy peace") trained my sensibility to the eccentric modulations of long-line composition displayed by Smart, Blake, Whitman, Jeffers, Rimbaud, Artaud and other precursors including now Edward Carpenter (whose *Towards Democracy* read me this year by his later lover Gavin Arthur struck me as the combine of Blake-visionary and Whitmanic-direct-notation nearest my own intuition that I'd ever stumbled upon). In fact I decided ruefully for 24 hours that I was like Carpenter just another fine minor Whitman necessary but forgettable.

But young minstrels have now arisen in the airwaves whose poetic forms outwardly resemble antique verse including regular stanzas refrains and rhymes: Dylan and Donovan and some fragments of the Rolling Stones because they *think* not only in words but also in music simultaneously have out of the necessities of their own space-age media and electric machinery tunes evolved a natural use of—a personal realistic imaginative rhymed verse. Principle of composition here is, however, unlike antique literary form, primarily spontaneous and improvised (in the studio if need be at the last minute), and prophetic in character in that tune and language are invoked shamanistically on the spot from the unconscious. This new ear is not dead because it's not only for eye-page, it's connected with a voice improvising, with hesitancies aloud, a living musician's ear. The old library poets had lost their voices; natural voice was rediscovered; and now natural song for physical voice. Oddly this fits Pound's paradigm tracing the degeneration of poesy from the Greek dance-foot chorus thru minstrel song thru 1900 abstract voiceless page. So now returned to song and song forms we may yet anticipate inspired creators like Shiva Krishna Chaitanya Mirabai and Ramakrishna who not only composed verse in ecstatic fits, but also chanted their verse in melody, and lifted themselves off the floor raised their arms and danced in time to manifest divine presence. Mantra repetition—a form of prayer in which a short magic formula containing various god names is chanted hypnotically—has entered Western consciousness and a new mantra-rock is formulated in the Byrds and Beatles.

Not being a musician from childhood my own *japa* and *kirtan*[5] is home made but not without influence on verbal composition practice. Introduction of tape recorder also catalyses changes in possibilities of composition via improvisation. A short fragment of longer trans-American voyage poetries is therefore composed directly on tape by voice, and then transcribed to page: page arrangement notates the thought-stops, breath-stops, runs of inspiration, changes of mind, start-ings and stoppings of the car.

WRITTEN: Sept. 10, 1966

FIRST PUBLISHED: Stephen Berg and Robert Mezey, eds., *Naked Poetry* (Indianapolis: Bobbs-Merrill Co., 1969).

Some Different Considerations in Mindful Arrangement of Open Verse Forms on the Page

1. Count of syllables (Marianne Moore, Kenneth Rexroth) (Creeley's mono syllabics)
2. Count of accents (traditional iambic etc. foot)
3. Measurement of vowel length: quantity (classical Greek and Latin, Swinburne experiments, Pound, Campion)
4. Breath stop (Creeley, Olson, Williams) (new breath, new line) (pause)
5. Units of mouth phrasing (pauses within same breath) (Ginsberg, Olson)
6. Divisions of mental ideas (Corso, Williams)
7. Typographical topography (aesthetic balances on page, symmetry, asymmetry)
8. Heartbeat (Duncan)
9. Conditions of original notation (line-length, verse length, bloc-shape) and writing materials (pocket notebook, booksize journal page, napkin, tape, typewriter, matchbook etc.) (Olson, Ginsberg etc. Kerouac especially)
10. Chance (arbitrary choice, impulse, fatigue, accident, interruption, sudden impatience or energy)

"Form" is what happens. All considerations are elements of a single "discipline" which is MINDFULNESS or conscious appreciation and awareness of the humors of line arrangements on the page, intelligence relating to the mental conception of the poem and its vocalization.

WRITTEN: April 2, 1977

FIRST PUBLISHED: Allen Ginsberg, *Composed on the Tongue* (Bolinas, CA: Grey Fox Press, 1980).

Fourteen Steps for Revising Poetry

1. Conception
2. Composition
3. Review it through several people's eyes
4. Review it with eye to idiomatic speech
5. Review it with eye to the condensation of syntax (blue pencil and transpose)
6. Check out all articles and prepositions: are they necessary and functional?
7. Review it for abstraction and substitute particular facts for reference (for example: "walking down the avenues" to "walking down 2nd Avenue")
8. Date the composition
9. Take a phrase from it and make up a title that's unique or curious or interesting sounding but realistic
10. Put quotations around speeches or referential slang "so to speak" phrases
11. Review it for weak spots you really don't like, but just left there for inertial reasons
12. Check for active versus inactive verbs (for example: "after the subway ride" instead of "after we rode the subway")
13. Chop it up in lines according to breath phrasing/ideas or units of thought within one breath, if any
14. Retype

WRITTEN: April 1, 1982

Unpublished.

Meditation and Poetics

EDITOR'S NOTE: This is the text of a speech given at the New York
Public Library in the winter of 1987.

It's an old tradition in the West among great poets that poetry is rarely
thought of as "just poetry." Real poetry practitioners are practitioners of
mind awareness, or practitioners of reality, expressing their fascination
with a phenomenal universe and trying to penetrate to the heart of it.
Poetics isn't mere picturesque dilettantism or egotistical expressionism
for craven motives grasping for sensation and flattery. Classical poetry is
a "process," or experiment—a probe into the nature of reality and the
nature of the mind.

That motif comes to a climax in both subject matter and method in
our own century. Recent artifacts in many fields of art are examples of
"process," or "work in progress," as with the preliminary title of Joyce's
last work, *Finnegans Wake*. Real poetry isn't consciously composed as
"poetry," as if one only sat down to compose a poem or a novel for publication. Some people do work that way: artists whose motivations are less
interesting than those of Shakespeare, Dante, Rimbaud, and Gertrude
Stein, or of certain surrealist verbal alchemists—Tristan Tzara, André
Breton, Antonin Artaud—or of the elders Pound and William Carlos
Williams, or, specifically in our own time, of William Burroughs and Jack
Kerouac. For most of "The Moderns," as with the Imagists of the twenties
and thirties in our century, the motive has been purification of mind and
speech. Thus we have the great verses of T. S. Eliot:

> Since our concern was speech, and speech impelled us
>   To purify the dialect of the tribe
>   And urge the mind to aftersight and foresight,
> Let me disclose the gifts reserved for age
>   To set a crown upon your lifetime's effort.
>   First, the cold friction of expiring sense
> Without enchantment, offering no promise
>   But bitter tastelessness of shadow fruit
>   As body and soul begin to fall asunder.

There's a common misconception among puritanical meditators and
puritanical businessmen, who think they've got "reality" in their hands,

that high poetics and art as practiced in the twentieth century are practiced as silly Bohemian indulgence, rather than for the reason that one practices mindfulness in meditation or accuracy in commerce. Western fine art and other meditation practices are brother-and-sister-related activities. (Which is quite different from the notion that East is East and West is West and never the twain shall meet—an idiot slogan denying the fact East and West the brain's the same.) It's an important insight to have so that as meditation practitioners and businessmen we don't become inhibited in expressing and probing ourselves through various art means that we've inherited—from poetry to music to tea ceremony to archery to horsemanship to cinema to jazz blues to painting, even New Wave electric music.

Major works of twentieth-century art are probes of consciousness—particular experiments with recollection or mindfulness, experiments with language and speech, experiments with forms. Modern art is an attempt to define or recognize or experience perception—pure perception. I'm taking the word "probe" for poetry—poetry as a probe into one subject or another—from the poet Gregory Corso. He speaks of poetry as a probe into Marriage, Hair, Mind, Death, Army, Police, which are the titles of some of his earlier poems. He uses poetry to take an individual word and probe all its possible variants. He'll take a concept like death, for instance, and pour every archetypal thought he's ever thought or could recollect having thought about death and lay them out in poetic form—making a whole mandala of thoughts about it.

Kerouac and I, following Arthur Rimbaud and Baudelaire, our great-grandfathers among hermetic poets and philosophers, were experimenting naively with what we thought of as "new reality," or "supreme reality." Actually that was a phrase in use in 1945; we were thinking in terms of a new vision or a new consciousness, after the little passage in Rimbaud's *A Season in Hell:* "Noël sur la terre!" "When shall we go beyond the shores and the mountains, to salute the birth of new work, new wisdom, the flight of tyrants and demons, end of superstition, to adore—the first!—Christmas on earth!" In fact, the phrase "new consciousness" circulated among Beat Generation writers as our poetic motif in the early fifties. The specific intention of that decade's poetry was the exploration of consciousness, which is why we were interested in psychedelic or mind-manifesting substances—not necessarily synthetic; they might also be herbs or cacti.

Kerouac's motive for his probe was disillusionment: the heavy experi-

ence of the lives, old age, sickness and death of his father and his older
brother, whose dying he experienced as he took care of them and
watched them in their beds, close to their deaths. As he wrote in *Visions
of Cody*, in 1951:

> I'm writing this book because we're all going to die—in the loneli-
> ness of my life, my father dead, my brother dead, my mother far
> away, my sister and wife far away, nothing here but my own tragic
> hands . . . that are now left to guide and disappear their own way
> into the common dark of all our death, sleeping in me raw bed,
> alone and stupid: with just this one pride and consolation: my
> heart broke in the general despair and opened up inwards to the
> Lord, I made a supplication in this dream.

As a motive for writing a giant novel, this passage from *Visions of Cody*
is a terrific stroke of awareness and *bodhisattva* heart, or outgoingness of
heart. So I'm speaking about the ground of poetry and purification of
motive. A few Buddhist *dharma* phrases correlate charmingly with the
process of Bohemian art of the twentieth century—notions like "Take a
non-totalitarian attitude," "Express yourself courageously," "Be outrageous to yourself," "Don't conform to your idea of what is expected but
conform to your present spontaneous mind, your raw awareness." That's
how *dharma* poets "make it new"—which was Pound's adjuration.

You need a certain deconditioning of attitude—a deconditioning of
rigidity and unyieldingness—so that you can get to the heart of your own
thought. That's parallel with traditional Buddhist ideas of renunciation—renunciation of hand-me-down conditioned conceptions of
mind. It's the meditative practice of "letting go of thought"—neither
pushing them away nor inviting them in, but, as you sit meditating,
watching the procession of thought forms pass by, rising, flowering and
dissolving, and disowning them, so to speak: you're not responsible any
more than you're responsible for the weather, because you can't tell in
advance what you're going to think next. Otherwise you'd be able to pre-
dict every thought, and that would be sad for you. There are some people whose thoughts are all predictable.

So it requires cultivation of tolerance towards one's own thoughts and
impulses and ideas—the tolerance necessary for the perception of one's
own mind, the kindness to the self necessary for acceptance of that pro-

cess of consciousness and for acceptance of the mind's raw contents, as in Walt Whitman's "Song of Myself," so that you can look from the outside into the skull and see what's there in your head.

The specific parallel to be drawn is to Keats' notion of "negative capability," written out in a letter to his brother. He was considering Shakespeare's character and asking what kind of quality went to form a man of achievement, especially in literature. "Negative capability," he wrote, "is when a man is capable of being in uncertainties, mysteries, doubts, without any irritable reaching out after fact and reason." This means the ability to hold contrary or even polar opposite ideas or conceptions in the mind without freaking out—to experience contradiction or conflict or chaos in the mind without any irritable grasping after facts.

The really interesting word here is "irritable," which in Buddhism we take to be the aggressive insistence on eliminating one concept as against another, so that you have to take a meat-ax to your opponent or yourself to resolve the contradictions—as the Marxists took a meat-ax to their own skulls at one point, and as the neo-conservatives at this point may take a meat-ax to their own inefficient skulls. A current example might be the maniacal insistence that the Sandinistas[6] are the force of evil and that our C.I.A. terrorists are patriots like George Washington. That's a completely polarized notion of the universe—the notion that everything is black and white.

A basic Buddhist idea from 150 A.D. is that "Form is no different from Emptiness, Emptiness no different from Form." That formulation is one that Keats and all subtle poets might appreciate. The American poets Philip Whalen, Gary Snyder, Kerouac and Burroughs in their work do appreciate this "highest perfect wisdom," both in their own intuition and from their study of *Prajnaparamita* texts.

As part of "purification" or "de-conditioning" we have the need for clear seeing or direct perception—perception of a young tree without an intervening veil of preconceived ideas; the surprise glimpse, let us say, or insight, or sudden Gestalt, or I suppose you could say *satori*, occasionally glimpsed as esthetic experience.

In our century Ezra Pound and William Carlos Williams constantly insist on direct perception of the materials of poetry, of the language itself that you're working with. The slogan here—and henceforth I'll use a series of slogans derived from various poets and yogis—is one out of

Pound: "Direct treatment of the thing." How do you interpret that phrase? Don't treat the object indirectly or symbolically, but look directly at it and choose spontaneously that aspect of it which is most immediately striking—the striking flash in consciousness or awareness, the most vivid, what sticks out in your mind—and notate that.

"Direct treatment of the 'thing' whether subjective or objective," is a famous axiom or principle that Pound pronounced around 1912. He derived that American application of twentieth-century insight from his study of Chinese Confucian, Taoist and Japanese Buddhist poetry. There was a Buddhist infusion into Western culture at the end of the nineteenth century, both in painting and in poetry. Pound put in order the papers of "the late professor Ernest Fenellosa," the celebrated essay on "The Chinese Written Character as a Medium for Poetry." Fenellosa/ Pound pointed out that in Chinese you were able to have a "direct treatment" of the object because the object was pictorially there via hieroglyph. Pound recommended the adaptation of the same idea: the Chinese poetic method as a corrective to the conceptual vagueness and sentimental abstraction of Western poetry. In a way he was asking for the intercession of the *bodhisattvas* of Buddhist poetry into Western poetics because he was calling for direct perception, direct contact without intervening conceptualization, a clear seeing attentiveness, which, as you may remember, echoing in your brain, is supposed to be one of the marks of Zen masters, as in their practice of gardening, tea ceremony, flower arranging or archery.

That idea was relatively rare in late-nineteenth-century academic Western poetry, though Pound also drew from advanced Western models—old Dante to the French modernist poets Jules Laforgue, Tristan Corbière and Rimbaud. The tradition was initiated by Baudelaire, who had updated the poetic consciousness of the nineteenth century to include the city, real estate, houses, carriages, traffic, machinery. As Walt Whitman said, "Bring the muse into the kitchen, Drag the muse into the kitchen? She's there, installed amidst the kitchenware."

Another slogan that evolved around the same time as Pound's and with the same motif was William Carlos Williams' famous "No ideas but in things." He repeats it in his epic *Paterson*, a little more clearly for those who haven't understood: "No ideas but in facts." Just the facts, ma'am. Don't give us your editorial; no general ideas. Just "give me a for instance"—correlate the conception with a real process or a particular action or a concrete thing, localized, immediate, palpable, practicable, involving direct sense contact.

In one of the immortal bard's lyrics, divine Shakespeare gives you nothing but things:

> When icicles hang by the wall
> And Dick the shepherd blows his nail
> And Tom bears logs into the hall,
> And milk comes frozen home in pail . . .
> And Marian's nose looks red and raw . . .

That was Shakespeare's vivid presentation of unmistakable winter. You don't need to make the generalization if you give the particular instances. A poet is like a Sherlock Holmes, assembling the phalanx of data from which to draw his editorial conclusion. William James' notion was of "the solidity of specificity." Kerouac's phrase for it was, "Details are the life of prose." To have it you've got to have "direct treatment of the thing." And that requires direct perception—mind capable of aware- ness, uncluttered by abstraction, the veil of conceptions parted to reveal significant details of the world's stage.

Williams has another way of saying it—homely advice to young poets and American art practitioners: "Write about things that are close to the nose." There's a poem of his, much quoted by Buddhist poets, called "Thursday." It goes like this:

> I have had my dream—like others—
> and it has come to nothing, so that
> I remain now carelessly
> with feet planted on the ground
> and look up at the sky—
> feeling my clothes about me,
> the weight of my body in my shoes,
> the rim of my hat, air passing in and out
> at my nose—and decide to dream no more.

Just try! Actually that one single poem is the intersection between the mind of meditation—the discipline of meditation, letting go of thoughts—and the Yankee practice of poetry after William James, where the poet is standing there, feeling the weight of his body in his shoes, aware of the air passing in and out of his nose. And since the title of this series of talks is "Spiritual Quests" we might make a little footnote here that "spirit" comes from the Latin *spiritus,* which means "breathing," and that the spiritual practices of the East are primarily involved with meditation, and that meditation practices usually begin with trying to increase one's awareness of the space around you, beginning with the fact that you're breathing. So generally you follow your breath, in Zen or in Tibetan style. It's a question of following the breath out from the tip of the nose to the end of the breath and then following it back into the stomach, perhaps, or the lower abdomen. So it's sort of charming that Williams arrived at this concept of his own: "air passing in and out at my nose—and decide to dream no more."

Another Pound phrase that leads the mind toward direct treatment of the thing, or clear seeing, is: "The natural object is always the adequate symbol." You don't have to go chasing after far-fetched symbols because direct perception will propose efficient language to you. And that relates to another very interesting statement, by the Tibetan lama poet Chögyam Trungpa: "Things are symbols of themselves." Pound means that the natural object is identical with what it is you're trying to symbolize in any case. Trungpa is saying that if you directly perceive a thing it's completely there, completely itself, completely revelatory of the eternal universe that it's in, or of your mind as it is.

In Kerouac's set of thirty slogans called "Belief and Technique for Modern Prose" there are a few mind-arrows, or mind-pointers, which are instruction on how to focus in, how to direct your mind to see things, whether it's "an old teacup in memory," or whether you're looking out a window, sketching verbally. Kerouac advised writers: "Don't think of words when you stop but to see picture better." William Blake's similar slogan is: "Labor well the Minute Particulars, attend to the Little-ones." It's very pretty actually; take care of the little baby facts. Blake continues:

He who would do good to another, must do it in Minute
    Particulars
General good is the plea of the scoundrel hypocrite and
    flatterer:
For Art and Science cannot exist but in minutely organized
    Particulars

A classic example of William Carlos Williams in America seeing minute particulars clearly, precisely, thoroughly, is in the famous and most obvious of Imagist poems, "The Red Wheelbarrow." Because the thing was seen so completely the poem seems to have penetrated throughout the culture, so that people who are not interested in poetry—high school kids or thick-headed businessmen—know this as the totem modern poem.

so much depends
upon
a red wheel
barrow
glazed with rain
water
beside the white
chickens.

That's considered the acme Imagist poem of direct perception. I think it was written in the twenties. It's not much, actually. Williams didn't think it was so much; he said, "An inconsequential poem—written in 2 minutes—as was (for instance) 'The Red Wheelbarrow' and most other short poems." But it became a sort of sacred object.

Why did he focus on that one image in his garden? Well, he probably didn't focus on it—it was just there and he saw it. And he remembered it. Vividness is self-selecting. In other words, he didn't prepare to see it, except that he had had a life's preparation in practicing awareness "close to the nose," trying to stay in his body and observe the space around him. That kind of spontaneous awareness has a Buddhist term for it: "the Unborn." For where does a thought come from? You can't trace it back to a womb, a thought is "unborn." Perception is unborn, in the sense that it spontaneously arises. Because even if you tried to trace your perceptions back to the source, you couldn't.

To catch the red wheelbarrow, however, you have to be practiced in poetics as well as practiced in ordinary mind. Flaubert was the prose initiator of that narrowing down of perception and the concretization of it with his phrase "The ordinary is the extraordinary." There's a very interesting formulation of that attitude of mind in writing poetry by the late Charles Olson, in his essay "Projective Verse." This is kind of caviar, but William Carlos Williams reprinted this famous essay for the transmission of his own ideas to another generation. It contains several slogans commonly used by most modern poets that relate to the idea of direct seeing or direct awareness of open mind and open form in poetry. Here's what Olson says:

> This is the problem which any poet who departs from closed form is especially confronted by. And it evolves a whole series of new recognitions. From the moment he ventures into FIELD COMPO-SITION [Olson means the field of the mind] . . . he can go by no track other than the one that the poem under hand declares for itself. Thus he has to behave, and be, instant by instant, aware of some several forces just now beginning to be examined. . . .

> The principle, the law which presides conspicuously over such composition and when obeyed is the reason why a projective poem can come into being. It is this: FORM IS NEVER MORE THAN AN EXTENSION OF CONTENT. (Or so it got phrased by one Robert Creeley, and it makes absolute sense to me, with this possible corollary, that right form, in any given poem, is the only and exclusively possible extension of the content under hand.) There it is, brothers, sitting there for USE.

> By "content" I think Olson means the sequence of perceptions. So the form—the form of a poem, the plot of a poem, the argument of a poem, the narrative of a poem—would correspond to the sequence of perceptions. If that seems opaque to you, the next paragraph from Olson's "Projective Verse" essay might explain more. He says this:

> Now the process of the thing, how the principle can be made so to shape the energies that the form is accomplished. And I think it could be boiled down to one statement (first pounded into my head by Edward Dahlberg): ONE PERCEPTION MUST IMMEDI-ATELY AND DIRECTLY LEAD TO A FURTHER PERCEPTION. It means exactly what it says, is a matter of, at all points . . . get on with it, keep moving, keep in, speed the nerves, their speed, the perceptions, theirs, the acts, the split-second acts [the decisions you make while scribbling], the whole business, keep it moving as fast as you can, citizen. And if you set up as a poet, USE, USE, USE the process at all points. In any given poem always, always one perception must, must, must [as with the mind] MOVE INSTANTER ON

ANOTHER! . . . So there we are, fast there's the dogma. And its excuse, its usableness, in practice. Which gets us . . . inside the machinery, now, 1950, of how projective verse is made.

I interpret that set of words—"one perception must move instanter on another"—as similar to the dharmic practice of letting go of thoughts and allowing fresh thoughts to arise and be registered, rather than hanging onto one exclusive image and forcing Reason to branch it out and extend it into a hung-up metaphor. That was the difference between the metaphysically inspired poetry of the thirties to the fifties in America after T. S. Eliot and the Open Form, practiced simultaneously by Ezra Pound and William Carlos Williams and later by Charles Olson and Robert Creeley. They let the mind loose. Actually, that's a phrase by one of the founders of our country: "The mind must be loose." That's John Adams, as reported by Robert Duncan in relation to poetics. Try that on the religious right. Leave the mind loose. One perception leads to another. So don't cling to perceptions, or fixate on impressions, or on visions of William Blake. As the young surrealist poet Philip Lamantia said when he was asked in 1958 to define "hip" as distinguishable from "square": Hip is "Don't get hung up."

So we have, as a ground of purification, letting go—the confidence to let your mind loose and observe your own perceptions and their discontinuities. You can't go back and change the sequence of the thoughts you had; you can't revise the process of thinking or deny what was thought, but thought obliterates itself anyway. You don't have to worry about that, you can go on to the next thought.

Robert Duncan once got up and walked across the room and then said, "I can't revise my steps once I've taken them." He was using that as an example to explain why he was interested in Gertrude Stein's writing, which was writing in the present moment, present time, present consciousness: what was going on in the grammar of her head during the time of composition without recourse to past memory or future planning.

Meditators have formulated a slogan that says, "Renunciation is a way to avoid conditioned mind." That means that meditation is practiced by constantly renouncing your mind, or "renouncing" your thoughts, or "letting go" of your thoughts. It doesn't mean letting go of your whole awareness—only that small part of your mind that's dependent on linear, logical thinking. It doesn't mean renouncing intellect, which has its proper place in Buddhism, as it does in Blake. It doesn't mean idiot wildness. It means expanding the area of awareness, so that your awareness surrounds your thoughts, rather than that you enter into thoughts like a dream. Thus the life of meditation and the life of art are both based on a similar conception of spontaneous mind. They both share renunciation as a way of avoiding a conditioned art work, or trite art, or repetition of other people's ideas.

Poets can avoid repetition of their obsessions. What it requires is confidence in the magic of chance. Chögyam Trungpa phrased this notion, "Magic is the total delight in chance." That also brings magic to poetry: chance thought, or the unborn thought, or the spontaneous thought, or the "first thought," or the thought spoken spontaneously with its conception—thought and word identical on the spot. It requires a certain amount of unselfconsciousness, like singing in the bathtub. It means not embarrassed, not jealous, not involved in one-upmanship, not mimicking, not imitating, above all not self-conscious. And that requires a certain amount of jumping out of yourself—courage and humor and openness and perspective and carelessness, in the sense of burning your mental bridges behind you, outreaching yourself; purification, so to speak, giving yourself permission to utter what you think, either simultaneously, or immediately thereafter, or ten years later.

That brings a kind of freshness and cleanness to both thought and utterance. William Carlos Williams has an interesting phrase about what's wrong when you don't allow that to happen: "There cannot be any kind of facile deception about it . . . prose with a dirty wash of a stale poem over it." Dirty wash of a stale poem over your own natural thought?

When I met Chögyam Trungpa in San Francisco in 1972 we were comparing our travels and our poetry. He had a heavy schedule and a long itinerary, and I said I was getting fatigued with mine. He said, "That's probably because you don't like your poetry."

So I said, "What do you know about poetry? How do you know I don't like my poetry?"

He said, "Why do you need a piece of paper? Don't you trust your own mind? Why don't you do like the classic poets? Milarepa made up his poems on the spot and other people copied them down."

That's actually the classical Buddhist practice among Zen masters and Tibetan lamas, like the author of "The Hundred Thousand Songs of

Milarepa." These songs are the most exquisite and hermetic as well as vulgar and folk-art-like works in all of Tibetan culture—classic folk poetry, known by every Tibetan. But Milarepa never could write. The method, again, was spontaneous mind, on-the-spot improvisation on the basis of meditative discipline.

What Trungpa said reminded me of a similar exchange that I had with Kerouac, who also urged me to be more spontaneous, less worried about my poetic practice. I was always worried about my poetry. Was it any good? Were the household dishes right, was the bed made? I remember Kerouac falling down drunk on the kitchen floor of 170 East Second Street in 1960, laughing up at me and saying, "Ginsberg, you're a hairy loss." That's something that he made up on the spot, a phrase that just came out of his mouth, and I was offended. A hairy loss! If you allow the active phrase to come to your mind, allow that out, you speak from a ground that can relate your inner perception to external phenomena, and thus join Heaven and Earth.

WRITTEN: Winter 1987

FIRST PUBLISHED: William Zinsser, ed., *Spiritual Quests* (Boston: Houghton Mifflin, 1988).

Exercises in Poetic Candor

1. Meditation instructions and five minutes sitting
2. Write down in chronologic sequence the main external perceptions and internal ruminations or chains of thought that passed thru your head.
3. Surprise Mind: "Nazi milk"
   Word associations with key word
   Seventeen syllable declarative sentence
4. Top ten most vivid recollections since childhood:
   Spots of Time: Wordsworth
   Vividness
5. Top ten fears

6. Top ten secrets you never told anybody

7. Top pleasures

8. Three-Part Short Poem:
   Waking from thoughts (Ground) (Sensation)
   What's the situation (Path) (Recognition)
   What's your reaction comment (Fruition) (Reaction)

9. Three panoramic landscapes, one breath verse apiece, total three verses, plus one switcheroo or capping thought, fourth verse

10. Confusion *samsara* to simplicity and clear mind in five twenty-four syllable verses

11. Haiku:
    Take one vivid moment, one spot of time
    Express the details in one sentence
    Reduce it to about seventeen syllables

12. Top ten wishes, top ten lies, top ten dreams; see Kenneth Koch *Wishes Lies Dreams* handbook

13. Rhyme—Take one word, rhyme it two more times then fill in the blank keeping to original rhyme, keeping to a regular syntax. Twelve-bar blues form.

Revision

14. Take the three-rhyme poem and cut out possessive articles and prepositions, conjunctions where you can: middle path, not too stilted short form, not excessively verbose.

WRITTEN: 1980s

Unpublished.

PART 7
Writers

WILLIAM BLAKE

Liner Notes to Blake Record

To Young Or Old Listeners

The songs were first composed on tape recorder, improvised on pump organ in farmhouse upstate N.Y. in two nights after returning from Democratic Convention 1968 Tear Gas Chicago. These are half the *Songs of Innocence and Experience* now finished to music; the rest will be completely tuned in another year.

Inspiration began 21 years, half my life ago, living in Harlem, in mind's outer ear I heard Blake's voice pronounce "Ah! Sun-flower" and "The Sick Rose" (and "A Little Girl Lost") and experienced an illumination of eternal consciousness, my own heart identical with the ancient heart of the universe.

It's taken two decades of vision fame, friends' deaths and apocalyptic history for me to materialize the spiritual illumination received thru these poems, without systematic study of Blake's life and only fragmentary study of later works. I *imagined* this music after 20 summers' musings over the rhythms.

William Blake (1757–1827) engraved his own picture plates, hand colored, and printed *Songs of Innocence and Experience* (1789–1794) only a couple dozen copies. Thus every word, every picture and every print of the book he made in his life bore the impress of his own intelligent body; there was no robot mechanical repetition in any copy. The title *Songs of Innocence and Experience* is literal; Blake used to sing them unaccompanied at his friends' houses.

The purpose in putting them to music was to articulate the significance of each holy and magic syllable of his poems; as if each syllable had intention. These are perfect verses, with no noise lost or extra accents for nothing. I tried to hear meanings of each line spoken intentionally and interestedly, and follow natural voice tones up or down according to different emphases and emotions vocalized as in daily intimate speech: I drew the latent tunes, up or down, out of talk-tones suggested by each syllable spoken with normal feeling.

> Piping
>> Down the
>>>>>> ey
>>>> Vall
>>>>>>>> Wi
>>>>>>>>>> ld:

Thus the flute pipes notes down from the hill into the deep valley floor with accurate melody.

Since a physiologic ecstatic experience had been catalyzed in my body by the physical arrangement of words in so small a poem as "Ah! Sun-flower," I determined long ago to think of poetry as a kind of machine that had a specific effect when planted inside a human body, an arrangement of picture mental associations that vibrated on the mind bank network; and an arrangement of related sounds and physical mouth movements that altered the habit functions of the neural network. Twentieth century French poet Antonin Artaud noted that certain sound vibrations, certain rhythmic frequencies of music or voice, might alter molecular patterns in the nervous system.

I had been led to hear by ear individual syllables and their spoken tonal intention by a whole American poetic tradition begun at turn of century with Pound who specified that for any prosody (measure of poetry rhythm) adequate to our real speech, the poet should train his ear "pay attention to the tone leading of vowels" instead of the tripping of stressed accents—i.e. hear the musical Aum vowel alterations of note and rhythm pattern, and not get hung up on voiced monotone stressed da dit da dit da dit da dits—like, "Thou too sail on O Ship of State." William Carlos Williams, Pound's friend, taught attention to raw spoken talk to learn the "for real" rhythms of American poetry. Later Basil Bunting sharpened my attention to vowels as solid objects in a verse line.

Ma Rainey, Pound, Dylan, Beatles, Ray Charles, Ed Sanders and other singers have returned language poesy to minstrelsy. As new generations understand and decipher poetical verses for gnostic-psychedelic flashes and practical artistic messages, I hope that musical articulation of Blake's poetry will be heard by the Pop Rock Music Mass Media

Electronic Illumination Democratic Ear and provide an eternal poesy standard by which to measure sublimity and sincerity in contemporary masters such as Bob Dylan, encouraging all souls to trust their own genius inspiration.

For the soul of the planet is wakening, the time of dissolution of material forms is here, our generation's trapped in imperial satanic cities and nations, and only the prophetic priestly consciousness of the bard—Blake, Whitman or our own new selves—can steady our gaze into the fiery eyes of the tygers of the wrath to come.

WRITTEN: Dec. 14–15, 1969

FIRST PUBLISHED: *Allen Ginsberg/William Blake: Songs of Innocence and Experience* (MGM Records, LP No. FTS3083, 1969).

Your Reason and Blake's System

The prophetic books are actually reflections of Blake's personal conflicts of the time. In *Jerusalem* (1820), there is a theme which is useful now: the argument between political anger—say, over the nuclear bomb—and a sense of compassion and mercy, and a realization that the world doesn't matter, or that if it does matter, there's no way of approaching it with anger. Blake was struggling with some of the same emotions we struggle with, which I assume are more or less common, for his revolutionary times—post French Revolution—and the destruction of idealism, radical disillusionment. There are similar revolutionary conditions now as in Blake's time, similar social and emotional problems. Blake's books are useful now as explorations of the same problems we have, somewhat related to the revolutionary fervor of the sixties in America and a subsequent so-called "disillusionment." So actually Blake is up to date in the psychology of wrath vs. pity, compassion vs. anger, that runs through all of his work and is visible for our own decade as well as his.

Blake knew Thomas Paine in England and in fact warned Paine to get out of London before the fuzz came to arrest him. So Paine left on the boat to France to join the French Revolution, just ahead of King George

III's police. Blake was contemporary; he was right in on the scene as most of us are in one way or another. He wasn't an isolated hermit, or the "mad Blake" that Wordsworth thought him. He was dealing with real people, real events.

I don't know how much Walt Whitman, who was a kindred nature to Blake, knew of him, but he asked that the door of his tomb be designed similar to the form in Blake's first illustration to *Jerusalem*. It's kind of an odd collocation of prophesy: old bards taking their lineage from each other.

In the *Song of Los* (1795) and *Book Of Urizen* (1794), there are long long passages describing the senses creating the world. Proceeding from an odd sort of really interesting physiology, Blake carried it out in blood and globular-veined detail. He was really an original in that. Blake is filled with neurological imagery:

> The roaring fires ran o'er the heav'ns
> In whirlwinds and cataracts of blood
> And o'er the dark deserts of Urizen
> Fires pour thro' the void on all sides
> On Urizens self-begotten armies.

It's very similar here in *Urizen* to the late 1970s problem the President had in deciding whether to employ the neutron bomb—whether to push forward on the vast nuclear plain or to withdraw. The paranoiac, self-limiting, territorial, comparing, reasoning, Urizenic mentality of the armaments makers and the Pentagon argues and pushes for defense against self-begotten armies. That is to say, if the Russians develop this particular type of bomb, then we have to compete with them. To a great extent, the Russian phantom is a projection from the American Urizenic mentality, just as the American phantom is a projection from the Russian Urizenic mentality, both of them by arithmetic and measure trying to balance and out-reason and out-construct architectural marvels that will threaten each other.

The division of Blake's final system is relatively simple. There's the body, *Tharmas*; there's emotion in the body, *Luvah*; there's imagination, *Urthona*; and there's reason, *Urizen*. Blake's basic conception is that if any single one of them "takes over," like Urizen, (which he thought was characteristic of the industrial scientific revolution), then all four parts of the entire human universe fall out of balance and that imbalance creates war and chaos. His analysis of the present Western industrial situation is that hyper-rationalism, Urizen, has taken over. In certain cases, such as revolution, Luvah (emotion) or Urthona (imagination) might take over primary power in a curious way and cause another kind of imbalance. Obviously, if Tharmas (the body) takes over without reason or imagination, and without genuine emotion, there'll be another catastrophe of muscle-bound brutishness. And if hypertrophic imagination takes over, it's like an acidhead taking his clothes off and running in front of cars, screaming "Stop the machines!" or Luvah (emotion) might drown the world in Jewish mother chicken soup. Obviously it's a very ordinary-mind notion that the raising of the whole man, *Albion*, requires a balance of imaginative faculty, emotional faculty, rational faculty and a firm body.

Urizen is the principle of excessively cutting intellect, a destructive or negative intellect so solidified or impacted that it doesn't allow for any feeling or bodily rest or richness or generosity of imaginative space. The present creators of nuclear power are absorbed in purely mental constructions without practical regard for fallout—radioactive waste or impossible stockpiles of unused plutonium. So with Urizen we're dealing with a contemporary mentality. I would say the triumph of the Urizenic mentality would probably be the neutron bomb in the sense that it destroys people and leaves architectural constructions intact. Overweening Urizen, the scoundrelish mental quality, involves abstracted judgment, limitation of senses and emotions, loss of imagination. Later, Blake associates Urizen with the Hebrew god Jehovah, the judging avenging Jehovah, the limiter, the knavish reasoner, bounded consciousness, guilty conscience. So the old Jehovaic heavy taskmaster is Urizen as well as Satan, the Satan whose mind is totally thick, whose conceptual and reasoning faculties are so egoistically solidified and world-dominant that his mind is opaque. He can't see through his mind nor can he see through the appearance of matter with eyes of feeling or imagination. In *Milton* (1840), Blake defines Satan as maximum opacity, or eyes in your head but you don't even see what's in front of you. The cause of Urizen's downfall to the state of Satan or error was the desire for more power, more territory, for dominion, the ego-centric desire for total mental control of nature—the condition of nuclear-power mentality. Urizen is motivated by foul ambition and cultivates "Satanic" self-deceit with its resultant hypocrisy such that he's constantly weeping over his own victims. He's jealous of man—his neutron bomb will destroy the human bodies but leave human architecture intact.

When Urizen sets himself up as God, he starts ordering everybody around. He commands Tharmas, he intimidates Luvah and he starts controlling Urthona, imagination, but he can't realistically "control" imagination. Poetic imagination always escapes Urizen in Blake's scheme. In fact, the drama of these prophetic books is in the development of the struggle between Urizen and the other *Three Zoas* or human qualities, and how occasionally *Los* (Urthona), the embodiment of imagination, gets a little tangled up but never gets completely subjugated by Urizen. There's always that escape clause in Blake's contract with eternity. The poetic imagination can get beyond appearances and that's why Blake insists the poetic imagination is primary, above the material senses. If we had to depend on material senses only for our poetry, we would endlessly repeat the same round of already-known experiences. In the beginning, Chapter One of *Urizen*:

> Lo! a shadow of horror is risen
> In eternity! Unknown, unprolific!

That's really great! Urizen is unprolific. He can't write poetry, he can't create anything, all he can do is criticize. Like our own rational conceptual insistences, so Urizen is born with anxiety, secrecy.

This book is Blake's first deep probe into the ultimate nature of the psyche in the creation of consciousness; actually it's Blake's book of Genesis for consciousness itself. There are a few other earlier books which deal with some similar symbols, but *Urizen* is the first deep classic probe in which Blake sets the stage for the mind-scape of the rest of his mythology. Blake, in fact, actually turns the Bible upside down: Jehovah, Elohim, those central authorities, become Satan—Lords of a materialistic universe—imprisoning the mind and imagination to moral law, binding them down in the ropes of ignorant reason. Blake illustrated Urizen bound in the heavy fishnet of his own thought-forms. This book was Blake's serious, somber, Beethovenian demonstration of how the scoundrelesque principle of "irritable reaching after fact and reason"[1] would create a hallucinatory universe around itself, going to complete excess and dragging everything with it, until its expansion was limited by its own self-contradiction. Finding a limit, it would have a form; that is, the limit of opacity would be its form. The notion has some familiar parallels, as in Blake's proverb "The path of excess leads to the palace of wisdom." That is, if you took crazy excess to its extreme, finally you'd reach a limit where excess would attack itself and manifest its own boundary. Reading *Urizen*, we understood an aspect of what Blake meant by the gnomic phrase "The path of excess leads to the palace of wisdom."

The imagery in *Urizen* is very similar to a lot of extraordinarily baroque Tibetan imagery describing the birth of ego or the appearance of ego in open space (*sunyata*, the void).[2] Blake's imagination and the imagination of Tibetan poetics and painted tankas are oddly similar, both in the same realm of mind-projection and exercise of three dimensional visualization. The Tibetan and Blakean traditions deal with extremely rarefied, subtle and very definite worlds of imagination. Both Blake's and Tibetan symbols serve as fixed images for meditation and contemplation of psychological archetypes. The "Urizenic" ego and the Tibetan *rudra*, egoic solidification, rationalistic, overly conceptualized mind, are functionally identical.

One of the most interesting alchemies in all of Blake is his conception of giving a "body to falsehood." He gives a body to that which is non-existent, to the lie, to the nonentity, to the illusion of selfhood, to error, to opacity. Why? So that it may be clearly seen by the senses and cast off forever. Did Blake originate this brilliant idea? There may be ancient Buddhist correlatives. He must give Urizen form, a body, so that error can be limited, recognized and annihilated. Blake follows this with the analytic strategy that if you want to understand Satan's secret, understand his system of ideas. If you want to get to the bottom of opacity or error or ignorance or however you want to deem your independent Satan, try to find out his system, wherefrom he comes, how he operates, why he's doing what he's doing, and what his function is. If you have his system, then you have his secret, and every Satan has a system. The reason Satan is opaque is ultimately irrational, self-contradictory, self-limiting. The reason Satan can't see what's in front of him is that his mind is so occupied with systematizing it doesn't notice events that don't fit into his system. Not only must you be able to confront Satan as his contestant, but also as his compassionate analyst: "The Reactor hath hid himself thro envy. I behold him. But you cannot behold him till he be reveald in his System" [*Jerusalem*, Ch II, Pl 43, 9–10].

If you read Blake's prophetic books naturally check out his pictures. We get a lot of intelligence out of Blake's own illustrations of his ideas. We can decipher his mind, visually. How much delicacy he put into each illustration! Just as in the prosody, his punctuation and eccentric capitalization, there's funny character in the paintings, there's tremendous wit, and there are exact suggestions how to interpret the poems. Sometimes the visualizations are completely at variance with anything we might guess. Sometimes they're humorously off-the-wall projections that we wouldn't have thought fit in with the poems but are real adornments, such as his human-faced Tygers. The illustrations give us new takes on how Blake views his subjects.

Urizen is one of Blake's really hard, tough, mental, dry-seed works— the poetry is terrific. Thereafter Blake unfolds his primordial mind and becomes mighty, rhetorically beautiful, golden tongued and syllabically interesting. Vowels become roarers and exquisite philosophic rhapsodies are introduced, that later turn visionary in *Milton* and throughout *Jerusalem.*

Blake was astonished by his own imagination.

WRITTEN: April 1978–March 2, 1988

FIRST PUBLISHED: Allen Ginsberg, *Your Reason and Blake's System* (New York: Hanuman Books, 1988).

WALT WHITMAN

On Walt Whitman, Composed on the Tongue
or
Taking a Walk Through Leaves of Grass

There was a man, Walt Whitman, who lived in the nineteenth century, in America, who began to define his own person, who began to tell his own secrets, who outlined his own body, and made an outline of his own mind, so other people could see it. He was sort of the prophet of American democracy in the sense that he got to be known as the good gray poet when he got to be an old, old man because he was so honest and so truthful and at the same time so enormous-voiced and bombastic that he sounded his "barbaric yawp over the roofs of the world," writing in New York City probably then, thinking of the skyline and roofs of Manhattan as it might have been in 1883 or so. He began announcing himself, and announcing person, with a big capital P, Person, self, or one's own nature, one's own original nature, what you really think when you're alone in bed, after everybody's gone home from the party or when you're looking in the mirror, shaving, or you're not shaving and you're looking in the mirror, looking at your long, white, aged beard, or if you're sitting on the toilet, or thinking to yourself "What happened to life?" "What happened to your Mommy?" or if you're just walking down the street, looking at people full of longing.

So he wrote a book called *Leaves of Grass*. (The text referred to here is the Modern Library edition: *Leaves of Grass and Selected Prose*, New York: Modern Library, Random House, Inc., 1950.) And the very first inscription, at the beginning of *Leaves of Grass*, was "One's-Self I Sing":

One's-Self I sing, a simple separate person,
Yet utter the word Democratic, the word En-Masse.
Of physiology from top to toe I sing,
Not physiognomy alone nor brain alone is worthy for the
   Muse, I say the Form complete is worthier far,

The Female equally with the Male I sing.
Of Life immense in passion, pulse, and power,
Cheerful, for freest action form'd under the laws divine,
The Modern Man I sing.

Well, that's kind of interesting. He starts with the female equally with the male, so he begins in the middle of the nineteenth century to begin saying "women's lib," actually, "The Female equally with the Male I sing." But he's going to talk about the body he says, of physiology from top to toe, so he's going to sing about the toes and the hair: modern man. This is on the very first page of his book *Leaves of Grass*.

Then, the next page, he has a little note, "To Foreign Lands":

I heard that you ask'd for something to prove this puzzle the
    New World,
And to define America, her athletic Democracy,
Therefore I send you my poems that you behold in them what
    you wanted.

An "athletic Democracy," so that was an idea. But what did he mean by that? He means people who are able to get up off their ass and get out and look up at the blue sky in the middle of the night and realize how big the universe is and how little, tiny America is, or, you know, how vast our souls are, and how small the state is, or the Capitol building, magnificent and glorious as it is, it's rendered the size of an ant's forefoot by the immensity of a cloud above it. And so, the soul that sees the cloud above the Capitol or the universe above the cloud, is the giant athletic soul, you could almost say. So, it's democracy, though, that is the key, which for him is meaning, in the long run, the love of comrades, that men will love men, women love women, men love women, women love men, but that there be a spontaneous tenderness between them as the basis of the democracy. "Athletic" probably ultimately for him means "erotic," people having sports in bed.

So he goes on, "To the States," announcing:

To the States or any one of them, or any city of the States, *Resist
    much, obey little,*
Once unquestioning obedience, once fully enslaved,

Once fully enslaved, no nation, state, city of this earth, ever
    afterward resumes its liberty.

Well, that's a warning to America, much needed later on, when as
Eisenhower, President a hundred years later, once warned, "Watch out
for the military-industrial complex which demands unquestioning obedience and slavery to military aggression." Fear, nuclear apocalypse,
unquestioning obedience like "Don't ask, maybe they know better than
you do." So this is a warning from Whitman about the difficulties of
democracy. Then he, like a *bodhisattva*, that is to say, someone who has
taken a vow to enlighten all beings in all the directions of space and in
all the three times—past, present, and future—has a little poem or song
to his fellow poets that would be born after him, that, like myself, will sit
in a recording studio reading his words aloud to be heard by ears
through some kind of movie/television/theater: "Poets to come! orators, singers,"—that must be, "orators," now who would that be, as "Thou
shalt not crucify mankind upon a cross of gold," that was William
Jennings Bryan, a great political orator; "singers," that must be Bob
Dylan; "musicians to come," that must be Mick Jagger; "Poets to come!
orators, singers, musicians to come . . ." "orators," that must be Kerouac.

Poets to come! orators, singers, musicians to come!
Not to-day is to justify me and answer what I am for,
But you, a new brood, native, athletic, continental, greater
    than before known,
Arouse! for you must justify me.
I myself but write one or two indicative words for the future,
I but advance a moment only to wheel and hurry back in the
    darkness.
I am a man who, sauntering along without fully stopping, turns
    a casual look upon you and then averts his face,
Leaving it to you to prove and define it,
Expecting the main things from you.

Ah, he wants somebody to pick him up in the street and make love to
him. But he wants to give that glance, so that you know he's open, but
what kind of love does he want?
    He wants a democratic love, and he wants an athletic love, he wants a

love from men, too, and he also wants a love in the imagination. He wants
an expansiveness, he wants communication, he wants some kind of vow
that everybody will cherish each other sacramentally. So he's going to
make the first breakthrough, which is what he's saying. So he's got
another little poem following that, "To You":

> Stranger, if you passing meet me and desire to speak to me,
>   why should you not speak to me?
> And why should I not speak to you?

Well, I don't know why not except everybody's too scared to be generally walking down the street, they might get hit for being a fairy or
something. Or, you know, be trying to pick you up or be a nut talking in
the subway, or somebody babbling to himself walking in the street. So
there's all these bag ladies and bag men, old Whitmans wandering
around with dirty white beards eating out of the garbage pail wanting to
talk to nobody actually. Those are the people that won't talk to anybody,
they just go around mumbling to themselves, they talk to themselves. But
he was willing to talk to anybody, he said. Of course he was living in a
time when there weren't too many people to talk to anyway, in the sense
of nineteenth-century America. Population was growing but there were
still lots of farms. There was still some sense of sport in the cities. Not a
total fear of being mugged by a junkie, I guess. I wonder what he
would've done with a junkie going along, "Hey, Mr. Whitman, you got
some smash? Got some spare change?" Or maybe he would have been
the one going around asking for spare change. Well why not? Spare, he's
looking for spare love, actually. Or spare affection. Or just spare openness, spare democracy. "You got any spare democracy, Mister?" Some
enthusiasm, a little bit of vitality, a little bit of that hard, gem-like flame
that artists burn with.

So, his major work is known as "Song of Myself." "Song of Myself" is a
long thing, about thirty-two pages of not such big type; he wrote a lot.
And this was a major statement, this was his declaration of his own
nature. Now, what is a declaration of nature for a guy? In the nineteenth
century, everybody was writing closed verse forms. They all went to
Germany for their education, like Longfellow, they went to Heidelberg
University, and they studied esoteric sociology and epistemology and lin-
guistics and ancient Greek and they thought back on the United States

romantically and wrote long poems about Hiawatha and the Indian maidens under the full moon near the Canadian lakes. Whitman actually just stated America and slugged it out with the beer carts along the Bowery and wandered up and down and sat afternoons in Pfaff's. Pfaff's was a bar he used to go to, a Bohemian hang-out, a downstairs beer hall, sort of like a German *bierstuben*. Bohemian friends used to meet there, probably like a gay gang, plus a newspaper gang, plus a theatrical gang, and the opera singers, and some of the dancers, a Broadway crowd sort of, way down, downtown though. And that was his hang-out. Probably down around Broadway and Third St., I think it was.

There he'd meet his friends, there he'd sit around and try to pick up people I guess or he'd write his articles. He was very naive at first. A young guy, he started out writing temperance novels and editing the *Brooklyn Eagle*, or some such newspaper from Brooklyn. Then, something happened to him in his thirties, about thirty-four, well, you know, crucifixion time, he realized he was going to die some day maybe, or that America was weird, or that he was weird, or maybe some kind of breakthrough of personal affection, maybe some kind of gay lib thing, anyway, he discovered his own mind and his own enthusiasm, his own expansiveness is the thing. The fact that his mind was so expansive that it was completely penitent. That it penetrated through curiosity and inquisitiveness into every crevasse and nook, every tree, bowl, every vagina, every anus, every mouth, every flower stamen, every exhaust pipe, every horse's ear and behind that he met, penetrated through the clouds; notice he wandered, he thought a lot, he wandered in his mind and he wasn't ashamed of what he thought.

So, Whitman was probably the first person in America who was not ashamed of the fact that he thought things that were as big as the universe. Or that were equal to the universe, or that fitted the universe. He wasn't ashamed of his mind or his body. So he wrote "Song of Myself," and it began tipping off where he was coming from and where he was going, saying that you, too, needn't be ashamed of your thoughts:

I celebrate myself, and sing myself,
And what I assume you shall assume,
For every atom belonging to me as good belongs to you.
I loafe and invite my soul,
I lean and loafe at my ease observing a spear of summer grass.

My tongue, every atom of my blood, form'd from this soil, this
    air,
Born here of parents born here from parents the same, and
    their parents the same,
I, now thirty-seven years old in perfect health begin,
Hoping to cease not till death.
Creeds and schools in abeyance,
Retiring back a while sufficed at what they are, but never
    forgotten,
I harbor for good or bad, I permit to speak at every hazard,
Nature without check with original energy.

Wow, what a thing to do!

So that's nineteenth century, and he's threatening to speak nature without check, with original energy. Well, who's willing to pick that one up? What does that mean, anyway? Means, born here from parents the same, so you can't accuse him of being un-American, he's 4th, 5th, 6th generation so he can say whatever he wants, on his own soil, on his own land, nobody can intimidate him, nobody can say "You didn't think that thought how dare you make up a thought like that and say you thought it." He just said what he actually thought.

So, Part 2 of "Song of Myself," going on with his original mind that he is presenting, and then he looks out at the drawing rooms of Brooklyn and lower Manhattan and the rich of his day, and the sophisticated culture of his day, and he sees that it's pretty shallow:

Houses and rooms are full of perfumes, the shelves are
    crowded with perfumes,
I breathe the fragrance myself and know it and like it,
The distillation would intoxicate me also, but I shall not let it.
The atmosphere is not a perfume, it has no taste of the
    distillation, it is odorless,
It is for my mouth forever, I am in love with it,
I will go to the bank by the wood and become undisguised and
    naked,
I am mad for it to be in contact with me.
The smoke of my own breath,
Echoes, ripples, buzz'd whispers, love-root, silk-thread, crotch
    and vine,

My respiration and inspiration, the beating of my heart, the
    passing of blood and air through my lungs,
The sniff of green leaves and dry leaves, and of the shore and
    dark-color'd sea-rocks, and of hay in the barn,
The sound of the belch'd words of my voice loos'd to the
    eddies of the wind,
A few light kisses, a few embraces, a reaching around of arms,
The play of shine and shade on the trees as the supple boughs
    wag,
The delight alone or in the rush of the streets, or along the
    fields and hill-sides,
The feeling of health, the full-noon trill, the song of me rising
    from bed and meeting the sun.
Have you reckon'd a thousand acres much? have you reckon'd
    the earth much?
Have you practis'd so long to learn to read?
Have you felt so proud to get at the meaning of poems?
Stop this day and night with me and you shall possess the
    origin of all poems,
You shall possess the good of the earth and sun, (there are
    millions of suns left,)
You shall no longer take things at second or third hand, nor
    look through the eyes of the dead, nor feed on the spectres
    in books,
You shall not look through my eyes either, nor take things from
    me,
You shall listen to all sides and filter them from your self.

So, what he's done here is he has completely possessed his own body,
he's gone over and realized he's breathing, that his heart is beating, that
he has roots that go from his crotch to his brain, he begins to sniff
around him and extend his thought around him to the sea, to the woods,
to the cities, recognizes his emotions, going all the way out to the millions of suns, then realizing that most of the time he and most everybody
else is taking things second- and third-hand from television, from *Time,
Newsweek, New York Times,* from the *Boulder Camera,* from the *Denver Post,*
from the *Minneapolis Star,* from the *Durham Gazette,* from the *Raleigh News
of the Dead,* from *Las Vegas Sporting Spectator,* from the *Manhattan Morbid
Chronicle,* but who actually looks out of their own eyes and sees the revo-

lutions in the trees in the fall or the bursting forth of tiny revolutions with each grass blade? Well, Whitman looked that way and recommended that everybody else look at the actual world around them rather than the abstract world they read about in the newspapers or saw as a pseudo-image/event, screened dots on television: "You shall listen to all sides and filter them from your self."

So, then what is he going to do now? What is he going to say next about where we all come from, where we are going?

> I have heard what the talkers were talking, the talk of the
>   beginning and the end,
> But I do not talk of the beginning or the end.
> There was never any more inception than there is now,
> Nor any more youth or age than there is now,
> And will never be any more perfection than there is now,
> Nor any more heaven or hell than there is now.

That's a great statement, very similar to what some of the Eastern, Oriental meditators, transcendentalists, or grounded Buddhists might say. Their notion is the unborn, that is to say, everything is here already, it wasn't born a billion years ago and slowly developed, it isn't going to be dead a billion years from now and slowly undevelop, it's just here, like a flower in the air. There's never going to be any more hell than there is now and never be any more understanding of heaven than there is right now in our own minds, with our own perception. So that means you can't postpone your acceptation and realization, you can't scream at your own eyes now, you've got to look out through your own eyes as Whitman said, hear with your own ears, smell with your own nose, touch with your own touch, fingers, taste with your own tongue, and be satisfied.

> I am satisfied—I see, dance, laugh, sing;
> As the hugging and loving bed-fellow sleeps at my side through
>   the night, and withdraws at the peep of the day with stealthy
>   tread,
> Leaving me baskets cover'd with white towels swelling the
>   house with their plenty,
> Shall I postpone my acceptation and realization and scream at
>   my eyes,

That they turn from gazing after and down the road,
And forthwith cipher and show me to a cent,
Exactly the value of one and exactly the value of two, and
    which is ahead?

So he's not interested in that kind of invidious comparison and competition. In the midst of "Song of Myself" he does come to a statement of what is the very nature of the mind, what is the nature of the human mind, his mind as he observed it in himself and when the mind is most open, most expanded, most realized, what relation is there between human beings and between man and nature. So I'll just read these little epiphanous moments showing, for one thing, his meditative view, this is the fourth part of "Song of Myself," and then an epiphany or ecstatic experience that he had. First of all, does he doubt himself? So, he says:

Trippers and askers surround me,
People I meet, the effect upon me of my early life or the ward
    and city I live in, or the nation,
The latest dates, discoveries, inventions, societies, authors old
    and new,
My dinner, dress, associates, looks, compliments, dues,
The real or fancied indifference of some man or woman I love,
The sickness of one of my folks or of myself, or ill-doing or loss
    or lack of money, or depressions or exaltations,
Battles, the horrors of fratricidal war, the fever of doubtful
    news, the fitful events;
These come to me days and nights and go from me again,
But they are not the Me myself.
Apart from the pulling and hauling stands what I am,
Stands amused, complacent, compassionating, idle, unitary,
Looks down, is erect, or bends an arm on an impalpable
    certain rest,
Looking with side-curved head curious what will come next,
Both in and out of the game and watching and wondering at it.
Backward I see in my own days where I sweated through fog
    with linguists and contenders,
I have no mockings or arguments, I witness and wait.

Now that's a real classical viewpoint, the last poet to really announce that was John Keats, who said he had a little idea about what made Shakespeare great. He said that was "negative capability." Which is to say, the possibility of seeing contending parties, seeing the Communists and Capitalists scream at each other, or the Buddhists and non-Buddhists, or the Muslims and Christians, or the Jews and the Arabs, or the self and the not-self, or your mommy and daddy, or yourself and your wife, or your baby and yourself. You can see them all screaming at each other, and you can see as a kind of comedic drama that you don't get tangled and lost in it, you don't enter into the daydream fantasy of being right and being one side or the other so completely that you go out and chop somebody's head off. Instead you just sort of watch yourself, you watch them in and out of the game at the same time, both in and out of the game, watching and wondering at it. That is to say, the ability to have contrary ideas in your head at the same time without it freaking out, without "an irritable reaching out after fact" or conclusions. Without an irritable reaching out. Naturally, you reach out and want to know more, but you don't get mad, crazed, say "I gotta know the answer, there is one answer and I, me, I have to have the one answer, me, my answer, me, answer." Well, you don't have to go through all that. Because maybe you don't know the answer, maybe there is no answer, maybe the question has no answer, maybe there is not even a question, though there may be perturbation and conflict. So, you could apply that, say, to the present Cold War situation where everyone wants to destroy the world in order to win victory over the Wrong (either side). Here, "apart from the pulling and hauling stands what I am," which is actually what we are, in the sense of nobody really believes all the stuff they talk, you know, you say it to hear what it sounds like most of the time. Even Whitman, I think, is just saying to hear what it sounds like because it's sort of the sound you might make when you're talking more frankly to yourself, or to friends. "Apart from the pulling and hauling stands what I am / Stands amused, complacent, compassionating," compassionating because both sides are right, and they don't even know it, both sides are wrong and they don't even know it. "Idle," he's not going to act on it, he's going to observe it, maybe go fry an egg. "Unitary," unitary is one thing, it is not divided up into this half of me is right and this half of me is wrong. "Looks down," well, you have to be looking down. "Is erect," straightens up, "bends an arm on an impalpable certain rest," maybe puts his arm down on the library desk, and thinks a little bit more, or spaces out. "Looking with side-curved head curious what will come next," come next out of his own mind he means or who will come into the door of the library. What plane, or when Mt. St. Helens will explode. Both in and out of the game, watching and wondering at it which is the best we can do actually. The best thing we can do is wonder at everything, it's so amazing. So, then what happens? If you take that attitude and open yourself up and allow yourself to admit everything, to hear everything, not to exclude, just be like the moon in the old Japanese haiku: "The autumn moon / shines kindly / on the flower-thief," or like Whitman's sun which shines on the common prostitute in his poem "To A Common Prostitute"—"Not till the sun excludes you do I exclude you." His mind is there, he's aware of her, she's aware of him and everybody's sitting around and internally scratching their head. So there is an epiphany out of this, or a rise, or a kind of exquisite awareness that intensifies.

Part 5 of "Song of Myself":

I believe in you my soul, the other I am must not abase itself to
   you,
And you must not be abased to the other.
Loafe with me on the grass, loose the stop from your throat,
Not words, not music or rhyme I want, not custom or lecture,
   not even the best,
Only the lull I like, the hum of your valvèd voice.
I mind how once we lay such a transparent summer morning,
How you settled your head athwart my hips and gently turn'd
   over upon me,
And parted the shirt from my bosom-bone, and plunged your
   tongue to my bare-stript heart,
And reach'd till you felt my beard, and reach'd till you held my
   feet.
Swiftly arose and spread around me the peace and knowledge
   that pass all the argument of the earth,
And I know that the hand of God is the promise of my own,
And I know that the spirit of God is the brother of my own,
And that all the men ever born are also my brothers, and the
   women my sisters and lovers,
And that a kelson of the creation is love,

And limitless are leaves stiff or drooping in the fields,
And brown ants in the little wells beneath them,
And mossy scabs of the worm fence, heap'd stones, elder,
   mullein and poke-weed.

So just out of that one experience of a touch with another person, of complete acceptance, his awareness spread throughout the space around him and he realized that that friendly touch, that friendly awareness was what bound the entire universe together and held everything suspended in gravity.

So given that, where could he go from here? Well, a long survey of America, which he did in "Song of Myself," in which he extended his own awareness to cover the entire basic spiritual awareness of America, trying to make an ideal America which would be an America of comradely awareness, acknowledgment of tenderness, acknowledgment of gentleness, acknowledgment of comradeship, acknowledgment of what he called adhesiveness. Because what he said was that if this country did not have some glue to keep people together, to bind them together, adhesiveness, some emotional bond, there was no possibility of democracy working, and we'd just be a lot of separate people fighting for advantage, military advantage, commercial advantage, iron advantage, coal advantage, silver advantage, gold, hunting up some kind of monopoly on molybdenum. On the other hand, there was a total democracy of feeling around, so in Part 11 of "Song of Myself":

Twenty-eight young men bathe by the shore,
Twenty-eight young men and all so friendly;
Twenty-eight years of womanly life, and all so lonesome.
She owns the fine house by the rise of the bank,
She hides handsome and richly drest aft the blinds of the window.
Which of the young men does she like the best?
Ah the homeliest of them is beautiful to her.
Where are you off to lady? for I see you,
You splash in the water there, yet stay stock still in your room.
Dancing and laughing along the beach came the twenty-ninth
   bather,
The rest did not see her, but she saw them and loved them.
The beards of the young men glisten'd with wet, it ran from
   their long hair,

Little streams pass'd all over their bodies.
An unseen hand also pass'd over their bodies,
It descended tremblingly from their temples and ribs.
The young men float on their backs, their white bellies bulge
  to the sun, they do not ask who seizes fast to them,
They do not know who puffs and declines with pendant and
  bending arch,
They do not think whom they souse with spray.

He pointed out the longing for closeness; erotic tenderness is of course implicit here, his own as well as in empathy, the spinster lady behind her curtains looking at the naked bathers. He pointed to that as basic to our bodies, basic to our minds, basic to our community, basic to our sociability, basic to our society, therefore basic to our politics. If that quality of compassion, erotic longing, tenderness, gentleness, was squelched, repressed, pushed back, denied, insulted, mocked, seen cynically, then the entire operation of democracy would be squelched, debased, mocked, seen cynically, made into a paranoid, mechano-megalopolis congregation of freaks afeard of each other. Because that may have been the very nature of the industrial civilization, that by the very roboting of work and homogenization of talk and imagery, unlike Whitman, people not speaking for themselves but talking falsely, as if they represented anything but themselves, like as if a President could represent anybody but his own mind, then there was going to be trouble. So, at one point he says human society is kind of messed up; so, Part 32 of "Song of Myself,"

I think I could turn, and live with animals, they are so placid
  and self-contain'd,
I stand and look at them long and long.
They do not sweat and whine about their condition,
They do not lie awake in the dark and weep for their sins,
They do not make me sick discussing their duty to God,
Not one is dissatisfied, not one is demented with the mania of
  owning things,
Not one kneels to another, nor to his kind that lived thousands
  of years ago,
Not one is respectable or unhappy over the whole earth.

Not one animal is respectable, in all of creation. All these human beings want to be respectable, but he's pointing out that not one elephant in Africa would ever dream of considering himself respectable.

So they show their relations to me and I accept them,
They bring me tokens of myself, they evince them plainly in
   their possession.

Then, what does he do in the city? He's lonesome, so there's a little one-line description of himself in the city, "Looking in at the shop-windows of Broadway the whole forenoon, flatting the flesh of my nose on the thick plate-glass." But then, also he can get out in his mind: "I go hunting polar furs and the seal, leaping chasms with a pike-pointed staff, clinging to topples of brittle and blue." He empathizes with everybody: "I am an old artillerist, I tell of my fort's bombardment, / I am there again." And in Part 34: "Now I tell what I knew in Texas in my early youth," and then he goes on with a long anecdote. Or, Part 35: "Would you hear of an old-time sea-fight," and he went on and on to that, telling about old-time sea-fights, and "Toward twelve there in the beams of the moon they surrender to us,"—the moony imagination. Then, maybe he's a sea fighter, or he's an Arctic explorer, or maybe he's a jerk. Part 37: "You laggards there on guard! look to your arms! / In at the conquer'd doors they crowd! I am posses'd!" He wasn't afraid of that, see: "Askers embody themselves in me and I am embodied in them, / I project my hat, sit shame-faced, and beg." That's like Bob Dylan in his film *Renaldo and Clara*, walking down the street and all of a sudden the camera catches him and stares him in the eye and he stares the camera in the eye and all of a sudden he shivers and puts out his right hand held by his left palm out, "Some change? Spare change of love? Spare change?" And so you have,

Enough! enough! enough!
Somehow I have been stunn'd. Stand back!
Give me a little time beyond my cuff'd head, slumbers, dreams,
   gaping,
I discover myself on the verge of a usual mistake.
That I could forget the mockers and insults!
That I could forget the trickling tears and the blows of the
   bludgeons and hammers!

That I could look with a separate look on my own crucifixion
and bloody crowning!

Ah, so he has suffered a bit here, he does empathize with all the beggars, the monstrous convicts with sweat twitching on their lips, but his
point here is that everybody so suffers, everybody is everybody else, in
the sense of having experienced in imagination or in real life all of the
non-respectable emotions of the elephants and the ants. So he says,

I am an acme of things accomplish'd, and I an encloser of
    things to be.
My feet strike an apex of the apices of the stairs,
On every step bunches of ages, and larger bunches between
    the steps,
All below duly travel'd, and still I mount and mount.
Rise after rise bow the phantoms behind me,
Afar down I see the huge first Nothing, I know I was even
    there,
I waited unseen and always, and slept through the lethargic
    mist,
And took my time, and took no hurt from the fetid carbon.
Long I was hugg'd close—long and long.
Immense have been the preparations for me.
Faithful and friendly the arms that have help'd me.
Cycles ferried my cradle, rowing and rowing like cheerful
    boatmen,
For room to me stars kept aside in their own rings,
They sent influences to look after what was to hold me.
Before I was born out of my mother generations guided me,
My embryo has never been torpid, nothing could overlay it.
For it the nebula cohered to an orb,
The long slow strata piled to rest it on,
Vast vegetables gave it sustenance,
Monstrous sauroids transported it in their mouths and
    deposited it with care.
All forces have been steadily employ'd to complete and delight
    me,
Now on this spot I stand with my robust soul.

So that's great, so he's here, he recognizes he's here:

My rendezvous is appointed, it is certain,
The Lord will be there and wait till I come on perfect terms,
The great Camerado, the lover true for whom I pine will be
    there.

So he says:

I have no chair, no church, no philosophy,
I lead no man to a dinner-table, library, exchange,
But each man and each woman of you I lead upon a knoll,
My left hand hooking you round the waist,
My right hand pointing to landscapes of continents and the
    public road.
Not I, not any one else can travel that road for you,
You must travel it for yourself.
It is not far, it is within reach,
Perhaps you have been on it since you were born and did not
    know,
Perhaps it is everywhere on water and on land.
Shoulder your duds dear son, and I will mine, and let us hasten
    forth,
Wonderful cities and free nations we shall fetch as we go.
If you tire, give me both burdens, and rest the chuff of your
    hand on my hip,
And in due time you shall repay the same service to me,
for after we start we never lie by again.

On the road, Walt Whitman, 1883 probably, prophesying what would
happen to America 100 years later.

So he comes to his conclusions at the end of the poem. He wants to
tell finally what he can get out of it all. Part 50 of "Song of Myself,"
approaching the end of the poem:

There is that in me—I do not know what it is—but I know it is
    in me.
Wrench'd and sweaty—calm and cool then my body becomes,

I sleep—I sleep long.

I do not know it—it is without name—it is a word unsaid,

It is not in any dictionary, utterance, symbol.

Something it swings on more than the earth I swing on,

To it the creation is the friend whose embracing awakes me.

Perhaps I might tell more. Outlines! I plead for my brothers
and sisters.

Do you see O my brothers and sisters?

It is not chaos or death—it is form, union, plan—it is eternal
life—it is Happiness.

And Part 51:

The past and present wilt—I have fill'd them, emptied them,

And proceed to fill my next fold of the future.

Listener up there! what have you to confide to me?

Look in my face while I snuff the sidle of evening,

(Talk honestly, no one else hears you, and I stay only a minute
longer.)

Do I contradict myself?

Very well then I contradict myself,

(I am large, I contain multitudes.)

I concentrate toward them that are nigh, I wait on the door-
slab.

Who has done his day's work? who will soonest be through with
his supper?

Who wishes to walk with me?

Will you speak before I am gone? will you prove already too
late?

Finally, Part 52, the last section, he'll make his last prophecy, dissolve himself into you the listener, the reader, and his poem will become a part of your consciousness:

The spotted hawk swoops by and accuses me, he complains of
my gab and my loitering.

I too am not a bit tamed, I too am untranslatable,

I sound my barbaric yawp over the roofs of the world.

The last scud of day holds back for me,
It flings my likeness after the rest and true as any on the
    shadow'd wilds,
It coaxes me to the vapor and the dusk.
I depart as air, I shake my white locks at the runaway sun,
I effuse my flesh in eddies, and drift it in lacy jags.
I bequeath myself to the dirt to grow from the grass I love,
If you want me again look for me under your boot-soles.
You will hardly know who I am or what I mean,
But I shall be good health to you nevertheless,
and filter and fibre your blood.
Failing to fetch me at first keep encouraged,
Missing me one place search another,
I stop somewhere waiting for you.

That's a very tearful, deep promise, "I stop somewhere waiting for you," so he's going to wait a long, long, long time, and have to go through a great deal of his own loves and fears before he actually finds a companion. What kind of companion does he want, what does he look for? "The expression of the face balks account . . ." and this is in the poem called "I Sing the Body Electric," in which he begins to describe his own body and other peoples' bodies in an intimate way, numbering all the parts, numbering all the emotions, and naming them and actually attempting to account, and give an accounting and itemization of all men. There is a little four or five lines of, just about, well, what does he look for?

The expression of the face balks account,
But the expression of a well-made man appears not only in his
    face,
It is in his limbs and joints also, it is curiously in the joints of
    his hips and wrists,
It is in his walk, the carriage of his neck, the flex of his waist
    and knees, dress does not hide him,
The strong sweet quality he has strikes through the cotton and
    broadcloth,
To see him pass conveys as much as the best poem, perhaps
    more,

You linger to see his back, and the back of his neck and
shoulder-side.

Well, everybody's done that, man or woman to each other, who is
interesting, who's got something going there. "Spontaneous me," he
says, and so he keeps walking around, "has native moments."
Finally he has a little short poem, "Native Moments," actually, defining what they are, when some authentic flash comes to him:

Native moments—when you come upon me—ah you are here
now,
Give me now libidinous joys only,
Give me the drench of my passions, give me life coarse and
rank,
To-day I go consort with Nature's darlings, to-night too,
I am for those who believe in loose delights, I share the
midnight orgies of young men,
I dance with the dancers and drink with the drinkers,
The echoes ring with our indecent calls, I pick out some low
person for my dearest friend,
He shall be lawless, rude, illiterate, he shall be one condemned
by others for deeds done,
I will play a part no longer, why should I exile myself from my
companions?
O you shunn'd persons, I at least do not shun you,
I come forthwith in your midst, I will be your poet,
I will be more to you than to any of the rest.

Well he is really declaring himself, declaring his own feelings, he's not
scared of them, like born for the first time in the world, recognizing his
own nature, recognizing the world. The last of the poems in the first part
of *Leaves of Grass* is "As Adam Early in the Morning":

As Adam early in the morning,
Walking forth from the bower refresh'd with sleep,
Behold me where I pass, hear my voice, approach,
Touch me, touch the palm of your hand to my body as I pass,
Be not afraid of my body.

Well, there is some false note there I guess, he really wants someone to love him, and he's not quite able to say it right. Still he does want to make democracy something that hangs together using the force of Eros, so, "For You O Democracy," in the "Calamus" section of *Leaves of Grass*:

Come, I will make the continent indissoluble,
I will make the most splendid race the sun ever shone upon,
I will make divine magnetic lands,
    With the love of comrades,
    With the life-long love of comrades.

Beatles, Rolling Stones, beatniks, the life-long love of comrades,

I will plant companionship thick as trees along all the rivers of
    America, and along the shores of the great lakes, and all
    over
    the prairies,
I will make inseparable cities with their arms about each
    other's necks,
    By the love of comrades,
    By the manly love of comrades,
For you these from me, O Democracy, to serve you ma femme!
For you, for you, I am trilling these songs.

Well, that's his statement of politics, actually, and, however, you never can tell, maybe he's just a big fairy egotist.

He's got a little poem "Are You the New Person Drawn toward Me?" in the "Calamus" section of *Leaves of Grass*, "Calamus," that is a section of *Leaves of Grass*; calamus has a forked root, oddly enough, it is a marsh plant, calamus grows, lives in marshes in the northeast, around Manhattan, in the old days on Long Island up near Cherry Valley³ where I live in the bogs. It has a somewhat manlike forked root.

The "Calamus" section of *Leaves of Grass* was that describing erotic pleasure and parts of the body, which when Whitman sent them to Ralph Waldo Emerson shocked the elder American prophet Emerson a bit, and he suggested that Whitman leave it out when he published the book because it was perhaps that people were not ready for it, America was not ready for it. Whitman, however, persisted and felt that that was an integral part of his message that if he was going to talk about honesty and frankness and openness and comradeship he did have to say the un-sayable, did have to talk about the people's bodies, did have to describe them with beauty and Greek levity and healthiness and hero-ism. So he did have to make heroes out of our private parts. So "Calamus" does include that but it's actually, nowadays reading, very tame. However, because he was so intent on his purpose, he was a little worried.

> Are you the new person drawn toward me?
> To begin with take warning, I am surely far different from what
>   you suppose;
> Do you suppose you will find in me your ideal?
> Do you think it is so easy to have me become your lover?
> Do you think the friendship of me would be unalloy'd
>   satisfaction?
> Do you think I am trusty and faithful?
> Do you see no further than this facade, this smooth and
>   tolerant manner of me?
> Do you suppose yourself advancing on real ground toward a
>   real heroic man?
> Have you no thought O dreamer that it may be all maya,
>   illusion?

I guess he's talking to himself. However, he's willing to trust his senses. So he says,

> Behold this swarthy face, these gray eyes,
> This beard, the white wool unclipt upon my neck,
> My brown hands and the silent manner of me without charm;
> Yet comes one a Manhattanese and ever at parting kisses me
>   lightly on the lips with robust love,
> And I on the crossing of the street or on the ship's deck give a
>   kiss in return,
> We observe that salute of American comrades land and sea,
> We are those two natural and nonchalant persons.

Okay, so he's proposing that the dear love of comrades and the unabashed affection between citizens be acknowledged as it stands rather than mocked. And then, of course, not to get people upset, so:

> I hear it was charged against me that I sought to destroy
> institutions;
> But really I am neither for nor against institutions,
> (What indeed have I in common with them? or what with the
> destruction of them?)
> Only I will establish in the Mannahatta and in every city of
> these States inland and seaboard,
> And in the fields and woods, and above every keel little or large
> that dents the water,
> Without edifices or rules or trustees or any argument,
> The institution of the dear love of comrades.

And that includes like the prairie grass everyone equal, so that there are ". . . those that look carelessly in the faces of Presidents and governors, as to say *Who are you?*" that's a little line from a poem called "The Prairie-Grass Dividing." So what's the big thrill like our big thrill nowadays? Well, here's my big thrill, here's Whitman's big thrill:

> A glimpse through an interstice caught,
> Of a crowd of workmen and drivers in a bar-room around the
> stove late of a winter night, and I unremark'd seated in a
> corner,
> Of a youth who loves me and whom I love, silently approaching
> and seating himself near, that he may hold me by the hand,
> A long while amid the noises coming and going, of drinking
> and oath and smutty jest,
> There we two, content, happy in being together, speaking little,
> perhaps not a word.

So that's a recognizable emotion between friends.
But there may be things that he doesn't want to say even, so he says:

> Earth, my likeness,
> Though you look so impassive, ample and spheric there,

I now suspect that is not all;
I now suspect there is something fierce in you eligible to burst
    forth,
For an athlete is enamour'd of me, and I of him,
But toward him there is something fierce and terrible in me
    eligible to burst forth,
I dare not tell it in words, not even in these songs.

So there's more to come and it'll come out of Whitman as he goes forward in his life, renouncing all formulas ". . . O bat-eyed and materialistic priests," (that's from "Song of the Open Road").

His next long poem is called "Salut au Monde!," saying, "Come on, let's go out, let's explore life, let's find out what's going on here. Let's look at the tents of the Kalmucks and the Baskirs, let's go out and see the African and Asiatic towns, go to the Ganges, let's go to the groves of Mona where the Druids walked and see the bodies of the gods and wait at Liverpool and Glasgow and Dublin and Marseilles, wait at Valparaiso, Panama, sail on the waters of Hindustan, the China Sea, all the way around the world, on the road." So it began:

O take my hand Walt Whitman!
Such gliding wonders! such sights and sounds!
Such join'd unended links, each hook'd to the next,
Each answering all, each sharing the earth with all.

—he's going to guide everybody around the world, spiritual trip around the world, like fuck in bed, but it will be in the spirit.

Then there's this very famous poem where he realizes, yeah, sure, but all that's transitory, it's going, there's not much, you know, like 20 years, 50 years, 70 years; then zap it's gone. So there is this great poem, in the middle of Manhattan looking over at Brooklyn on the Brooklyn ferry, called "Crossing Brooklyn Ferry," realizing, okay, he's had these feelings, everybody has these kinds of feelings, everybody rarely has the chance to experience them, much less say them aloud, much less propose them as politics, much less offer to save the nation with feeling and at the same time it's in the appearances of life even though it was very rare for people to understand that, except that at the deepest moment of their life they do understand that. And, looking at the vast apparition of

Manhattan and the masts of ships around it and the sunset and the sea-gulls, what more does he have to ask than the immensity of universe around him and the river on which he's riding and the feelings which he's aware of and the ability he has to call these feelings out to other people from his time to the future. He says:

We understand then do we not?
What I promis'd without mentioning it, have you not accepted?
What the study could not teach—what the preaching could not
    accomplish is accomplish'd, is it not?
Flow on, river! flow with the flood-tide, and ebb with the ebb-
    tide!
Frolic on, crested and scallop-edg'd waves!
Gorgeous clouds of the sunset! drench with your splendor me,
    or the men and women generations after me!
Cross from shore to shore, countless crowds of passengers!
Stand up, tall masts of Mannahatta! stand up, beautiful hills of
    Brooklyn!
Throb, baffled and curious brain! throw out questions and
    answers!
Suspend here and everywhere, eternal float of solution!
Gaze, loving and thirsting eyes, in the house or street or public
    assembly!
Sound out, voices of young men! loudly and musically call me
    by my nighest name!
Live, old life! play the part that looks back on the actor or
    actress!
Play the old role, the role that is great or small according as
    one makes it!
Consider, you who peruse me, whether I may not in unknown
    ways be looking upon you;
Be firm, rail over the river, to support those who lean idly, yet
    haste with the hasting current;
Fly on, sea-birds! fly sideways, or wheel in large circles high in
    the air,
Receive the summer sky, you water, and faithfully hold it till all
    downcast eyes have time to take it from you!
Diverge, fine spokes of light, from the shape of my head, or
    any one's head, in the sunlit water!

Come on, ships from the lower bay! pass up or down, white-
    sail'd schooners, sloops, lighters!
Flaunt away, flags of all nations! be duly lower'd at sunset!
Burn high your fires, foundry chimneys! cast black shadows at
    nightfall! cast red and yellow light over the tops of the houses!
Appearances, now or henceforth, indicate what you are,
You necessary film, continue to envelop the soul,
About my body for me, and your body for you, be hung our
    divinest aromas,
Thrive, cities—bring your freight, bring your shows, ample and
    sufficient rivers,
Expand, being than which none else is perhaps more spiritual,
Keep your places, objects than which none else is more lasting.

That's very subtle, you see from the sunshine halo, aureole, aura
around the hair in the sunshine reflected in the water. He's even noticing, his noticing is so exquisite and ethereal and fine that he's got massive masts of the aureole of the light of the sun reflected shining in water
and reflected in people's hair around him.

You have waited, you always wait, you dumb, beautiful
    ministers,
We receive you with free sense at last, and are insatiate
    henceforward,
Not you any more shall be able to foil us, or withhold
    yourselves from us,
We use you, and do not cast you aside—we plant you
    permanently within us,
We fathom you not—we love you—there is perfection in you
    also,
You furnish your parts toward eternity,
Great or small, you furnish your parts toward the soul.

He needs from that, after "Crossing Brooklyn Ferry," he needs someone to answer him, so his next long poem is "Song of the Answerer," in
which he imagines the answerer, he is the answerer, what can be
answered he answers and what cannot be answered he shows how it cannot be answered and that goes on and on and on and praises the words
of true poems of the true poets which do not merely please:

> The true poets are not followers of beauty but the august
>   masters of beauty;
> The greatness of sons is the exuding of the greatness of
>   mothers and fathers,
> The words of true poems are the tuft and final applause of
>   science.

Well, he'll go on and then there's a great tragedy coming up ahead. He's passed through California and he's written about lonesome Kansas and he's written about birds of passage and a song of the rolling earth and he's written about the ocean and then back to his birthplace in Long Island looking at the city, a vision of birth continuous and death continuous. Again, sort of an ecstatic acknowledgment of the continuity of feeling from generation to generation as the continuity of birth that no matter what the appearances, there always is a rebirth of delight, of feeling of acknowledgment, of the spaciousness of glittery sunlight on the ocean. And that's the famous poem "Sea-Drift: Out of the Cradle Endlessly Rocking"

> Out of the cradle endlessly rocking,
> Out of the mocking-bird's throat, the musical shuttle,
> Out of the Ninth-month midnight,
> Over the sterile sands and the fields beyond, where the child
>   leaving his bed wander'd alone, bareheaded, barefoot,
> Down from the shower'd halo,
> Up from the mystic play of shadows twining and twisting as if
>   they were alive,
> Out from the patches of briers and blackberries,
> From the memories of the bird that chanted to me,
> From your memories sad brother, from the fitful risings and
>   fallings I heard,
> From under that yellow half-moon late-risen and swollen as if
>   with tears,
> From those beginning notes of yearning and love there in the
>   mist,
> From the thousand responses of my heart never to cease,
> From the myriad thence-arous'd words,
> From the word stronger and more delicious than any,
> From such as now they start the scene revisiting,

As a flock, twittering, rising, or overhead passing,
Borne hither, ere all eludes me, hurriedly,
A man, yet by these tears a little boy again,
Throwing myself on the sand, confronting the waves,
I, chanter of pains and joys, uniter of here and hereafter,
Taking all hints to use them, but swiftly leaping beyond them,
A reminiscence sing.

Of course, the form there is a classical form: "Of Man's First Disobedience, and the Fruit / Of that Forbidden Tree, whose mortal taste / Brought Death into the World, and all our woe . . . Sing Heav'nly Muse," that's John Milton's opening of *Paradise Lost*. Or the opening of Homer's *Iliad*: "Sing O goddess of the wrath of Achilles, Peleus' son, the ruinous wrath that brought down countless woes upon the heads of the Achaeans and sent many brave souls hurrying down to Hades and many a hero left for prey to dogs and vultures . . ." or something like that. Again, in that same long, long, long breath of realization that ends with an accomplished trumpet call, almost to sing the personal, I mean, ". . . a reminiscence sing," and then it's a reminiscence of a whisper of death, when he was young at the oceanside. "Sea-Drift," "Tears," "On the Beach at Night Alone," "The World Below the Brine," "Song for All Seas, All Ships," those are some of the titles of the poems of that era—that was up until about 1854. Then, a few prophecies of the presidents, and some patriotic songs, and more awareness of the problems of America as it was going into the Civil War. Then, in the Civil War he himself following his instincts, followed the soldiers, went to Washington, worked in hospitals, took care of dying men, was out on the battlefields as a nurse and then in the hospitals in Washington, D.C. as a nurse, saw Abe Lincoln walking around Washington likely enough at 4 A.M.; as Whitman was walking around on his own mission of mercy or mercies of mission, he wrote a lot of poems, like "A Sight in Camp in the Daybreak Gray and Dim"—this is a little, say, a snapshot, the same theme of human divinity in the midst of the degradation of horror and war.

A sight in camp in the daybreak gray and dim,
As from my tent I emerge so early sleepless,
As slow I walk in the cool fresh air the path near by the hospital
    tent,

Three forms I see on stretchers lying, brought out there
    untended lying,
Over each the blanket spread, ample brownish woolen blanket,
Gray and heavy blanket, folding, covering all.

So, he worked as a wound-dresser, taking care of the wounds of the injured and the dying in the Civil War. Having the same delicate, emotional relationships with the people he met as:

O tan-faced prairie-boy,
Before you came to camp came many a welcome gift,
Praises and presents came and nourishing food, till at last
    among the recruits,
You came, taciturn, with nothing to give—we but look'd on
    each other,
When lo! more than all the gifts of the world you gave me.

Funny, his idea of America, "tan-faced prairie-boy," full of feeling and awareness, not at all a stereotyped television Barbie doll.

Then, in the midst of the tragedies of the war and the visions of death he had, the actual dying, memories of President Lincoln who was shot, and so his great old elegy for Lincoln, which most every kid in America knew back in the '20s and '30s, with its very beautiful description of the passing of Lincoln's coffin on railroad through lanes and streets, through the cities and through the states and with processions, seas of silence, seas of faces and unbared heads, the coffin of Lincoln mourned and in the middle of this poem a recognition of death in a way that had not been proposed in America before. Just as he had accepted the feelings of life, there was the appearance and feelings of death, the awareness of death that he had to tally finally. So there's this great italicized song in Part 14 of "When Lilacs Last in the Dooryard Bloom'd," from "Memories of President Lincoln."

Actually, the whole of "When Lilacs Last in the Dooryard Bloom'd" is so beautiful that it would be worth reading, but it's so long that I can't do it and also it's so beautiful that I'm afraid I'll cry if I read it. "When Lilacs Last in the Dooryard Bloom'd,"—which is a very interesting title because I visited Whitman's house in Camden, New Jersey, and in the back yard in the old brick house on Mickle Street where he lived the last years of his life, though not likely where he wrote this poem, there were lilacs blooming in the back yard, blooming by the outhouse which was right outside the back door in the garden.

1

When lilacs last in the dooryard bloom'd,
And the great star early droop'd in the western sky in the
    night,
I mourn'd, and yet shall mourn with ever-returning spring.
Ever-returning spring, trinity sure to me you bring,
Lilac blooming perennial and drooping star in the west,
And thought of him I love.

2

O powerful western fallen star!
O shades of night—O moody, tearful night!
O great star disappear'd—O the black murk that hides the
    star!
O cruel hands that hold me powerless—O helpless soul of me!
O harsh surrounding cloud that will not free my soul.

3

In the dooryard fronting an old farm-house near the white-
    wash'd palings,
Stands the lilac-bush tall-growing with heart-shaped leaves of
    rich green,
With many a pointed blossom rising delicate, with the perfume
    strong I love,
With every leaf a miracle—and from this bush in the dooryard,
With delicate-color'd blossoms and heart-shaped leaves of rich
    green,
A sprig with its flower I break.

5

Over the breast of the spring, the land, amid cities,
Amid lanes and through old woods, where lately the violets
    peep'd from the ground, spotting the gray debris,
Amid the grass in the fields each side of the lanes, passing the
    endless grass,

Passing the yellow-spear'd wheat, every grain from its shroud in
    the dark-brown fields uprisen,
Passing the apple-tree blows of white and pink in the orchards,
Carrying a corpse to where it shall rest in the grave,
Night and day journeys a coffin.

6
Coffin that passes through lanes and streets,
Through day and night with the great cloud darkening the
    land,
With the pomp of the inloop'd flags with the cities draped in
    black,
With the show of the States themselves as of crape-veil'd
    women standing,
With processions long and winding and the flambeaus of the
    night,
With the countless torches lit, with the silent sea of faces and
    the unbared head,
With the waiting depot, the arriving coffin, and the sombre
    faces,
With dirges through the night, with the thousand voices rising
    strong and solemn,
With all the mournful voices of the dirges pour'd around the
    coffin,
The dim-lit churches and the shuddering organs—where amid
    these you journey,
With the tolling tolling bells' perpetual clang,
Here, coffin that slowly passes,
I give you my sprig of lilac.

[Hymn to Death]
Come lovely and soothing death,
Undulate round the world, serenely arriving, arriving,
In the day, in the night, to all, to each,
Sooner or later delicate death.
Prais'd be the fathomless universe,
For life and joy, and for objects and knowledge curious,
And for love, sweet love—but praise! praise! praise!
For the sure-enwinding arms of cool-enfolding death.

Dark mother always gliding near with soft feet,
Have none chanted for thee a chant of fullest welcome?
Then I chant it for thee, I glorify thee above all,
I bring thee a song that when thou must indeed come, come
     unfalteringly.
Approach strong deliveress,
When it is so, when thou hast taken them I joyously sing the dead,
Lost in the loving floating ocean of thee,
Laved in the flood of thy bliss O death.
From me to thee glad serenades,
Dances for thee I propose saluting thee, adornments and feastings for thee,
And the sights of the open landscape and the high-spread sky are
     fitting,
And life and the fields, and the huge and thoughtful night.
The night in silence under many a star,
The ocean shore and the husky whispering wave whose voice I know,
And the soul turning to thee O vast and well-veil'd death,
And the body gratefully nestling close to thee.
Over the tree-tops I float thee a song,
Over the rising and sinking waves, over the myriad fields and the
     prairies wide,
Over the dense-pack'd cities all and the teeming wharves and ways,
I float this carol with joy, with joy to thee O death.

Then Whitman grew older, traveled, extended his imagination to blue Ontario shore, began to see the declining of his own physical body in a series of poems called "Autumn Rivulets." He wrote about the compost, as Peter Orlovsky did a hundred years later. So Whitman wrote:

Behold this compost! behold it well!
Perhaps every mite has once form'd part of a sick person—yet
     behold!
The grass of spring covers the prairies,
The bean bursts noiselessly through the mould in the garden,
The delicate spear of the onion pierces upward,

So, after the carol to death there is a realization of the recycling in the compost, the recycling of soul, the recycling of body, the inevitability of passage, transitoriness, of things entering the earth and emerging from the earth, and he wrote poems about the city dead-house, too. So these were all autumn rivulets. He wrote his poem to the singer in prison, and "Outlines for a Tomb."

Incidentally, he took his own tomb at that point, made up a little drawing of a tomb for himself which he took from the opening page of William Blake's last great prophetic book, *Jerusalem*, of a man entering a stone, open door, stone pillars on each side, stone floor, stone arch, a triangular arch on top with a great stone door opened, a man carrying a great globe of light. A consciousness entering into this dark, he can't see what's in it, he's going in, passing through with a big black hat. Whitman designed this tomb for himself, which is now standing in Camden, New Jersey, in exactly the same image as the Blake. He wrote little poems to his own tomb then and to the negative and began to consider the negative, how do you recompost the negative?

So, the line I was quoting from "To a Common Prostitute," that line occurs here:

Be composed—be at ease with me—I am Walt Whitman,
   liberal and lusty as Nature,
Not till the sun excludes you do I exclude you,
Not till the waters refuse to glisten for you and the leaves to
   rustle for you, do my words refuse to glisten and rustle for
   you.
My girl I appoint with you an appointment, and I charge you
   that you make preparation to be worthy to meet me,
And I charge you that you be patient and perfect till I come.
Till then I salute you with a significant look that you do not
   forget me.

That's a good way to be kind to your neighbor, and to acknowledge the varying vocations.

He took a trip out to Kansas and wrote funny little poems about the encroaching civilization that was beginning to cover the prairies. There is a little tiny poem that I've quoted, "The Prairie States":

A newer garden of creation, no primal solitude,
Dense, joyous, modern, populous millions, cities and farms,
With iron interlaced, composite, tied, many in one,

By all the world contributed—freedom's and law's and thrift's
    society,
The crown and teeming paradise, so far, of time's
    accumulations,
To justify the past.

So that was ambitious and hopeful thought, he might have had some
change of mind if he saw Kansas during the Vietnam War, with army
bases and airplane bases and "iron interlaced" above the plains there,
horrific iron.

He wrote a great poem now beginning to go into a recognition of the
Orient and recognition of the ancient wisdoms of death that were understood there, that is, the acceptance of death as well as the acceptance of
life, seeing an identity between his own extended empathy and sympathy
and compassion, and the ancient empathies and sympathies and com-
passions of the meditators of the Himalayas.

There's a very interesting section in "Passage to India," interesting to
those of us who already made that passage ourselves, either mentally or
physically. Remember, in the nineteenth century lots and lots of poets
and philosophers in America were interested in transcendentalism and
oriental wisdom and Brahma and the Hindus and the romantic, glamorous wisdom of the East, the Brook Farm experiment, many people and
Bronson Alcott were interested in Western gnosticism, and Bronson
Alcott went to England to buy up the neo-Platonic and hermetic translations of Thomas Taylor, the Platonist, translations which were from
Greek Orphic mysteries and Dionysian mysteries, that were also read by
the great British transcendental mystic poets like Coleridge, Shelley,
William Blake, those same books were brought to Brook Farm and then
translations by Thomas Taylor of ancient hermetic Greek texts were circulated by Bronson Alcott to Emerson and to Thoreau and Hawthorne.
So there was this movement of transcendentalism and a recognition of
the exotic East, there was the opening of Japan around that time. There
was Lafcadio Hearn, maybe thirty years later, going to Japan and making
great collections of Japanese art to bring to Boston to impress the New
Englanders in the second wave of Oriental understanding thirty years
later, but even in Europe at that time, Japanese prints by Hiroshige were
circulating and were eyed by Gauguin and Van Gogh, who began imitating their flat surfaces and their bright colors. So, a whole new calligraphy

of the mind was beginning to be discovered by the West—in the same time that the West was peddling opium in China, oddly enough, that was the trade exchange, opium for meditation.

However, Whitman reflected that in "Passage to India":

Lo soul, the retrospect brought forward,
The old, most populous, wealthiest of earth's lands,
The streams of the Indus and the Ganges and their many
    affluents,
(I my shores of America walking to-day behold, resuming all,)
The tale of Alexander on his warlike marches suddenly dying,
On one side China and on the other side Persia and Arabia,
To the south the great seas and the bay of Bengal,
The flowing literatures, tremendous epics, religions, castes,
Old occult Brahma interminably far back, the tender and
    junior Buddha,
Central and southern empires and all their belongings,
    possessors,
The wars of Tamerlane, the reign of Aurungzebe,
The traders, ruler, explorers, Moslems, Venetians, Byzantium,
    the Arabs, Portuguese,
The first travelers famous yet, Marco Polo, Batouta the Moor,
Doubts to be solv'd, the map incognita, blanks to be fill'd,
The foot of man unstay'd, the hands never at rest,
Thyself O soul that will not brook a challenge.

So he acknowledged that transcendence, like D. H. Lawrence a hundred years later, wrote about the great ship of death that goes forward to explore: "O we can wait no longer, / We too take ship O soul, . . ." Talking about going through the soul as well as going through the world.

However he sees that most of the world is asleep, alas. So there's this long poem "The Sleepers." This is like middle age now, it's really getting deeper on him now and death is coming a bit into his mind as he gets into his 50s and 60s. Also the fact that most of the living on the world are the living dead or the sleepers:

I wander all night in my vision,
Stepping with light feet, swiftly and noiselessly stepping and
    stopping,

Bending with open eyes over the shut eyes of sleepers,
Wandering and confused, lost to myself, ill-assorted,
    contradictory,
Pausing, gazing, bending, and stopping.
How solemn they look there, stretch'd and still,
How quiet they breathe, the little children in their cradles.

Well, they all sleep, so he moves on, and says at the end of all these sleepers,

I too pass from the night,
I stay a while away O night, but I return to you again and love
    you.
Why should I be afraid to trust myself to you?
I am not afraid, I have been well brought forward by you,
I love the rich running day, but I do not desert her in whom I
    lay so long,
I know not how I came of you and I know not where I go with
    you but I know I came well and shall go well.
I will stop only a time with the night, and rise betimes,
I will duly pass the day O my mother, and duly return to you.

So he's now beginning to think of the future, what's going to happen to him.

Then the next set of poems in *Leaves of Grass* is called "Whispers of Heavenly Death," very interesting, beginning to get more and more close to the grand subject of all poetry. "Quicksand Years" is a very charming little statement on that. Now he's beginning to doubt himself a little bit:

Quicksand years that whirl me I know not whither,
Your schemes, politics, fail, lines give way, substances mock and
    elude me,
Only the theme I sing, the great and strong-possess'd soul,
    eludes not,
One's-self must never give way—that is the final substance—
    that out of all is sure,
Out of politics, triumphs, battles, life, what at last finally
    remains?
When shows break up what but One's-Self is sure?

Well, how does he know that? That one's self is even sure, well, he's going to get older, we'll see what happens next.

That's an interesting thing, because now he realized that it is the notion of an unconquerable self or soul that all along has sustained him, but that, too, will dissolve and as a great poet he's going to let it dissolve. He has a few thoughts about the dissolution, also, incidentally, just as of his soul, of the soul of the nation, the dissolution of democracy, and in those days, of public opinion. Well, here's what he's got to say, "Thoughts," he's not going to give it a title, you know. It's all about Watergate basically:

> Of public opinion,
> Of a calm and cool fiat sooner or later, (how impassive! how
>   certain and final!)
> Of the President with pale face asking secretly to himself, *What
>   will the people say at last?*
> Of the frivolous Judge—of the corrupt Congressman,
>   Governor, Mayor—of such as these standing helpless and
>   exposed,

So that prophesied way in advance, even the President of the United States someday must stand naked, [as stated by] Bob Dylan.

"So long!" finally he says to all these thoughts. It's toward the end of *Leaves of Grass*, in fact, I think it's the last great poem in *Leaves of Grass*, salutation and farewell and summary, conclusion, triumph, disillusion, giving up, taking it all on, giving it all over to you who are listening. "So Long!":

> To conclude, I announce what comes after me.
> I remember I said before my leaves sprang at all,
> I would raise my voice jocund and strong with reference to
>   consummations.

But he wasn't dead yet, actually, he was only 70. So now he's got to go through the actual dying, so how does he do that? How does he take that? What has he got to say about that? Well, there are some really interesting "Sands at Seventy" thoughts, giving out, he was quite ill and old in his 70s, in the sense of old in the body, gallstones, paralysis, uremia probably, emphysema, great many of his heart difficulties. I think his autopsy, according to a poem by Jonathan Williams I once read, showed him to have been universal in his illnesses near death as he was in his healths in life. So, little poems, then, just whatever he could write now, his great major work over, and yet the little trickle drops of wisdom of a man of 70 are exquisite and curious.

As I sit writing here, sick and grown old,
Not my least burden is that dulness of the years, querilities,
Ungracious glooms, aches, lethargy, constipation, whimpering
    ennui,
May filter in my daily songs.

And he's got a little poem to his canary bird, he's stuck in his little bedroom up in Camden, on Mickle Street, in a little house with low ceilings. So, he's sitting there talking to his canary bird, "Did we count great, O soul, to penetrate the themes of mighty books . . . ?" Then "Queries to My Seventieth Year": "Approaching, nearing, curious, / Thou dim, uncertain spectre—bringest thou life or death?" Well, everything wasn't bad, he had his first dandelion, springtime:

Simple and fresh and fair from winter's close emerging,
As if no artifice of fashion, business, politics, had ever been,
Forth from its sunny nook of shelter'd grass—innocent,
    golden, calm as the dawn,
The spring's first dandelion shows its trustful face.

So he had that same witty awareness, even lying in his sickbed.
Then people began exploring the North Pole, and he was amazed at that:

Of that blithe throat of thine from arctic bleak and blank,
I'll mind the lesson, solitary bird—let me too welcome chilling
    drifts,
E'en the profoundest chill, as now—a torpid pulse, a brain
    unnerv'd,
Old age land-lock'd within its winter bay—(cold, cold, O cold!)
These snowy hairs, my feeble arm, my frozen feet,

For them thy faith, thy rule I take, and grave it to the last;
Not summer's zones alone—not chants of youth, or south's
      warm tides alone,
But held by sluggish floes, pack'd in the northern ice, the
      cumulus of years,
These with gay heart I also sing.

Well, that's what wisdom brings, he's no longer dependent on that youthful self, in fact the self is dissolving as it will in these last poems. "To Get the Final Lilt of Songs," he says in "Sands at Seventy":

To get the final lilt of songs,
To penetrate the inmost lore of poets—to know the mighty
      ones,
Job, Homer, Eschylus, Dante, Shakespere, Tennyson, Emerson;
To diagnose the shifting-delicate tints of love and pride and
      doubt—to truly understand,
To encompass these, the last keen faculty and entrance-price,
Old age, and what it brings from all its past experiences.

So, you need that, otherwise you ain't gonna learn nuttin' if you don't grow old and die, you just know what you have in your mind when you think you've got the world by the crotch.

An odd lament for the aborigines, an Iroquois term "*Yonnondio*," the sense of the word is *lament for the aborigines,* Whitman has a little note here, ". . . an Iroquois term; and has been used for a personal name." It's an odd little political poem at the end, warning us of Black Mesa, of the Four Corners, of the civilization's destruction of the land and the original natives there.

A song, a poem of itself—the word itself a dirge,
Amid the wilds, the rocks, the storm and wintry night,
To me such misty, strange tableaux the syllables calling up;
Yonnondio—I see, far in the west or north, a limitless ravine,
      with plains and mountains dark,
I see swarms of stalwart chieftains, medicine-men, and warriors,
As flitting by like clouds of ghosts, they pass and are gone in
      the twilight,

So he's also saying as he dies, so may all the machinery of the civilization, so there's nothing for anybody to get too high and mighty about.

But he's got to give thanks in old age. For what?

Thanks in old age—thanks ere I go,
For health, the midday sun, the impalpable air—for life, mere
    life,
For precious ever-lingering memories, (of you my mother
    dear—you father—you, brothers, sisters, friends,)
For all my days—not those of peace alone—the days of war the
    same,
For gentle words, caresses, gifts from foreign lands,
For shelter, wine and meat—for sweet appreciation,
(You distant, dim unknown—or young or old—countless,
    unspecified, readers belov'd,
We never met, and ne'er shall meet—and yet our souls
    embrace, long, close and long;)
For beings, groups, love, deeds, words, books—for colors,
    forms,
For all the brave strong men—devoted, hardy men—who've
    forward sprung in freedom's help, all years, all lands,
For braver, stronger, more devoted men—(a special laurel ere I
    go, to life's war's chosen ones,
The cannoneers of song and thought—the great artillerists—
    the foremost leaders, captains of the soul:)
As soldier from an ended war return'd—As traveler out of
    myriads, to the long procession retrospective,
Thanks—joyful thanks!—a soldier's, traveler's thanks.

But there is also "Stronger Lessons"—is everything thanks for the memories and thanks for the good times, and thanks for the gifts and thanks for the loves? "Stronger Lessons":

Have you learn'd lessons only of those who admired you, and
    were tender with you, and stood aside for you?
Have you not learn'd great lessons from those who reject you,
    and brace themselves against you? or who treat you with
    contempt, or dispute the passage with you?

That's a good piece of advice of how to alchemize fear to bliss, how to alchemize contrariety to harmony, how to ride with the punches, so to speak. But what is it all about? So he's got finally, twilight, not quite sure about that old self. "Twilight":

> The soft voluptuous opiate shades,
> The sun just gone, the eager light dispell'd—(I too will soon be
>   gone, dispell'd,)
> A haze—nirwana—rest and night—oblivion.

But there are still a few thoughts left in his mind before he goes off into that rest and night.

> You lingering sparse leaves of me on winter-nearing boughs,
> And I some well-shorn tree of field or orchard-row;
> You tokens diminute and lorn—(not now the flush of May, or
>   July clover-bloom—no grain of August now;)
> You pallid banner-staves—you pennants valueless—you
>   overstay'd of time,
> Yet my soul-dearest leaves confirming all the rest,
> The faithfulest—hardiest—last.

Well, what has he done, he wonders, with his life? So he says farewell to all of his earlier poems.

> Now precedent songs, farewell—by every name farewell,
> (Trains of a staggering line in many a strange procession,
>   waggons,
> From ups and downs—with intervals—from elder years, mid-
>   age, or youth,)
> "In Cabin'd Ships," or "Thee Old Cause" or "Poets to Come"
> Or "Paumanok," "Song of Myself," "Calamus," or "Adam,"
> Or "Beat! Beat! Drums" or "To the Leaven'd Soil they Trod,"
> Or "Captain! My Captain!" "Kosmos," "Quicksand Years," or
>   "Thoughts,"
> "Thou Mother with thy Equal Brood," and many, many more
>   unspecified,
> From fibre heart of mine—from throat and tongue—(My life's
>   hot pulsing blood,

The personal urge and form for me—not merely paper,
   automatic type and ink,)
Each song of mine—each utterance in the past—having its
   long, long history,
Of life or death, or soldier's wound, of country's loss or safety,
(O heaven! what flash and started endless train of all!
   compared indeed to that!
What wretched shred e'en at the best of all!)

Then, having summed up his life, well, just waiting around, "An
Evening Lull":

After a week of physical anguish,
Unrest and pain, and feverish heat,
Toward the ending day a calm and lull comes on,
Three hours of peace and soothing rest of brain.

Then, "After the Supper and Talk" is the last of the poems of "Sands
at Seventy," and perhaps his last.

After the supper and talk—after the day is done,
As a friend from friends his final withdrawal prolonging,
Good-bye and Good-bye with emotional lips repeating,
(So hard for his hand to release those hands—no more will
   they meet,
No more for communion of sorrow and joy, of old and
   young,
A far-stretching journey awaits him, to return no more,)
Shunning, postponing severance—seeking to ward off the last
   word ever so little,
E'en at the exit-door turning—charges superfluous calling
   back—e'en as he descends the steps,
Something to eke out a minute additional—shadows of
   nightfall deepening,
Farewells, messages lessening—dimmer the forthgoer's visage
   and form,
Soon to be lost for aye in the darkness—loth, O so loth to
   depart!
Garrulous to the very last.

So, that was goodbye my fancy, but that wasn't his last word, no, because he lived on. So he's got, what, "Good-Bye My Fancy," "Second Annex," "Preface Note to the Second Annex," where he says:

> Reader, you must allow a little fun here—for one reason there are too many of the following poemets about death, &c., and for another the passing hours (July 5, 1890) are so sunny-fine. And old as I am I feel to-day almost a part of some frolicsome wave, or for sporting yet like a kid or kitten— . . .

Still there are a couple of little last poems. "My 71st Year":

> After surmounting three-score and ten,
> With all their chances, changes, losses, sorrows,
> My parents' deaths, the vagaries of my life, the many tearing
>   passions of me, the war of '63 and '4,
> As some old broken soldier, after a long, hot, wearying march,
>   or haply after battle,
> To-day at twilight, hobbling, answering company roll-call, *Here,*
>   with vital voice,
> Reporting yet, saluting yet the Officer over all.

Then at last he'll have another comment on his work: "Long, Long Hence":

> After a long, long course, hundreds of years, denials,
> Accumulations, rous'd love and joy and thought,
> Hopes, wishes, aspirations, ponderings, victories, myriads of
>   readers,
> Coating, compassing, covering—after ages' and ages'
>   encrustations,
> Then only may these songs reach fruition.

Well, that's actually what happened to him in the sense that his work was little famous, not much read and a bit put down in the years after his death, to the point of . . . or to the situation that when I went to Columbia College in 1945, between '44 and '49, by scholars and academic poets and by professors and their ilk and by the Cold War soldiers and warriors of those days, Whitman was considered some lonesome, foolish crank who'd lived in poverty and likely Bohemian dissplendor, having cantankerous affairs with jerks of all nations, in his mind. Not to be considered a major personage like the witty dimwits of mid-town Manhattan who worked for *Time, Life,* CIA, *Newsweek,* and their own egos.

Whitman, still clinging on, recognized what it was that was his victory, the commonplace, ordinary mind, as it is known around the world. "The Commonplace":

> The commonplace I sing;
> How cheap is health! how cheap nobility!
> Abstinence, no falsehood, no gluttony, lust;
> The open air I sing, freedom, toleration,
> (Take here the mainest lesson—less from books—less from the
>   schools,)
> The common day and night—the common earth and waters,
> Your farm—your work, trade, occupation,
> The democratic wisdom underneath, like solid ground for all.

So he knew what the basis was where everybody could stand, which was where we all actually are, and was recognizable in our own bodies in our own thoughts in our own work in our own nation, in our own local particulars. A wisdom that was inherited by Ezra Pound and William Carlos Williams and whole generations of poets after Walt Whitman who had discovered that common ground of self and dissolution of self, common ground of his own mind and the common ground of city pavement he walked on with his fellow citizens and the common ground of their emotions between them.

At the end, there is "'The Rounded Catalogue Divine Complete,'" he says:

> The devilish and the dark, the dying and diseas'd,
> The countless (nineteen-twentieths) low and evil, crude and
>   savage,
> The crazed prisoners in jail, the horrible, rank, malignant,
> Venom and filth, serpents, the ravenous sharks, liars, the
>   dissolute;

(What is the part the wicked and the loathsome bear within
    earth's orbic scheme?)
Newts, crawling things in slime and mud, poisons,
The barren soil, the evil men, the slag and hideous rot.

Okay, so he says, finally, in the "Purport" to *Leaves of Grass,* his entire book, "Not to exclude or demarcate, or pick out evils from their formidable masses (even to expose them,) / But add, fuse, complete, extend—and celebrate the immortal and the good . . ." So what was there unexpressed, actually, in his life? He has a little poem, almost his last here, "The Unexpress'd":

How dare one say it?
After the cycles, poems, singers, plays,
Vaunted Ionia's, India's—Homer, Shakspere—the long, long
    times, thick dotted roads, areas,
The shining clusters and the Milky Ways of stars—Nature's
    pulses reap'd,
All retrospective passions, heroes, war, love, adoration,
All ages' plummets dropt to their utmost depth,
All human lives, throats, wishes, brains—all experiences'
    utterance;
After the countless songs, or long or short, all tongues, all
    lands,
Still something not yet told in poesy's voice or print—
    something lacking,
(Who knows? the best yet unexpress'd and lacking.)

So, if there is yet unexpressed form, there'll be unseen buds for the future. His next-to-the-last poem: "Unseen Buds": "Unseen buds, infinite . . ." of course he's garrulous to the very last, as he's said,

Unseen buds, infinite, hidden well,
Under the snow and ice, under the darkness, in every square
    or cubic inch,
Germinal, exquisite, in delicate lace, microscopic, unborn,
Like babes in wombs, latent, folded, compact, sleeping;
Billions of billions, and trillions of trillions of them waiting,

(On earth and in the sea—the universe—the stars there in the
   heavens,)
Urging slowly, surely forward, forming endless,
And waiting ever more, forever more behind.

So he can with good conscience say farewell to his part, to his own
fancy, to his own imagination, to his own life's work, to his own life,
"Good-Bye My Fancy!"

Good-bye my Fancy!
Farewell dear mate, dear love!
I'm going away, I know not where,
Or to what fortune, or whether I may ever see you again,
So Good-bye my Fancy.
Now for my last—let me look back a moment;
The slower fainter ticking of the clock is in me,
Exit, nightfall, and soon the heart-thud stopping.
Long have we lived, joy'd, caress'd together;
Delightful!—now separation—Good-bye my Fancy.
Yet let me not be too hasty,
Long indeed have we lived, slept, filter'd, become really
   blended into one;
Then if we die we die together, (yes, we'll remain one,)
If we go anywhere we'll go together to meet what happens,
May-be we'll be better off and blither, and learn something,
May-be it is yourself now really ushering me to the true songs,
   (who knows?)
May-be it is you the mortal knob really undoing, turning—so
   now finally,
Good-bye—and hail! my Fancy.

And that's counted as almost his last poem, but then he didn't die, he
had to go on, there's more. He had to keep going, poor fellow, thinking,
putting it all out, *Old Age Echoes*. To be at all, he's amazed at it, and he's
there, so what can you do? Remember all the dirty deeds he did? "Of
Many a Smutch'd Deed Reminiscent":

Full of wickedness, I—of many a smutch'd deed reminiscent—
　　of worse deeds capable,
Yet I look composedly upon nature, drink day and night the
　　joys of life, and await death with perfect equanimity,
Because of my tender and boundless love for him I love and
　　because of his boundless love for me.

Well, that's something fine to figure on, but his actual last poem after writing something about death's valley, and there are poems about death's valley and "Nay Tell Me Not Today the Publish'd Shame," he's got an account of the horrible politics going on there as he was dying. Last: "A Thought of Columbus," it's a forward-looking thing about exploration, navigation, going on into worlds unknown, unconquered, etc. "A Thought of Columbus," not his most moving poem, not his greatest poem, but on the other hand his last poem as listed, and so maybe his last thoughts:

The mystery of mysteries, the crude and hurried ceaseless
　　flame, spontaneous, bearing on itself.
The bubble and the huge, round, concrete orb!
A breath of Deity, as thence the bulging universe unfolding!
The many issuing cycles from their precedent minute!
The eras of the soul incepting in an hour,
Haply the widest, farthest evolutions of the world and man.
Thousands and thousands of miles hence, and now four
　　centuries back,
A mortal impulse thrilling its brain cell,
Reck'd or unreck'd, the birth can no longer be postpon'd:
A phantom of the moment, mystic, stalking, sudden,
Only a silent thought, yet toppling down of more than walls of
　　brass or stone.
(A flutter at the darkness' edge as if old Time's and Space's
　　secret near revealing.)
A thought! a definite thought works out in shape.
Four hundred years roll on.
The rapid cumulus—trade, navigation, war, peace, democracy,
　　roll on;
The restless armies and the fleets of time following their

leader—the old camps of ages pitch'd in newer, larger areas,
The tangl'd, long-deferr'd éclaircissement of human life and
    hopes boldly begins untying,
As here to-day up-grows the Western World.
(An added word yet to my song, far Discoverer, as ne'er before
    sent back to son of earth–
If still thou hearest, hear me,
Voicing as now—lands, races, arts, bravas to thee,
O'er the long backward path to thee—one vast consensus
    north, south, east, west,
Soul plaudits! acclamation! reverent echoes!
One manifold, huge memory to thee! oceans and lands!
The modern world to thee and thought of thee!)

So, he ended on a heroic historic note, congratulating the explorer,
himself really, or the Columbus in himself, and the Columbus in all of us
for seeking outward in our spiritual journey looking for not even truth,
because it wasn't truth he was proposing, except the truth of the fact that
we are here with our lusts and delights, our givings up and grabbings,
growings into trouble and marriage and birth and growings into coffins
and earth and unbirth. Good character, all in all, the kind of character
that if a nation were composed of such liberal, large-minded gentlemen
of the old school or young, large-bodied persons with free emotions and
funny thoughts and tender looks, there might be the possibility of this
nation and other nations surviving on the planet, but to survive, we'd
have to take on some of that large magnanimity that Whitman yawped
over the roof tops of the world.

WRITTEN: May 31, 1980

FIRST PUBLISHED: Jim Perlman, Ed Folsom, and Dan Campion, eds., *Walt Whitman, The Measure of His Song* (Minneapolis: Holy Cow! Press, 1981).

Whitman's Influence: A Mountain Too Vast to Be Seen

Like Poe, Whitman's breakthru from official conventional nationalist identity to personal self, to subject, subjectivity, to candor of person, sacredness of the unique eccentric curious solitary personal conscious-ness changed written imaginative conception of the individual around the whole world, and inspired a democratic revolution of mental nature from Leningrad and Paris to Shanghai and Tokyo.

Like Poe, who introduced modern self-consciousness to Baudelaire and Dostoyevsky, so Whitman's exposure of a new self of man and woman empowered every particular soul who heard his long breathed inspiration, "I celebrate myself, and sing myself / And what I assume you shall assume . . ."

This expansive person and expanded verse line affected continental literary consciousness by the turn of the century, Emile Verhaeren in Belgian French, Paul Claudel later with extended strophic verse. The Russian Futurists adapted Whitman's bold personism—vide Mayakovsky's *Cloud in Trousers*, Blok's *The Twelve*, Khlebnikoff's vocal experimentation. Perhaps thru the French, Japanese and Chinese poets reinvented verse forms and personality of poet—Guo Moro and Ai Qing particularly, introduced Whitmanic afflatus and expanded verse line to China by 1919. And Ezra Pound also said "I make a pact with you Walt Whitman" in introducing modernism to American English poetry by World War I—thereby catalyzing renewal of all world poetries. What was Whitman's effect on Italian Futurists? On Marinetti and Ungaretti?

In *Democratic Vistas* Whitman warned that unless American material-ism were to be enlightened by some spiritual influence, the United States would turn into "the fabled damned of nations." His spiritual medicine or antidote to poisonous materialism was "adhesiveness," a generous affection between citizens. In his preface to *Leaves of Grass* he prescribed "candor" as the necessary virtue of "poets and orators to come."

The Good Grey Poet's own affection and candor led to the excellent tender erotic verse in the "Calamus" section of *Leaves of Grass*, prophesy-ing a gay liberation for American and world literature.

His "Passage to India" predicted a meeting of Eastern and Western thought in our twentieth century, a pragmatic transcendentalism that's come true with the flavor of meditation practice in American poetry as we approach the second millennium's end.

His image of universal transitoriness in "Crossing Brooklyn Ferry" has transmitted itself across a century. As the Tibetan lama, the Venerable Chögyam Trungpa, Rinpoche, remarked, Whitman's writing equals Buddhist sutras in this perception.

"When Lilacs Last in the Dooryard Bloom'd," his threnody for Lincoln, salutes Death with romantic vigor equal to his salutation to Life, "Salut au Monde."

And his "Sands at Seventy," "Good-Bye My Fancy" and "Old Age Echoes" are marvelous short poems of old age, describing with equanimity the "querilities . . . constipation . . . whimpering ennui" of body and mind approaching death, signaling farewell, waving goodbye, "garrulous to the very last." These late lesser known poems are among his most vividly appealing, and prefigure the brief clear-eyed sketches of his poetic grandchildren the Imagist and Objectivist poets William Carlos Williams and Charles Reznikoff. Such poems serve as candid models for my own verse to this day.

WRITTEN: Jan. 28, 1992

FIRST PUBLISHED: *Sulfur,* no. 31 (Fall 1992) pp. 229–230.

WILLIAM CARLOS WILLIAMS

Williams in a World of Objects

Accuracy. Williams' accuracy. The phrase "clamp your mind down on objects" is his. The phrase "no ideas but in things" is his. It means, "no *general* ideas in your poetry." Don't put out any abstract ideas about things, but present the things themselves that give you the ideas. Let's try and understand what Williams is trying to say and then we'll propose a different theory. Here are three lines from "Dance Russe":

> And the sun is a flame-white disc
> in silken mists
> above shining trees,—

Now he is being very fair there. He is just telling you what you can see. He's not laying a trip on you about the sun in general. Here he puts your eyes on the sun in one specific kind of day so that you can see it with your own eyes. He is saying "just put down the details of the things you see in front of you." If you can't begin there, what good are any ideas. Begin with what the sense offers. If you can't do that, you'll have to go to astronomy. But astronomy is based on observations of some kind.

Suppose a dying man! If you can't *see* the dying man in front of you, you can't see what is wrong with your behavior toward him. Here is not a *change* of ideas; it's a change of *directive stance*. Once understood, Williams' phrase becomes a basic building block, for a system maybe, or a reference point for a complete system in itself or usable with other systems. But until the phrase ["no ideas but in things"] is understood in itself, there is no common ground to begin with. In the lines from the poem, what's the one common ground we begin with? We've got the sun, an orange ball going down over the maple tree, or the sun just as we see it. How artfully can we describe what we see, so that it is common ground, where everybody is in the same place, so that one can use it like a reference point. It may be fictional but it is the common ground. If we don't have any reference point in the physical world, then what have we got? Here's one common reference point at least: everybody's breathing. That's where Buddhism starts—at that one place and moves from there. Starts at one place that everybody can locate: the tip of the nose where everybody is breathing in and out. Start close to the nose. That is a reality where everybody is or can be: we must begin where we are.

Williams got into this because *reality* had become so confusing in the twentieth century, and poetry had got so freaked out that it was strange: he didn't know what poetry was! He didn't know what anything was! But he knew where his nose was and could begin there. He gave up all ideas [meaning abstractions] and started with things themselves. Naturally everybody sees things differently: The word is not The Thing. The word "word," a concept in itself, is an abstraction, an idea. The entire world is fictional. "Words themselves are ideas!": There is a little double-dealing in that phrase. But everybody can come down to the same place and begin there: the one place where *everybody* can be. There is only one place where everybody can be.

The question is, Where are we going to begin? [The answer is] let's begin with what we can see in front of us. Williams was looking for a place where everybody could begin together in poetry because everything was new; a new continent, newly discovered, newly invaded with European ideas plastered all over it. He was trying to clean up the slate and start all over again. That's why he wrote a book called *In the American Grain,* trying to reach American history, to see what fresh planet we'd come upon. "The natural object is always the adequate symbol": That's Pound's way of saying the same thing: "Don't bother with abstractions." In other words, no poetry but in "for instances," no ideas but in things. He would say you could include feelings, but you'd have to deal with them as observed things and not get lost. It is very similar to the process of meditation: paying attention to the breaths, wandering off into a daydream, and then becoming unconscious of the mind moving into the daydream, of the breaths, and then you could describe the thought you had but you no longer are obsessed by it or lost in it. Don't lose perspective. There is always the home base to touch back on. He's saying let's fill with *our* attention the things that other people can see and fill with *their* attention. Then we can both check our consciousness, one against another, and see where we are, like triangulating the stars.

Here's two short poems:

Goodnight
In brilliant gas light
I turn the kitchen spigot
and watch the water plash
into the clean white sink.
On the grooved drain-board
to one side is
a glass filled with parsley—
crisped green.
    Waiting
for the water to freshen—
I glance at the spotless floor—:
a pair of rubber sandals
lie side by side
under the wall-table
all is in order for the night.
Waiting, with a glass in my hand
—three girls in crimson satin
pass close before me on
the murmurous background of
the crowded opera—
    it is
memory playing the clown—
three vague, meaningless girls
full of smells and
the rustling sounds of
cloth rubbing on cloth and
little slippers on carpet—
high-school French
spoken in a loud voice!

Parsley in a glass
still and shining
brings me back.
I take a drink and
yawn deliciously.
I am ready for bed.

He brings us through the whole process.

The mundaneness is interesting, to me, because it sees so clearly that it becomes crisp in meaning, still and shining. The water glass suddenly is a totemic object. It becomes a symbol of itself, of his investment in his attention in that object: *it* becomes a symbol of itself also.

Because he sees it so clearly, he notices what about the object that shines, what's particular about the object that could be written down in a word—he sees the object without association. That's characteristic of visionary moments: you get supernatural visions by giving up supernatural visions; just looking at what is in front of you. You are not superimposing another idea or another image on the image that's already there.

The poem "Thursday" shows that he really is a Buddhist:

I have had my dream—like others—
and it has come to nothing, so that
I remain now carelessly
with feet planted on the ground
and look up at the sky—
feeling my clothes about me,
the weight of my body in my shoes,
the rim of my hat, air passing in and out
at my nose—and decide to dream no more.

When I discovered this poem, I realized its thematic Buddhism: the practice we were doing and the pragmatic practice had intersected and there was a common ground. Williams had arrived at the same place that everybody else was studying and got there early and on his own: it reconfirmed my feelings that he was some kind of a saint of perception.

This is a beginning: to understand his basic principle and then extend it as we have to. Well, you can be mindful of generalizations if you are mindful of the particulars out of which you draw: *No ideas but in facts!*

II

Williams is the clearest and simplest and most direct when trying to tie the mind down, to bring the imagination down to earth again and put all of his intensity and all of his energy into seeing what is actually there, what anybody can see in the light of day: no imagination except what he's conscious of as daydreams while looking directly at people, cars, horses, bushes, maple trees, or Rutherford, New Jersey. He's a doctor. Let's start with a couple of his early sketches:

Late for Summer Weather

He has on
an old light grey fedora
She a black beret

He a dirty sweater
She an old blue coat
that fits her tight

Grey flapping pants
Red skirt and
broken down black pumps

Fat Lost Ambling
nowhere through
the upper town they kick

their way through
heaps of
fallen maple leaves

still green—and
crisp as dollar bills
Nothing to do. Hot cha!

Proletarian Portrait

A big young bareheaded woman
in an apron

Her hair slicked back standing
on the street

One stockinged foot toeing
the sidewalk

Her shoe in her hand. Looking
intently into it

She pulls out the paper insole
to find the nail

That has been hurting her

Williams was a friend of Reznikoff's. They were practicing the same poetics together trying to get it to boil down to the direct presentation of the object that they were writing about with no excess words. They composed their poems out of the elements of natural speech, their own speech, as heard on the porch or in talk over the kitchen table. Poetry that would be identical to spoken conversation that you could actually hear as regular conversation and not recognize it as poetry at all unless you suddenly dug that there was something going on, curiously sharp and fresh that was smart people talking.

Here's the doctor, maybe out on a call:

The Young Housewife
At ten a.m. the young housewife
moves about in negligee behind
the wooden walls of her husband's house.
I pass solitary in my car.

Then again she comes to the curb
to call the ice-man, fish-man, and stands
shy, uncorseted, tucking in
stray ends of hair, and I compare her
to a fallen leaf.

The noiseless wheels of my car
rush with a crackling sound over
dried leaves as I bow and pass smiling.

So, what's the use of being so flat and prosaic? Or, what's the purpose of trying to make poetry out of the objects seen under the aspect of ordinary minds? Generally we don't see ordinary objects at all. We are filled with daydream fantasy so that we don't see what is in front of us. We are not aware of what is close to the nose, and we don't even appreciate what everyday tables and chairs have to offer in terms of service for food or a place to sit; in terms of the centuries of maturing that it took to give us a place for the food. Zeroing in on actuality with the ordinary mind and abandoning any thought of heaven, illumination; giving up any attempt to manipulate the universe to make it better than it is; but, instead, coming down to earth and being willing to relate to what is actually here without trying to change the universe or alter it from the one which we can see, smell, taste, touch, hear and think about. Williams' work as a poet is very similar to Zen Buddhist mindfulness practice, because it clamps the mind down on objects and brings the practitioner into direct relations with whatever he can find in front of him without making a big deal about it; without satisfying some ego ambition to have something more princely or less painful than what already *is*.

Williams was good friends with extraordinary people: Pound, H.D., Marianne Moore. They all knew each other at the University of Pennsylvania I believe. But Williams was a square. He always thought Pound was a little cranky and crazy. Williams was kind of naive; square but inside he was such a humane man. Since he learned to deal with what was around him he learned to sympathize, empathize. His growth was totally self-made, totally natural. He had the idea of going in that direction very early and just kept working at it. He had the idea [about poetry] and thought about working on it, like going through medical school. Going through poetry and developing his focus was just like going through medical school. He deliberately stayed in Rutherford, New Jersey, and wrote poetry about the local landscape, using local language. He wanted to be a provincial from the point of view of really being there where he was; really knowing his ground. He wanted to know his roots, know who the iceman and fishman were; know the housewife; he wanted to know his town—his whole body in a sense. A strange idea; he might have got it from some literary sources like Guy de Maupassant; Keats might have given him some hints.

He was dealing with actual birth rather than literary birth, actual eyes, hair, etc. He was somebody no different from ourselves, actually, somebody you don't have to worry about pulling a fast metaphysical trick on you and declaring another universe. That's the whole point; dealing with *this* universe. And that was a fantastic discovery: that you can actually make poetry by dealing with this universe instead of creating another one.

WRITTEN: Fall 1976

FIRST PUBLISHED: Carroll Terrell, ed., *William Carlos Williams: Man and   Poet* (Orono, ME: National Poetry Foundation, 1983).

JACK KEROUAC

The *Dharma Bums* Review

EDITOR'S NOTE: Allen Ginsberg's book review of Jack Kerouac's book *The Dharma Bums* appeared long after the enthusiasm of the wonderful *New York Times* book review of *On the Road* by Gilbert Millstein had cooled and several subsequent attacks on Kerouac's books had taken place.

A few facts to clear up a lot of bullshit. *On the Road* was written around 1950, in the space of several weeks, mostly on benny,[4] an extraordinary project, sort of a flash of inspiration on a new approach to prose, an attempt to tell completely, all at once, everything on his mind in relation to the hero Dean Moriarity, spill it all out at once and follow the convolutions of the active mind for direction as to the "structure of the confession." And discover the rhythm of the mind at work at high speed in prose. An attempt to trap the prose of truth mind by means of a highly scientific attack on new prose method. The result was a magnificent single paragraph several blocks long, rolling, like the road itself, the length of an entire onionskin teletype roll. The sadness that this was never published in its most exciting form—its original discovery—but hacked and punctuated and broken—the rhythms and swing of it broken—by presumptuous literary critics in publishing houses. The original mad version is greater than the published version, the manuscript still exists and someday when everybody's dead [will] be published as it is. Its greatness (like the opening pages of Miller's [*Tropic of*] *Cancer*)—the great spirit of adventure into poetic composition. And great tender delicacy of language.

The long lines of "Howl" are piddling compared to the sustained imagic rhythms of that magnificent endless paragraph. Some of the original, a lot of it, can be seen in the published version though. The book took 7–8 years to appear in mutilated form. By then Kerouac had disappeared down that road and was invisible, magic art car soul.

The conception for such prose came from the hero of the road himself, Moriarty's prototype, who sent Kerouac a long wild introspective 40-singlespace-page letter. It's been lost, by me, I think.

The next step (after the rejection of the original *Road*) was to redo the subject, chronological account of the hero's life, in regular gothic-Melvillian prose.

That was started with one magic chapter about a Denver football field. But then Kerouac said, fuck publishing and literary preconceptions, I want something I can *read*, some interesting prose, for my old age. *Visions of Neal* and *Dr. Sax* (1951–53) and another dozen subsequent books (prose, poetry, biography, meditation, translation, sketching, novels, nouvelles, fragments of brown wrapping paper, golden parchments scribbled at midnight, strange notebooks in Mexico and Desolation Peak and Ozone Park) follow.

Writing is like piano playing, the more you do it the more you know how to play a piano. And improvise, like Bach.

Not a mechanical process: the mechanical and artless practice would have been to go on writing regular novels with regular type form and dull prose. Well, I don't know why I'm arguing.

Too many critics (all incomplete because they themselves do not know how to write). Pound said not to take advice from someone who had not himself produced a masterpiece.

Am I writing for *The Village Voice* or the ear of God? In a monster mechanical mass-medium age full of horrible people with wires in their heads, the explanation is hard to make; after everybody's cash-conscious egotistical book-reviewing trend-spotting brother has bespoke his own opinion.

It's all gibberish, everything that has been said. There's not many competent explainers, I'm speaking of the Beat Generation, which after all is quite an angelic idea. As to what non-writers, journalists, etc., have made of it, as usual—well, it's their bad poetry not Kerouac's.

Be that as it may, *The Subterraneans* (1953) and *The Dharma Bums* (1958) are sketchy evidence of the prose pilgrimage he's made.

The virtue of *The Subterraneans* was that it was, at last, published, completely his own prose, no changes.

An account of his method of prose (written 1953) about the time of the composition of *The Subterraneans* was reprinted in *Evergreen Review,* vol. 2, no. 8 (Spring 1959) from *Black Mountain Review,* no. 7 (Autumn 1957).

Essentials of Spontaneous Prose

SET-UP The object is set before the mind, either in reality, as in sketching (before a landscape or teacup or old face) or is set in the memory wherein it becomes the sketching from memory of a definite image-object.

PROCEDURE Time being of the essence in the purity of speech, sketching language is undisturbed flow from the mind of personal secret idea-words, *blowing* (as per jazz musician) on subject of image.

METHOD No periods separating sentence-structures already arbitrarily riddled by false colons and timid usually needless commas—but the vigorous space dash separating rhetorical breathing (as jazz musician drawing breath between outblown phrases)—"measured pauses which are the essentials of our speech"—"divisions of the *sounds* we hear"—"time and how to note it down." (William Carlos Williams)

SCOPING Not "selectivity" of expression but following free deviation (association) of mind into limitless blow-on-subject seas of thought, swimming in sea of English with no discipline other than rhythms of rhetorical exhalation and expostulated statement, like a fist coming down on a table with each complete utterance, bang! (the space dash)—Blow as deep as you want—write as deeply, fish as far down as you want, satisfy yourself first, then reader cannot fail to receive telepathic shock and meaning-excitement by same laws operating in his own human mind.

LAG IN PROCEDURE No pause to think of proper word but the infantile pileup of scatological buildup words till satisfaction is gained, which will turn out to be a great appending rhythm to the thought and be in accordance with Great Law of timing.

TIMING Nothing is muddy that *runs in time* and to laws of *time*—Shakespearean stress of dramatic need to speak now in own unalterable way or forever hold tongue—*no revisions* (except obvious rational mistakes, such as names or *calculated* insertions in act of not writing but *inserting*).

CENTER OF INTEREST Begin not from preconceived idea of what to say about image but from jewel center of interest in subject of image at *moment* of writing, and write outwards swimming in sea of language to peripheral release and exhaustion—Do not afterthink except for poetic or P.S. reasons. Never afterthink to "improve" or defray impressions, as, the best writing is always the most painful personal wrung-out tossed from cradle warm protective mind—tap from yourself the song of yourself, *blow!—now!—your* way is your only way— "good"—or "bad"—always honest, ("ludicrous"), spontaneous, "confessional" interesting, because not "crafted." Craft *is* craft.

STRUCTURE OF WORK Modern bizarre structures (science fiction, etc.) arise from language being dead, "different" themes give illusion of "new" life. Follow roughly outlines in outfanning movement over subject, as river rock, so mindflow over jewel-center need (run your mind over it, *once*) arriving at pivot, where what was dim-formed "beginning" becomes sharp-necessitating "ending" and language shortens in race to wire of time-race of work, following laws of Deep Form, to conclusion last words, last trickle—Night is The End.

MENTAL STATE If possible write "without consciousness" in semi-trance (as Yeats' later "trance writing") allowing subconscious to admit in own uninhibited interesting necessary and so "modern" language what conscious art would censor, and write excitedly, swiftly, with writing-or-typing-cramps, in accordance (as from center to periphery) with laws of orgasm, Reich's "beclouding of consciousness." *Come* from within, out—to relaxed and said.

An excellent sample of the kind of sentence, the peculiar kind of rhythm, the appropriate alterations of square syntax, the juicy kind of imagery, the intimacy and juxtaposition of strange eternal detail, the very modernity of the thought, the very individuality (and therefore universality) of the specific sense perceptions, are to be found, for instance, in the long sentence that winds from the 6th line of p. 34 to the 13th line of p. 35 in *The Subterraneans* as follows:

—Ended when she got home to her sisters' house in Oakland and they were furious at her anyway but she told them off and did strange things; she noticed for instance the complicated wiring her eldest sister had done to connect the TV and the radio to the kitchen plug in the ramshackle wood upstairs of their cottage near Seventh and Pine the railroad sooty wood and gargoyle porches like tinder in the sham scrapple slums, the yard nothing but a lot with broken rocks and black wood showing where hoboes Tokay'd last night before moving off across the meatpacking yard to the Mainline rail Tracy-bound thru vast endless impossible

Brooklyn-Oakland full of telephone poles and crap and on Saturday nights the wild Negro bars full of whores and the Mexicans Ya-Yaaing in their own saloons and the cop car cruising the long sad avenue riddled with drinkers and the glitter of broken bottles (now in the wood house where she was raised in terror Mardou is squatting against the wall looking at the wires in the half dark and she hears herself speak and doesn't understand why she's saying it except that it must be said, come out, because that day earlier when in her wandering she finally got to wild Third Street among the lines of slugging winos and the bloody drunken Indians with bandages rolling out of alleys and the 10¢ movie house with three features and little children of skid row hotels running on the sidewalk and the pawnshops and the Negro chickenshack jukeboxes and she stood in drowsy sun suddenly listening to bop as if for the first time as it poured out, the intention of the musicians and of the horns and instruments suddenly a mystical unity expressing itself in waves like sinister and again electricity but screaming with palpable aliveness the direct word from the vibration, the interchanges of statement, the levels of waving intimation, the smile in sound, the same living insinuation in the way her sister'd arranged those wires wriggled entangled and fraught with intention, innocent looking but actually behind the mask of casual life completely by agreement the mawkish mouth almost sneering snakes of electricity purposely placed she'd been seeing all day and hearing in the music and saw now in the wires), "What are you trying to do actually electrocute me?" so the sisters could see something was really wrong, worse than the youngest of the Fox sisters who was alcoholic and made the wild street and got arrested regularly by the vice squad, some nameless horrible yawning wrong, "She smokes dope, she hangs out with all those queer guys with beards in the City."

Spontaneous Bop Prosody, a nickname one might give to this kind of writing—that is to say, read aloud and notice how the motion of the sentence corresponds to the motion of actual excited talk.

It takes enormous art (being a genius and writing a lot) to get to that point in prose. (And trusting God.)

Bop because, partly, in listening to the new improvisatory freedoms of progressive musicians, one develops an ear for one's own actual sounds. One does not force them into the old rhythm. Unless one wishes to protect one's old emotions by falsifying the new ones and making them fit the forms of the old.

Jack [is] very concerned with the rhythm of his sentences, he enjoys that like he enjoys jazz, Bach, Buddhism, or the rhythm in Shakespeare, apropos of whom he oft remarks: "Genius is *funny*." The combinations of words and the rhythmic variations make masters laugh together (much as the two dopey sages giggling over a Chinese parchment—a picture in the Freer Gallery [Washington, DC]). All this ties in with the half-century-old struggle for the development of an American prosody to match our own speech and thinking rhythms. It's all quite traditional actually you see. Thus William Carlos Williams has preached the tradition of "invention."

All this is quite obvious except to those who are not involved with the radical problems of artistic form.

Dharma Bums is a late and recent book, he's weary of the world and prose. Extraordinary mystic testament, however, and record of various inner signposts on the road to understanding of the illusion of being.

The sentences are shorter (shorter than the great flowing inventive sentences of *Dr. Sax*), almost as if he were writing a book of a thousand *haikus*—Buddhist visionary at times. He's had an actual religious experience over a prolonged period of time. This book puts it, for convenience, in the form of a novel about another interesting friend. The passages of solitary meditation are the best I'd say. The wildest sentence, perhaps:

"Suddenly came the drenching fall rains, all-night rain, millions of acres of Bo-trees being washed and washed, and in my attic millennial rats wisely sleeping."

Now that's a very strange sentence, an oddly personal associative jump in the middle of it to the eternal rats. Not many prose writers alive (Céline, Genet, a few others) would have the freedom and intelligence to trust their own minds, remember they made that jump, not censor it but write it down and discover its beauty. That's what I look for in Kerouac's prose. He's gone very far out in discovering (or remembering, or transcribing) the perfect patterns that his own mind makes, and trusting them, and seeing their importance—to rhythm, to imagery, to the very structure of the "novel."

In this, in the present American scene in prose, he is the great master innovator. There are others (Robert Creeley, maybe I don't understand what he's doing in prose though his poetry is perfect I know). And our legendary unpublished Wm. S. Burroughs.

A few other notes. The meditation in the woods, published originally in *Chicago Review,* Zen issue, is an excellent sincere long passage. Reading it one wonders how anybody but a boor can vision Kerouac as anything but a gentle, intelligent, suffering prose saint. The abuse he's taken is disgusting, and the technical ignorance of most of his reviewers both pro and con is scandalous.

There has not been criticism that has examined his prose purpose— nor his hip-beat insight and style—nor, finally, his holy content. It takes one to find one. Don't expect much understanding from academic journalists who, for all their pretense at civilization, have learned little but wicked opinion.

I'm only vomiting up some of the horror of literature. Hacks in every direction. And a nation brainwashed by hacks. I begin to see why Pound went paranoiac, if he did. It's the same situation as 1910. There is a great revolution, innovation, in poetry and prose and going on now—continuing. That the academies have learned so little in the meantime—I feel betrayed. I'll stop before I go mad.

Book ends with a great holy Blah! At last America has a new visionary poet. So let us talk of Angels.

WRITTEN: 1958

FIRST PUBLISHED: *Village Voice* (Nov. 12, 1958) pp. 3–5.

The Great Rememberer

EDITOR'S NOTE: Written as the introduction to Jack Kerouac's *Visions of Cody* published after his death by McGraw-Hill in 1973. Cody is a thinly veiled pseudonym for Neal Cassady. Specific references are to that book.

Two noble men, Americans, perished younger than old whitebeard prophets' wrinkled gay eye archetypes might've imagined like Whitman. The death of America in their early stop—untimely tears—for loves glimpsed and not fulfilled—not completely fulfilled, some kind of withdrawal from the promised tender nation—Larimer Street[5] down, green lights glimmering, Denver surrounded by Honeywell warplants, IBM war calculators, selfish air bases, botanical mortal brain factories—Robot buildings downtown lifted under crescent moon—The small hands gestured to belly and titty, under backstairs decades ago, seeking release to each other, trembling sexual tenderness discovered first times . . . before the wars began . . . 1939 Denver's mysterious glimpses of earth life unfolding on side streets in United States—Perfectly captured nostalgia by Jack Kerouac *Visions of Cody* (Neal) . . . Peace protester adolescents from Cherry High with neck kiss bruises sit and weep on Denver Capitol Hill lawn, hundreds of Neal and Jack souls mortal lamblike sighing over the nation now, 1972.

Mortal America's here . . . disappearing elevateds, diners, iceboxes, dusty hat racks preserved from oblivion . . . Larimer Street itself this year in ruins resurrected spectral thru *Visions of Cody*—And the poolhall itself gone to parking lot and Fun Adult Movies the heritage of Neal's sex fantasies on the bench watching Watson shoot snooker—

By this prose preserved for a younger generation appreciative of the Bowery camp and thirties hair consciousness destroyed by real estate speculators on war-growth economy.

I don't think it is possible to proceed further in America without first understanding Kerouac's tender brooding compassion for bygone scene and personal individuality oddity'd therein. Bypassing Kerouac one bypasses the mortal heart, sung in prose vowels; the book a giant mantra of appreciation and adoration of an American man, one striving heroic soul, Kerouac's judgment on Neal Cassady was confirmed by later Kesey history.

"I saw the flash of their mouths, like the mouths of minstrels, as they ate."

High generous prose moments, I reread this book 19 years later—the *shabda* (sound waves) passage, "like ants in orchestras." Hector's Cafeteria food description a Homeric hymn. "All you do is head straight for the grave." Robert Duncan circa '55 was impressed by the passages reflecting shiny auto fenders in plateglass.—"Lord, I scribbled hymns to you"—nobody else says anything like that, not Mailer Genet Céline . . . "hundreds of death-conscious boys."

I worship Jack's candid observation of inner consciousness manifested in solitude, the girl eating in Cafeteria, a complete world *satori*. Here as distinct from his critic P.,[6] Kerouac is present in the world solitary musing, observing actual event, "mind clamped down on objects" completely anonymous, in a single universe of perception with no mental maneuvers or self-conscious manipulation of any reader's mind (he's writing for no reader but his own intelligent self)—completely *here*, watching the world—not generalizing in a study, but sketching solitude Mannahatta's cafeteria—"She just blew her nose daintily with a napkin; has private personal sad manners, at least externally, by which she makes her own formal existence known to herself . . ."

Great ringing historical lines: "I accept lostness forever. Everything belongs to me because I am poor." Complete prophecy Dream 1951–1973: "A Ritz Yale Club Party . . . hundreds of kids in leather jackets instead of big tuxedo . . . everybody smoking marijuana, wailing a new decade in one wild *crowd*" . . . in a single parenthesis, a whole American future style's prophesied. This book, then, an education on perceptions of the mind person: "and I dig *you* as we together dig the lostness and the fact that of course nothing's ever to be gained but death." Thus a panoramic consciousness, "The wide surroundment brooding over him . . ." (Kerouac'd been reading Melville's *Pierre*), "long ago in the red sun."

"The unspeakable visions of the individual . . . the joy of downtown city night . . . the red brick wall behind the red neons . . . the poor hidden brick of America . . . the center of the grief . . . America's a lonely crockashit . . . And so I struggle in the dark with the enormity of my soul, trying desperately to be a great rememberer redeeming life from darkness."

Thousands of children now, millions of children now, orphaned in America by the war, crying for the United States to repent and love them again.

The Tape: a new section of the novel, begins, if anybody doesn't know, how could they? Cody (Neal) telling Jack the story of what it was like summer 1947, Cody and myself hitched from Denver to New Waverly Texas to Bull Hubbard's (Bill Burroughs) marijuana garden farm in E. Texas bayou country; recollection for the great rememberer of our "Green Automobile" vow. Of course Cody wasn't entirely romantically frank with Jack—We vowed to own and accept each other's bodies and souls and help each other into heaven, while on earth, one person. And the incident of the bed never did get told—though it dominates 30 pages of conversation: Cody and I had no mutual Texas bed to sleep together in, I was eager, so tried to build one out of 2 army cots with Huck's (Huncke's) help a miserable symbolic failure, sagged in the middle. "I couldn't stand him touching me," says Cody somewhere. He didn't help build the love bed, though I pleaded.

The entire tape section's a set of nights on newly discovered grass, (incidentally, Neal spent several years in jail a decade later, and lost his family type railroad job he revered so stably for years, as result of giving a couple joints to a carfull of agents who gave him a ride to work. So he was an early "political prisoner.") wherein these souls explored the mind blanks impressions that tea creates: that's the subject, unaltered and unadorned—halts, switches, emptiness, quixotic chatters, summary piths, exactly reproduced, significant because:

1) Vocal familiar friendly teahead life talk had never been transcribed and examined consciously (like Warhol 20 years later examined Campbell's Soup cans).

2) Despite monotony, the gaps and changes (like Warhol watching Empire State Building all night) are dramatic.

3) It leads somewhere, like life.

4) It's interesting if you want the characters' reality.

5) It's real.

6) It's art because at that point in progress of Jack's art he began transcribing *first* thoughts of true mind in American speech, and as objective sample of that teahead-high speech of his model hero, he placed uncorrected tape central in his book, actual sample-reality he was otherwere rhapsodizing.

Art lies in the consciousness of doing the thing, in the attention to the happening, in the sacramentalization of everyday reality, the God-worship in the present conversation, no matter what. Thus the tape may be read not as hung-up which it sometimes is to the stranger, but as a spontaneous ritual performed once and never repeated, in full consciousness that every yawn and syllable uttered would be eternal . . . the tape coheres together with serious solemn discussion of their lives.

Jack Kerouac's style of transcription of taped conversation is, also, impeccably accurate in syntax punctuation—separation of elements for clarity . . . labeling of voices, parenthesizing of interruption. A model to study.

Concluding we see the beauty of the tapes that Jack cherished, that they are inclusive samples of complete exchange of information and love thoughts between two men, each giving his mind history to the other—The remarkable situation, which we are privileged to witness thru these creaky tapes transcribed by now dead hand, is—of Kerouac the great rememberer on quiet evenings 1950 to 1951 with Neal Cassady, the great experiencer and Midwest driver and talker, gossiping intimately of their eternities—here's representative sample of these evenings, and we can take as model their exchange and see that our own lives also have secrets, mysteries, explanations and love equal to those of feeble, seeking heroes past—Another generation has followed, perhaps surpassed, Neal and Jack conversing in midnight intimacy—if it hasn't discovered that "huge confessional night" then this tape transcript is fit model. If it's surpassed—more coherent these days—I doubt it!?! But then, this is ancient history—if history's interesting now that America has near destroyed the human compassionate world still surviving as in fragments of bewildering conversation between these two dead souls.

There follows an "Imitation of the Tape in Heaven," taking off from black preacher calling Jesus in the night, inspired rhythmic babble, gemmy little fragments of literature, by now K.'d obviously given up entirely on American Lit., and let his mind loose. Thus proceeds analysis of his fall from college window innocence, and American innocence too—where the "alienation" is now obvious and frightful filled with Jelly Bombs Fragmentation Nazi Electronic Good American in 1951–52 Jack saw it as a change of insouciance, going into a bar . . . something as subtle as that . . . "There's no neighborhood any more"—and that's his first *Town and the City* tragic theme. "Beyond this old honesty there can only be thieves," and that means Nixon and Bebe Rebozo. So that "Looking at a man in the eye is now queer." A perfect expression (p. 262) in Whitmanic terms, of what went wrong with American males, muscle biceps tensely meet on the street: "Low panhandler homosexual dopefiend nigger Communist" paranoia.

• • •

Later an explanation for this journey across U.S. is given complete: "At the junction of the state line of Colorado . . . go moan for man . . . go thou, go thous, die hence; and of Cody report you well and truly"— What American poet ever had more sad and beautiful directions, commands from the god muse? more prophetic, yet more anonymously erranded?

Thence into the book, a new Neal after *On the Road*—That period is covered in *Visions of Cody* for those who'd ever wish'd a historic sequel— What happened to Dean Pomeroy, settled and married—? Kerouac's golden dreams come true—and a prophecy:

"War will be impossible when marijuana becomes legal." How truly lovely the primitive faith, in depths of 1951 cop-lobbied national dope fiend hallucination, that his private experience of grass would become, as it *did,* a national experience?

"*Everything always all right*"—afternoons together, Americans, working on the railroad—at that time no guilt, even the sticky hot tar and rail smoke soot a sort of golden afternoon's honest perfume—before the murder of Indians came to consciousness in America. Way before Neal's bust, this was just before Dulles and Ike and everyone Spellman started Vietnam War Indochina.

Heavenly Cody soliloquizes: "Our common death in this skeletal earth and billion particle'd grey moth void one empty huge horror and glory isn't it awful . . . Adieu Sweet Jack, the air of life is permeated with roses all the time," he has Neal say and himself reply, "I heard you, I sure do know it now," to Neal's speech, "I love you, man, you've got to dig that; boy you've got to know." Whitman's adhesiveness! Sociability without genital sexuality between them, but adoration and love, light as America promised in love.

The New Consciousness is early pronounced here, an old consciousness already forgotten since the good grey bard's 19th century yore; and among these prophecies the reader finds Kerouac's completely *written* peyote text, total explanations of states of consciousness, "This thing is the realization of suicide, your mind tells you how you can die, take your pick; I see"—perfect mind-changes of peyote recorded, a brilliant contribution to the literature, and early O hippies, how early his tragic common sense and un-drunk humanity squinting undismayed dismayed at the cactus "with his big lizard hide and poison hole buttons with wild hair, grooking in the desert to eat our hearts alive, ach. . . . Cody, this is

the end of the heart." Follows the funniest description of Mr. Peyote writ
ever.

And after peyote vision of their life together in moth-wracked joyful
trembling stomach-ghost-horror glory—he begins to try nail down the
exact places and visions he loved Neal in.* [*The bus station photograph described p. 343, Neal in pinstripe suit—can be seen p. 22 *Scenes
Along the Road*, Ed. Ann Charters. Portents/Gotham Book Mart, New
York City, 1970.] And "the great spindly tin-like crane towers of transter-
ritorial electric power wires . . . pagodas of Japan hung in a grey mist . . .
marching to the beat of Bethlehem steel hammers" can still be seen year
after year speeding north on Bayshore beneath San Francisco's hills,
where Neal and Jack worked the railroad.

At last, reveal'd, Kerouac's memory of the time Cody fuck'd the car
driving "pansy" they traveled east with—This reference alas was excised
from *On the Road* thus removing one dimension of American hero and
misleading thousands of highschool boys for decades—A vigorous
description and very Shakespeare-funny's given, though Jack in the toilet watching quoting Céline, "It's not in my line, probably should have
got into the act for his own happy good, not drunk himself to death later
with sinful visions like 'at one point it appeared Cody had thrown him
over legs in the air like a dead hen' . . . ouch . . . No wonder, 'Slam-bang-
ing sodomies that made me sick.'" Well I enjoyed both Cody and Jack,
many times in many ways jolly bodily and in soul love, and wish Jack had
been physically tenderer to Cody or vice versa, done 'em both good,
some love balm over that bleak manly power they had, displayed, were
forced to endure and die with.

"I'm writing this book because we're all going to die . . . my heart broke
in the general despair and opened up inwards to the Lord, I made a supplication in this dream." This is the most sincere and holy writing I know
of our age—at the same time for pre-Buddhist Jack, a complete display
of knowledge of Noble Truths he soon discovered in Goddard's *Buddhist
Bible*.

Yet Jack had another 18 years ahead with Neal on earth, neither was
dead ("Neal is Dead"), except this vision book was all out effort to understand early in the midst of life, what Jack's yearning and Neal's response
and both their mortal American energy was all about, was directed to—

but only time could tell, and both got tired *several* times—Jack went on to write not only *Dr. Sax* but *Mexico City Blues* in the next year and then *The Subterraneans* and *Springtime Mary (Maggie Cassidy)* and more and more and more climaxed 5 years later with some fame, and the brilliant Buddhist exposition *Dharma Bums,* and also *Desolation Angels* later, to keep the perfect chronicle going—"rack my hand with labor of Nada"— and many poems—not to speak of his *Book of Dreams* and giant as-yet-unpublished *Some of the Dharma,* 1000 pages of haikus, meditations, readings, commentaries on *Prajnaparamita* and Diamond Sutras, brain-thinks, *Samadhi*[7] notes, scholarship in the Void—reading Shakespeare and Melville all the while and listening to Bach's St. Matthew's Passion evermore—

Saying farewell to Cody, Jack was saying farewell to the world, both of them gave up several times—but at that 1952 time both of them were at their wits' ends with the world and America—the "Beat Generation" was about that time formulated, the Vietnam War just about to be continued American bodied (as 'twas already funded American dollar'd via opium pushing France and French-Corsican intelligence agencies)—two years after completion of this book Neal lived in a quiet home, receptive and friendly but by then entered into a blank new insistent religiosity, "like Billy Sunday in a suit" epistled Jack, namely Edgar Cayce study—which reincarnation philosophy drove Jack to study Buddhism; a new phase not even recorded or mentioned in this vast essay on Early or Middle Neal.

I remember the sleepless epiphanies of 1948—everywhere in America brain-consciousness was waking up, from Times Square to the banks of Willamette River to Berkeley's groves of Academe: little *samadhis* and appreciations of intimate spaciness that might later be explain'd and followed as the Crazy Wisdom of Rinzai Zen or the Whispered Transmission of Red Hat Vajrayana Path Doctrine, or Coyote's empty yell in the Sierras. Out of Burroughs' copy of Spengler Kerouac arrived at the conception of "Fellaheen Eternal Country Life"—Country *samadhi* for Jack, country Ken and consciousness latent discovered in Mexico as our heroes crossed the border: immediate recognition of Biblical Patriarch Type in Mexic Fellaheen fathers: the Bible those days the only immediate American mind-entry to primeval earth-consciousness non-machine populace that inhabits 80 per cent of the world—"Jeremiacal hoboes lounge, shepherds by trade ... I can see the hand of God. The future's in Fellaheen. At

Actopan this biblical plateau begins—it's reached by the mountain of faith only. I know that I will someday live in a land like this. I did long ago." heartbreaking prophecy. And intelligent Neal'd said, "What they want has already crumbled in a rubbish heap—they want banks."

Jack Kerouac didn't write this book for money, he wrote it for love, he *gave* it away to the world; not even for fame, but as an explanation and prayer to his fellow mortals, and gods—with naked motive, and humble piety search—that's what makes *Visions of Cody* a work of primitive genius that grooks next to Douanier Rousseau's visions, and sits well-libraried beside Thomas Wolfe's *Time and River* (which Thos. Mann from his European eminence said was the great prose of America) and sits beside Tolstoi for its *prayers*. A La La Ho!

So we see the end of the American road is the U.S. boy's conscious discovery of the eternal natural man, primitive, ancient Biblical or Josephaic Shepherd or Khartoum Mongolian Gothic Celtic: thus the magic political formulation idiotically stark sanely presented on p. 387—A quote from the mustached Vice Regent Consul of Empire next to a quote from Jackey Keracky:

"*False nonsense*"—*Acheson, 1952*

"*You've got to legalize the Fellaheen*"—*Duluoz, 1952*

And why this paean to Neal? It's a consistent panegyric to heroism of mind, to the American Person that Whitman sought to adore. And now, "The holy Coast is done, the holy Road is over." Jack thought Cody'd gone back to California marriage, would settle down be silent and die of old age—little he knew the psychedelic bus, as if *On the Road* were transported to heaven, would ride on the road again through America, the great vehicle painted rainbow colored as *Mahayana* illusion with its tantric Kool-Aid and celestial passengers playing their Merry Pranks "Further" thru the land, "A Vote for Goldwater is a Vote for Fun" sign painted on bus-side, en route to find sad drunken Jack, enthusiastic but speechless high bring him to acid apartment on Park Avenue crowded at midnight with 50 Prankster bus passengers all cynically expectant jester-dressed and starry eyed worshipping—the old red faced W. C. Fields Toad Guru trembling shy hungover sick potbellied master tenderly came back to the city afraid to drink himself to death—a Park Avenue apartment the site for Great Union Reunion Kerouac Cassady Kesey and friends all together at last once in New York under unofficial mock but real Klieg lights with microphones reverb feedback wires snaking all over th'electrified household living room floor 86th St. upper East Side—an American flag draped over couch, on which shocked Jack refused to sit—Kesey respectful welcoming and silent, fatherly timid host, myself marveling and sad, it was all out of my hands now, history was even out of Jack's hands now, he'd already written it 15 years before, he could only watch hopelessly one of his more magically colored prophecy shows, the hope show of ghost wisdoms made modern chemical and mechanic, in this *Kali Yuga,* he knew the worser death gloom to come, already on him in his alcohol ridden trembling no longer sexually tender corpus—anyway, O clouds over Tetons, great rain clouds over Idaho, lowbellied cumulus over Gros Ventre rain!—the conversation in that brilliant lit apartment Manhattan 1967 was sparse halting sad disappointing yet absolutely real, and thus recorded on tape as Jack already did, as well as (new era technology 15 years later Spenglerean time) on film! O rain spoils't thou man's toys and images? Washest time? And then the bright vast bus on the magic road went honking up to Dr. Leary's Millbrook tantric mansion, what eras're ushered in on us?

The last pages say, "All America marching to this last land." The book was a dirge for America, for its heroes' deaths too, but then who could know except in the unconscious—A dirge for the American hope that Jack (and his hero Neal) carried so valiantly through the land after Whitman—an America of pioneers and generosity—and selfish glooms and exploitations implicit in the pioneers' entry into foreign Indian and moose lands—but the great betrayal of that manly America was made by the pseudo-heroic pseudo-responsible masculines of Army and industry and advertising and construction and transport and toilets and wars.

Last pages—how tender—"Adios King!" a farewell to all the promises of America, an explanation and prayer for innocence, a tearful renunciation of victory and accomplishment, a humility in the face of "the necessary blankness of men" in hopeless America, hopeless World, in hopeless wheel of Heaven, a compassionate farewell to love and the companion, Adios King.

WRITTEN: May 17–June 9, 1972

FIRST PUBLISHED: *University Review,* no. 25 (Nov. 1972) pp. 20–22, 36. Reprinted as introduction to Jack Kerouac, *Visions of Cody* (New York: McGraw-Hill, 1973).

Kerouac's Ethic

I

Preamble

Visiting Tristan Tzara at his Paris apartment in 1957, he opened a notebook where he kept documents and showed Gregory Corso and myself a long letter of imprecation to him from Antonin Artaud, accusing him of being a custodian of a museum, an archivist, and not a true dada poet. The letter was marked with spit, cigarettes, curses, some of Artaud's sperm and some of his blood, and was sent from Rodez hospital asylum before Artaud's death.

Once Kerouac came to visit Peter Orlovsky on East Second Street in New York, in 1959, very late at night, drunk, banging on the front door disturbing the household. Peter Orlovsky's sister Marie, who was studying to be a nurse, was living in a little side room off our kitchen, and Kerouac made a lot of drunken noise, then opened the door to the room of this young, innocent, virgin girl and frightened her. I got outraged and told him to shut up and behave himself and he fell down on the floor laughing at me and said: "Ginsberg, you're a hairy loss."

He would phone very late at night since he couldn't receive visitors at his house. There were a few times when I and other friends wanted to come to see him in the mid-sixties and late sixties—once with the poet John Wieners, who had just come out of a mental hospital. We called ahead by phone every half hour to Cape Cod where he was living and he kept encouraging us to come because I hadn't seen him for a year. But when we got there all the lights in the house were out and he wouldn't answer the door. Later, he said it was because his mother refused to admit anybody and so Kerouac went and hid in the back yard, frightened among the garbage bins, afraid to appear at the door and turn us away, but trapped between his mother's obsessions and his own openness. He actually did want to see us but was afraid of his mother, and what he said to me later was: "My mother is as crazy as your mother was, except I'm not going to throw her to the dogs of eternity like you threw yours." So, he was guilt-bound to stay with her and take care of her, participate and empathize with her and exercise enormous generosity of temperament which in some respect was suicidal for him.

I remember visiting earlier, in the late fifties, his house in Northport, Long Island, and we sat by the television set and there was a retrospective news broadcast about Hitler and the concentration camps. Kerouac and his mother were both drinking. She was also a great tippler, both were drunk, and they began arguing among themselves. And then some German refugee came on the screen and talked about the Holocaust and Kerouac's mother said in front of me: "They're still complaining about Hitler, it's too bad he didn't finish them off." Kerouac agreed with her. I sat there and nodded. Then he said to her, "You dirty cunt, why did you say that?" And she said, "You fucking prick, you heard me say that before." And then began an argument of violence and filth such as I had never heard in any household in my life. I was actually shocked.

I suddenly realized the relationship between them: they were a bunch of drunks together, actually talking totally uninhibitedly like down-home peasants, not restrained at all in their family squabbles fired by alcohol. Not a calm maternal scene but a weird companionship. Many of his friends "disapproved" and thought he would do better out in the world with us. I even bought a farm in New York state as a refuge for him in case he was able to make his break from the family. But poet Philip Whalen pointed out to us, "There's nobody else that could take care of him except his mother. So it's probably a good thing that he's there with her, because otherwise he might die in the city."

Kerouac kept saying, he couldn't come to New York City, to Manhattan. He was afraid he would get drunk and bang his head and break his skull on the sidewalk curb. That's something that did happen to him when he came in, drank, and got into arguments and fights in the San Remo Bar. And he was incapable of fighting back. Not that he was weak but he simply wouldn't strike another person; he believed in the Lamb and so lived that through. There were situations where people attacked him, out of inquisitiveness or jealousy or natural alcoholic anger or irritability—jealousy primarily. Then there was one incident where he actually was down on the sidewalk with a big huge man literally banging his head on the sidewalk. Kerouac said it "did something to his brain," scrambled his brains permanently. So, he was afraid to come into the metropolis after that.

Whalen's remark had a great deal of insight. Whalen also said: "His

[Kerouac's] life was hardly a tragedy," that he'd produced so much and created a huge mythology and great literature and also a great lineage of intelligence in writing.

Late at night toward the end of the sixties, most of our communication was in the form of telephone calls, usually in the middle of the night. Sometimes, two or three a.m., he would be alone at home, lonesome, drinking, and finally get up the spirit to pick up the phone and make long distance calls to his friends. Sometimes to John Clellon Holmes, sometimes to Lucien Carr, often to me or Robert Frank, to whoever he knew in the city. Usually the calls were mockingly abusive, insulting. He'd constantly rag me for being a city intellectual Jew, make fun of my eyeglasses, ask me to suck his cock on the telephone. The older he got, the more gross in alcohol, the more insistent he was that I get down and suck his cock; the more he stank, the fatter, the more obese, the more drunken, the more insistent he was.

There was an adventure with the writer Paul Bowles, Tennessee Williams and John Gielgud the actor, at the very elegant Johnny Nicholson's restaurant on 57th Street sometime in the early sixties, where he insisted that the very dignified gay musician writer Paul Bowles show everybody his prick. Kerouac would talk about nothing but that for the whole elegant supper; he got underneath finally and overturned the entire marble round table still yelling that Bowles should show his prick. Alas, Bowles didn't have the courage or the humor to do so and satisfy him.

In the phone calls, along with insults, were very intelligent trenchant remarks always. Finally, I realized he was toying, playing, trying to see if he could get a rise out of me, trying to see if he could get me angry. Usually he did, but at one point I realized that this was almost like a Zen master's tactics for trying to break through my sense of self-importance. And so finally I said, "Kerouac if you don't shut up, I'll call your mother to the phone and tell her that her cunt is full of shit." He said, "You will?" And I said, "Yes, bring her over to the phone." Then he started laughing. And from then on, the conversation was very serious about Rimbaud and literature. So this was a seemingly vicious but playful mask. He was capable of a kind of bone-deep humor, but as I remember it in hindsight, despite my irritation at the time, it was always a lesson such as I learned later from another great drinker, the Tibetan lama Chögyam Trungpa (who also died at the age of 47 of alcohol).

There is a trenchancy in that alcoholic insight that sometimes is useful, and in the hands or in the mind or mouth of someone like Kerouac for me was always a teaching rather than pure insult. What that kind of bitterness or black humor did to him is nothing I can account for and, obviously, it killed him. But on the other hand there was always an intelligence there that, as I saw it, was actually really sublime. When I began insulting his mother, he began to ease off and take it easy and start talking straight. But until I was willing to counter his insult with a direct insult to him, he would pursue it and pursue it, and I think that is characteristic of many drinkers.

II

Kerouac's Ethic in the Light of his Buddhism

I was asked to approach the topic of Kerouac's ethic. It wasn't a subject that I chose, but it might be proper to reflect in this context on his Buddhism.[8] His interest in Buddhism began after he spent time with Neal Cassady, who had taken an interest in the local California variety of New Age Spiritualism, particularly the work of Edgar Cayce. Kerouac mocked Cassady as a sort of home-made American "Billy Sunday with a suit" for praising Cayce, who went into trance-states of sleep and then read what were called the Akashic records, and gave medical advice to the petitioners who came to ask him questions with answers which involve reincarnation. So, Kerouac was interested in going back to the original historic sources. He went to the library in San Jose, California and read a book called *A Buddhist Bible,* edited by Dwight Goddard—a very good anthology of classic Buddhist texts. Kerouac read them very deeply, memorized many of them and then went on to do other reading and other research and actually became a learned Buddhist intuitive scholar. A practitioner like the poet Gary Snyder, who studied Japanese Zen *in situ* in Daitoku-Ju monastery, later thought that Kerouac was quite brilliant and if faced by Koan exercises, would probably solve them very fast. So Kerouac did have an intelligent grasp of Eastern thought, also a learned grasp, and that's something most people don't realize.

His introduction to it, for me, was in the form of letters reminding me that suffering was the basis of existence, which is the first Noble Truth in Buddhism, and the first characteristic of existence in that category known as the Three Marks of Existence or Three Characteristics of Existence. Well, this is basic, so let us get to the ultimate nature of existence.

I was at the time a more or less left-wing liberal progressive intellectual and I was insulted that Kerouac should be telling me that the real basis of existence was suffering. I thought this was a personal insult and didn't realize he was simply telling me what he had realized as the basic nature of life.

There is this doctrine in Buddhism of the Three Marks of Existence: first, that existence contains suffering; in Yiddish, existence contains *tsores*, serious difficulty. Born, as Gregory Corso says, in "a hairy bag of water," there's going to be some difficulty before you leave your body, some irritability or discomfort. If you don't like the word "suffering," then you have to accept that existence contains some "discomfort." The traditional definition is that, being born, the inevitable ultimate consequence is old age, sickness and death, well described by Kerouac. This is inevitable. Most people don't want to look at it in advance, but Kerouac had seen that with his father and with Gérard [his brother], and he knew that lesson very clearly.

The second characteristic of existence as described in Buddha-*Dharma*, is impermanence—the transitoriness of our condition; the fact that what we have here is like a dream, in the sense that it is real while it is here. And so, Kerouac would say to me, "Come back in a million years and tell me if this is real." He had the sense of the reality of existence and at the same time the unreality of existence. To Western minds this is a contradiction and an impossibility. But actually, it is not impossible because it is true; this universe is real, and is at the same time unreal. This is known in Buddhism as a co-emergent wisdom, the fact that form and emptiness are identical. These are just basic Buddhist ideas. You'll find the terminology of "*sunyata*," emptiness, within form, running through all of Kerouac's middle period writing, especially in *Mexico City Blues*. The idea of transitoriness, of impermanence, is not a Himalayan idea, and not an Oriental idea, it's a classic Western idea. For, as Gregory Corso paraphrases Heraclitus, "You can't step in the same river once." You remember Heraclitus' "You can't step in the same river twice"? So Corso put it one poetic move ahead, you can't step in the same river "once." Or if you read the Western poet Percy Bysshe Shelley's poem *Mutability*, you realize this is an old Western idea as well as an old Eastern idea.

What Kerouac was discovering was not some strange Oriental notion alien to the Canuck or Western mind. He was exploring the basis of mind itself as it's known in the West as in the East, except that he saw the Buddhist formulations as being perhaps more sophisticated than the monotheistic formulations of the West. Nevertheless there were non-theistic formulations of the same thing in writers that he read like Lucretius and Montaigne.

So, the third aspect of existence or third mark of existence is *Anatma—Atman*: self; *Anatma*: no permanent self. That comes from the second mark, no permanence of any kind. All the foundations of existence are transitory, or as Kerouac paraphrased traditional Buddhist terminology, "All the constituents of being are transitory," all the building blocks of being are transitory. That being so, there is no permanent self-hood, no permanent me me me me me, and no permanent Great Me in Heaven. There is no reference point at all. There is nothing but open space or, as it is known to existentialists, the void. *Sunyata,* as it is known in the Orient; open and accommodating space. The notion of the void in the West may be claustrophobic and dark mainly thanks to Jean-Paul Sartre's unfortunate mescaline experience in *La Nausée,* when he saw the tree roots and felt a claustrophobic fear, a "bummer" as we know it in later terminology. But that sense of bummer is a very Western and theistic notion. In the East, the notion of "open space" or "accommodating space" is considered a liberation from the limitation of horizon or boundary wherein a theistic God image is the ultimate reference point. Or to put it very simply, when Chögyam Trungpa, who appreciated Kerouac's writings a great deal, was asked by his son: "Daddy, is there a God?" Trungpa said: "No." And his son said: "Whew!" That sigh of relief might have solved many of Kerouac's problems.

So, he introduced me to Buddhism in the form of song. As you may know, Kerouac admired Frank Sinatra for his crooning enunciation, for his oratory, for his clarity of speech, for the precision with which he emphasized consonants and the intonations with which he pronounced the affective emotional content of his vowels. And so, like Frank Sinatra, the first direct Buddhist word I heard from Kerouac's mouth after letters, was his singing of the Three Refuges. So, that would be the next step.

This is basic to Kerouac's understanding of Buddhism. It goes: "In *Buddha* I take my refuge, in *Dharma* I take my refuge, in *sangha* I take my refuge" (repeated three times). *Buddha* may be defined here as wakened mind; clear, not sleeping, not daydreaming but clear, aware of this space. *Dharma,* the intellectual explanation and exposition of the state of awakeness—historically, through Sutra discourses and through understanding of the theory. *Sangha* is the assembled fellow awakened meditators, in the sense that this is a Kerouac *Sangha.* So what he did is sing in Sanskrit to me: "*Buddham Saranam Gochamee, Dhammam Saranam Gochamee, Sangham Saranam Gochamee,*" etc. So, he sang that like Frank Sinatra in 1952. And that first introduced me to the delicacy and softness of his Buddhism aside from the tough truth of suffering, transitoriness, and no permanent Allen Ginsberg or permanent Kerouac.

Following that are the Four Noble Truths which he refers to in his writing very often and which readers read but without inquiring further about what these Four Noble Truths are, although in various essays Kerouac expounds them. We should pay sufficient respect to Kerouac (unlike his interrogators on television and in the media) to inquire: "What did he mean by the Four Noble Truths? What are these Four Noble Truths that he speaks of continually?" Perhaps they should be presented here as part of an exposition of Kerouac's ethics, because this refers directly to the central ethics we find in *Dharma Bums, Mexico City Blues, Some of the Dharma, Wake Up,* his unpublished biography of Buddha, *Desolation Angels,* and continuing even through later works more charged with monotheistic Catholic notions of Sacred Heart in relation to suffering.

The Four Noble Truths (based on the Three Marks of Existence) are as follows. First, existence contains suffering. Second Noble Truth: suffering is caused by ignorance of the conditions in which we exist—ignorance of the transitoriness and ignorance of *Anatma,* the empty nature of the situation, so that everybody is afraid of a permanent condition of suffering and doesn't realize that suffering itself is transitory, impermanent. There is no permanent Hell, there is no permanent Heaven. Therefore, the suffering that we sense during this transition of life is not a permanent condition that we need to be afraid of. It's not where we're going to end up. We end liberated from the suffering either by death, or in life, by waking up to the nature of our situation and not clinging and grasping, screaming and being angry, resentful, irritable or insulted by our existence.

It is possible to take our existence as a "sacred world," to take this place as open space rather than claustrophobic dark void. It is possible to take a friendly relationship to our ego natures, it is possible to appreciate the esthetic play of forms in emptiness, and to exist in this place like majestic kings of our own consciousness. But to do that, we would have to give up grasping to make everything come out the way we daydream it should, according to our Jewish-Canuck idea. So, suffering is caused by ignorance, or suffering exaggerated by ignorance or ignorant grasping and clinging to our notion of what we think should be, is what causes the "suffering of suffering." The suffering itself is not so bad, it's the resentment against suffering that is the real pain. This is where I think Kerouac got caught as a Catholic, ultimately, because I don't think he overcame that fear of the First Noble Truth.

The Third Noble Truth says there is an end to suffering, there is a way out of it. And the Fourth Noble Truth is called the Eightfold Path out of suffering, which Kerouac repeated over and over again in his poems and in his writings. The Eightfold Path is as follows: first, Right Understanding, Right View as it is called, Right Perspective on the whole scene of consciousness and space, which is the realization of suffering and the realization of transitoriness and the realization that there is no permanent ego. Right View, then, leads to the Right Aspiration or Right Ambition or the ambition to overcome the obstacle of ignorance and greed and passion and clinging, and to get out of the fix.

Third after Right Aspiration comes Right Speech, speech that is in line or coordinated with an understanding of the basic situation. This is distinct from, let us say, the problem that Kerouac came to later within the suffering of grasping for a permanent reference point in a Catholic God, who will save you and take you to Heaven, or who might condemn you to Hell: a sense of permanent doom or a permanent bliss that you are going to come to. So, Right Speech, not creating more mental garbage, not creating more mental fog for others or yourself.

From Right Speech, the fourth step is Right Activity, not messing up the universe with an insistence that other people follow you towards your obsessive wars, either wars against God or for God or for Hitler or against Hitler or for your mother or against your mother.

From Right Action comes Right Labor, a right kind of work so you don't get a job in the atom bomb industry and help blow up the world.

From Right Labor comes Right Mindfulness, the awareness of what is around you unobstructed by guilt over what are you doing, saying, thinking and working at.

From Right Mindfulness comes Right Energy, waking up in the morning happy with what you are going to do, not obstructed by your own garbage. And from Right Energy comes Right *Samadhi* or Right Meditation or basically being here where you are, unchanged, without guilt. Being able to exist without credentials, not needing an excuse to be here on earth, existing with the earth, co-eternal with the earth or existing simultaneously with the earth without apology any more than the sun has to apologize.

Here we come to Walt Whitman's original American proclamation of this condition. This was also in line with Kerouac's understanding. So, from this comes a term which Kerouac pronounced over and over again in his poetry, the "*Bodhisattva.*" Here's the formula: the *bodhisattva* makes a very clear set of simple vows.

First: sentient beings are numberless. I vow to liberate them all (dogs, worms, kitty cats, mommys, mémères, myself, Ginsberg, innumerable in the universe). I vow to illuminate all, is the purpose of Kerouac's writing and the ultimate ethic of his writing. Second: obstacles are countless, I vow to cut through them. My own neuroses are countless, my own graspings are countless, one's own aggression is inexhaustible. Yet, one vows to relate to it, to acknowledge it, to work on it, to cut through it and open up and admit the existence of other sentient beings into one's universe and relate to them in an honest way.

Third of the four vows of the *bodhisattva*: *Dharma* gates are uncountable, I vow to enter every gate. *Dharma* gates are situations in which to practice wakeful mind, situations to enter into without being afraid, including the situation of birth and death, the situation of writing Dharmic works for America as Kerouac did, the situation of not being afraid to be corny and display Sacred Heart in relation to Kerouac's prose. It's the disposition to allow our own emotion and tears and sense of suffering, to allow mutual confidence in each other with our most sensitive feelings, as Kerouac confided to us his most sensitive feelings: "Gates of *Dharma* are endless, I vow not to boycott anyone." No boycott of any situation but total openness toward all situations.

And last of all, Buddha path, or path of awakened mind, is infinite, endless, you never can finish with it, it's too long. I vow to follow through anyway: though Buddha path is endless, I vow to follow through. These are the Four *Bodhisattva* vows.

Now, when you take the *bodhisattva* vow it doesn't mean you can do it. It only means that this is the direction in which you would like to go. This is your ideal. This is your compass, or this is your inclination, or this is your heart's desire even if you can't accomplish it. As you might declare your love for a girl even though you know she won't sleep with you. Still, that doesn't prevent you from loving her. So, you need not be prevented from being a *bodhisattva* for fear that you'll not be able to accomplish these four vows, because if that's a heart's desire, that's sufficient for you to take that vow. It's a compass point or a direction or an indication of desire, and a vow to go in that direction. No permanent Heaven, no punishment of permanent Hell for that. So, this then leads to the next: Highest Perfect Wisdom, or "*Prajnaparamita,*" the ultimate philosophical and ethical statement of Zen Buddhism and Tibetan Buddhism, found in a text which Kerouac knew very well, the *Heart Sutra.*

Kerouac mentions, "*Anuttara Samyak Sambodhi.*" He used that phrase any number of times including in *Mexico City Blues*: "I attained absolutely nothing . . ." (111th chorus). "I didn't attain nothing when I attained Highest Perfect Wisdom, it was empty delightful bolony" (190th chorus). So, *Anuttara Samyak Sambodhi* is related to Highest Perfect Wisdom Sutra; in Sanskrit, *Prajnaparamita. Prajna* is wisdom, *Para* as in "parapsychology" is big or over, *Mita* is virtue. *Prajnaparamita* is a statement, a chant chanted every morning by Gary Snyder and Philip Whalen and other Zen Buddhists when they sit down to meditate.

To summarize the gist, it says *Avalokitesvara* (down-glancing-Lord-of-mercy) *Bodhisattva* dwelled in meditation on Highest Perfect Wisdom, when he realized that all the five heaps (*Skandas*) of consciousness we have were empty, this relieved every suffering. Then this discourse continues: *Shariputra,* form is emptiness, form is no different from emptiness, emptiness no different from form, form is the emptiness, emptiness is the form. Sensation, thought, imagination, consciousness are also like this. *Shariputra* (student), this is the original character of everything. Not born, not annihilated, not tainted, not pure, does not increase, does not decrease . . . No eye, no ear, no nose, no tongue, no body, no mind, no color, no sound, no smell, no taste, no touch, no object; no eye, no world of eyes until we come to no world of consciousness. No ignorance, also no combat against ignorance . . . no suffering, no cause of suffering, no *Nirvana*, no path, no wisdom, also no attainment because no attainment. Therefore every *bodhisattva* depends on Highest Perfect Wisdom because mind is no obstacle, because of no obstacle fear does not exist. Go beyond screwy views, attain *Nirvana*. Past, present and future, every Buddha depends on this Highest Perfect Wisdom . . . Therefore, I know *Prajnaparamita* is the great holy *mantram*, the untainted mantram, the supreme mantram, the incomparable mantram, is capable of assuaging all suffering. True because not false. Therefore he proclaimed *Prajnaparamita* mantram, and said mantram goes: *Gate Gate Paragate Parasamgate Bodhi Svâha!* Gone, gone, gone over the top, gone all the way over the top to the other shore, wakened mind. Salutations.

That's a summary of the text of *Prajnaparamita*: "Highest Perfect Wisdom" *Heart Sutra*. Most of Kerouac's mind-late poetry depends on some glimpse or some understanding of that statement, as both an ethic and a philosophical take on reality and appearance. Once you get that terminology down, you'll be able to read his *Mexico City Blues* very easily and see how funny they are, what a good representation of the mind they are and how trenchant philosophically.

Hardly any of the critics who wrote about him or interlocutors who'd interviewed him, and rarely any of the biographers who read to interpret him, have had the inquisitiveness to go into his Buddhism and learn what the basis of it is. But it could be summarized in one sentence which Kerouac often quoted from the *Vajraheddika*, or *Diamond Sutra*:

> All conceptions as to the existence of the self, as well as all conceptions as to the non-existence of the self; as well as all conceptions as to the existence of a supreme self, as well as all conceptions as to the non-existence of the supreme self, are equally arbitrary, being only conceptions.

It's not very far from the notion that William Burroughs laid on Kerouac in 1945 when he gave him a copy of Alfred Korzybski's *Science and Sanity*, the basic foundation work in general semantics. When Kerouac and I first visited Burroughs, he physically gave us his library: Oswald Spengler's *Decline of the West*, Jean Cocteau's *Opium*, Rimbaud's *Season in Hell* and *Illuminations*, William Blake's *Songs of Innocence and Experience*, Kafka's *Castle*. Among others I remember the big huge volume of *Science and Sanity*. The theme was: don't confuse words (and ideas) with events. This table is not a table. This is not a finger, it's called a finger but it is what it is. I "am" Allen Ginsberg or *my name* is Allen Ginsberg, but I am not "Allen Ginsberg." I'm me, or whatever I am. Allen Ginsberg is the label, Kerouac is the label for that masque of perceptions and consciousness, but it isn't a "thing" that you can *limit* by abstraction or generalization or definition. So, he was leaving the universe open. The slogan is to avoid "the *is* of identity."

Unfortunately, Kerouac had no teacher in the lineage of Zen or classical Buddhism. And so the one thing lacking was the tool, the instrument to realize the sort of substratum of all this exposition, namely the sitting practice of meditation—to actually take in his body the notion of emptiness or examine it as a process of mind, through the practice of classical meditation as handed down in immemorial "ear-whispered" tradition.

However, Kerouac was very intelligent and knew that substratum almost intuitively. You can tell that from his writing, from his poetry with its metaphors of emptiness and the description of vast spaciousness, which is the same thing as emptiness. You can see it at the end of *The Town and the City*, the vision of the football field, the clouds above the football field, the sun going down behind the clouds and the vaster spaces beyond in the sky. Beginning with microscopic detail and ending with the macroscopic view of the entire spacious universe.

The sense of "panoramic awareness" runs though all of Kerouac's descriptions of landscape. You always find him focusing on Neal Cassady at the pool table or the snooker table with the camera receding as it does at the end of the movie *Les Enfants du Paradis*. Remember when the camera recedes above the buildings, above the Ferris wheel, until we see the vast crowd receding in a much vaster space?

Kerouac, however, lacked specific instruction in the actual method of meditation practice in Zen. This, basically, is to follow the breath and take a friendly attitude toward one's thoughts, but bring the mind back to attention to the breath. Kerouac had worked out his own form of sitting practice which involved squeezing his anus, closing his eyes, and trying to see a golden light.

He had some kind of *satori* from that. But the instruction one gets in ancient sitting practice is: as soon as you see your thoughts, renounce them, let go. Don't cling to thought, don't try and sanctify it, don't try and make it a reference point, keep the space of mind open. As Blake says, "He who binds to himself a joy / does the winged life destroy / He who kisses the joy as it flies / lives in eternity's sunrise."

Kerouac's *satori* was clinging both to despair of suffering, fear of suffering, and permanent Hell, fear of a permanent Heaven: "I am only an Apache / smoking hashi, in old Cabashy / by the lamp," humorously frozen in a kind of horrible hashish Hell. He constantly refers to that image: "Pieces of the Buddha material frozen and sliced microscopically in morgues of the North . . . skeletons of heroes . . . fingers and joints . . . elephants of kindness as being torn apart by vultures." So obsessed was he with the suffering he encountered that he wasn't able to let go. I think the alcohol amplified that suffering, left him prey to the phantasm of the monotheistic imposition which Blake had denounced as being "Six thousand years of sleep" for Western civilization.

That's the basis, simply paying attention to the ongoing process of breath while it's proceeding, and taking a friendly attitude towards your thought forms. Not inviting them in, not pushing them away, allowing them to take care of themselves, but keeping your attention on the actual physical space around you, the flow of the outbreath. That's Tibetan style meditation. Gary Snyder never did teach him Zen Buddhist style in 1955, '56 and '57, because of some odd miscommunication. Though Gary Snyder had practiced, there was never any communication about the actual techniques of the sitting-practice of meditation.

So, we have a contrast here, ethically and philosophically, between non-theistic Buddhist space-awareness or awareness practice, and theistic Catholicism's contemplation of or fixation on the Cross of suffering.

As Jack grew older, in despair and lacking the means to calm his mind and let go of the suffering, he tended more and more to grasp at the Cross. And so, in his later years, he made many paintings of the Cross, of cardinals, popes, of Christ crucified, of Mary; seeing himself on the Cross, and finally conceiving of himself as being crucified. He was undergoing crucifixion in the mortification of his body as he drank. Nonetheless, he did have this quality of negative capability, the ability to hold opposite ideas in his mind without "an irritable reaching out after fact and reason," which John Keats proposed as the true mind of the Shakespearean poet.

"I am Canuck, I am from Lowell, I am Jewish, I am Palestinian, I am, I am the finger, I am the name": Kerouac was not heavily entangled in such fixed identity.

We owe it to Burroughs somewhat for having cut Kerouac loose from that "is of identity" in the mid-1940s, so that Kerouac had the ability to empathize with the old transvestite queen and become "one of the world's / great bullshitters, / girls," as he says in his *Mexico City Blues*. "Darling! Red hot / That kind of camping / I don't object to / unless its kept within reason" (74th chorus). He could empathize with the all-American boy, football hero. He could empathize with the Canuck *joual*-speaking provincial naïf. He could empathize with the sophisticated European Breton speaking Canadian-American. He could be a sophisticated *littérateur* or an old drunk alternatively. He could be country bumpkin, he could be as Thomas Wolfe, or he could empathize with William Burroughs as a "non-Wolfean" European sophisticate. So, in the end, his poetry and his prose become a perfect manifestation of his mind.

That was the whole point of the spontaneous prosody. And the great Tibetan Lama Chögyam Trungpa, examining Kerouac's poetry, said: "It's a perfect manifestation of mind," and that's why at Naropa Institute in Boulder Colorado, we originated the Jack Kerouac School of Disembodied Poetics in 1974. "Disembodied," because Kerouac was dead. His work is accepted in the Buddhist community as a great manifestation of poetic mind; true to the nature of mind as understood traditionally by Buddhist theories of spontaneous mind, how to achieve and how to use it.

I'd like to conclude by quoting from Kerouac's late analysis of the nature of mind and writing, to show how far he went. It's from a little pirate Zeta Press (1985) reprint, a pamphlet entitled *Last Words* containing an essay called "The First Word," dated January 1967, perhaps originally printed in *Escapade* or some other cheap pop magazine:

In the Surangama Sutra, Gautama Buddha says: "If you are now desirous of more perfectly understanding Supreme Enlightenment, you must learn to answer questions spontaneously and with no recourse to discriminate thinking. For the Tathagathas (the passers-through) in the ten quarters of the universes, because of the straight-forwardness of their minds and the spontaneity of their mentations, have ever remained, from beginningless time to endless time, of one pure Suchness with the enlightening nature of pure Mind Essence."

Then Kerouac continues:

. . . which is pretty strange old news. You can also find pretty much the same thing in Mark 13:11. "Take no thought beforehand what ye shall speak, neither do you premeditate: but whatsoever shall be given to you in that hour, that speak ye: for it is not ye that speak but the Holy Ghost!" Mozart and Blake often felt they weren't pushing their own pens, it was the "Muse" singing and pushing.

. . . In another sense spontaneous, or ad lib, artistic writing imitates as best it can the flow of the mind as it moves in its space-time continuum, in this sense, it may really be called Space Age Prose someday because when astronauts are flowing through space and time they too have no chance to stop and reconsider and go back. It may be they won't be reading anything else but spontaneous writing when they do get out there, the science of the language to fit their science of movement.

Then he adds something very interesting about his most extreme and auditorily exquisite prose experiment, *Old Angel Midnight,* originally called *Lucien Midnight.* In *Old Lucien Midnight* Kerouac tried to go all the way into the realm of pure "*shabda,*" Sound, and hear the spontaneous babble inside his brain and write that down. Actually, in his movie (*Pull My Daisy*), there are some "Midnight" passages—which are, I think, among the most beautiful of his writings, the caviar or cream of his prose. But here, in 1967, in his older age, he's reconsidering, and even criticizing himself:

But I'd gone so far to the edges of language where the babble of the subconscious begins, because words "come from the Holy Ghost" first in a form of a babble which suddenly by its sound indicates the word truly intended (in describing the stormy sea in *Desolate Angels,* I heard the sound *Peligrosso* for "Peligrosso Roar" without knowing what it meant, wrote it down involuntarily, late found out, it means "dangerous" in Spanish)—I began to rely too much on babble in my nervous race away from cantish clichés, chased the proton too close with my microscope, ended up rav-ingly enslaved to sounds, become unclear and dull as in my ulti-mate lit'ry experiment "Old Angel Midnight" . . . There's a delicate balancing point between bombast and babble.

And now my hand doesn't move as fast as it used to, and so many critics have laughed at me for those 16 originally-styled volumes of mine published in 16 languages and 42 countries, never for one moment calling me "sensitive" or artistically dignified but an unlet-tered literary hoodlum with diarrhea of the mouth, I'm having to retreat closer back to the bombast (empty abstraction) of this world and make my meaning plainer, i.e., dimmer, but the Space Age of the future won't bother with any of my "later" works if any, or with any of those millions of other things written today that all sound alike.

To break through the barrier of language with WORDS, you have to be in orbit around your mind, and I may go up again if I regain my strength. It may sound vain but I've been wrestling with this angelic problem with at least as much discipline as Jacob.

FIRST PUBLISHED: Pierre Anctil and others, eds. *Un Homme Grand* (Ottawa: Carleton University Press, 1990).

To America: Kerouac's *Pomes All Sizes*

He was Poet:—*You guys call yourselves poets, write little short lines, I'm a poet but I write lines paragraphs and pages and many pages long.* Thus he wrote in mid-fifties, a letter from Mexico City enclosing a scroll of his *Blues.*

Thus his ear auditing Burroughs' naked prose poetry: "Motel . . . motel . . . motel . . . broken neon arabesque . . . loneliness moans across the continent like fog horns over still oily tidal rivers . . ."[9]

His ear followed the road of sound: ". . . the mad road, keening in a seizure of tarpaulin power." He didn't know what the phrase meant, as he wrote it, later realized that "tarpaulin" covered truck gondolas piled with logs or pipes.

His ear came from reading and music: Thomas Wolfe, Herman

Melville, Shakespeare, C. F. Atkinson's translation of Spengler's Germanic portentous sound in *The Decline of the West,* Sir Thomas Browne, Rabelais, Shelley, Poe, Hart Crane—a romantic ear. And modern Whitman, Eliot, Pound, Céline, and Genet. Soul from Dostoyevsky and Gogol. Music from Bach's *St. Matthew's Passion* to Thelonious Monk's *Mysterioso.*

His influence is world wide, not only in spirit, with beat planetary youth culture, but poetic, technical. It woke Bob Dylan to world minstrelry: "How do you know Kerouac's poetry?" I asked Mr. Dylan after we improvised songs and read some *Mexico City Blues* choruses over Kerouac's gravestone 1976 Lowell's Edson Cemetery, cameras on us walking side by side under high trees and shifting clouds as we disappeared down distant aisles of gravestones. *Someone handed me* Mexico City Blues *in St. Paul in 1959 and it blew my mind!* Why? I asked. Dylan answered that it was the first poetry that spoke his own language.

My own poetry's always been modeled on Kerouac's practice of tracing his mind's thoughts and sounds directly on the page. Poetry can be "writing the mind," the Venerable Chögyam Trungpa phrased it, corollary to his slogan "First thought, best thought," itself parallel to Kerouac's formulation "Mind is shapely, Art is shapely." Reading *Mexico City Blues* to that great Buddhist teacher from the front carseat on a long drive Karme Chöling Retreat Center (1972 called Tail of the Tiger) [Vermont] to New York, Trungpa laughed all the way . . . "Anger doesn't like to be reminded of fits . . . The wheel of the quivering meat conception . . . The doll like way she stands / bowlegged in my dreams waiting to serve me . . . Don't ignore other parts of the mind . . ." As we got out of the car he stood on the pavement and said *It's a perfect exposition of mind.*

The next day, *I kept hearing Kerouac's voice all night, or yours and Anne Waldman's* . . . He said it'd given him a new idea of American poetry, for his own poetry . . . thus Trungpa Rinpoche's last decade's open form international spontaneous style *First Thought Best Thought* poetry collection (Boston: Shambhala, 1983). Thus two years later the "Jack Kerouac School of Disembodied Poetics" was founded with Naropa Institute, certainly a center for meeting of classical Eastern wisdom meditative practice with Western alert spontaneous candid thought, healthy synthesis of Eastern and Western mind, at last these twain've met *forever Hallelujah Svaha!*

But back to America in mid-1950s—the scroll of *Mexico City Blues* arrived at our cottage in Berkeley and inspired poet Philip Whalen (presently Whalen Sensei, Abbot of San Francisco Hartford Street Zen Center) to write *Big Baby Buddha Golden 65 feet high* ("Big high song for somebody"). Philip Lamantia, authentic surrealist American poet, had already delighted in Kerouac's catholic tender mind Big Sur 1950 on peyote.

Gary Snyder preparing to go to Japan was impressed by Kerouac's intuitive familiarity with *dharma* sutra and its manifestation in *Blues*: *When I first saw* Mexico City Blues *I was immediately taken by the ease of it, the effortless way it moved on—apparently effortless—at the same time there was some constant surprise arising in the words, always something happening with the words. You can see the mind at work, see the mind in it. Each poem was complete in itself, each had a similar mode of movement, each like a little stanza born. In the year [1955] I was getting to know Jack, I was touched by* Mexico City Blues *and Whitman, the same influence at that time, struck by poems Kerouac published in the Berkeley Bussei.*

Michael McClure was inspired to the later ditties of *September Blackberries. It's the sheer beauty of his treatment of everyday as divine world . . . the smallest voice was equal to the most heroic chunk of matter . . . In addition I was illuminated, thrilled, deeply moved by seeing the natural unplanned growth of them, poem after poem, each with a life of its own. "Morphine Junkey" to "Mission on Mercy" to "Gerard as Child" was preparation for me to write my own visions.*

There's a movement thru space of an energy, a system that acts to organize that system. You see Kerouac's flow, you can follow his spiritual energy as the system moves along acting to organize itself into a great religious poem. He's the model from which the spirit drives outward organizing itself into a previously nonexistent structure—equivalent to life, it's like a living being, Mexico City Blues.

In addition, done with grace because of its lack of pretentiousness—the most insignificant equal to the most significant, which is the divine grace.

Actually my own major work, unpublished, is Fleas—*Kerouac was my mental model . . . Kerouac's* Mexico City Blues *and Pound's* Cantos *are a similar experience for me . . . I began to write things fast as I could, write at typewriter . . . the spirit organizes itself—it's turned into 250 stanza rhyming autobiography not published . . . I vowed not to censor it, so not ever ever publish—the writing blithely completely idiot cartoon Skeltonic rhyming—now released from constraint.*

All San Francisco Renaissance poets were curious, interested, impressed, sometimes inspired by Kerouac's solitary autochthonous strength, ear, Kerouac's sound, his unobstructed grasp of American idiom. Thus Robert Duncan's astonishment at Kerouac's *List of Essentials* in "Belief and Technique for Modern Prose" I'd tacked on my wall when he visited Marconi Hotel, North Beach 1955.

Robert Creeley speaks of that time: *Jack had an extraordinary ear, that impeccable ear that could hear patterns and make patterns in the sounds and rhythms of the language as spoken. Extraordinary ear, in the way he could manage such a live and insistently natural structure. Jack was a genius at the register of the speaking voice, a human voice talking. Its effect on my poetry? He gave an absolute measure of what the range of that kind of writing was.*

Before that the standards ranged from Cummings to Prévert, but with Kerouac we had a human voice, not as imitation, but as fact of that voice talking. That he could do it in both poetry and prose interested me.

Anthologies?—Same confusion of critics as with Lawrence, the constant problem of falling between two stools, prose and poetry. He was classified as "novelist" despite the evidence of Brakeman on Railroad, Mexico City Blues, *and* Visions of Cody *that the distinction between the two forms was in certain writers artificial—they are inseparable.*

As Creeley points out, *Kerouac's simultaneous ability in prose and poetry like Hardy, like Lawrence, like Joyce, like Jean Genet, like Burroughs, proposes questions that are more fruitful to contemplate rather than to dismiss: "Oh I didn't know he wrote poetry?"... or "Oh, he's famous for his novels"... or "Oh, it's just prose put in short lines"... or "Oh, he's mainly a prose writer isn't he?"*

Kerouac "was a writer" as Burroughs remarked; that is, he *wrote*. He practiced writing, and for him writing was a sacred practice as he himself prayed, "I made a supplication in this dream." Holy recollected visions of mortal existence with panoramic scope of suffering and transitoriness—Buddhist sympathy and Catholic compassion—gave motif constantly lofty and playful—the very mind of poetry. So Olson championed Kerouac from a distance. And Lew Welch drove across America with him writing haikus.

The second generation of New York School, well versed in the spontaneous sophistications of O'Hara and Ashbery, recognized Kerouac's genius and were influenced by this Americana spontaneity—Ted Berrigan and Aram Saroyan notably, who interviewed him for *Paris Review*, Tom Clark and Anne Waldman, themselves powers at St Mark's Poetry Project, inherited some of Kerouac's energy and intelligence in U.S. ordinary mind—sacred mind, pop art mind, Bop mind. And LeRoi

Jones (Amiri Baraka) who liberated a world of African American verse, also caught some of Jack Kerouac's mind and musical vibration and publicly praised Kerouac's theoretic rationale of authentic oral spontaneity. And certainly it was Kerouac who collaborated with William Burroughs in Burroughs' first "hardboiled' fiction back in 1945 and passed the romantic "gemlike flame" of sacred prose-poetry, home made, personal, spontaneous, to Burroughs himself, Kerouac was a catalyst there. And how many would-be poets, ordinary poets, and genius poets in U.S. found Kerouac's legend and texts a model inspiration?

Certainly a colossus, for his poetry books and parallel prosepoetry passages in novels (whether the still life sketches of first 150 pages of *Visions of Cody,* or the shroud at the window of *Dr Sax,* or the ear babble of *Old Angel Midnight*) or the haikus, playful snapshots and matured musings in the present posthumously published *Pomes All Sizes.* Kerouac is a major perhaps the major seminal poet of the latter half of U.S. twentieth century—and mayhap thru his imprint on Dylan and myself among others a poetic influence over the entire planet. Jack Kerouac was above all a poets' poet, as well as a people's poet and an ivory tower poet, like Rimbaud legended to youth round the world.

Alas a poet not yet appreciated by the Academy. What's that "Academy"? Let us say, the Academy as represented by major English-language college anthologies used in the quarter century or so since Kerouac's death 1969.

1960s *New American Poetry* introduced Kerouac to the world of anthology (as well as myself, O'Hara, Ashbery, Corso, Koch, Olson, Creeley, Wieners, Snyder, Levertov etc.). Following that—total amnesia! But look in 1990's Norton, Macmillan, Harvard, Oxford, Heath textbooks, etc., etc. lined up row after row in college bookstores, arriving at English department mailboxes, heavy tomes authored by professors from sea to shining sea, published with groaning labor by the heaviest of textbook publishers, we find poet after poet influenced consciously by Kerouac, or swept up unconsciously into the cultural stream of self-empowerment—initiated by Kerouac—academic poets with loosened verse, minority poets of all colors indebted to Kerouac's bardic breakthru—but where's a text of Kerouac? Nowhere to be found to astonish and delight youngsters who open these classroom books. Mediocre poets mix with modern great names, experimental poets mix with re-formalist pigmies, first rate ordinary versifiers mix with multicultural identity boosters. But Kerouac the author-catalyst of this American literary revolution? Not yet to be found in "establishment" anthologies!

He'll be read in volumes like this, which Kerouac himself prepared before his death for City Lights Books, publisher of his outlandish classic original *Book of Dreams* (1961), and first posthumous *Scattered Poems* (1971). Lawrence Ferlinghetti speaks: *I was influenced by Kerouac years later, not in the '50s, by* Mexico City Blues—*I stole quite a few images from him. I've used that "quivering meat wheel" in the end, in my unpublished notebooks, but didn't react to it at first, didn't publish it . . . I remember, from Jack's French poems, I picked up on how you can blend the French and English, and did that in some of my poems. He's a hero to French Canadian writers, not only to prose, but among poets too, the father of Canuck poetry.*

Here's a treasure, in the main stream of American literature, random as this collection is, of notebook jottings, little magazine items—a grab bag, containing lovely familiar classic Kerouacisms, nostalgic gathas from 1955 Berkeley cottage days, pure sober tender Kerouac of yore, pithy exquisite later drunken laments and bitter nuts and verses. *Pomes All Sizes*—modest title—to be appreciated by cognoscenti and literate strangers—more valuable for being 'isolato,' original, unrecognized, exactly because such beauty's too personal to be noticed by literature's officialdom—"mis-noticed"—socio-politically "inconvenient" to include in the exasperating parade of college-wise-notable acceptable poetry collections by professionals and editors.

"This prophecy Merlin shall make for I live before his time": Till Kerouac as poet's understood, his formal verse beauty visible to scholars, and his surprise mind tenderness taken straight-forwardly and felt by vulnerable professors, the teaching of American literature'll never get on the right track, a conscious breath of U.S. poetry be neglected, the nation won't exhale its own compassionate spirit, hordes of literary bureaucrats will continue to snuffle shallow inspiration and new generations'll be turned off to poetry except for individual chance in finding this original Kerouac book or works by Kerouac fellow traveler poets like-minded and lighthearted on the same road announced by Walt Whitman.

WRITTEN: March 14, 1992

FIRST PUBLISHED: Introduction to Jack Kerouac, *Pomes All Sizes* (San Francisco: City Lights, 1992).

WILLIAM S. BURROUGHS

William S. Burroughs Academy Blurbs
[Written As a Nomination for Membership]

William Seward Burroughs, invisible man, explorer of souls and cities; whose exact-prosed *Junky* showed process of police-state chemical conditioning; whose classic *Naked Lunch* broke down legal barriers to deconditioning from heavy metal planetary hypnosis practiced by authoritarian word-manipulators including C.I.A. fronting for the Nova Mob; whose trilogy *Soft Machine, Nova Express* and *Ticket That Exploded* cut up post-atomic consciousness and traced back along word-lines to the Nova Mob's Image Bank power centers; whose *The Job* summarized de-conditioning techniques that had inspired three decades of poets musicians artists to world-revolution of consciousness characteristic of Beat Hip and later longhair generations; whose *The Wild Boys* and *Exterminator!* continue literary exploration of dense worlds of international consciousness, amounting to home-made, individualistic, self invented Yankee *tantra*.

WRITTEN: Feb. 15, 1975

FIRST PUBLISHED: 1977 ballot, American Academy and Institute of Arts and Letters, Department of Literature, New York, 1976.

William Seward Burroughs is a prose-poet with an extraordinary ear for assonance and speech styles, a naked eye for hypnotic detail, and an innovator of forms, forms ideas and moods in novels and cultural symbols.

WRITTEN: June 1982

Junky: **An Appreciation**

The reader, after a cursory glance at this book, will discover that the author is no ordinary junky. He seems to have taken pains to disguise the fact that he is also a man with a background that might astonish many of his readers.

Born just before the twenties, of a respectable middle-class family in a large Midwestern city—a family whose name is a household word in America for the inventions and commercial exploits of its 19th-century forebears—he received a good education at a private school where he was known as an aloof, and shy aristocrat with phenomenal scholarly aptitudes and a startling penchant for wildness. His first literary venture was a history of Rome, done (in true 19th-century manner) from common Latin sources, at the age of 18. Having set a record for scholarship at this school he was sent to Harvard, where he studied English literature. Little is known of his experiences there, except that he was supposed to have kept a ferret on a chain in his rooms, and a portrait of his family house on the wall. When questioned about the latter his invariable remark, with an offhand gesture of the palm, was "Yes isn't it hideous?" Only one literary specimen remains from his graduate school days, a 20-page playlet set on a sinking ship in the middle of the Atlantic, with several of his acquaintances cast in various roles of hysteria, terror, malice, and last-minute turpitude.

On his graduation in the early thirties, considering that he had said all he had to say literarily in the aforementioned charade, he studied anthropology, again at Harvard, specializing in Aztec and Mayan archaeology.

Returning to his home city he found no career to his liking and took to drinking, riding around the river sections with his contemporaries on summer drunks, and studying yoga. Presumably he had no formal instruction in the latter discipline, since on being challenged to prove its efficacy, he announced that he was impervious to pain and demonstrated this by cutting off a finger. This exploit led to his incarceration in a private sanitarium nearby, from which he was soon released, as he seemed composed and cognizant of his surroundings.

His next move, in true American style, was the Grand Tour of Europe. He spent a year in Europe and North Africa before returning to America. His favorite books, which he carried around with him, included Pareto and Spengler, Cocteau's *Opium,* a copy of Baudelaire, a paperbacked volume of Shakespeare's tragedies, and (later) W. B. Yeats' *A Vision.*

Returning to America he brought with him a bride, whom he had met during one year's abortive career as a medical student in Middle Europe. Bride and groom separated immediately on landing in New York, the purpose of the marriage having been to obtain citizenship for the Jewish lady, supposed also to have been a baroness.

Then followed a tour of U.S. cities, hotel room to hotel room; from New York, through the South and Midwest, with long stops during the early forties in Chicago and New York. This was made possible by a small private income from his family.

It was in Chicago that the author first began to explore the underworld, while working as a professional pest exterminator in that city's slum areas. However, certain other less criminal but nonetheless subterranean vices, treated in the later sections of the book, had already been discovered in his youth in America and travels in Europe.

One other important moment of background may be mentioned: the author's second wife,[10] who appears briefly in the New Orleans section of the book. The common-law marriage, which began in the late forties, ended with her untimely death as the result of a drinking accident in a Latin American country in 1950.

The subject of *Junky* is drugs and the drug world; it is not in any sense a complete autobiography, though many personal details relating to the main subject have been included. It is the autobiography of one aspect of the author's life, and obviously cannot be taken as an account of the whole man, as the last pages of the Prologue will demonstrate.

In that respect, the author has done what he set out to do: to give a fairly representative and accurate picture of the junk world in the late forties and early fifties and all it involves; a true picture, given for the first time in America, of that vast underground life which recently has been much publicized. It is a notable accomplishment; there is no sentimentality here, no attempt at self-exculpation besides the most candid, no romanticizing of the circumstances, the dreariness, the horror, the mechanical beatness and evil of the junk life as lived. It is a true account of its pleasures, such as they are; a relentless and perspicacious account of the characters that inhabit the junk world, with their likeness and unlikeness to the known average of the culture; a systematic history of the events of a habit, the cravings, the jailings, the night errands, the day boredoms.

We are fortunate that we have a historian, however firmly he has taken his position on the other side of the dark wall of normal gratification, who is able to give us these facts in a manner of writing which shows signs of literary maturity; a style which is direct, personal, very characteristic, very literal, highly selective, intense and economical in its imagery. It would be too great a presumption to compare such a localized world of horror as that of junk, with the universal Inferno of Dante; and yet that comparison, for certain spareness of manner and realistic use of simile, is what may happily arise in the mind of the trained reader.

It remains to be said that the publisher presents this book to the public for its originality of style and content in dealing with a highly controversial subject. Very little real information is obtainable on this subject, and most of it is romanticized and hyped up or distorted for mass commercial purposes. This book has the advantage of being both real and readable. It is an important document; an archive of the underground; a true history of the true horrors of a vice. It makes clear what even the most foolish may understand.

WRITTEN: April 12, 1952

Unpublished.

Junky: Introduction

Bill Burroughs and I had known each other since X-mas 1944, and at the beginning of the '50s were in deep correspondence. I had always respected him as elder and wiser than myself, and in first years' acquaintance was amazed that he treated me with respect at all. As time wore on and our fortunes altered—me to solitary bughouse for awhile, he to his own tragedies and travels—I became more bold in presuming on his shyness, as I intuited it, and encouraged him to write more prose. By then Kerouac and I considered ourselves poet/writers in destiny, and Bill was too diffident to make such extravagant theater of self. In any case he responded to my letters with chapters of *Junky,* I think begun as curious sketching but soon conceived on his part—to my thrilled surprise—as continuing workmanlike fragments of a book, narrative on a subject. So the bulk of the manuscript arrived sequentially in the mail, some to Paterson, New Jersey. I thought I was encouraging him. It occurs to me that he may have been encouraging me to keep in active contact with the world, as I was rusticating at my parents' house after eight months in mental hospital as result of hippie contretemps with law.

This took place over quarter century ago, and I don't remember structure of our correspondence—which continued for years, continent to continent and coast to coast, and was the method whereby we assembled books not only of *Junky* but also *Yage Letters, Queer* (as yet unpublished), and much of *Naked Lunch.* Shamefully, Burroughs has destroyed much of his personal epistles of the mid-'50s which I entrusted to his archival care—letters of a more pronouncedly affectionate nature than he usually displays to public—so, alas, that charming aspect of the otherwise Invisible Inspector Lee has been forever obscured behind the Belles Lettristic Curtain.

Once the manuscript was complete, I began taking it around to various classmates in college or mental hospital who had succeeded in establishing themselves in publishing—an ambition which was mine also, frustrated; and thus incompetent in worldly matters, I conceived of myself as a secret literary agent. Jason Epstein read the manuscript of Burroughs' *Junky* (of course he knew Burroughs by legend from Columbia days) and concluded that had it been written by Winston Churchill, it would be interesting; but since Burroughs' prose was "undistinguished" (a point I argued with as much as I could in his Doubleday office, but felt faint surrounded by so much reality . . . mustard gas of sinister intelligent editors . . . my own paranoia or inexperience with the great dumbness of business buildings of New York) the book was not of interest to publish. That season I was also carrying around Kerouac's Proustian chapters from *Visions of Cody* that later developed into the vision of *On the Road.* And I carried *On the Road* from one publishing office to another. Louis Simpson, himself recovering from nervous breakdown at Bobbs-Merrill, found no artistic merit in the manuscripts either.

By grand chance, my companion from N.Y. State Psychiatric Institute, Carl Solomon, was given a job by his uncle, Mr. A. A. Wyn of Ace Books.

Solomon had the literary taste and humor for these documents—
though on the rebound from his own Dadaist, Lettriste and Paranoiac-
Critical literary extravagances, he, like Simpson, distrusted the criminal
or vagabond romanticism of Burroughs and Kerouac. (I was myself at
the time a nice Jewish boy with one foot in middle-class writing careful
revised rhymed metaphysical verse—not quite.) Certainly these books
indicated we were in the middle of an identity crisis prefiguring nervous
breakdown for the whole United States. On the other hand Ace Books'
paperback line was mostly commercial schlupp with an occasional
French Romance or hardboiled novel nervously slipped into the list by
Carl, while Uncle winked his eye.

Editor Solomon felt that we (us guys, Bill, Jack, myself) didn't care, as
he did, about the real Paranoia of such publishing—it was not part of
our situation as it was of his—Carl's context of family and psychiatrists,
publishing house responsibilities, nervousness at being thought mentally ill by his uncle—so that it took bravery on his part to put out "this
type of thing," a book on junk, and give Kerouac $250 advance for a
prose novel. "The damn thing almost gave me a nervous breakdown—
buildup of fear and terror, to work with that material."

There was at the time—not unknown to the present with its leftover
vibrations of police state paranoia cultivated by narcotics bureaus—a
very heavy implicit thought-form, or assumption: that if you talked aloud
about "tea" (much less junk) on the bus or subway, you might be
arrested—even if you were only discussing a change in the law. It was just
about illegal to talk about dope. A decade later you still couldn't get away
with national public TV discussion of the laws without the narcotics
bureau and FCC intruding with canned film clips weeks later denouncing the debate. That's history. But the fear and terror that Solomon
refers to was so real that it had been internalized in the publishing industry, and so, before the book could be printed, all sorts of disclaimers had
to be interleaved with the text—lest the publisher be implicated criminally with the author, lest the public be misled by arbitrary opinions of
the author which were at variance with "recognized medical authority"—at the time a forcible captive of the narcotics bureau (20,000 doctors arraigned for trying to treat junkies, thousands fined and jailed
1935–1953, in what N.Y. County Medical Association called "a war on
doctors").

The simple and basic fact is that, in cahoots with organized crime, the

Narcotics Bureaus were involved in under-the-table peddling of dope, and so had built up myths reinforcing "criminalization" of addicts rather than medical treatment. The motive was pure and simple: greed for money, salaries, blackmail and illegal profits, at the expense of citizens who were classified by press and police as "Fiends." The historic working relationship between police and syndicate bureaucracies had by early 1970s been documented by various official reports and books (notably N.Y.'s 1972 Knapp Commission Report and *The Politics of Opium in Indochina* by Al McCoy).

Because the subject—*in medias res*—was considered so outré, Burroughs was asked to contribute a preface explaining that he was from distinguished family background—anonymously William Lee—and giving some hint how some supposedly normal citizen could arrive at being a dope fiend, to soften the blow for readers, censors, reviewers, police, critical eyes in walls and publishers' rows, god knows who. Carl wrote a worried introduction pretending to be the voice of sanity introducing the book on the part of the publishers. Perhaps he was. A certain literary description of Texas agricultural society was excised as not being germane to the funky harsh non-literary subject matter. And I repeat, crucial medico-political statements of fact or opinion by Wm. Lee were on the spot (in parentheses) disclaimed (by Editor).

As agent I negotiated a contract approving all these obscurations, and delivering Burroughs an advance of $800 on an edition of 100,000 copies printed back-to-back—69'd so to speak—with another book on drugs, by an ex-narcotics agent. Certainly a shabby package; on the other hand, given our naïveté, a kind of brave miracle that the text actually was printed and read over the next decade by a million *cognoscenti*—who did appreciate the intelligent fact, the clear perception, precise bare language, direct syntax and mind pictures—as well as the enormous sociological grasp, culture-revolutionary attitude toward bureaucracy and law, and the stoic cold-humor'd eye on crime.

WRITTEN: Sept. 19, 1976

FIRST PUBLISHED: William Burroughs, *Junky* (New York: Penguin, 1977).

Recollections of Burroughs Letters

I adore the writer of these letters full of black humor and suffering querulousness. Kerouac at this time called Burroughs "the most intelligent man in America" and decades later I'd say he was right. At least I can't think of anyone more basically to the point. "Genius is funny," Kerouac also said, thinking Shakespeare. I burst out laughing 25 years later, reading Burroughs' directions to Seymour Wyse where to "find the action" (letter May 30, 1956).

But a few paragraphs on the circumstances of these letters might be useful. We'd known each other since 1945, we lived together for a few months 1953 in idyllic pre-Viet-war Lower East Side between Avenues B and C on East 7th Street, visited by Kerouac, Corso and other friends, had assembled the text of *Yage Letters* and *Queer* and had a love affair. In the end, despite my admiration and affection for my teacher, I had rejected his body. "I don't want your ugly old cock." Harsh words for a young man, something I wouldn't want anyone to say to me. But he had pushed me to it, after long ambivalence, by offering, nay, threatening to "schlupp" with me, i.e. devour my soul parasitically, as Bradley the Buyer does to the District Supervisor in *Naked Lunch*. This word was part of an exquisite black-humorous fantasy on Bill B.'s part, hardly the thing to woo a scared lad (I was bodily ungainly anyway), and a parody of his feelings, lest his desire be considered offensive. So he wooed with extravagant self-deprecatory suggestiveness. It scared me, the responsibility to be his love connection. Unlimited sensitivity and vulnerability, I understood at the time, and respected, idolized. Not sure if some monstrous Crab Nebula ambassador was behind his implacable love, I reacted with naive impatience one afternoon on the NE corner of E. 7th Street and Avenue B, "I don't want . . . ," affronting his trust boorishly, in rude panic—I ever regret the wound I dealt his heart.

We decided to separate for a season. We'd been spiritual-literary friends since Kerouac and I had decided to visit him in 1945 to pay our respects and inquire after his soul. Among close friends, *Junky, Yage Letters, Pull My Daisy, The Green Automobile, The First Third, On the Road, Visions of Cody, Subterreaneans* had already been written and "published in heaven" if not on earth—we stayed still faithful to the star on each other's forehead, still sacramental life-companions despite disturbance of erotic rapport. I loved Bill and he loved me, as I still do decades later. Wouldn't you?

So he sailed to Europe, eventually Tangier, and I hitchhiked to visit his earlier boyfriend Marker in Jacksonville, then spent Xmas with Burroughs' parents living in Palm Beach, stayed in Yucatan and Chiapas half a year, then trained to San Jose in the Bay Area near San Francisco to meet Neal Cassady (with whom I was erotically enamored as much as Bill was heart-aching for me) and Kerouac.

In this context of trust, love, and heartache we continued a correspondence already years old (*Junky* and *Yage Letters* already were composed from his half the previous three years' epistles). The reader will thus recognize many of the "routines," that later became *Naked Lunch,* as conscious projections of Burroughs' love fantasies—further explanations and parodies and models of our ideal love schlupp together.

I was somewhat resistant, so much of his fantasy consists of a parody of his invasion of my body and brain. At the time I was experimenting with heterosexual amity and was shacked up with a fellow worker girl in the market research and advertising world of Nob Hill and smart San Francisco Montgomery Street. This appeared as a terrible affront to Bill's hope of marriage of heart and soul with me; I was just trying out my capacity for love of all kinds and accommodation to Commercial Society. I made direct heart exchange with Peter Orlovsky within a year.

The bulk of letters written to San Francisco from Tangier are Bill's faithful record of his heroic battle with depression and junk, Burroughs transcending his own condition to examine world condition, prophesying and articulating a post-nuclear psychology. Exploring his own soul, till he reached the bottom, he emptied his soul out and entered at last the open blue space of "Benevolent indifferent attentiveness" characteristic of later phases of his art.

These letters are a record of Burroughs' suffering from a "Dark Night of the Soul," the necessary experience of recognition and purification, or clearing out, of love-wounded fantasy. A chronicle of Burroughs at his most vulnerable, "the invisible man" at his most visible tender, in a self-humbling open-hearted phase, longing and desirous, offering body and inmost self-regard for inspection and acceptance. A tremendous sweetness and willingness comes through, as in the letter to Jack Aug. 18, 1954 and one to myself May 17, 1955—"I am having Serious difficulties with my novel. I tell you the novel form is completely inadequate to express what I have to say. I don't know if I can find a form. I am very gloomy as to the prospects of publication. And I'm not like you, Jack, I need an audience, of course, a small audience. But I still need publication for development . . ." "Wish you were here as I could do with some outside help."

I was inadequate to answer this weight of love—not smart enough to be the object on which he lavished such inventive genius—not open-hearted enough to give him what he needed, wanted, and deserved—a dearer answer than I gave. I felt ashamed of my own shallowness. My own letters in return for his have not survived, I'm almost glad, they'd show the poverty of my own art and superficial appreciation of his attentive devotion to me. His letters go through phases of suit and rejection, somewhat similar in structure to Shakespeare's sonnet sequence to his boyfriend Mr. W.H. First evidence of cut-up is displayed as reunion between us approaches, after 4 years. Here Burroughs the letter writer person (Jan. 31, 1957) nearly merges with the routines that pass before his eyes. The letters merge with the novel, the life merges with the art. He has won through, become one with his imagination, and begins to assume gigantic solitary proportions as artist alone in the universe, some-what mysterious, somewhat dehumanized behind mask of artists, more aloof, and later more outrageous than ever. By 1961, our next reunion in Tangier, he was a hash-eating rambunctious machete-swinging holy laughing terror, cutting up his prose and "all apparent sensory phenom-ena."

Alas! the most extravagant passages, abject letters of complete schlupp-longing, and prophetic curse at my ingratitude, have been cen-sored by the author. A red heart valentine center has been removed—the elder distinguished Mr. B. of the preface to this volume has judged himself (and me?) too harshly and excised some evidence of sentimen-tal romance from this collection as edited and printed here—lines blue-penciled in various letters, a few pages irrevocably burnt.

Despite emendations, Burroughs' presentations of these epistolary confessions is an act of benevolence. They are revealing, personal, wild, sensitive, foolish, sublime, sweet and self-deceiving, frank and soft. How can he stand such a self-portrait, so many decades later? Yet he's given himself away—the strange Burroughs that Kerouac and I knew, the gentle melancholy Blue Boy, the proud elegant sissy, the old charmer, the intelli-gent dear. I kept his letters, snapshots, envelopes in black springboard binders, the text of *Naked Lunch* ("an endless novel which will drive every-body mad") accumulated till 1957 when I was free to join Bill and Kerouac in Tangier. Jack lived two floors above Bill's at the Villa Mouniria in a balcony room overlooking the Straits of Gibraltar. He had begun retyping the preliminary assemblage of texts and letters which compose *Naked Lunch*. I was to bring my entire manuscript—hundreds of pages, in chronological order of invention, to Tangier. There all of us were to sit together and assemble a final manuscript. The difficulty was that Dr. Benway and other characters introduced from 1953 on were refined and developed from letter to letter with new adventures and routines and additional skits and episodes. How to weave it all together? My idea was to present it chronologically, so that the theme or plot would be the actual development, in time, of the ideas as they changed through 3–4 years, visible to the reader, one superimposed on another, developing and integrating with each other, as they did in the letters, accounting B.'s changes of psyche, and extension of fantasy—the mad doctor in his operating room superimposed on purple-assed baboon motorcyclist superimposed on Roosevelt's cabinet massacres invented earlier in N.Y. '53.

The problem of compositional structure was never resolved that season—Kerouac completed one section of typing, I began retyping another, separating personal-letter matter from imaginative improvisation and fantasy and "routine" matter. Alan Ansen arrived, and with more powerful typist genius took on the greater burden of preparing the manuscript. So when it was time after several months—half a year?—for me and Peter to leave on our first visit of Europe, I entrusted the two springboard binders to Ansen, who in his apartment of those years in Venice and later in Athens housed a rare collection of manuscripts, incunabula—Auden's letters and drafts of *Age of Anxiety*, correspondence with Thomas Mann on Wagner's prosody.

The final editing arrangement of *Naked Lunch* in Paris two years later was a dramatic accident. Sinclair Beiles, Burroughs' friend working with Olympia Press, said that Maurice Girodias wanted to publish the entire book on the basis of his reading of sections prepared for Chicago's *Big Table* magazine. Girodias' message was that the manuscript had to be ready for printer in two weeks. By Burroughs' account: "We worked away, sending pieces to the printer as soon as they were typed up. When we got proofs back Beiles said, 'I don't think anything needs to be done at all.' The way it came off the typewriter was the way it worked. I looked at it and said, 'I think you're right.' Only one change was made—the placement of the first passage on the detectives (Hauser and O'Brien) shifted toward the end. From the time that Girodias sent Sinclair over saying I want to publish the novel to its printing was only one month."

At the time I was proud, pleased and inspired to receive the letters, which were shared with Neal and Jack and Philip Whalen and Gary Snyder and Robert Creeley.[11] If nothing else of my own history survives, I'd be happily remembered as the sympathetic kid to whom W. S. Burroughs addressed his tender intelligence in these letters containing major sketches of *Naked Lunch*. This is the heart of the man behind *Naked Lunch*, and the years of its creation—a classic example of struggling artist—and inspiration for all writers working in the vast solitude of art.

The literary-historical record will be filled out by reference to *As Ever* and *Straight Hearts Delight*, contemporary letters (circa 1953–60) between Neal Cassady and self, and Peter and self. Publication of correspondence with Kerouac and Corso will give ampler realistic picture of those decades' thoughts and unconditional friendship.

WRITTEN: Feb.–April 1981

FIRST PUBLISHED: Introduction to William Burroughs, *Letters to Allen Ginsberg* (New York: Full Court Press, 1982).

William S. Burroughs Nobel Prize

[Recommendation Essay]

For Nobel Prize for Literature I propose William Seward Burroughs, Member of American Academy of Arts and Letters, Commander of l'Ordre des Arts et Lettres, France: "Invisible Man," explorer of souls and cities, whose exact-prosed *Junky* demonstrated process of police-state chemical conditioning; whose once-censored 1950s classic *Naked Lunch* broke down legal barriers to de-conditioning from heavy metal planetary hypnosis practiced by authoritarian word-manipulators fronting for the world-destroying "Nova Mob." His '60s trilogy *Soft Machine, Nova Express* and *Ticket That Exploded* cut up post-atomic consciousness and traced back along word-lines to the Nova Mob's Image Bank power-centers; his *The Job* and *Third Mind* summarized de-conditioning techniques that had inspired three decades of poets musicians artists to the world-revolution of mentality characteristic of Beat Hip and later longhair generations. William Burroughs' *The Wild Boys*, and *Exterminator!* continued literary exploration of dense worlds of international consciousness, amounting to a home-made, individualistic, self invented international Tantra. Subsequent 80s trilogy of novels ending with *The Western Lands* grounded Burroughs' research in history; later in 90s the books *Queer* and *Interzone* and in his 80th year his novel of dreams, *My Education*, brought his account of the world up to date. His continued influence, world wide from Europe thru China, on writing, music lyric, and politics on the latest pre-millennial generation perhaps surpasses that of any other literary figure of this last half century.

WRITTEN: ca. 1995

Unpublished.

GREGORY CORSO

Corso Academy Blurb

Captain Poetry. His City Lights 1958 *Gasoline* recharged the San Francisco Poetry Renaissance. His New Directions *Happy Birthday of Death, Long Live Man,* and *Elegaic Feelings American* spanned 1960 Beat Generation to 1980s tailor'd velvet-verse maturity as *Herald of the Autochthonic Spirit,* and 1990s *Mindfield: New and Selected Poems.* A loner divine *poete maudit* hitherto scandalously unlaurelled by any native prize, his muse's wild fame extends translated round the world. Gregory Corso examples a revolutionary of the spirit, the opposite of hypocrisy. Of himself he said, "I have better taste than life." Without him all else would be too straight.

WRITTEN: 1994

FIRST PUBLISHED: 1994 ballot, American Academy and Institute of Arts and Letters, Department of Literature, New York, 1994.

Introduction to *Gasoline*

Open this book as you would a box of crazy toys, take in your hands a refinement of beauty out of a destructive atmosphere. These combinations are imaginary and pure, in accordance with Corso's individual (therefore universal) DESIRE.

All his own originality! What's his connection, but his own beauty? Such weird haiku-like juxtapositions aren't in the American book. Ah! but the real classic tradition—from Aristotle's description of metaphor to the wildness of his Shelley—and Apollinaire, Lorca, Mayakovsky. Corso is a great word-slinger, first naked sign of a poet, a scientific master of mad mouthfuls of language. He wants a surface hilarious with ellipses, jumps of the strangest phrasing picked off the streets of his mind like "mad children of soda caps."

This is his great *sound*: "O drop that fire engine out of your mouth!"

Crazier: "Dirty Ears aims a knife at me, I pump him full of lost watches."

What nerve! "You, Mexico, you have no Chicago, no white-blonde moll." ("H. G. Wells," unpublished.)

He gets pure abstract poetry, the inside sound of language alone.

But what is he *saying*? Who cares? It's said! "Outside by a Halloween fire, wise on a charred log, an old man is dictating to the heir of the Goon."

This heir sometimes transcribes perfect modern lyrics anyone can dig: "Italian Extravaganza," "Birthplace Revisited," "Last Gangster," "Mad Yak," "Furnished Room," "Haarlem," "Last Night I Drove a Car," "Ecce Homo," "Hello."

A rare sad goonish knowledge with reality—a hip piss on reality also—he prefers his dreams. Why not? His heaven is poetry. He explains at length in the great unpublished "Power":

I do not sing of dictatorial power.
The stiff arm of dictatorship is symbolic of awful power.
In my room I have gathered enough gasoline and evidence to
    allow dictators inexhaustible power.
Am I the stiff arm of Costa Rica?
Do I wear red and green in Chrysler Squads?
Do I hate my people?
Will they forgive me their taxes?
Am I to be shot at the racetrack? Do they plot now?

. . . .

Beautiful people, you too are power. I remember your power.
I have not forgotten you in the snows of Bavaria skiing down
    on the sleeping village with flares and carbines,
I have not forgotten you rubbing your greasy hands on my
    aircraft, signing your obscure names on the blockbuster!
No!
I have not forgotten the bazooka you decked with palm
    fastened on the shoulder of a black man aimed at a tank full
    of Aryans!

Nor have I forgotten the grenade, the fear and emergency it
  spread throughout your brother's trench.
You are power, beautiful people!
. . . .
Power is not to be dropped from a plane
A hat is power
The world is power
Being afraid is power
Standing on a streetcorner waiting for no one is power
The demon is not as powerful as walking across the street
The angel is not as powerful as looking and then not looking.

What a solitary dignitary! He's got the angelic power of making autonomous poems, like god making brooks.

"With me automaticism is an entranced moment in which the mind accelerates a constant hour of mind-foolery, mind-genius, mind-madness . . ."

"When Bird Parker or Miles Davis blow a standard piece of music, they break off into other own-self little unstandard sounds—well, that's my way with poetry—X Y and Z, call it automatic—I call it a standard flow (because at the offset words are standard) that is intentionally distracted diverted into my own sound. Of course many will say a poem written on that order is unpolished, etc.—that's just what I want them to be—because I have made them truly my own—which is inevitably something NEW—like all good spontaneous jazz, newness is acceptable and expected—by hip people who listen."

"Don't Shoot The Warthog!" The mind has taken a leap in language. He curses like a brook, pure poetry. "I screamed the name: Beauty!" We're the fabled damned if we put it down. He's probably the greatest poet in America, and he's starving in Europe.

WRITTEN: Oct. 1957

FIRST PUBLISHED: Gregory Corso, *Gasoline* (San Francisco: City Lights, 1958).

ON CORSO'S VIRTUES

Gregory Corso's an aphoristic poet, and a poet of ideas. What modern poets write with such terse clarity that their verses stick in the mind without effort? Certainly Yeats, Pound, Williams, Eliot, Kerouac, Creeley, Dylan and Corso have that quality.

Corso's handling of ideas is unique, as in various one-word-title-poems ("Power," "Bomb," "Marriage," "Army," "Police," "Hair," "Death," "Clown" and later "Friend"). He distills the essence of archetypal concepts, recycling them with humor to make them new, examining, contrasting and alchemizing common vernacular notions into mind-blowing (deconstructive or de-conditioning) insights. In this mode, his late 1950s poems (like Kerouac's 1951–52 scriptures on "Joan [Crawford] Rawshanks in the Fog" and "Neal and The Three Stooges") manifest a precursor Pop artistry, the realized notice of quotidian artifacts.

Poetic *philosophe*, Corso's uncanny insight mixes wisdom and logopoeia. "I'd a humor save me from amateur philosophy," he writes: "Fish is animalized water"—"knowing my words to be the acquainted prophecy of all men / and my unwords no less an acquaintanceship"— "Nothing sits on nothing in a nothing of many nothings a nothing king"— "I found God a gigantic fly paper"—"Standing on a street corner waiting for no one is Power"—"A star / is as far / as the eye / can see / and / as near / as my eye / is to me"—"And how can I trust them / who pollute the sky / with heavens / the below with hells."

As poetic craftsman, Corso is impeccable. His revision process, which he calls "tailoring," generally elision and condensation, yields gist-phrasing, extraordinary mind-jump humor. Clown sounds of circus, abstracted from plethora are reduced to perfect expression, "Tang-a-lang boom. Fife feef! Toot!" Quick sketch, sharp mind scissors.

As engineer of ideas, certain concepts recur retailored for nuance, such as "I shall never know my death," (i.e. dead he won't know it) and "You can't step in the same river once."

His late work, "The Whole Mess . . . Almost" is a masterpiece of experience, the grand poetic abstractions Truth, Love, God, Faith Hope Charity, Beauty, Money, Death, and Humor are animated in a single poem with brilliant and intimate familiarity.

As poetic wordslinger he has command of idiomatic simplicity, to wit: "A hat is power," "fried shoes" or:

O Bomb I love you
I want to kiss your clank   eat your boom
You are a paean an acme of scream
a lyric hat of Mister Thunder

as well as exuberant invention as "an astrologer dabbling in dragon prose":

. . . Bomb
from your belly outflock vulturic salutations
Battle forth your spangled hyena finger stumps
along the brink of Paradise

Corso also excels as political philosophe; his many years as classic artist wanderer dwelling in European hotels, castles, and streets gives him perspective on North America. His crucial position in world cultural revolution mid-twentieth century as originator of the "Beat Generation" literary movement, along with Kerouac, Burroughs, Orlovsky and others, grants him an experience inside history few bards of politicians have known. Readers of the poem cluster "Elegiac Feelings American" will appreciate Corso's generational insight into Empire sickness. Earlier poems like "Power," "Bomb," "Army," and many brief expatriate lyrics prove Corso to be Shelley's natural prophet among "unacknowledged legislators of the world."

Corso is a poet's Poet, his verse pure velvet, close to John Keats for our time, exquisitely delicate in manners of the muse. He has been and always will be a popular poet, awakener of youth, puzzlement and pleasure for sophisticated elder bibliophiles, "Immortal" as immortal is, Captain Poetry exampling revolution of spirit, his "poetry the opposite of hypocrisy," a loner, laughably unlaurelled by native prizes, divine Poet Maudit, rascal poet Villonesque and Rimbaudian whose wild fame's extended for decades around the world from France to China, world poet.

WRITTEN: March 1989

FIRST PUBLISHED: Foreword to Gregory Corso, *Mindfield* (Santa Barbara: Black Sparrow Press, 1989).

PETER ORLOVSKY

Peter Orlovsky *Clean Asshole Poems* Blurb

First harvest of 1958–1978 eternal decades' poetry by Peter Orlovsky, born July 8, 1933, in the vanished Women's Infirmary in Lower East Side N.Y. Sometime ambulance attendant, farmer, house-cleaner, silkscreen handyman, newsboy, postal clerk and instructor at Kerouac School of Poetics, he was discharged from military after telling government psychiatrist, "An army is an army against love." Witness of the '50s San Francisco Poetry Renaissance, he was portrayed by Jack Kerouac as hospital nurse saint Simon Darlovsky among *Desolation Angels,* learned driving speech from Neal Cassady and taught heart in return, partook of psychedelic revolution a pillar of strength with Timothy Leary and Charles Olson, companioned Kerouac and William Burroughs in Tangier, was one of the first American poets to make modern passage to India in early '60s accompanying Gary Snyder and Allen Ginsberg, studied sarod, banjo and guitar, read poetry in Chicago and at Harvard Columbia Princeton Yale and New York's St. Mark's Poetry Project, survived speed and junk hells, sang in jail at anti-war protest and political convention occasions, was published in historic *Beatitude* and Don Allen anthologies of *The New American Poetry,* played self in early underground Robert Frank movies, traveled with Dylan's *Rolling Thunder Review,* farmed solitary upstate New York ten years organic and Herculean, fed and nursed decades of poetry families. An experienced Buddhist sitter and Vajrayana meditation practitioner, his *Dharma* name is "Ocean of Generosity." After 20 years of shy genius this first poem book's published on earth.

WRITTEN: Aug. 27, 1978

FIRST PUBLISHED: Peter Orlovsky, *Clean Asshole Poems and Smiling Vegetable Songs* (San Francisco: City Lights, 1978).

CARL SOLOMON

Carl Solomon *Emergency Messages* Blurb

Carl Solomon's brilliance as mass observer of cosmopolitan political movements and esthetic options is once again proved in this volume of sophisticated communiqués from megalopolis, advice to the lovelorn, sane letters to crazy *littérateurs*, home front manifestos, cold war burlesque, and mental vaudeville essays. Combining the old world humor of the Bronx and continental brevity of Parisian wit he continues to enrich the genre of *belles-lettres* common to Lord Chesterfield and La Rochefoucauld.

FIRST PUBLISHED: Carl Solomon, *Emergency Messages* (New York: Paragon, 1988).

HERBERT HUNCKE

Blurb for Herbert Huncke's *Journal*

The first published chapters of Herbert Huncke's confessions manifest such naked tolerance beaten into his human soul by the law's savage rejection of him junk-sick that all freaks of law, nature and man's self are treated with just compassion in pure awkward American prose narrative fragments equal in delicacy of expression to Sherwood Anderson's Merciful Ones.

FIRST PUBLISHED: Herbert Huncke, *Huncke's Journal* (New York: Poets Press, 1965).

On Huncke's Book

If universe is a dream-illusion as gnostics and Buddhists chant, one alien, one stranger, one caller of the great call, one knower, one enlightened being waking in the midst of dream can shiver the fundament of Kosmos with his lone realization—because it is the only verifiable thing among myriads of phantom phenomena.

> *O go way Man I can*
> *hypnotize this Nation*
> *I can shake the Earth's foundation*
> *with the Maple Leaf Rag*

The whole stage-scenery of Moloch's altar—Time, Life, Fortune, Pentagon, Madison Avenue, Wall Street, Treasury Department, St. Patrick's Cathedral, Wrigley Building and all—shuddered evanescent in the sunset when *The Evening Sun Turned Crimson*, when Herbert E. Huncke's consciousness was opened.

Toward the end of the planetary conflict then called World War Two Mr. Huncke was a familiar Stranger hustling around Times Square 42nd Street New York, so alien in fact that several years later the Police themselves banned him from the street as a creep. A number of subtle revolutions had begun by that time: a change in national music to variable rhythmic base called Bop, a corresponding change in poetic prosody (William Carlos Williams' variable American foot), hip styles of diction and posture and hand-gesture signaling revolution of consciousness from Harlem and 52nd Street jazz meccas, breakthroughs of cosmic consciousness (or planetary consciousness if the latter phrase is more acceptable to city-minded critics) occurring to Whitmanic isolatos in myriad cities of these States, drug-induced ecstasies and hallucinations passing from black and red subcultural hands into the heads of scholarly whites, changes in body-awareness and recognition of sexual tendernesses heretofore acknowledged by Sherwood Anderson in the same provincial American ken as prophet Walt Whitman. Herbert Huncke on Times Square quite literally embodied all these hustling tendencies in his solitary frame, and was to be found in 1945 passing on subways from Harlem to Broadway scoring for drugs, music, incense, lovers, Benzedrine inhalers, second story furniture, coffee, all night vigils in 42nd Street Horn and Hardart and Bickford Cafeterias, encountering curious and beautiful solitaries of New York dawn, in one season selling newspapers, in another serving as a connection for the venerable Dr Alfred Kinsey pursuing his investigations of the sexual revolution statisticised for credibility, and in one Fall of the mid-forties appearing as companion on the streets to Jack Kerouac, William Burroughs, myself and others.

Huncke's figure appears variously in Clellon Holmes' novel *Go*, there is an excellent early portrait in Kerouac's first *bildungsroman, The Town and The City*, fugitive glimpses of Huncke as Gotham morphinist appear in William Lee's *Junky*, Burroughs' dry first classic of prose. He walked on the snowbank docks with shoes full of blood into the middle of my own rhapsody, *Howl*, and is glimpsed in short sketches by Herb Gold, Carl Solomon and Irving Rosenthal scattered thru subsequent decades.

As far as I know the ethos of what's charmingly hip, and the first pronunciation of the word itself to my fellow ears, first came consciously from Huncke's lips; and the first information and ritual of the emergent hip subculture passed through Huncke's person. Not that he invented this style of late twentieth century individualistic illumination and naked perception—but that in his anonymity and holy creephood in New York he was the sensitive vehicle for a veritable new consciousness which spread through him to others sensitized by their dislocation from history and thence to entire generations of a nation renewing itself for fear of apocalyptic judgment. So in the grand *karma* of robotic civilizations it may be that the humblest, most afflicted, most persecuted, most suffering lowly junkie hustling some change in the all-night movie is the initiate of a glory transcending his nation's consciousness that will swiftly draw that nation to its knees in tearful self-forgiveness.

One incidental condition of the junkie—Huncke in particular—should be understood (as it has not been in the mass hallucinations of Treasury Department propaganda multiplied millionfold by collaborators such as *The Readers Digest* and the *Daily News*)—that the junk "problem" as it exists circa 1970 is the result of a sadistic self-serving conspiracy by Narcotics Bureaus and Mafia to perpetuate their own business, which is supervising the black market in junk and selling junk, which both groups conjoined have done for decades. Though the Supreme Court in its 1925 *Lindner Decision* specified that the original junkie-registration laws were *not* intended to prevent doctors from ethical maintenance treatment of junkies (as successfully practiced with modifications to this day in Great Britain), agents of Government have illegally and forcibly blackmailed, trapped, propagandized, strong-armed and snow-jobbed everybody in the socio-medical field of junkdom to impotent silence and political futility. Given this context, little known by the liberal public, Herbert Huncke emerges as one of the early political victims of the evolving Police State in America.

Given the remarkable person of Herbert Huncke in his history, our history, we have here his own prose, documentation of stages of his own consciousness, recordings of experiences, fragments of meditation, confessions, journals, anecdotes, characters, stories. Kerouac always maintained that he was a great storyteller—having sat by candlelight on 115th Street NY in an apartment we all shared decades ago to listen to the sea-tale of the "big dinge nut." My own favorite fragment is "In the Park" which in tradition of Sherwood Anderson articulates not only the character of inhuman psyche of the whole official nation but also the human magnanimity and benevolent indifferent compassion of the story-teller—the very *curiosity* of man—that makes this storyteller the conscience of the nation. That same compassion for the isolato which has always been native to the eccentric American genius from Melville thru Whitman thru Anderson comes through in Huncke's characters of "Elsie," "The Tattooed Woman," "Alvarez" and "Cuba," and in his uniquely planetary descriptions of city sunrises and dusks. Dawn colors in a solar system which might be seen from a speedy Mars, but fatigued earth eyes register and human hand writes compassionately for the information of odd sleeping fellow citizens. Later episodes (in chronology, this prose was begun in fragments at the end of the forties) describe the meta-amphetamine civilization of the Lower East Side, and therein Huncke's literality coincides with Poe's old demonic dreaminess.

Like Anderson and like Poe, Huncke writes weird personal prose—provincial, awkwardly literate—the same characteristic exaggerated into insane rhetoric in Melville's *Pierre* makes that much unread book a funny delight to prose cognoscenti. Huncke's prose proceeds from his midnight mouth, that is, literal storytelling, just talking—for that reason it is both awkward and pure. There are traces of old highfalutin literary half-style that give a gentlemanly antiquity to the writer's character—Poe-esque or Chinese Moderne fustian of the thirties and Prohibition. What is excellent as prose in *The Evening Sun Turned Crimson* is naked city man speech, clear and magnanimous as personal conversation. The book is memorable for these traces of American tongue, and remarkable for its chapters of American History.

WRITTEN: Sept. 18, 1968

FIRST PUBLISHED: *Unspeakable Visions of the Individual,* vol. 3, no. 1–2 (1973) pp. 20–23.

MICHAEL MCCLURE

Michael McClure Guggenheim Recommendation

McClure certainly genius in thought and writing it out; began "Death of 100 Whales" first pamphlet published 17 yrs ago sharp prophetic cry on mechanic butchery of philosophers of deep thus with Gary Snyder introduced new-generation ecological preoccupations to new consciousness manifested in poetics of his contemporaries including myself and Kerouac and incidentally influenced Bob Dylan in direction of intellectual poetry. Skipping the decade and half, Dylan presenting McClure with autoharp late '60s started McClure on to music/poetry composition which increasingly influences contemporaries again including myself to tune our lyric words to actual song. Back in time, *Dark Brown* erotic odes were in late '50s a public breakthru of heterosexual Whitmanic nature person expression among contemporaries. His poetry productions from Grove's *A Book of Torture* to recent *Star* Delacorte Press showed increase of wisdom and information "ecological, ethnological and biological" as McClure's application for money states it; and this latter area of study is really McClure's professional academe—he's worked long with expert philosophers and scientists and avant-garde publicists and poets to master biological-universe view of man personality and his own nature and thought, and spread thought among citizenry. Extraordinary work published *Meat Science Essays,* even more extraordinary his unpublished information-and-observation filled biology-poetry giant book-essay "Wolf Net." That is he's a hard worker, in his present mature decade a classical Goethean professional writer unlike myself and sloppier contemporaries—McClure gets up early each morn and doth write hours and hours before lunch. Studies, writes, reads, attends, walks on hills with specimen-glasses butterfly nets odd sampling cases and professors of nature, for information for his intelligence's wolf-net.

His history as dramatist—beginning with *succès de scandale, Billy the Kid*—is exemplary, inasmuch as he began with obscure devotion to his fancy and wrote plays for literary merit and experiment, plays which years later came to fame, and thereafter wrote and published *even more interesting* plays now recently published (in part) as *Gargoyle Cartoons,* eminently actable probably commercial someday, but already acted much in Bay Area with fame of them reaching Lower East Side NY stages and Texas dormitories. Invention, fancy, gorgeous language, funny scenery, detailed droll descriptive instructions, free man's wit, work of happy Rabelaisian energy now so rare in America. Historically *Billy the Kid* was stage-erotic breakthru as *Dark Brown* was poetry erotic breakthru as *Hundred Whales* was philosophic-poetry breakthru.

What next? Prose, even prose! amazing, McClure's extended himself also, for years, to the novel, current madcap autobiographical at first with *Mad Cub* texts, couple early novels influenced (in spontaneity and redis-covery of American Memory thrills) by Kerouac—for McClure is one of the few contemporaries to have understood Kerouac as literary poet—and learned some joyous classic invention therefrom—but beyond that the exquisite *detailed* prose (with informed biologic metaphor-cement page after page) of McClure's novel *The Adept* published 1971 makes me think that in his maturity this poet has become a rare great novelist—in any case I class *The Adept* as a certain swift classic novel of its day, comparable to *Day of the Locust,* yet more enlightened as to prose and humane glory. If I think of prose in US since this last year—considering *Meat Science* and *Wolf Net* as prose essays, and *Mad Cub* as a rare high spirited energetic beginning—then with the *Adept* novel, I realize that McClure is one of our few Genius prose writers—high art prose—that is, with Burroughs, Selby, Kerouac and a few others, an *original.* My tastes though my own are not solipsistic, I refer to the above small "pantheon" of "originals" because McClure has achieved his own equal originality and beauty, and I can't even say that about my own prose, and very few others. He's *readable* as most even good literature is now not, given the inundation of mechanically reproduced texts we all see.

Thus we have a McClure poet, a McClure natural philosopher, a McClure dramatist, and a McClure *prosateur* and novelist. Hardly anyone in America with equal range and sharpness, liveness. What more? The secret McClure! that is I have seen whole vast manuscripts of *books* of rare poetry—stylistically unified separate books—unpublished—hard worker.

WRITTEN: Dec. 29, 1971

Unpublished.

GARY SNYDER

_____

My Mythic Thumbnail Biography of Gary Snyder

Grew up among Northwest lumberjacks, Indians, Wobblies[12] and intellectuals, met William Carlos Williams 1950 Reed College with friends Lew Welch and Philip Whalen. Meditated as early 1950s fire lookout Washington State, trail crew worker Yosemite National Park, graduate student Oriental languages U. Cal. Berkeley 1952–56. American literary cultural hero since his central participation in mid-'50s San Francisco open-form Poetry Renaissance and Beat Generation literary movement, Snyder's figure served as model for fictional protagonist Japhy Ryder in Kerouac's longhair-rucksack revolution breakthrough novel _The Dharma Bums,_ 1958. Left for Japan 1956 to spend dozen years in monastic and householder study, writing, and _zazen,_ later seasons in company of wife poet Joanne Kyger with whom made _Dharma_ pilgrimage India. Snyder ripened as wilderness philosopher activist, integrating ecological planet karma with Native-American Poetry's indigenous household view. Built house in ponderosa-black oak parklike woods 3,000 feet high Western slope Sierras, working with wife Masa Uehara and sons Kai and Gen for two decades. Translated Stockholm to Beijing, Snyder notably furthered Ezra Pound's ideogrammatic lineage. Like Pound, key figure in the adaptation of Oriental Wisdom arts to the West, he translated Chinese and Japanese Classic gnomic texts, by-product of three decades' Zen practice. Traveled widely China to Alaska wilds; founded Ring of Bone _Zendo,_ named for late poet companion Lew Welch, on San Juan Ridge; joined by Carole Koda 1988; completing midlife tome on poetics of wilderness as of November 14, 1989.

FIRST PUBLISHED: Jon Halper, ed., _Gary Snyder: Dimensions of a Life_ (San Francisco: Sierra Club Books, 1991).

Gary Snyder Recommendation

I've known Gary Snyder as poet, Buddhist practitioner and nature citizen for almost 40 years. The elder poet Kenneth Rexroth introduced us in 1955, praising him as an accomplished disciplined poet and meditator. Together with other poets (Philip Whalen now Sensei, or Zen teacher, Michael McClure, Jack Kerouac, Gregory Corso and others) we participated in poetry readings and cultural-literary activities that became known as San Francisco Poetry Renaissance, and later, Beat Generation literary movement. All of us were poets but Snyder's distinction was that he had the disciplines of Chinese and Japanese language, Zen meditation, and expertise in Northwest Amerindian Culture, as well as woodsmanship and mountain climbing. A picture of him at that time, drawn as prototype hero of Kerouac's novel *Dharma Bums,* influenced successive generations of young Americans (and Chinese and Russians) toward an adventurous modern nature citizenship and ecological consciousness.

The San Francisco literary movement has especially strong echoes today in U.S. (and 'round the world) as inspiration for the spread of poetry readings in cafés, universities, theaters and clubs, restoring contemporary poetry to its vocal dimension and democratic popularity.

Snyder left U.S.A. in mid-'50s for training in Zen monasteries in Japan, contributed to translation of the classic koan text *Zen Dust* under aegis of first Zen Institute at Dai-toku-ji Monastery in Japan where he studied under Miura Roshi and others for a decade before returning home permanently to practice an American Zen. He continued his studies with Aitken Roshi, and organized and founded Ring of Bone *Zendo* in the Sierras to serve as sitting place for a number of intellectuals who gathered 'round him as a community in San Juan Ridge near Nevada City, California. That site continues with a permanent Zen teacher, on Snyder's property adjacent to large rustic house where he raised a family 1968 to this day, without electricity. Snyder provided energy with solar apparatus over the years, and with ecologically oriented number of friends formed a construction company, voting community and woodland preservation association in his home region San Juan Ridge. Thus he practiced what he preached.

Networking with an amazing number of biologists, woodsmen, western U.S. Culture scholars, anthropologists and scientific seed and grain specialists, Snyder became a leader in evolution of a bioregional "politics" or cultural philosophy for "Turtle Island," his North America.

All this time as prolific poet, he wrote book after book of original verse, each book a steppingstone to study of mind, nature and the city. Their titles are classics to several generations: *Han Shan's Cold Mountain Poems, Rip Rap, Regarding Wave, Earth House Hold, Left Out in the Rain, No Nature*, etc. Profound, original and in the open form tradition of Modernists Ezra Pound and William Carlos Williams (whom he met at Reed College), Snyder was recognized early as a major American poet with international influence, received a Pulitzer Prize, and was elected to the American Academy of Arts and Letters.

Living many years on modest means, growing some of his own food, laboring on his land, philosophically allied with his friend poet Wendell Berry, and sustaining his family with celebrated poetry readings at universities and ecological conferences, he accepted a professorship at UC Davis in the last decade.

I should say, personally, that a great deal of my own education and thinking regarding hypertechnology's relation to a natural world comes directly from Snyder—he's a kind of American guru for many of my own and succeeding generations, is universally respected and listened to by his peers, popular among older and younger scholars as well among punk and grunge youths, a curious intelligentsia for whom he is a totemic figure, a leader, forerunner, avant-garde nature thinker, activist and major poet.

I should mention his activism—both in poetry and person—in anti war and ecological conferences from Berkeley to Stockholm, and as democratically innovative Chairman of Governor Brown's state arts commission. I'm sure the *Dictionary of Literary Biography* can supply information on that aspect of his life.

Gary Snyder is one of the most virtuous, visionarily inspired as well as intellectually grounded American poets of this half century, a legend in his own lifetime because of his physical exertion, poetic creation, and social-philosophical formulations in defense of nature in his many books of essays and poems. His poetic career is one of the glories of our culture, and as he approaches conclusion of his lifelong epic poem "Mountains and Rivers Without End," he is at the height of his powers.

WRITTEN: ca. 1994

Unpublished.

KENNETH REXROTH

Kenneth Rexroth: 1905–1982

Kenneth Rexroth was born in South Bend, Indiana, on December 22, 1905. Both his parents died when he was young. In 1918 he was taken by an aunt to Chicago to live. He wrote his first poems when he was fifteen, and in the exciting city that Chicago was then, mostly on his own, he studied painting at the Art Institute of Chicago; the natural sciences by sitting in on classes at the University of Chicago; and all kinds of music, classical, ethnic, and jazz, the latter at first hand in the dives and black clubs of the city. He became a political man simply as a natural means of survival: he liked to know how things worked, and in Chicago, and later San Francisco, got his information by first-hand observation of political machines in operation. "I write prose for money, and to put my ideas in order," he said. He also once said, "I write poetry to seduce women, and to overthrow the capitalistic system."

In Chicago, while still in his teens, he helped run a nightclub called The Green Mask, where poets, including himself and Langston Hughes, among others, read to jazz. During his Chicago years he also worked as a farm hand, a factory worker, and an attendant in an insane asylum. In 1927 Rexroth and his first wife, Andrée, moved to San Francisco, where he settled in for a lifelong stay, worked his way through the leftist views towards what was essentially an anarchist position in politics, and where he first defined the kind of poetry he recognized as true for him:

(it was to be) a revolt against rhetoric and symbolism in poetry, a return to direct statement, simple, clear images, unpretentious themes, fidelity to objectively verifiable experience, strict avoidance of sentimentality.

Out of this program Rexroth evolved what was basically a quantitative verse whose measure consisted of simple count of syllables per line, with variations allowed; how many syllables per line, be it seven, eleven, or whatever, derived from whatever feeling he was dealing with. It was a musical system. (The number of stresses per line was where he left himself utterly free to play—he "went on his nerve.") On occasion he could be, as William Carlos Williams wrote of him, "a moralist with his hand at the trigger, ready to fire at the turn of a hair."

His colleague Louis Zukofsky had included him in the famous Objectivist issue of *Poetry* magazine in 1931 (an earlier wave of open form poetics), but Rexroth was no joiner—he was both a generous man, and an abrasive one. He was an outspoken lover, and a good mad hater. City-bred, he loved nature, and knew its workings, he knew the names of the flowers and trees and the migration paths of birds. He climbed mountains, and knew the stories of their rock formations, just as in literature he knew the great stories of the chair: the names and stories of writers of many cultures, which men and women he thought of as his contemporaries. His favorite poets perhaps included more women than men. In his books *Bird In The Bush, Assays,* and *Classics Revisited,* he makes Chinese and Japanese and French, Spanish, Greek and Latin writers come alive as any writer writing now is alive. Those books have been read in and out of universities for thirty years, and continue to be read.

His translations, notably *100 Poems from the Chinese* and *100 Poems from the Japanese,* and his [Pierre] Reverdy translations, are present on every poetry lover's bookshelves.

A quarter century before his death, he was one of a community of older poets primarily responsible for encouraging public acceptance of that group of writers associated with the "San Francisco Renaissance," and thus helped supervise the transition of American poetics from closed to open form. In this role he was mentor and friend to the literary circle that included West Coast bards Robert Duncan, Michael McClure, Philip Lamantia, Philip Whalen and Gary Snyder, as well as Denise Levertov, Robert Creeley, Gregory Corso, Jack Kerouac and myself, visiting from the East in the mid-1950s.

His major books remain: *The Collected Shorter Poems,* and *The Collected Longer Poems,* from New Directions; the outrageous *In Defense of the Earth,* with its love poems to Andrée, and his shocking and controversially anti-bourgeois-Philistine *Thou Shalt Not Kill,* an elegy for Dylan Thomas. He told much of his own story in his dazzling tall-tale autobiography, *An Autobiographical Novel.* On phonograph records, that scornful, tender, abrasive and musical voice continues to tell its story, and name names of human loves, and curse the despicable.

Charles Olson said, "That Rexroth, there's no accounting for him, but that long poem of his, *The Dragon and the Unicorn,* that's really something! He gets the whole thing down there!"[13]

WRITTEN: 1982

FIRST PUBLISHED: *Proceedings of the American Academy and Institute of Arts and Letters,* 2nd series, no. 34 (1983).

ROBERT DUNCAN

Robert Duncan [Obit]

I heard Robert Duncan read entire *[The] Opening of the Field* one night
late 1959 at Intersection Coffee House up Grant Street, a corner store-
front full of intimate friends mixed with a few strangers in San Francisco
aware of his manners loves and complete devotion to the word:

        It is across great scars of wrong
     I reach toward the song of kindred men
     and strike again the naked string
  old Whitman sang from.

He listened with lifted finger marking time as a conductor and then
spoke, his tremulous voice cadenced to heart-beat, expounding inner
shifting forms of thought as improvised on the page, discontinuities, correspondences and rapturous wonderings of inspiration. He seemed to
express his being completely, I was awed by a continuous prescience.

WRITTEN: Feb. 14, 1988

FIRST PUBLISHED: Poetry Flash, no. 180 (March 1988) p. 3.

ROBERT CREELEY

The Collected Poems of Robert Creeley Blurb

From the first clear grounded 1940s insight snapshots of "For Love" through his recent decade experiments with syllable by syllable intelligence, Robert Creeley has created a noble life body of poetry that extends the work of his predecessors Pound, Williams, Zukofsky, and Olson and provides like them a method for his successors in exploring our new American poetic consciousness.

WRITTEN: 1982

FIRST PUBLISHED: Robert Creeley, *The Collected Poems* (Berkeley: University of California Press, 1982).

On Creeley's Ear Mind

Creeley reading at Naropa Institute late summer 1976 at "Jack Kerouac School of Disembodied Poetics" I was the host doubly nervous my own sneaky karma and Creeley's present drunkenness—He sat onstage at table, boom armed microphone across from his face above notebooks newly carried back from Japan and Korea. Creeley read new work for connoisseurs of ear—short lines spotted down the small notebook pages, separated by a line or a star between different entries. His mustache and blind eye too far from the microphone, I couldn't hear him altogether, I kept hearing syllable by syllable his mouth, his words, but not the continuity, despairing shakes of the head to indicate what he read was incomprehensible if it wasn't immediately totally comprehensible, it was so simple . . . his voice fading as he looked around to find my face or another's friendly understanding or at least hearing or trying to hear, in the wings or audience. Occasionally he grabbed the microphone and squeezed it cruelly, making a rutting electric sound, disgusted with its intervention on the actual breath, the local word. I went up onstage and held microphone closer to his mouth, looking over his manuscript, leaning in close to him, so I could follow the text as he spoke.

I was astonished at the closeness of his speech with its hesitancies word by word to the forms of his writing. It seemed that, in his specialized— i.e. personal, unique, home-made, close to the nose, close to the grain, actual—world of writing and speech, the forms he wrote were precise notations of the way his mind thoughts occurred to him, as he noticed them, and the way they'd be uttered out loud. Of course Creeley's famous for his precise exactitude of form—the personal—and I'd written or spoken about it before—but I'd never realized it so clearly. The main principle seemed to be that his mind moved syllable by syllable—as if his basic unit of thought was the syllable—as if thought-forms could be broken down further than picture image, further than thought-breath or thought-phrase or idea-phrase or speech-phrase or breath-clause or whatever larger unit Kerouac or Olson or Duncan or Williams or others have used, could be broken down below words themselves even, to syllables, one by one moving forward in time, one by one at a time left on the page to tell what change mind went thru in the head at the desk or with pen in hand on the lap on a ship or a plane or in bed, slow as a live clock, monosyllable by monosyllable. Remember this was a Buddhist institute specialized in observation of phenomena of thought-forms and here Creeley was exhibiting his own personal objective yoga as it were of speech-mindfulness, a completely unique universe uncovered by his awareness of the syllable as basic atom or brick of poetic mind. What was rare to experience was how much the entire set of mind, the set up, represented in the beginning of the poem, was modified by each new single-breath'd syllable. So each one word syllable modified by hindsight all the previous words. Of course that's universal in speech, but to hear speech so bare that the modifications of mind syllable by syllable were apparent, were the theme and play of the poem, was like raw mind discovery to me anew, like rediscovering Cézanne's method of creating space, or Poussin's arrangement of planes or Pound's quantity of vowels. And I knew this theme before but had never experienced it so directly as this reading in 1976. I was overjoyed at the clarity of the demonstration of the power of syllables as a measure of the poetic line, and wondered how many of the audience, puzzled by Creeley's quirkiness of manner at microphone or distracted by my own or his histrionics, heard what he was laying down.

WRITTEN: Feb. 22, 1977

FIRST PUBLISHED: *Boundary 2,* vol. 6–7, no. 3–1 (Spring/Fall 1978) pp. 443–445.

JOHN WIENERS

Foreword to John Wieners' *Selected Poems*

John Wieners speaks with Keatsian eloquence, pathos, substantiality, the sound of immortality in auto exhaust same as nightingale. He presents emotion on the spot—despair, nostalgia, bliss of love, dissatisfaction, flesh pressing on flesh. And *Glamor,* coming from desire for *Glamour.* "Paris Vancouver Hyannis Avignon New York and the Antilles" ("The Windows").

It's thrilling to watch the drama develop! After *The Hotel Wentley's* commitment to the moment of love, of street, of drug, glamors of the underworld, Wieners then gives us retrospect of "The Acts of Youth," his supreme tragic American poem in rhymeless quatrain form. According to mode and morale of 19th century gnostic idealism, it ends with "Infinite particles of the divine sun."

Practical realism in the midst of glamor: "as we lie abed waiting for the pills to take effect." And practical realism in art, in relation to the moment of composition, an imprint of eternal prescience: "And the hand trembles / at the next word to put down." The poet's love-or-drug-hallucinated eye stares on reality, space, leaves him awake as sun rises to notice "The color of the grass on Boston Common at dawn" ("A Series").

As that youthful idealism of *The Hotel Wentley Poems* dissolves in *Ace of Pentacles,* we see his intelligence delve deeper and deeper into the hole, or void, created by his imagination of an impossible love. This is chronicled in *Pressed Wafer, Asylum Poems,* and *Nerves*—three magisterial books of poetry that stand among the few truthful monuments of the late 1960s era.

There is a disciplined effort of spontaneity wherein we can read his mind. He leaves evidence of it in the casual conscious breaks in the verse—the urgency to remember what is being thought, capture the flash of enchantment in the mind pictures that pass, leaving words behind, arranged on the page the way they came, as thoughts rose clear enough to indite; so move by move we see his awareness of the line, the helplessness of the line, the inevitability of the line, displayed. Naked line, raw line, vulnerable line, a line of pain so fine it cannot be altered by primping or rouging (i.e., correcting); his thought already was there, and left its mark:

> There is a new cross in the wind, and it is our
> minds, imagination, will
> where the discovery is made
> of how to pass the night, how to share the gift
> of love, our bodies, which is true
> illumination
> of the present instant.
> ("The blind see only this world . . . ")

And the story's rumored, that may never be told, of his romance with the European lady of means; his idyll like Rilke in a stately castle; the conception of a child—and the intrusion of another reality, abortion of his seed, rejection by the unique feminine glamor girl that could attract his romantic devotion.

John Wieners explains his condition clearly and early: "Poetry is a trance / of make-believe." And "it's a condition of gradual loss / of reality until there's only left / this shattering of the world" ("Concentration"). What's unique is the precise analysis of his situation, a common one for all of us, not only poets. "The shattering of the world" is universal, not merely Wieners' condition. He suffered it acutely, early, and without relief, but he does express, with strength, youth and clarity, the experience of one's grandmother, or old uncle, adrift in home for the aged, where one's world's taken away, or "Sunday evening / when one's parents feel old" ("Determination"). And it is this "Concentration" and "Determination" to persist in poetry that makes him poet amid the ruin of his life, of all our lives.

John Wieners' glory is solitary, as pure poet—a man reduced to loneness in poetry, without worldly distractions—and a man become one with his poetry. A life in contrast to the fluff and ambition of Pulitzer, National Book Awardees, Poetry Medallists from the American Arts and Letters and Poetry Academies—harmless bureaucratic functionaries among themselves, until the holders of these titles deny the pure genius of poets like John Wieners, in favor of society-minded misfits who drink flatter fuck and get interviewed, sucking up the attention of the young, who are misled into the study of minor poetry—till such books as this emerge from obscurity of decades, to reveal the true light of genius in the poem. And if this curse falls on myself, so be it, that John Wieners' genius may shine forth and be proclaimed by the authority of my own fame deserved or not.

Amazing how, though clinging to an emotional abstraction, or fixation, that takes him away from "reality" or himself, still details of the real world in all its sordid sacred flash remain vivid: "in gray mid-Manhattan / in mid-morning mist / as taxis splash through rain" ("Consolation"). Yet he knows that the emotional strategy of clinging can't last: "mad truth of these trysts to lose / in time their hidden passion and meaning" ("Deprivation"). This is of course a prophecy of what'll happen in his own poetry. How counter that strategy?

This book tells the story, a novel-like development of the drama—as in Shakespeare's sonnets, of the growth and decay of his singular passion.

"Feminine Soliloquy" coherently explains his fix, and his behavior. In the pit of his hell, he analyzes the odd steps that left him bereft— development of fantasy onanistic love since he was 12. This is one of the great analytic confessions I know of in U.S. literature. Written circa 1969, it explains the course of tragedy since *Wentley Poems* classics 1958.

"Love-Life" tells the result of this hopeless love: "Though the gift has gone. / The handwriting changed. / And the mind broken in two. / By such aimless arrow."

Now, "Reading in Bed," in order "to write a poem" one has "to pore over one's past / recall ultimate orders one has since doubted / in despair." He's set up an impossible situation for himself. This leads to a nervous condition: "I have sat here so often / in nervous trembling / this might be found out, with / a thousand pills in my stomach" ("On the Back to the Cover of *The Algeria Poems*").

Where to go from here? That's the drama of the book. What development possible in this familiar stasis? That's the plot up to the end of *Nerves*. Next, a new definition of poetry's function for him: "Poetry is some way / of keeping in touch, / something to do / against staring at the wall, blankly. / It's some way / of filling loneliness / without politics" ("Determination").

So, *Behind the State Capitol,* a different book of the shattered mind, inventing a thousand re-combinations. A thousand pieces, a thousand personae, a thousand pictures floating over the world.

Then in mental hospital another breakthrough, to social realization, "Children of the Working Class": an attack on God's created reality, on the lot and fate of the mad—a sudden awareness of a whole class of sufferers like himself, by what divine or human reason, outcast and deformed in America.

Later we find further political statement, "After Dinner on Pinckney Street," "How can a poor person matter in this world?" And an analysis of family and communal poverty that makes us all poor.

Behind the State Capitol makes an ideogrammatic picture of his mind, with a widening of subjects, and dissociation as method, after Charles Olson's dictum "One perception must directly lead to another." We have magical use of language, flashes of the mind working to subvert order, any order, and are left where we began—with the mystery of inspiration, the enigma of the poem.

Parallel with *State Capitol* (circa 1972–75) a number of poems of complete loneliness emerge, with various definitions of poetic friendship, rejection of false fame, estimates of the condition of middle and old age occupied by solitary art (e.g. "To Sleep Alone," "For Ed Dorn," "After the Orgasm," "Here for the Night"). Then Wieners fell into eight years of relative silence, curtly telling his friends "Poetry is not on my calendar" and "I am living out the logical conclusion of my books." And these were out of print.

By 1983, with the intervention of the editor of this book,[14] poet Wieners began a new deliberation. He restates his spiritual themes, this time more playfully, with in fact comic treatment of the dilemma, almost Chaplinesque, the poet arrived to his own state of maturity.

Wieners always has an oddly humorous aesthetic floating on the surface of his somber reverie, or New Yorker glamor daydream. The puns and doubleplay or words almost dreamlike themselves suggest a mortal tangle too true and deep to be recognized in the gossip columns, a world of meat, drink, gambling, rich hotels, transvestite fellatio, married aristocrats, shopping, masturbation, tormented Pilgrim spirits. Tremendous morbid wit, derived from his stubborn resilient strain of New England genius (Emily Dickinson to Robert Creeley), is evident in swerve and switch of verse line and subject, last line moral, afterthought, or poem title.

WRITTEN: July 1, 1985

FIRST PUBLISHED: John Wieners, *Selected Poems 1958–1984* (Santa Barbara: Black Sparrow Press, 1986).

DIANE DI PRIMA

Pieces of a Song by Diane di Prima Blurb

Diane di Prima, revolutionary activist of the 1960s' Beat literary renaissance, heroic in life and poetics: a learned humorous bohemian, classically educated, and twentieth-century radical, her writing, informed by Buddhist equanimity, is exemplary in imagist, political and mystical modes. A great woman poet in second half of American century, she broke barriers of race-class identity, delivered a major body of verse brilliant in its particularity.

FIRST PUBLISHED: Diane di Prima, *Pieces of a Song* (San Francisco: City Lights, 1990).

LAWRENCE FERLINGHETTI

Lawrence Ferlinghetti Academy Blurb

Lawrence Ferlinghetti's poetry strikes a universal characteristic nostalgic bohemian tone, internationally recognizable, translated into several dozen languages round the world. A most popularly read literary poet in his own nation, readers over the planet welcome him as representative non-official American culture hero. Celebrated prose and poetries include mid-fifties *Pictures of the Gone World,* and *Coney Island of the Mind,* his novels including *Love in the Days of Rage* (1988) and a dozen books of poetry thru recent *These Are My Rivers: New and Selected Poems 1955–1993.* Mr. Ferlinghetti would be a welcome populist addition to our contemporary pantheon.

<small>WRITTEN:</small> 1995

<small>FIRST PUBLISHED:</small> 1995 ballot, American Academy and Institute of Arts and Letters, Department of Literature, New York, 1995.

ANNE WALDMAN

Makeup on Empty Space by Anne Waldman Blurb

Anne Waldman is a poet orator, her body is an instrument for vocalization, her voice a trembling flame rising out of a strong body, her texts the accurate energetic fine notations of words with spoken music latent in mindful arrangement on the page. She is a power, an executive of vast poetry projects and mind schools in America, a rhythmic pioneer on the road of loud sound that came from Homer Sappho and leads to future epic space mouth, she's a cultivated Buddhist meditator, an international subtle *Tantrika,* an activist of tender brain vibrations.

FIRST PUBLISHED: Anne Waldman, *Makeup on Empty Space* (West Branch, IA: Toothpaste Press, 1984).

ALAN ANSEN

Contact Highs by Alan Ansen Blurb

Ansen is the most delicate hippopotamus of poets with his monstrous classical versifications—he gets conversational fatness 'into stricter order' by use of weird echosyllabics, polyphony, strict rhymeless pindarics, self-annihilating sestinas, mono-amphisbaenic and echo rhyme, skeltonics, versicles and alcaics coherent palindromes and such like master eccentricities—a hangup on forms which interestingly pushes academic models beyond polite limits into the area of lunatic personal genius—This is an amazing book, with many sad poems.

FIRST PUBLISHED: Alan Ansen, *Contact Highs* (Elmwood Park, IL: Dalkey Archive Press, 1989).

RAY BREMSER

————————

Ray Bremser and His Poetry

Ray Bremser born 1934 Jersey City grade school armed robbery age 19 Bordentown Reformatory six years there completed high school and *Poems of Madness* forwarded with correspondence to this A. Ginsberg and that G. Corso in Paris. Released 1958 published in *Yugen* magazine and Don Allen *New American Poetry* anthology gave readings Princeton Brown and Washington DC tour with fellow poets Living Theatre, married Bonnie (nee Frazer.)

Philadelphia TV pro-marijuana-legalization speech inspired Bordentown parole investigation. After six months Trenton State Prison (*Blues for Bonnie,* 1960) for "getting married without permission" intervention by the late Dr. William Carlos Williams and lawyers secured release. Romance with fuzz continued, Bremser immediately re-arrested bailed out then indicted for Jersey City armed robbery on I presume false/mistaken identification. Poet wife and child fled to Mexico half-year, abducted/deported to Laredo Texas as fugitive, wild palms. Bailed out again returned to Mexico anonymous another half-year. Rearrived in States to publish poetry 1962 busted in N.Y. "traces of marijuana in his address book" charge dismissed, held on Jersey robbery warrant bailed out crossed river and spent 3 months in can waiting. Inept lawyer unfriendly police and jury conviction alas 3 years as of Feb. 1963 expensive Kafkian appeal pending, so passeth over a year to now.

In Bremser poetry we have powerful curious Hoboken language, crank-blat phrasing, rhythmic motion that moves forward in sections to climaxes of feeling. Imagination shifts in and out of heard-about places in space and rime, American primitive, jailhouse primitive, and dramatizes key ideas—personal empathy with Egypt and a Pop Art approach to Platonic archetypes. Where is the truth in this? The truth here is the realized expression of emotional awareness. Poesy a rhythmic articulation of feeling, emotional physiology vocalized. Now the piper's piped, but had no human reward in his America—thus he goes wild, piping inhumanely.

> I passed out at this point and woke again amidst rowers . . .
> I pretend to pure dislocation and end in the palace of a
> great queen
> Whose bath has been drawn against logic . . .

Also he's funny: on funk, funky. Echoes of amphetamine echolalia—the line carried out through its last mental pip-squeak of idea-rhythm. A mouth hopped up with unnatural dactyls, or some kind of many-footed Greek measure.

> The zeal of gospel, elation
> Wham/Cymbal/Wham

The later writing is very jazzy, scatting related to Monk Coltraine Taylor Charles as well as meth-freak head noises. Awe of the universe enters into the poetry which is a big pile-up of words sometimes into Hart Crane-ish clang-lines.

> Great edible crotch full of hermitage lore
> and excusable gloom!

That takes a certain genius. But the real measure of inspiration is the opening up of the bardic breath and the summoning forward of rhythmic power from the breast for the sustained light of proclamation that climaxes the *Poems of Madness.*

WRITTEN: May 27, 1964

FIRST PUBLISHED: Ray Bremser, *Poems of Madness* (New York: Paper Book Gallery, 1965).

AUTHOR'S NOTE: Bremser in N.Y. lived with Elvin Jones and other great rhythmic artisans, and retains his spectacular oral gifts among American poets. Originally presented by Don Allen in his historic *New American Poetry.*

Resurrecting his genius, his texts—while he's still alive—would be happy denouement of this assemblage. This text was a press release on behalf of publication of his book *Angel*.

I realize these essays are time bombs, meant to explode their intelligence to future generations when and if scholars have time to follow the threads of information presented here, "wind up into a gold ball / in Jerusalem's wall!"

ANTLER

Antler *Factory* Blurb

Factory inspired me to laughter near tears, I think it's the most enlightening and magnanimous American poem I've seen since "Howl" of my own generation, and I haven't been as thrilled by any single giant work by anyone of '60s and '70s decades as I was by your continuing inventions and visionary transparency. . . . Nakedness honesty beautified by your self-confidence and self-regard and healthy exuberance, that exuberance a sign of genius, *bodhisattva* wit . . . seems you have developed your sincerity and natural truth and come through to eternal poetic ground, unquestionable and clear. . . . More fineness than I thought probable to see again in my lifetime from younger solitary unknown self-inspirer U.S. poet—I guess it's so beautiful to see because it appears inevitable as death, that breakthrough of beauty you've allowed yrself and me.

FIRST PUBLISHED: Antler, *Factory* (San Francisco: City Lights, 1980).

Antler's "Last Words"

The author of this book born Jan. 29, 1946 was raised in Wauwatosa, Wisconsin as Brad Burdick and given his life pseudonym Antler at summer camp ceremonies by friends in his 18th year. The poems in this monumental first book were written from his 22nd year to the mid 1970s while he dwelled mid-American in Milwaukee and traveled in solitude (or in company with Jeff Poniewaz his poet friend from those years to these) in North Woods Quetico—Superior Canoe country. At certain periods in this relatively noiseless and studious early life he studied in universities at Wisconsin and Iowa and he labored at Continental Can Company Plant #77 along the Milwaukee river, "the largest can company in the world under one roof."

With these few facts known, the reader may enter Antler's world in this book, and stand silent with admiration in a giant cavern created complete with logical stalagmites and stupendous stalactites, secret rooms and passageways, including ancient and modern graffiti—a vast space of poetic mind with myriad definite, resolved formations inside one skull, detailed in such way as might extend to infinity! Well thought out universe or, more down to earth, like a marvelously architected and productive can factory.

The major poem *Factory* seems to me a modern original classic in the tradition of Walt Whitman's realistic breath line of American poetics, and the unique single long poem that I know of in this genre created in postwar America since *Howl* that has complete formal unity, brilliance of conception and detail, logical grounding and trunk-like solidity of idea, branching out with brilliant conceptions, and details naturally delicate as exfoliation of leaves from a healthy tree; a major poem built solid as a brick shithouse. The "mystical" erotic conversion experience outside the factory has power and particularity like Whitman's confessional, sincerity, exuberance, and grandeur in Section 5 of "Song of Myself." Antler's section XII is a clear spacious imitation of the universe as we know it personally.

I mind how once we lay such a transparent summer morning,
How you settled your head athwart my hips and gently turn'd
    over upon me,
And parted the shirt from my bosom-bone, and plunged your
    tongue to my bare-stript heart,
And reach'd till you felt my beard, and reach'd till you held my
    feet.
Swiftly arose and spread around me the peace and knowledge
    that pass all the argument of the earth, . . .

"Exuberance is beauty" and an exuberant catalogue of factory made products devours the poet's imagination up to the realization that his poem will be reproduced in a poem printing factory. All his words will be "last words" henceforth.

An element of comedy in the improvisation of maddening logical extensions of key ideas keeps the composition from mechanic rigidity. The very mechanical nature of human mind and conditional activities is played on, parodied and transcended with desperate exaggeration of affairs which turn out to be real: "Factories that make toy coffins and toy plutonium." The conception is a giant toy, a toy weapon of mindfulness in the midst of the hallucinatory solidification of the Satanic mill that cans the human universe. Here's a prophecy beyond the Factory to Eden with space of eons of mind to swallow the anger against repetitious aluminum.

WRITTEN: 1980

Unpublished.

ANDY CLAUSEN

―――――――――

Introduction to *Without Doubt* by Andy Clausen

Andy Clausen's character voice is heroic, a *vox populi* of the democratic unconscious, a "divine average" thinking workman persona. As "one of the rough," a Whitmanic laborer, precisely a union hodcarrier long-standing, his bardic populism's grounded on long years' painful sturdy experience earning family bread by the sweat of his brow. His comments on the enthusiastic sixties, defensive seventies, unjust eighties, and bullying nineties present a genuine authority in America not voiced much in little magazine print, less in newspapers of record, never in political theatrics through Oval Office airwaves. The expensive bullshit of government TV poetics suffers diminution of credibility placed side by side with Mr. Clausen's direct information and sad raw insight. Would he were, I'd take my chance on a President Clausen!

As Clausen's experience of American hope and greed's authentic, so swift language is the second marvel of his verse. Some kind of native exuberance, an inventiveness of word-play juxtaposition and concept construction's always struck me (and poet familiars Gregory Corso and Philip Whalen, Sensei) as hitting the telepathic nail on the head.

"The derelict women poets are coming!"
  (*They Are Coming*)
". . . the inch nudged ten ton door / of Dickenson . . ."
  (*The Challenge*)
"the hay mulch wet as a car wash sponge"
  (*In Gorky*)
"protectors of stowaway Honor"
  (*Wail Bar Night*)
"a garbage eating role model"
  (*O the Fugacious*)

"cattle bewildered by neon galactics"
>(*Granny's New White China*)

A third specialty of his poetry is the run-on extended breath mental word riff (got from Kerouac, Cassady, and minstrel Dylan, the "chains of flashing images"):

"O night simple everyday magic night
Hoist thy iron true hammer!"
>(*Wail Bar Night*)

"Is not the miracle of pumping loins
produce this thinking feeling baby enough?"
>(*Baptism Enough*)

"red nosed busted blue derelicts
supported by lampposts and buildings
in the typewriter rain"
>(*Sacred Relics*)

"A purple boiling Coxey's Army
   charges out my chest like molten
      slag a volcanic smelter"
>(*O the Fugacious*)

A fourth charm and highlight of this writing is the self contained anecdotal vignette, particularly in the poems *Soldiers of Christ, Small Part of the Be-Bop Bill Story, Old Man, Ramona,* and "She Walks By The Crew." When he gets going in improvisation, the frank friendly extravagance of his metaphor and word-connection gives Andy Clausen's poetry a reading interest rare in poetry of any generation.

Hardly a primitive, though; he'd inherited some of Neal Cassady's optimistic energy through direct contact, had spent years in literary streets and coffeehouses, Bay Area, Austin, Northwest, and New York atmospheres; hosted and intermingled with many elder poets; taught at Naropa Institute's Poetics School during long residence in Boulder with family—even more recently's gone around the world, expanded the horizon of his work through Alaskan oilspill labors, Himalayan *mantrayan* contacts, and mitteleuropean post-cold-war sophistications to include audience with Czech President-Philosopher Havel before returning to the union bricks and coffeehouses of the Bay Area.

His forebears? Walt Whitman, Jack London and Jack Kerouac of course, but also Gregory Corso's tailored high style word paradox; also Mayakovsky's epic and Velimir Khlebnikov's big sound Zaum, and

American worksong. Oddly enough this Americanist archetype is also solid Belgian born, and that nativity flavors the genius of his tongue.

His poems' enjoyable energies flash wise.

WRITTEN: March 4, 1991

FIRST PUBLISHED: Andy Clausen, *Without Doubt* (Oakland, CA: Zeitgeist Press, 1991).

DAVID COPE

Foreword to *Quiet Lives* by David Cope

I have been much absorbed in David Cope's poetry as necessary continuation of tradition of lucid grounded sane objectivism in poetry following the visually solid practice of Charles Reznikoff and William Carlos Williams. Though the notions of "objectivism" were common for many decades among U.S. poets, there is not a great body of direct-sighted "close to the nose" examples of poems that hit a certain ideal objectivist mark—"No ideas but in things" consisting of "minute particulars" in which "the natural object is always the adequate symbol," works of language wherein "the mind is clamped down on objects," and where these "Things are symbols of themselves." The poets I named above specialized in this refined experiment, and Pound touched on the subject as did Zukofsky and Bunting, and lesser but interesting figures such as Marsden Hartley in his little known poetry, and more romantic writers such as D. H. Lawrence. In this area of phanopoeiac "focus," the sketching of particulars by which a motif is recognizably significant, David Cope has made, by the beginning of his third decade, the largest body of such work that I know of among poets of his own generation.

FIRST PUBLISHED: David Cope, *Quiet Lives* (Clifton, NJ: Humana Press, 1983).

EDITOR'S NOTE: This blurb from the dust jacket of the same volume.

Cope's out there in the provinces writing about . . . America where it is . . . He creates tiny movie pictures in your mind . . . the only younger poet I know who has that rare special genius . . . so simple, it's deceptive. There's no romantic fireworks. It's just straight reality.

ELIOT KATZ

Space by Eliot Katz, an Introduction

Another classic New Jersey Bard! Eloquent and poetic orator presenting working youth's psychoeconomic dilemmas with superior and uncanny analytic insight and happy exuberance, the very persona of E. Katz himself. Poet, printer, humorist, 80s generation political activist, his verses bespeak the colloquial heart of world tragedy and hope from his haunts, New Brunswick U.S.A.

I've known Eliot Katz for about ten years, and I've seen his poetry grow. In style and substance, he follows in the Whitmanic democratic tradition. Beyond that, he's developed a unique blend of literary influences: Romantics, Dickinson, Williams, surrealists, Brecht, Beats, modern feminist- and ecology-conscious poets, African-American and Latin American political modes. He uses a long-line oratorical form with lyrical passion, makes odd philosophical probes, populist humoresques, registers moments of contemplation and imagination. He's clear about minute particulars and works with American idiom. What's remarkable is the unabashed quest for spiritual health and enlightenment in a world otherwise depressed. Imaginative and sprightly conversations with dinosaurs, spirits, and UFO creatures give "E. Katz" an alternative "distanced" perspective on late–20th century planet Earth; even blueprints proposed for social transformation, American *glasnost* and *perestroika*! E. Katz has created his own original poetics for personal observation, animated discourse, critical insight, fantasy and communal vision.

FIRST PUBLISHED: Eliot Katz, *Space and Other Poems* (Orono, ME: Northern Lights, 1990).

PART 8
Further
Appreciations

ROBERT LAVIGNE

Robert LaVigne Exhibit

I was wandering around in Fosters,[1] Polk and Sutter, lonely 3 years ago looking for someone, I didn't know who, with a star on his forehead, as my dreams told me there would be, somewhere that night, perhaps in Polk Gulch, I saw Robert LaVigne looking poor and interesting with a beard, talking with a table full of what I thought were intimate sweet old friend bohemians, and wanted to get in on a new group, whatever they were, in the promise (always fulfilled where there's hope in the art star and the soul flash) something beautiful would happen, I'd end up that night in some angelic bed, or drunk maybe sad in littered apartment—anyway, embarrassed, went up and talked to him because he had a beard.

Later walking up Polk to his house to see his pictures we talked about art—poetry as a science of a kind, with a history of discoveries and changes (metrics)—and he seemed to think on that level, with painting. Also I began to see that though I was used to (and didn't too much like, then) the painters I half knew in NY, [Larry] Rivers, etc.—he alone in San Francisco leading a lone and very personal existence devotion of his own by the hand, was working on somewhat similar lines as they—he was interested in Bonnard (I know little about painting ways but remembered the sophisticated schools in NY around De Kooning then also had similar taste)—we talked about Cézanne—I had a theory of space ellipse in Cézanne which I manufactured in the basement of NY Museum of Modern Art high on T [marijuana] looking at the "View of Garonne" drawing—he understood all that, or I thought he did—all this to say that we had long interesting theoretical conversation, I was amazed at his seriousness, almost religious, toward his art, and thought him a sure and trustful brother. First picture I saw in his Gough Street house was a huge naked portrait of Peter Orlovsky—I looked in its eyes and was shocked by love.

A few weeks later I moved up into Gough Street and we all got involved in great magical personality hassles and all night portraits and endless friendships. While I was around in San Francisco the next year and a half or longer I watched his work week after week. The thing that most amazed me was the way he developed, by long drawn out intuitive phases—I guess everybody does that, good or bad—but here as in any really good artist, or as in my ideal of how it should work, like in Yeats, I saw him experimenting, phase after phase, all intimately tied up with his own psychic or soulful development, all expressions one after another like a biography—and getting hung on this or that technical problem, and carrying out infinite or anyway numberless variations of the same, spontaneously, one after another—then maybe a period of depression and then sudden new impulse and a new series—I remember several of them, which have been seen and unappreciated around San Francisco while I was there—"The Dangerous Garden," which hung in The Place, also a series of abstract box within box perspective drawings which ended (the last of the series) with a crazy fourth dimensional spiral—like the breakup of the piano sonata Beethoven Op. 111 form—this hung at City Lights, mostly unsold (I bought some); also the delicate Iris series—he sat a week or two and drew successive stages of the bloom and death of an iris in a bottle in his room at the Wentley [Hotel]—a great poetic story, full of suspense and observation—I always liked the delicate observation of his tender drawing, and death was in it too;—all this to say his inner development has beautiful drama. Toward the end of our stay in San Francisco there was the great idea of a huge historic picture of the scene in Fosters [Cafeteria], with the now dead Natalie Jackson seated naked in a chair perhaps, and all the people we knew, fixed in some sweet and final attitude in eternity on his canvas. It came out of sketches he'd done already, one which I grabbed, and an earlier fine narrow canvas (his landlord alas took for rent)—all sorts of space tricks with mirrors and elliptical spacejumps between huge nearby coffeecups and faraway San Francisco businessmen-lautrecian-groaner soup eaters—added to this the lovers of Fosters in their time. Well god knows where this painting is progressed to by this time, he wrote he had done more and I wish I could see it. Also I hear of a new series with new advanced strange theories brought down to some simplicity called the "Battle of Four Lakes"—he went to Washington and painted there with family solitude all last year.

Now a new exhibit—I wonder if anyone in San Francisco will pick up on his genius this time. If I were there I'd try to write about it precisely—as I did, composing a long private poem for him to hang on The Place wall with the "Dangerous Garden"—pointing out exactly the details I see in the pictures—but I'm too far away—so leave it there, having tried to sketch the background and his nature as a person, a painter who wears the golden crown with all its rusty diamonds, some kind of king without a name. I wish with all those drear streets and yelling about art and poetry and beat and renaissance, it will be recognized that this is it—going on right now, still, with all its poverty and having to work with no real hope of reward—unless people give him back the same tender understanding he has given them in his painting. But he's naked, and a great painter, and will be so in any case. I wish I were there to cry at his opening—the years are too short to let them go by without understanding.

WRITTEN: May 25, 1958

FIRST PUBLISHED: exhibition flyer, *Robert LaVigne: An Exhibition of Selected Works* (San Francisco: Lion Bookstore, July 11, 1958).

PHILIP LAMANTIA

Lamantia As Forerunner

Philip Lamantia and I share old friendship and similarity of sources—
our insight into an American *voice*, its *mechano hells* (his words): our
longing for breakthrough into the more natural universe of self, all our
true feelings: our prayer, public communication, poetry. His interest in
techniques of surreal composition notoriously antedates mine and surpasses my practice in a quality of untouched-news, nervous scatting,
street moment purity—his imagination zapping in all directs of vision at
once in a cafeteria—prosodic hesitancies and speedballs—the impatience, petulance, unhesitant declaration, machinegunning at mirrors
nakedly—that make his *line* his mantric own.

Since I'm cited as stylistic authority I authoritatively declare Lamantia
an American original, soothsayer even as Poe, genius in the language of
Whitman, native companion and teacher to myself. "And for years I have
been absorbed in contemplation of the golden roseate auricular gong-
tongue emanating from his black and curly skull. Why not." Says Philip
Whalen, and many poets his admirers Michael McClure and Robert
Creeley others have spoken—thus I've composed this prose returning to
Lamantia the last word:

There is no agrarian program it is all economic war!
I make war! I declare this tribe, cool! this nation, spared!
    this stupidity unlimited, put down! this slumbering beauty,
    waked up!
    this heap, fuckup, dead bitch—run down, put down,
finished!
    I liquidate by magic!

WRITTEN: ca. fall 1963

FIRST PUBLISHED: Excerpts published as a blurb for Philip Lamantia, *The Blood of the Air* (San Francisco: Four Seasons Foundation, 1970).

AUTHOR'S NOTE: I was college companion to Richard Howard in late 1940s early 1950s, we had been close, so a decade later I was dismayed by his flippancy in reviewing a work by Philip Lamantia, certainly a rare poet. He had met and was inspired directly by the Surrealist teachers who came to N.Y. during WWII Breton, Calas, etc. I thought Howard might understand the genre—being a specialist in French translation—and recognize Lamantia's unique role as an authentic inheritor of surrealist lineage in home grown American context. Philip Whalen at hand in S.F. when I typed this reply, so I quoted him for authority and assumed the syntax and diction of the letter would appear noticeably eccentric in the somewhat dull context of *Poetry* magazine, I hoped the humor of the praise be appreciated both for its seriousness and its style of Whitmanic megalomania. It may take a few more decades to sink into the thick head of Academy.

HENRI MICHAUX

On Henri Michaux

In 1948 in a polite madhouse where I stayed nearly a year with Carl
Solomon for company, I encountered many rare texts unfamiliar to me
as a student of modern French at Columbia University. I had been fed a
diet of Maurice Barrès for syntactical study, and other dreary prose and
poetry I have already forgotten: M. Solomon in our retreat provided me
with documents from the hand of Jacques Vadré, Rigault, Genet for
the first time (Céline I had already studied with Burroughs half decade
earlier, and a decade later we made an afternoon's company together
with the rheumy gay eyed old gentleman in Meudon), also poetry
of Schwitters, Artaud's *pour en finir avec le jugement de dieu* and other
penetrant verse/prophecy and hollow-cheeked photos in *Kra,* Isou's
Aggregation, etc. (We performed certain of his sound-letter pieces in the
hospital common room to the approval of random patients and nurses),
writings of Crevel and Desnos, and Henri Michaux's *Barbarian in Asia*
and fragmentary plumes.

I had tender contact with the American poetry teacher William Carlos
Williams and so expected much of my elders: frankness, vulnerability,
courtesy, information; and so in Paris in 1958 wanted to look in the eyes
of three living men maybe more, Cocteau also happily alive then though
I never found him, certainly not be in the same city and fail to seek out
Céline and Genet both masters of prose-poetry and Michaux who had
solitarily emerged sane and *renaissant* as a courageous human prophet
after his research into psychedelic drugs. Genet was hidden or away in
Corsica studying meat or in Amsterdam studying Rembrandt. I sent
Michaux a polite note around the corner from Rue Git-Le-Coeur[2] where
I stayed, I said I was a *jeune poète Américaine* who had much experience in
the same hallucinogenic field as himself, and would like to exchange
information with him. (He was the first substantial poet I had the opportunity to encounter who did know something about honorific use of

drugs—all the younger American poets by that time, unbeknownst to their French contemporaries, had done extensive research into the fields of consciousness that could be catalyzed by peyote and hashish and mescaline. But we had no elder soul in America to check our senses with.)

Michaux had a reputation for being a fine recluse so that I was surprised when I received a note that he would come to visit on a certain afternoon, and more surprised when a sharp eyed elderly man entered my dingy hotel room while I was washing my feet in the sink.

He sat on the bed, I explained to him the tradition of peyote experiment in the US of the last decade, I think he was happily surprised to find that unknown company existed in the world. I was delighted by his affection and praise of Artaud as *poet,* and his sympathetic description of the revelatory physical sound of Artaud's voice. One thing I concluded was that Michaux apparently diffident and solitary was like all geniuses a man full of natural sympathy who could be trusted to approve enthusiasm, heart, common humor or any humane crankiness as long as it was unaffected. He had no reason to give me time and be courteous except that he was intelligent and responsive to my own intelligent curiosity.

It reaffirmed a sense of traditional value—sincerity?—that I found affirmed in William Carlos Williams' eyes.

I asked what younger French poets he recommended, he said there wasn't much, perhaps Bonnefoi, more maybe visionary in Joyce Mansour. Bonnefoi's *Douve* he recommended. We mostly talked about Artaud's *Radio Diffusion Française* performance, and some gossip about mescaline—I gave him copies of my own book *Howl* and Corso's *Gasoline.* I think we went around the corner to Place St. Michel and had tea with Gregory Corso who was living with me. But we had little time at this first meeting; sufficient to see that he was a benevolent presence on the planet.

We met briefly once again, again he had the courtesy to come to our hotel (or perhaps he wanted his house kept quiet) where he met Wm. Burroughs—he'd happily looked into the books; I don't think he got much out of my English, but he certainly was sensitive to Gregory Corso's language and laughed quoting a line he'd *noticed* which pleased him "mad children of soda caps"—"children of soda caps?"—I thought it was a funny phrase too, remarkable and inevitable that a superior French language-man should dig it. He had brought *Tourbillion De L'infini* as a farewell gift. "Would you please sign it?" I asked. I think he was amused that the young U.S. barbarian would be affected by such gestures, and did write a note in the flyleaf. But Corso and Burroughs wanted to read the book and so I left for US without it, never saw it again.

I heard from Burroughs that the two met occasionally, chancing on each other in local cafés. Burroughs had begun to cut-up his own language to escape it; and alter his consciousness. He wrote that Michaux, hurrying by like the White Rabbit, stopped to report that in some dream or hallucinogen reverie, he had found Burroughs there imperturbably waiting. "I've been there all along," affirmed Burroughs. Lovely, though it was Mr. Burroughs' story.

Several years later, after some horrific experiences with LSD in America, I passed thru Paris again, on way to India. We had lunch in an odd cafe a mile away where he appointed to meet me. "I am less interested in the visions that people have with the drugs, now I am more interested in how they manifest their experience after-ward, what they do with it later." That was his reasonable sense of things at the time, 1961.

Returned from India and in Paris 1965, with Gregory Corso again, I went into his hallway and left a note at the door; we missed each other for days, finally returning from St. Germain along Rue St. Jacques Gregory spied him crossing the street, and yelled (like a Lower East Side New York gang boy to a Jewish delicatessen owner) "Hey! Henry!"

Henry crossed the street, "Did you get my note?" "No did you get mine?" "I sent you a note making a date tomorrow," and while we talked grouped around a lamppost, oddly met on the planet again, M. Michaux noticed out of the corner of his eye that, half way across the narrow street, a rich young lady tourist journalist had pointed a camera at us. He sidestepped and averted his face. I myself, new to fame, assumed we'd been recognized; though in fact it was fortunate to have the adventitious street encounter imprinted in permanent shadow. "Dear Poet Ginsberg" said Michaux naively, "they are undoubtedly interested in your picture. I must step aside." I was embarrassed, I was afraid he'd think we had been searching him out on the streets with a camera entourage, had found and trapped him, and were ready to charter a plane back to America with all our images captured together for some *Life* magazine of another eternity. I was about to say, "But I mean . . . No, I think they're coming to get *you*," but was too confused and ashamed to say anything. The lady meanwhile was giving us instructions, was she asking us to look at her and smile?

"Will you gentlemen please get out of the way, I am trying to take a photograph of the carriage entrance behind you?"

"No no," said Michaux, "Please M. Ginsberg, it is for you alone this photo"—he hadn't heard or yet comprehended her and was still earnest on retreating from my brash conspiracy.

"I say, gentlemen *please*, move from the doorway so I can snap my picture," the lady importuned. Michaux's face lighted up with Chinese absurdity and delight and we moved on like Chaplinesque exquisite heroes, pathetically bowing and showing the path to each other.

Meanwhile, far from having a chartered plane in abeyance, we had no place to stay, and little money for food; we all returned to our senses and Michaux like kindly father offered a few thousand francs which I was ashamed to accept. We made an appointment for lunch next day.

And went, of all places this time, to La Coupole[3] in a taxi and ate shell-fish and rare meat, and talked about India.

"But where is all the immortal poetry of young France? I did read Bonnefoi but it was all abstract! What did you mean Monsieur Bonnefoi?"

"Oh, I just told you that Monsieur was interesting, mystic, you asked what poetry there was, I thought it was a polite literary question for a literary voyager; a literary answer." He seemed dismayed that there was no spiritual invention renewed in Paris; I saw a lone dignified, fine-haired skull seven years later.

Gregory was slightly ill, some American infection, and he left early; then I begged Michaux to accompany me to the Libraire Mistral—I was staying in the smelly book-lined guest room upstairs overlooking Notre Dame (sleeping late into the morning, after wandering around lonesome and lovesick for strangers from Fiacre to La Pergola till dawn, to wake surrounded by beaded girls reading books on Red China)—I had begun chanting mantram in India, accompanying myself on tiny finger-cymbals and wanted at last to manifest for Michaux a new thing for both of us—perhaps related to his desire years ago to see the results in action of quotidian consciousness integrating some psychedelic depth—any way, I wanted to SING to Michaux, like a poet should, finally.

This singing is part of the practice of *Bhakti* Yoga devotional Yoga, where it is understood that in this *Kali Yuga* age of destruction breath, meditation, mind, intelligence and works are hopeless to raise the soul out of its materialist mire—only sheer joy will save us. Only sheer delight! So we sat, late afternoon, he perhaps wondering at my awkward purpose, in a room strange to him, Seine flowing behind the iron window-grate, mid summer, his face no older than I first remember him but now more hesitant, softer and kinder of eye—confused! As I was confused! Happily all there was left to do was sing *Hari Krishna Hari Krishna Krishna Krishna Hari Hari Hari Rama Hari Rama Rama Rama Hari Hari,* the Hindu *japa maha* mantra, and *Om A Ra Ba Tsa Na De De De De De De* a Tibetan meaningless syllabic mantra designed to occupy the mind while circumambulating temples or cradling children in the arm.

Salutations to self, the lovely teacher.

WRITTEN: Dec. 1965

FIRST PUBLISHED: Introduction to Henri Michaux, *By Surprise* (New York: Hanuman Books, 1987).

JEAN GENET

Genet's Commencement Discourse

May Day 1970 at Yale satisfied the most ancient traditions of Academy when school strike shut down Establishment social classes and 20,000—30,000 youths assembled with black men, church men, bohemian and professor elders to sit under grassy sky before a wooden platform raised under the portentous stone columns of New Haven's imitation-classic Courthouse—What Blake would have made of that priestly facade!—to hear Jean Genet, most eminent prosateur of Europe and saintly thinker of France, most shy poet of twentieth century slipped criminally into forbidden America through Canada border, standing flanked by clownish tragic reality of revolution of consciousness and body in America—Yippie Saints Rubin Hoffman, peaceful Saint Dellinger, many musical and professorial politic thinkers, black philosopher street theorists and actionaries, and great Big Man leader of New Haven Panthers that day—deliver his historic psychopolitical *Commencement Discourse* to the Academy and Polis of America, to youthful lovers of all lands' races, and especially to the tender terrified whites assembled under the eye of metal-armed masked robot national armies and gas-weaponed police—all of us black and white now scholars in Hell! on New Haven's green—pronouncing the very terms of the desired merciful survival armistice and union between black and white races in America that might bring peace to the entire world.

M. Genet appeared short, round headed, white skull'd, pink faced with energetic cigar, drest in Amerindian style brown leather-thonged jacket, he spoke first into the microphone in French, explaining (as I remember, myself sitting far left of the iron-pole joint-footed platform accepting burning grass reefer stubs from varicolor-shirted youths thick bearded seated round, long haired and short naked-minded newborn scholars of police-state reality, apocalyptic biblical revolution for millennium our mortal lot—) his presence in America and introducing his text, which he explained would be read for him in English by Mr. Big Man (whose name Genet pronounced happily Beeg Man)—And so after a page, Mr. Big Man bent to the microphone, and straining over the fresh English/American translation read Genet's sentences in gentle and firm voice. Genet had not been advertised for that first day's convocation; many newsmen had not yet arrived to the giant crowd nor were aware that Genet's person and prose were fortunately and intelligently the first offering of the afternoon, and many inattentive folk on the green didn't know that Big Man's speech was Genet's composition.

The exquisite common sense of Genet's document on racism was immediately apparent—to those of us whose consciousness attended his classic language while we eyed the bannered mass multitude seated on ground, batteries of cameras TV'd in front circle, FBI window-telescopes in high floors of bank department edifices walled over New Haven Green—black flag and red, scroll'd cannabis leaf insignia and 50-starred stripes, helicopter passed roaring overhead—and the Panthers and their righteous cause and the grievous, mean, bitter murderous injustice dealt them by our Government was explained again clearly once for all and established irrevocably in conscience and consciousness in *white terms* unmistakable, and in language that commanded a new "delicacy of heart" as the next political dimension of white reality, confronted with age old bestiality and desensitization of heart that had shrouded white mind for 400 years of contemptible histrionics.

Genet's prayer for himself, for ourselves, remarkably included this tender odd affirmation for all: "Personally, I place a certain trust in man's nature, even the nature of the most limited man."

The complete text of this class discourse, a true commencement exercise marking the historic graduation of white mentality to a "delicacy of heart" hitherto forbidden in fear and greed by universities and press, church, foundation, unions and advertising freakdoms, and fumbling, conspiring, dangerous, trembling criminal police agents.

WRITTEN: June 1970

FIRST PUBLISHED: Introduction to Jean Genet, *May Day Speech* (San Francisco: City Lights, 1970).

W. H. AUDEN

––––––––––––

Remembering Auden

We met first at Earl Hall, Columbia University, 1945, when he read to students. I accompanied him on the subway to Sheridan Square, wondering if he'd invite me to his Cornelia Street apartment and seduce me. He didn't. Years later in Ischia at a garden table, 1957, I said I thought there was a social revolution at hand, he poo-pooed it, and I drunkenly yelled at him, indignant, "You ought to be ashamed of yourself discouraging young hope and energy!" I was outraged, intemperate, tipsy and self-righteous. Oddly, years later, he apologized to me for having been too off-handed with me. Actually I'd made pilgrimage to Ischia to see him and I'd intruded at his restaurant wine leisure dusk.

Auden was very fussy, sort of generous, but fussy. In the sixties I used to go visit him every year or two, have tea. Soon after I came back from India I went to see him with a harmonium and started singing Hare Krishna and various mantras and he sat and listened, but he was uncomfortable, like pinned wriggling to the wall, and having to be polite and really mind-wandering and not really interested in my great display of knowledge, because I was laying this trip on him.

The next time I went to see him I brought my harmonium wanting to sing some Blake songs. He said, "Oh, no no no no, I just can't stand people singing to me like that, makes me terribly embarrassed. I can't sit here and have people singing. I'm quiet and prefer to listen to them in a concert hall, or on a record. Don't sing, have some tea, have some tea, please. You'll embarrass me."

I think he got a little bit silly. When he was last in New York he was doing some work with a cartoonist making some funny little poems. So instead of my singing to him, he wanted me to look at those. I was full of big serious mantras and Blake and spiritual trippiness and he wanted me to look at all those funny little household domestic verses about how silly and comfy the Victorians were. Summer 1973 in London we all read together—Basil Bunting and Auden and myself and MacDiarmid at Queen Elizabeth Hall and he read some very great poems saying farewell to his body, farewell to his eyes, to his senses one by one, evaluating them and putting them in place, dissociating himself from permanent identification with his senses, and preparing his soul to meet his ultimate empty nature God. So there was an individualistic solitary complete objectivity that he arrived at.

Apparently he was very domestic, but his apartment was a complete mess, there were papers all over, books piled up on end tables and shelves, just like a real artist's.

I had a couple of funny run-ins with him different times, and always had a very uneasy time with him, I always felt like a fool, trying to lay a trip on him culture-political or otherwise. Once we had a big happy agreement about marijuana should be legalized. He said "Liquor is much worse, quite right quite right. I do think . . . end all this fuss."

He must have been lonely, because he said he was afraid he'd drop dead in his apartment and have a heart attack and nobody would find him. Quite true because he did have a final heart attack a year later. I don't know if he encouraged local friendliness or not, but every time I called him up he'd make a date for about a week later, and he'd be there and be expecting me and have tea ready.

WRITTEN: 1973

FIRST PUBLISHED: *Drummer,* no. 282 (Feb. 12, 1974) p. 3.

JOHN LENNON AND YOKO ONO

Visas for Lennon and Ono

It is with great pleasure that we wish to add P.E.N. Club American Center's great Roc's voice to the vast chorus of poetic larks and ambassadorial editorial owls who've already raised cries throbbing to heav'n that American shores, woods and lakes not be banned to the great Swan of Liverpool John Lennon poet-musician (in the line of descent of Campion, Waller and Dowland fellow language-ayre minstrels celebrated in the great tree of Britain's poesy) and his paramour-wife conceptual authoress Yoko Ono, birds of a feather.

Such mighty creatures as these who've winged o'er Atlantic's deeps to Mannahatta Isle are threatened to be cast hence for once consuming hemp leafs in their home nesting ground. So tiny a natural peccadillo, and so great a cage, as large as the world, to keep them out of America!

May all the chorus of singing creatures on Turtle Island (North America) bid them welcome to stay immigrant here including even the lonely near-extinct Federal Bald Eagle.

WRITTEN: ca. 1972

FIRST PUBLISHED: *Berkeley Barb,* vol. 15, no. 12 (Oct. 6–12, 1972) p. 2.

Lennon/Ono and Poetic Tradition

There's a poetic event taking place consequent on the genius minstrelsy of Lennon, Dylan and others—namely, that (as Ezra Pound and Bessie Smith prophesied) poetry has been returned through music back to the human body. In mid-twentieth century, American-English poetry had been cut off from the body, as 'twere a thinking head: not talking, not singing, not chanting, not praying aloud but only murmuring in the mind.

So, Lennon's particularly interesting, in English minstrel's tradition—remember, Shakespeare wrote songs, "With a Hey and a Ho and a Hey nonny-o . . . with Hey! with Hey! The thrush and the jay."

Dowland, Campion and Waller wrote exquisite verses, tuned to Renaissance guitars—(God knows, mandolins or harpsichords?), William Blake wrote *a cappella* "Songs of Innocence and of Experience." As Pound chanted in Canto LXXXI,

> Lawes and Jenkyns guard thy rest
> Dolmetsch ever be thy guest . . .
> Then resolve me, tell me aright
> If Waller saying or Dowland played . . .
> And for 180 years almost nothing.

So, Blake wrote songs around the time of the American Revolution and for "180 years almost nothing," in white culture music until the Beatles sang a most perfect modern European poem in English language at the end of the Sergeant Pepper album. "A Day in the Life" is a twentieth century poem: style Guillaume Apollinaire, "Zone." Readers are urged to compare the two texts for similar intelligence in syntax, punctuation, condensation, surrealistic juxtaposition of quotidian and urban details (combs, taxis, Albert Halls, car crash). As Apollinaire's "Zone" could be placed in an anthology of twentieth century world poetry, so can "Day in the Life."

And, as Bertolt Brecht and early Auden lyrics on social circumstances have already found their way into anthologies so, with intelligent editorship, will Lennon's more secret social writings settle by their own weight into anthologies of classic, contemporary verse. Lennon, knowingly (or intuitively as in most true artist's work) has proceeded in the 1970s USA to the same poetic territory as Bertolt Brecht in his social-attack opera masterpiece *libretti: Three-penny Opera* and *Mahagonny.*

Both Brecht's and Lennon's genius has been to take pop social-revolutionary slogans (some invented by himself and Yoko Ono, some gathered in from the air as Shakespeare gathered London phrases) and fill out verses around them that stick in the mind, with dramatic personal meaning for poet and poetess; phrases digested through their own genius and rhymed socially in a popular manner that is absolutely not stereo-typed or trite, but transformed into pungent rhythm, as choppy, sharp, penetrant and art-wise as social Rimbaud or Brecht.

Dull minds observing Lennon transform himself into an angry *bodhisattva* of song for the masses have mistaken his verse to be over-simplistic. On the contrary, it's an ancient perfectly subtle, humble, artful simplicity: the condensation of common, social language into hard strong human personal verse. The dangers of oversimplification are obvious, but Lennon and Ono's approach has been humble and brilliant simultaneous. Every stanza they sing has a weird personal twist that lifts it above doddering rhymed social realist poetry and Nixon-era reactionary rock-schlock and individualizes "Progressive" communal emotion. (I'm thinking of lyrics and music on albums starting with *John Lennon/Plastic Ono Band* to *Sometime in New York*.)[4]

Lennon/Ono has grasped some principle of *mantra* more directly than other electrical artists and applied such in consciously transformed Americanese for purposes of political consciousness revolution-evolution. Notoriously successful with "Give Peace a Chance": a workable mantra. (Conversation with Lennon in Syracuse in '71 clarified the fact that Lennon *intended* the song as mantra: Peace Mantra, based somewhat on his experience and familiarity with Hare Krishna esoteric mantra usage.) Later Xmas song provided new Xmas mantra.

To sum up, Lennon/Ono is a conscious poet coherently adapting traditional poetic song devices to new consciousness, new technology electronic mass ear education: one brilliant development of modern poetry, completely realized. If Lennon/Ono disappear tomorrow to heaven, they'd take an immortal laurel crown (traditional poetic gift of the muses) to the pearly gates, great work finished.

WRITTEN: Jan. 1973

FIRST PUBLISHED: *Changes,* no. 86 (1974) p. 13.

Beatles Essay

I remember the precise moment, the precise night I went to this place in New York City called the Dom[5] and they turned on "I Want to Hold Your Hand," and I heard that high, yodeling alto sound of the OOOH that went right through my skull, and I realized it was going to go through the skull of Western civilization. I began dancing in public the first time in my life complete delight and abandon, no self-conscious wall-flower anxieties.

It was joyful rhythm, generosity, the openness, youthfulness and communality of their voices. They were four guys who were a gang, and they loved and appreciated each other. I remember realizing that night at the Dom that black dancing had been brought back to the white West, people were going to return to their bodies that Americans were going to shake their ass.

The Beatles changed American consciousness, they introduced a new note of complete masculinity allied with complete tenderness and vulnerability. And when that note was accepted in America, it did more than anything or anyone to prepare us for some kind of open-minded, open-hearted relationship with each other—and the rest of the world.

WRITTEN: Jan. 1984

FIRST PUBLISHED: *Rolling Stone,* no. 415 (Feb. 16, 1984) p. 22.

ANDY WARHOL

Andy Warhol [Festschrift]

Despite the coolness of Warhol's art attitudes, surface unemotionality, advertising texture, and multiples method, there was (as in Burroughs' cut-up procedure for prose composition) an advantage: an almost spiritual nonattachment, or appearance of nonattachment, since ultimately Warhol's private mortal reference was to the supreme *kitsch* of the Catholic Church.

Yet in practice Warhol provided an opportunity to review archetypal U.S. images, grocery containers, movie stars, and most-wanted-criminal posters, etc.; and see them isolated epiphanous with new eyes, "the doors of perception" cleansed of associations or with associations rememberable but oddly irrelevant to the actual images enlarged for inspection.

His autobiography presents also an almost Zen-like nonattachment—except for crucial instances where Warhol's preferences and straightforward predilections are declared. His method of relating to film censorship was Taoist—let go of one banned film and produce another, faster than censors could catch up.

Kerouac, Corso, Orlovsky, and myself cavorted and talked on his *Couch*; he didn't participate much in the moment, simply left the camera turned on, and I've never managed to see the picture. Yet it's the only existing picture with all four of us in the frame on earth.

Was his enormous wealth, by-product of his own genius and communal effort, recycled in any large part back to the artistic community he inhabited?

In the long run, effort to evade egocentric subjectivity by making cool anonymous art is unnecessary. Friendly relationship to a tamed transparent ego encourages more passionate intensity without disillusioning backfires. Some Marxists aimed at puritanically egoless aesthetics, often with suicidal or secret power-mad consequences.

FIRST PUBLISHED: Kynaston McShine, ed., *Andy Warhol, A Retrospective* (New York: Museum of Modern Art, 1989).

CHÖGYAM TRUNGPA

Introduction to *First Thought Best Thought*

As lineage holder in ear-whispered *Kagyü* transmission of Tibetan Buddhist practice of wakefulness, Chögyam Trungpa is *Rinpoche* or "Precious Jewel" of millennial practical information on attitudes and practices of mind speech and body that Western poets over the same millennia have explored, individually, fitfully, as far as they were able—searching thru cities, scenes, seasons, manuscripts, libraries, back alleys, whorehouses, churches, drawing rooms, revolutionary cells, opium dens, merchant's rooms in Harrar, salons in Lissadell.

Rimbaud, drawing on the magician Eliphas Levi and hashishien back-alleys of Paris, rediscovered "Alchemy of the Verb" and other Western magics including home-made colors of vowels and "long reasoned derangement of all the senses" as part of his scheme to arrive at the unknown as poet-seer. His conception of poet as visionary savant is unbeatable ambition no Western poet can bypass, though as in the lives of Rimbaud and Kerouac, mature suffering, the First Noble Truth of existence, may be the destined end of ambitious magic. Some reality is arrived at: "Charity is that key—This inspiration proves that I have dreamed! . . . I who called myself angel or seer, exempt from all morality, I am returned to the soil with a duty to seek and rough reality to embrace! Peasant!"

Rimbaud, still a model of the beautiful poet, concluded his life's last year with the following letters: "In the long run our life is a horror, an endless horror! What are we alive for?" . . . "My life is over, all I am now is a motionless stump." Generations later poets are still trying to change reality with the revolution of the word, a twentieth century preoccupation drawing on Western gnostic sources.

Some compromise with Absolute Truth had to be made in twentieth century poetics: William Carlos Williams thru Kerouac, poets were willing to work with relative truth, the sight at hand, accurate perception of appearance, accurate reportage of consciousness—although Hart Crane and some rock poets continued to force the issue of self-immolation as means of becoming one with phenomena.

As part of the aesthetics of working with relative truth, an American idiom developed (born out of the spacious pragmatism of Whitman in dealing with his own ego): the acceptance of actual poetic (poesis: making) behavior of the mind as model, subject, and measure of literary form and content. Mind is shapely, art is shapely. Gertrude Stein's style thus merges literary artifact with present consciousness during the time of composition. Put another way: the sequence of events of poet's mind, accidents of mind, provide the highlights, jumps and plot of poetry. As to the muse, "She's there, installed amid the kitchenware" as Whitman celebrated the change from absolute heroic to relative honesty in poetic method. Thus we inherited our world of poetry in twentieth century.

Thirst for some absolute truth still lurks behind this shift, thus bullfighting, drugs, God, communism, realpolitik or revolution, drink, suburb or Bohemia, sex, grassroots communalism, ecology or Amerindian ground, blasts of eternal vision, death's skull, even various apocalypses or extraterrestrial paranoias and delights recur as our preoccupation, and have been epic'd. Brave energies of fear, joy or anomie, not much certainty; yet there's been honest effort to display what can be seen of naked mind, and that's led to an amazingly open style of poetry which includes snow-blinding Sierras and rain-diamonded traffic lights, as mind's-eye does. An international style, based on facts, has emerged, perhaps the most relaxed poetic mode ever. Still, no certainty emerges but ultimate suffering, accelerating change, and perhaps some vast glimpse of universal soullessness. Has the poetic seer failed? Or perhaps succeeded at arriving at a place of beat bleakness where the ego of poetry is annihilated?

At last! To the rescue! Carrying the panoply of 25 centuries of wakened mind-consciousness "where glorious radiant Howdahs / are being carried by elephants / through groves of flowing milk / past paradises of Waterfall / into the valley of bright gems / be rubying an antique ocean / floor of undiscovered splendor / in the heart of un happiness."[6] And whozat? The poet of absolute sanity and resolution, "having drunk the hot blood of the ego." The author is a reincarnated Tibetan Lama trained from age 2 in various ancient practices aimed at concentrating attention, focusing perception, minding thought-forms to transparency, profounding awareness, vasting consciousness, annihilating ego, and immolating ego-mind in phenomena: a wizard in control of day-dream, conscious visualization and thought projection, vocal sound vibration, outward application of insight, practice of natural virtues, and a very admiral of oceanic scholarship thereof.

The dramatic situation of someone who has realized the world as pure mind, and gone beyond attachment to ego to return to the world and work with universal ignorance, confront the spiritual-materialist daydream of Western world—and tell it in modernist poetry—provides the historic excitement this book puts in our laps.

To focus on one aspect of the drama, consider the progression of style, from early poems adapted out of Tibetan formal-classic modes, to the free-wheeling personism improvisations of the poems of 1975, which reflect guru mind's wily means of adapting techniques of imagism, post-surrealist humor, modernist slang, subjective frankness and egoism, hip "finger-painting," and tenderhearted spontaneities as adornments of tantric statement. We see respect and appreciation given to the "projective field" of modern Western poetry; this is a teaching in itself, which few past "gurus" have been able to manifest in their mistier mystic musings. Something has jerked forward here, into focus, visible, in our own language: rare perceptions dealt with in our own terms.

By hindsight the classical style poems become precious exhibitions of cultural starting place and intention for the poet, Chögyam, "the stray dog."

For those familiar with advanced Buddhist practice and doctrine, the solidified symbolisms of early poems are significant teachings, or statements of method, attitude, and experience, as in "The Zen Teacher," where horse, boat and stick may represent *Hinayana Mahayana* and *Vajrayana* attitudes of wakefulness. Quite thrilling, unusual, to find a contemporary poet who's master of an ancient "system." Within my memory, it was academically fashionable to say that the twentieth century lacked the culture for great poetry, not possessing, as Dante's time did, a "system" of cultural assumptions on which to hang an epic. But it seemed too late to go back and clothe the skeleton of God, though Eliot, Claudel and others yearned nostalgic for such divine certainty.

Chögyam Trungpa, however, does have a classical system working for him to make "the snakeknot of conceptual mind uncoil in air." *Vajrayana* Buddhist symbolism is at his disposal, including the notion of "Absolute

Truth"—a property hitherto unclaimable since Plato kicked the poets out of his republic. Tho' Keats did propose redeeming truth as beauty. Blake created a symbolic sacred world in many ways parallel to *Vajrayana*. How do other poet friends look in this light, faced with contest from within their ranks by poet who's also lineage holder of the most esoteric teachings of the East? Will Auden seem amateur, pursuing testy quasi-Christian personal conclusions? Does Eliot quote Buddha, Krishna and Christ like a country vicar? How do I sit, charlatan pedant full of resentful Ginsberghood, posed by contemporary media as cultural guru? Does Yeats gasp like a beached fish in the tin air of Theosophy's "Secret Doctrines" version of the Great East? Whereas "Chögyam writing a poem is like a king inspecting his Soldiers." Well, Well!

What will poetry readers think of that bardic boast? Diamond Macho the *Kalevala* song men wouldn't match, tho' they might threaten to sing each other into a swamp.[7] What image of poet! What would angelic Shelly've said? What would Blake warn? "I must make a system of my own, or be enslaved by another man's"? On Mt. Ida the Muses look up astonished by this bolt of lightning thru blue cloudless sky.

This book is evidence of a Buddha-natured child taking first verbal steps age 35, in totally other language direction than he spoke age 10, talking side of mouth slang: redneck, hippie, chamber of commerce, good citizen, Oxfordian aesthete slang, like a dream *bodhisattva* with thousand eyes and mouths talking turkey.

Thus poems of June 1972 approach the theme of personal love using open Western forms and "first thought best thought" improvisatory technique—statements which mediate between the formality of *Dharma* Master and a man immersed in relative truth. Phrases return and re-echo in mind: "Take a thistle to bed, / And make love to it." The following "Letter to Marpa," classical theme, is done in smooth mixture of old and new styles: "Ordering Damema to serve beer for a break." If you know the wife of Marpa (translator and early founder of *Kagyü* Lineage) and Trungpa Rinpoche, this poem's a historic prophecy of transplantation of lineage to America in American terms: awesome knowledge and self-aware humor are explicit in the poem.

"Nameless Child": "hearing the pearl dust crunch between his teeth" is startling statement of egolessness, "unborn nature" of consciousness, done in traditional style. The next experiment is with gnomic haiku-like riddles, developing 7 November 1972 into precise American style "red wheelbarrow" snapshots. "Skiing in a red and blue outfit, drinking cold beer," etc. Thru these we see ordinary mind of the poet, whose specialty as Eastern teacher is ordinary mind.

Years later ordinary egoless mind says in response to anxiety-ridden ecology freaks, "Glory be to the rain / That brought down / Concentrated pollution / On the roof of my car / In the parking lot." Amazing chance to see his thought process step by step, link by link, cutting through solidifications of opinion and fixations on "Badgoodgood / goodbadbad" and attachment to this and that humorless image the poems July 1974, including "Ginsberg being Pedantic."

This method of first-thought concatenations develops in a series of tipsy essays in modern style—some dealing with serious personal matters. By September 1974, in "Supplication to the Emperor," ancient wisdom transmission heritage is wedded to powerful modern "surrealist" style.

These poems are dictated amidst an ocean of other activities including the utterance of masses of books of *Dharma* exposition—as the Tibetan imagery says "a mountain of jewels"—exactly true of this strange poet in our midst, noticing our "Aluminum-rim black leather executive chairs."

What's odd, adventurous, inventive, mind-blowing, is the combination of classical occasion (visit of head of *Kagyü* Order, His Holiness Gyalwa Karmapa, to North America) treated in authentic post-Apollinaire recognizably American-minded style ("Supplication to the Emperor").

Poignant and powerful then, the re-echoes of liturgical style that reappear in 1974, the poet in midst of struggle with the flypaper of modern centerless-minded poetics (as in an unpublished text, "Homage to *Samantabhadra*," 11 November 1974):

I am a mad Yogi.
Since I have no beginning, no end,
I am known as the ocean of Dharma.
I am the primordial madman;
I am primordially drunk.
Since all comes from me,
I am the only son of the only Guru.

By February 1975, a series of poems in entirely modern style indicate absorption of the lively fashion of versifying developed in the U.S. after models of Christopher Smart and Apollinaire, and transmitted in U.S.

'50s to '70s by Corso, the "List Poem" spoken of by Anne Waldman and others—see the cadenzas punning and joking on the word palm (25 February 1975), the "best minds" commentary of the same day, and subsequent love poems. In "Dying Laughing" there's an ironic commentary on modern poetic mind, "scattered thoughts are the best you can do . . . That the whole universe / could be exasperated / And die laughing."

There follows a series of portraits—"characters" as T. S. Eliot termed certain of William Carlos Williams' poems on persons—thumbnail sketches of his students, their natures exposed to x-ray humorous advice—"If you're going to tickle me, be gentle . . . But titillating enough to stimulate my system with your feminine healthy shining well-trimmed nail just so . . ."

Of the famous situation of guru playing with disciples this is rare honest private occasion made public where you can see the inside story and its humanity and innocence, its true teaching and bone quick insight. Tiny details of personality, irritating seen in greater space, along with tiny details of resolution of problems of egoic self-consciousness proposed by subjects of the portraits—this one composed March 1975:

. . . jalapeño dumpling
Bitten by Alice's white teeth,
Which are lubricated by feminine saliva

There's an odd reminder of Kurt Schwitters' *Anne Blume* here, or: the love poem dated 7 March 1975:

As she turns her head
From the little irritation of long flowing hair
She says, Mmmm.
But on the other hand she is somewhat perturbed;
Not knowing whether she is glamorous or ugly

A number of successful complete poems follow, the poetic ground having been prepared, the improvisational practice having been taken seriously, thus "Victory Chatter" is fruition of poetic path begun consciously much earlier. The details in the mind of the "good general" of *dharma* battle are recognizable. A number of poems like "Missing the Point" have extra flavor of inside gossip on attitudes and thought processes of the professional teacher, "Lingering thought / Tells me / My private secretary is really drunk" and have sort of Chinese Royal tone; might've been written in 14th century Kahm slang. "RMDC": "Dead or alive, I have no regrets." An up-to-date playfulness develops, mind-plays of obvious charm, even naïveté, as in writings by Marsden Hartley or Samuel Greenberg's not-well-known classics.

"Report from Loveland," July 1975: The whole *dharma* is given in Disneyesque parody of everyday perplexity's bourgeois life. By that month's end, the writings are well-formed shapes with one subject. The "1135 10th St." lady friend poem is a series of exquisitely courteous and penetrant, yet funny, first thoughts, where mind's mixed with *dharma* and every noticed detail points in a unified direction. Can you, by following first thoughts, arrive at a rounded complete one-subject poem, but crazy-poetic still, like: "fresh air / Which turns into a well-cared-for garden / Free from lawnmowers and insecticides?"

In "Aurora 7 #11" the poet emerges complete whole, teacher and self, talking to the world his world, face to face, completely out of the closet poetically so to speak, without losing poetic dignity as tantric lama and guru: "Here comes Chögyie / Chögyie's for all / Take Chögyie as yours / Chögyam says: lots of love! / I'm yours!"

I must say, that there is something healthy about the American idiom as it's been charmed into being by Williams, Kerouac, Creeley and others, a frankness of person and accuracy to thought-forms and speech that may've been unheard of in other cultures, a freestyle stick-your-neck-out mortal humor of the "Far West." When the Great East enters this body speech and mind there is a ravishing combination of total anarchy and total discipline.

Well, has the transition been made, by this poet, from absolute truth expressed thru symbols ("riding on the white horse of *Dharmata*")[8] to relative truth nail'd down in devotional commitment to the American ground he's set out to transvalue and conquer?—In the drama of this book, yes, the author Chögyam, with all his *Vajra* perfections, is the drunk poet on his throne in the Rockies proclaiming "Chögyie is yours." What will Walt Whitman's expansive children do faced with such a person?

WRITTEN: 1976, revised 1983

FIRST PUBLISHED: Chögyam Trungpa, *First Thought Best Thought* (Boulder, CO: Shambhala, 1984).

ROBERT FRANK

Robert Frank to 1985—A Man

A quality of loneliness in Robert Frank's pictures is visible in Zurich's polished top hat, the little two-legged chair in Paris in 1949, or where Robert later 1950 watching the crowd pass staring at polished shoes on the legs stretched out of fine trouser cuffs lying on the street, someone's heart attack? Nobody at the corner of Rue De Santé's prison wall monolith—What was Frank doing in outskirts of Paris 1949 in a misty field where a horse stared beside its hay at some kids signaling, running to the path in fields near Porte de Clingnancourt? The lone beggar his cross stick and hat on a paper on a stone balustrade under night's streetlamp? Immediately visible, a man mixed up with his loneliness.

Difficult to maintain continuous awareness, consciousness of frame and space, tonal range, chance casualty half recognized—to look at the world thru an old Leica for years, reduce one's eyes to that attention— focus swiftly, "invisibly," as Kerouac noticed, shoot from the hip—turn the eye aside then click chance in the "windows on another time, on another place." And the camera itself was a mixed machine, with Zeiss lens on Leitz body, "not well adjusted," Frank remarked, so that sprocket holes cut inside the frame.

He had classical training in Zurich under Wolgensinger, an industrial photographer with old world technology and middle European workman's heritage—apprenticed at 17 to learn to light long steel-ribbed leviathan factory-hangers with magnesium flares—learn the chemistry of film and developer, learn large Universal View Camera work—

Always, a curiosity about cameras—he liked my little cheap Olympus XA. His printmaker Mr. Sid Kaplan, who taught photography at New School, could show me and did the different knacks of the classic Rolleiflex, all its sprigots and sights, upside-down focus eye-level, and mirrored lens and cap for auto portrait focus—delayed click—Robert smiled at his proficiency.

Summer 1984 I had visited with Berenice Abbott in Maine, she said,

All these young photographers with little cameras click click click think they can get something . . . You need to take time and prepare a photograph, and use big frame to get that tiny detail in panoramic scope.

So I bought a used 1950s Rolleiflex, and said to Robert "I learned something from her." He smiled and said, "Maybe I could show you something too."

Why had he quit still photography? He said he was tired of looking at life thru Leica lens, had used up the variety; and also was disturbed at the exploitation or commercialization of his work, after photography'd become art business investment. And anyway in the early 1970s he'd sold his prints—all made to date—with no further right to make and sell more—in exchange for ten years middle range income: He'd been raising money for movies, for 25 years to the time I speak of, 1984—

I'd known Robert F. as art family friend since I'd worked under his eye at 16 mm. camera *Pull My Daisy* 1958—Walter Gutman, painter financier angel, Zero Mostel big Kafkian comedian, and Robert's patron U.S. spiritual friend protector, Walker Evans, visiting.

Walker Evans, an aristocrat by nature, wondering what R. Frank, his brilliant protégé, was doing with those Bohemians, and had offered to preface Grove Press edition of *The Americans*. But Robert chose Kerouac as writer, an eccentric lonely choice. As Robert had invented a new way of lonely solitary chance conscious seeing, in the little Leica format (formerly not considered true photo art?). Spontaneous glance—accident truth—"First thought, best thought," similar to Tibetan Vajrayana spontaneous primordial mind and Kerouac's improvised *Visions of Cody* rhapsody.

Berenice Abbott 1985 alive said, "I love that Robert Frank, of all the younger photographers he's so interesting, and honest—I'd like to see him again"—They'd finally met in N.Y. hotel a year before, she aged 86, but he left her hotel room after brief meeting—a conversation interrupted by arrival of dealers and collectors.

Returning from India 1963 I was more or less broke, so Robert hired me to his house daily, I wrote a cinematic script for my *Kaddish* one scene a day—Robert paid me $10 an hour or so, or $15 a scene. A subsidy gratefully received, and under his encouraging direction I finished a model script, then at Robert's suggestion, wrote scenes from present time to be interweaved with original narrative, flashes forward. I hadn't thought of that. The poem was an account of my mother's nervous breakdowns and death in a mental hospital. But Robert couldn't raise money to film *Kaddish*, so he started shooting my roommate Peter and his mental hospital brother Julius Orlovsky in New York, in Central Park at night, in Kansas wheat fields and a Kansas City night rock club, actual life with improvisations including a scene in our apartment East 5th Street Lower East Side where I played a waiter's role. Joseph Chaikin played Julius for awhile when in mid-film Julius wandered away, lost—we found him months later in a provincial hospital north of Berkeley. Frank at that time, mid '60s, had a silent Arriflex movie camera.

His daughter Andrea grown up was killed in a plane crash.

He broke up with sculptor wife Mary Frank, they moved out from their great 8 room European family style solid walled apartment (a famous fortress) on 86th Street Broadway—He kept his film negative files in a closet I saw at the time, he could find things, had some kind of a system, it was difficult always to locate exactly the negative—he still needed to set them in permanent order, that was done decades later.

His son Pablo black-haired angelic had played David Amram's French horn in 1958 at round table in artist co-director Al Leslie's loft where Kerouac came to watch *Pull My Daisy* filmed. Gregory Corso poet played Kerouac persona role, Amram played Donovan a simple S.F. hippie cheerful composite invention, Larry Rivers painter supposedly playing the character "Neal Cassady" from Kerouac's earlier autonomous script (still unpublished) "The Beat Generation"—we did first of 3 acts playable, varying improvisation from Kerouac's model—

So Robert Frank's dear son Pablo grown up, working with stranger synthetic chemical iridescent photoprints later had cancer, operation, struck a blow by life, years in help hospitals, later Bronx State across a huge muddy field from an elevated subway stop, later recovery. Some kind of reverse *Kaddish* come true, I had always wondered at his interest in my own family story and Peter Orlovsky's.

He thought I seemed to have survived and kept busy, gave me credit for knowing what I was doing as an artist, or middle aged man—saw I lived somewhat on the edge of slum Lower East Side half prosperity in apartment house penury East 12th Street New York—I was greatly surprised at his glum approval, after nearly 3 decades' friendship, we were both "survivors," at least had no mortal noxious habits, and were still artists, solitary and alone—other friends were rich artists. As Frank was alone till he married June Leaf sculptor and resettled his life, solitary as Mabou, Nova Scotia in retirement—1969. He's made many subjective films, some amazingly funny like his collaboration with Rudy Wurlitzer *Energy and How to Get It* (Burroughs as C.I.A. Army Intelligence Chief deciding not to invest in Robert Golka, who had a scheme for creating electricity for nothing [bypassing nuke bombs], a little Edison's rival Nicola Tessla).

And *Cocksucker Blues* before that—invited to preview showing in tiny room at Screen Building Broadway and 48th Street. I sat next to Frank, Mick Jagger sat in back row with lady friend—it opened with Jagger lying in bed, filmed from above, a mirrored ceiling, playing with himself hand inside his long pants—and odd scenes of junkies in hotel airplane cabins sticking hypodevices in arms—a startling accurate documentary disillusioned and brilliant—afterward, going down on the elevator tall Jagger said "It's a fucking good film, Robert, but if it shows in America we'll never be allowed in the country"—immigration customs border U.S.A. Robert replied that there was no English foreign born person shooting up, only Americans who wouldn't have trouble with a passport or visa. Thereafter a contest between the two artists—the decision some year or 2 years later, Robert could show *Cocksucker Blues* at college or festival if he were present, as part of show of his life work. So Robert traveled and taught, and continued to make movies.

He came to Naropa Institute 1982 somewhat reluctantly, invited to improvise a film at "Jack Kerouac *On the Road* Celebration 1957–1982—25th Anniversary of Publication"—many video and movie cameras there interviewed talking heads—Robert took his silent Eclair sound-movie camera to his house porch, residence of the scholars and poets attending invited as friends of art and Kerouac—himself, Carl Solomon, street poets Ray Bremser and Jack Micheline, Burroughs, Corso again after 25 years, Edie Kerouac Parker, Ken Kesey, Abbie Hoffman, myself, and Peter Orlovsky—sat on the corner-railing coffee morning verandah, and filmed natural conversation. Really, friendly candid companions exaggerated and conscious of his present cinematic attention. Yet still on their own ground eternity in time visible captured in moving image in Chautauqua Park Boulder. Later he was glad he'd come and made 28 minute film.

Several years later with lighter weight J.V.C. video that, he said, was easier to carry on his shoulder, the film camera too heavy for his age, hard work for his body at 58—anyway, video had the improvised quality of still film—the scratch of a chair pulled along the floor as Robert filmed me reading him *White Shroud*, a 1983 epilogue to *Kaddish,* for the first time—shifting the video eye to Peter Orlovsky entering the small room as his name came up in the poetic text and I pronounced it—easy to visit each other's house and make simple records, I later photographed Robert (using Olympus XA he said was sufficiently good lens and service—) in 2nd Avenue restaurants and at home. Cameras and film, he pointed out, were increasingly made for amateurs, simplified, he recommended I try out Zeiss Lens Yashica 1984 totally automatic, I did, it's curious—still have to master its tendency to bulge, when you fix focus and change the frame-balance.

Robert Frank writes—brief lonely honest event sentiment-filled prose—letters, even signal slogans on his Polaroid negatives—

Asked 1982 if he would do cover photo for my *First Blues* music record album, he said, apologetically, with friendly odd glance—"Well it's a continuation of earlier work we did, old long project. So it feels OK." Three years later I asked for back cover portrait *Collected Poems 1947–1980* Harper and Row, he agreed, I came down to his new carpentered studio in an old Bowery brick run-down house on Bleecker Street—he used an early 1970s Polaroid model #195 that gives big negatives—3" x 4½"—as well as instant print, so you can check your object image at same time, and vary the frame balance. Same time I snapped his picture as he kneeled to get the right close portrait-angle from slightly below eye-level—and Peter Orlovsky (head cut off in Frank's photo of me) with my Olympus XA snapped ourselves ensemble in a frame which included the near-Bowery Yippie side street afternoon window-front passers-by and brick boarded-up factory lofts across the curbs—.

Robert Frank as a teacher: as I have prints made, many by Canadian carpenter-photographer-friend Brian Graham whom Robert met in Nova Scotia, Robert looks at what I bring by Bleecker Street, points out one or another he likes—occasionally suggests a cropping, rarely—and says with a rueful smile, "Well you're moving fast" in the world of *Aperture,* Holly Solomon Gallery, N.Y. Public Library Print Collection. He shuffles thru 30–40 photos fast, says what he likes—sometimes surprising me with his view choices, allows me to appreciate what I wasn't sure of, has his own eye. He said "You seem to know what subject you want to take" as I showed him new big prints of 1953 negatives Kerouac and Burroughs, 1984 Robert Frank close face arm raised (I'd said "Hold still a minute") after midnite in Kiev restaurant we went to on 2nd Ave and 7th Street 1984—or with Pablo by the sink my living room East 12th St. 4 flights upstairs a Sunday family visit.

Kindly teacher, with hesitant humorous trust in himself—and others—still alive together for awhile—for What?

FIRST PUBLISHED: Introduction to Robert Frank, *New York to Nova Scotia* (Boston: Little, Brown and Co., 1986).

PHILIP GLASS

Hydrogen Jukebox

Philip Glass and I visited India at different times and were influenced by Indian music, Indian philosophy and Indian meditation forms. Particularly Buddhist since we're Buddhist practitioners.

I imagine part of his move toward a more comprehensible less hyper-intellectual more devotional melodic form is part of his practical activity as a Buddhist *Mahayana* meditator who's worked with the *bodhisattva* vow, which is, to begin with, that sentient beings are numberless—one vows to liberate all.

Thus you can't dwell totally in a completely abstract music form that limits communication of intelligence. You really have to talk to the denizens of not only the world of the Gods and the human world but also the denizens of the hungry ghosts world, the cold hells and hot hells, the animal indifference world, the angry warrior world—as well as the god worlds. So you're moved to make a music that penetrates all these psychological worlds at once, quite a large audience.

Ultimately, the motif of the opera, the underpinning, the secret message, secret activity of the opera, is to relieve human suffering by communicating some kind of enlightened awareness of various themes, topics, obsessions, neuroses, difficulties problems perplexities that we encounter as we end the millennium, nineteen ninety, end and last decade of the century.

So this "melodrama" is a millennial survey of what's up—what's on our minds, what's the pertinent American and Planet News? Constructing the opera, we had the idea of the decline of empire, or Fall of America as "empire," and even perhaps the loss of a planet over the next few hundred years. We made a list of things we wanted to cover, that we all think about—he and I and Jerome Serlin the scenarist—common questions. There was of course Buddhism, meditation. There was sex, sexual revolution, in my case awareness of homosexuality and gay lib. There was the notion of corruption in politics, and corruption of empire at the top—which is represented in "NSA Dope Calypso," second act climax. There are the themes of art, rock 'n' roll, travel, east meets west, meditation and ecology, which is on everyone's mind. And war, of course, peace, pacifism.

Philip Glass had a very definite idea that we should cover public issues as well as completely subjective private life including family history and interior meditative solitude as well as newspaper headline metropolis, external common language.

Having decided these topics, we then found texts which covered them, and put a mosaic or tapestry together. So the opera's interlinked, hooked together thematically, though it's not a "linear" story. Maybe more like slow motion music video, in a sense. So we began with heart prophecy of the Fall of America on a train, introducing the notion of travel, and war, sung to "Who is the enemy, year after year," what's going on, how come all the bombs, "what's the picture decade after decade," whether from Vietnam or Granada or Panama, Iraq or what'll be next, Peru? Nicaragua? take your choice. Then we focus on one big central war, "Yahweh and Allah Battle," the Middle East.

Following that a switcheroo to interior reverie, going back to the subjective, we find ourselves in India, you know, meditative subjectivity, here a fragment from Calcutta, a little personal scene, Peter Orlovsky's birthday in 1962 age 29. Then traveling east to west, returning to America, surveying planetary ecological damage from a plane. Might be ecological damage or it might be the hydrocarbon smog of Los Angeles, or it might be post nuclear wreckage. We move from San Francisco through Denver through Chicago back to the east coast. Then shifting to the center of America, we make a unilateral declaration of the end of the war, a duet between myself and Philip Glass, in performance that was the end of act one, taped, with pantomime by the singers directed by Anne Carlson, as well as projection spectral scenery by Jerome Serlin. So we had a four part collaboration.

The second half begins centering in on Moloch, Part II of "Howl": the hyper-industrialized, hyper-technological Moloch consumes the planet, everyone's thwarted desensitized or robotized by the inanimate conditioning hypnosis machine we've built around us. Then some statistics: the age of the universe, the age of the earth, and a few other hokey num-bers. Then having presented the problem, we present the medicine—several haikus, written on meditation retreat in the Rocky Mountains it so happens. Haiku perception in calm and peace with a very sweet aria, much applauded in performance, with a singer sitting on a Zen *zafu* and *zabutan,* in meditative posture.

Then returning to family, "To Aunt Rose," a poem that's in many anthologies, set very beautifully to music, staged with a lot of photographs of my family, my Aunt Rose, my Aunt Honey, my mother and father and myself in Woodstock 1936. Then the gay lib theme, "The Green Automobile," travel again, back across America, looking for love, the lover behind the poem, in this case actually, Neal Cassady, now quite well known as the inspiration for Kerouac's *On the Road* hero, as well as Ken Kesey's psychedelic bus driver.

Then the climax of the opera, the "National Security Agency Dope Calypso," interleaved with the poem "Violence," which names Richard Secord, Oliver North, George Bush, Donald Gregg, General Noriega, drug cartel accountant Juan Milian Rodriguez, and Felix Rodriguez of the CIA as co-actors in U.S. government intelligence "off the shelf" operations drawing on cocaine and marijuana smuggling to fund Contra arms, which one has read about in newspapers of record, I assume. All the information's "real," taken straight from the *Washington Post, New York Times, Los Angeles Times* and Senator Kerry's Subcommittee investigating government involvement with dope pushing simultaneous with the fraudulent so-called war on drugs. During that scene a flag was projected on the backstage drop, smoke came up out of the flag, all these celestial dummy politicians danced madly on stage. That climax established the prettiest and most powerful part—and the most hypnotic musically I would say for me—I often wake up on my pillow hearing that "anvil chorus."

Then comes the post nuclear moment—a series of codas which end the opera. First "Everybody's Fantasy," some skeletons hold hands trying to get across the stage after the nuke blast. "I walked outside / and the bomb'd dropped / lots of Plutonium / all over the Lower East Side." Then a return to primordial civilization in the Central Australian Desert, using the single verse forms of Aboriginal songmen, singing during a nuclear winter, on stage, snow coming down. Last song, a Buddhist-American threnody or hymn "Father Death Blues," written on the death of my father, philosophic reconciliation and peace, emotionally very calm, in six part harmony a cappella, quite sublime actually, as the finale for the opera. So that's the plot.

WRITTEN: Nov. 23, 1991

FIRST PUBLISHED: liner notes, Philip Glass, *Hydrogen Jukebox* (Electra Nonesuch, compact disc #79286–2, 1993).

HIRO YAMAGATA

Hiro Yamagata's Holy Ghost XX Century Automobiles

I never learned to drive—how do people overcome panic at intersections, or speeding freeways and superhighways, autobahns, bridges? Thousands of motors on wheels revving up noisy crisscrossing clover-leafed borders at 80 MPH? What would I do, Thump, a bloody body dangling over my hood, skull crushed, intestines dripping over the fender?

Meanwhile the Sphinx is losing the rest of his nose, the Acropolis' columns are pitted, David's been taken indoors in Florence, cars hoot up alleys by the Bargello, the Bible says brimstone falls from heaven at Apocalypse time, sulfuric acid rain eats away Notre Dame's gargoyle mouths, petrol exhaust rises to Paris' skies, a thin brown layer of gas floats over every city in the world, Mexico, New York, Denver, Beijing, Los Angeles, Kyoto.

Persian Gulf reefs clogged with petroleum, more than a hundred thousand teenagers bombed to death in Baghdad, desert sands, Ur, Sumer—Petrochemical Nightmare! The planet revved up on fossil fuel, bigtime wars pivot round Middle East's petroleum "Concession States." Israel Iraq Iran Saudi Yemen Bahrein Kuwait Lebanon are battlegrounds for rights to subterranean oily lakes that power the metropolises of the world. We continue our dirty work, colonizing every continent, reducing the mass of humanity to "underdeveloped" fools supplying raw materials and labor while the ecosystems that bore them are destroyed. Mile by mile, hectare by hectare, forest by forest, river by river chemicalled, gigantic cities spread tentacles of highway trucks and acid rain on subcontinents' polluted Edens.

Billions of carbon bodies, a hundred million years of trees, fireflies, liquid fish and animals' remains sucked out of earth's hide run through energy machines that spew them out into the atmosphere. The *karma* of a billion years' conifers and mosquitoes, pterodactyls, stegosauri and dragonflies, roaches, giant lizards, waterbugs, enormous ferns—all fumed into the air, cyclic eons of life resurrected and exhausted into the thin layer of planet oxygen.

We can't kill the planet. Asteroids, moons, volcanoes, ice ages come and go, seeds sprout, mastodons freeze, tropics turn arctic, poles reverse their charges, the brontosaurus sprouts wings, the planet's got another couple billion years to breathe, clouds swirling round like TV speedup weather reports—"The sun's not eternal, that's why there's the blues." So the sun's got another 12 billion years (I once heard) before it runs down, eats itself up, sucked into its black hole, lots of leisure time to recuperate from the human virus and its fossil pneumonia.

Not that I don't ride cars myself, fly jet planes, turn on the petro-chemical lightswitch, or eat cauliflowers grown with fossil fertilizers and nitrates that pollute the waters—or enjoy Lower East Side apartment steamheat in freezing New York wintertime, plug in amps to read eco-logical poetry in Harvard auditoriums, waste huge forests to read the *Times,* or publish ravings such as this—as Gregory Corso said, "No good news can be written on bad news."

We won't kill the planet but we might well suicide the human race, wipe ourselves out with the help of the World Bank—jungle industrial-ization brings ecocide, ecocide brings genocide in Amazon, Borneo, Far West, Far East, USA.

We can only destroy ourselves and a lot of mammals birds and fish—maybe not extinguish the entire gene pool, just blank out portions of our own, other species', vegetable germs, whales or birdies. They'll come back, maybe we'll come back gnashing our teeth, starting fires, inventing the wheel, or taking it easy, four hours a day for hunting and gathering food shelter and amusement. Neanderthal folk had bigger brains than we have—crammed full of info on local flora and fauna, minute particu-lars re their bioregional territories. They knew more about quality leisure time than we do.

So now we're stuck with a science that doesn't know how to wipe its own half ass—witness the impossible task of cleaning out old Rockwell Corporation's abandoned plutonium bomb trigger plant at Rocky Flats, 15 miles from this table whereon I write. This monstrosity, a fossil remains of an "American Century," is a waste dump employing increas-ing thousands of laborers to contain its transuranic elements lest they migrate outward in vast underground plumes to poison the soil under universities and downtowns of the Denver Rockies' Front Range region.

Yes, we're stuck with a Frankenstein civilization we grew up in, that nour-
ished our flesh and minds at the expense of billions of underclass sentient beings.

What to do? The *Bosatsu* vows point a way—to do whatever's in our
power to relieve the mass of sentient suffering, to dissolve the illusion of
permanent solidity of our selfhood and the pains of extreme views:
Eternalism (America and Japan will last forever! Our science will
progress eternally till everyone on the planet is drinking milk! eating
cow steak and zipping around the equator in 10 billion Mercedes Benzes
by the year 3000 AD!) or nihilism (The world's a wreck, whadda I care—
might as well burn down the rest of it while I'm alive—After me the del-
uge! I got mine! Screw Africa Asia South America the Arctic Poles the
future).

Middle Path, we won't wreck the planet only ourselves. Knowing that,
we can look into our own eyes and calm the anger ignorance disease that
drives our multinational machine. Can acknowledge our own material
lust and resentment, calm down a bit and take classic steps to purify our
consciousness—recognize our own wreckage, regret wrong actions,
repair what loss we can, and not repeat wreckage where we have control.
Admittedly we don't have much control. On the margin we control, can
relieve our bit of the great drag breakdown of false civilization.
"Benevolent indifferent attentiveness," a "choiceless awareness" of our
own grief and despair at what we've done gives rise to compassion for
ourselves. That extends to the world's inhabitants, transforming grief to
energetic action for everyone's benefit.

Catholics confess and ask absolution, Buddhists wipe out a billion
years of *karma* with an empty thought, Moslems lift their hands and give
the grief over to Allah. Artists take nightmare and paint it up for what it
is: dream, illusion, transitory Maya, flowers in the air, bubbles on a
stream, rainbow clouds. How turn "Waste to Treasure"? How alchemize
"Shit to Roses"?

The private automobile's the symbolic villain of this subjective essay,
perhaps objectively symbolic of all East and Western hyperindustrialized
villainy. This little bubble of speed on high tech gearshifts rubber wheels
and fossil fuels liberates the rich to flit around earth, escaping boredom
stuck in slums bidonvilles bustees and shanty towns of the upper class. A
mass of humanity howls on garbage mountains and urban ashpits, left
behind.

OK Hiro Yamagata's taken the most brilliant of all cars—in his view—
the long outmoded Mercedes Benz Cabriolet 220—an aristocrat of capitalist cars, luxurious toy of the tasteful racy rich—and rescued it from
oblivion, alchemized the wreckage to exemplary totemhood.
Cannibalizing the bodies of dozens or hundreds of such cars, he's
reversed time's ravage of these wearouts. Not quite mass produced, not
quite singular and unreplica'd, with old handcraft style and artisan
comeliness, sleek modish dated chic and charm—Yamagata's resurrected this mid-century's last gasp of "innocent" mechanical beauty.

With an eccentric idea, the use of the "ultimate" car for floral arrangements or sky and ocean waves usually reserved for Japanese fans, screens
or exquisite nightclub wallpaper, the artist's imagination's run wild on
hood and fender canvas. Paint the universe itself! Paint the high class vil-
lainous machine with 1960s flowerpowered lilies orchids daisies, Fijian
blossoms, porcelain bugs and butterflies, graffitian tattoos, funky hallucinatory flowers on the carapace of a fine-tuned German machine.
Disney meets Hitler, Mickey Mouse wraps up the Nazis, (i.e., not to be
chauvinistic about German politics) free imagination meets naive indus-
trialization. In any case Japanese and German modern technologic
"Idealism" is subjected to the extremist sophisticated whims of a highly
competent individual artist with the Herculean means to undertake symbolic cleaning of the liquid-looking horseless carriage's Augean Stables.

Appropriately this creation and exhibition takes place in Los Angeles
where over half century ago General Motors bought up and destroyed
Charlie Chaplin's and the Keystone Kops' mass transit trolley system to
clear the way for its car products I saw their clean hallucinatory "World
of the Future" (with no ecological fumes, made of plaster) in the New
York World's Fair's 1939 Perisphere. A commercial hallucination that's
turned into a material nightmare! "Only the imagination is real," said
William Carlos Williams.

My 88 year old stepmother still drives, that's her desperate last mobil-
ity. Not driving, I ride taxis in Manhattan, as before congestive heart failure 1990, I "Put on my tie in a taxi, short of breath, rushing to meditate."
In my first long poem "The Green Automobile," I imagined a motor
vehicle crossing the 1953 continent to see my boyfriend Neal Cassady. I
backseat drive, at 68 I want comfort, have twice hired a limo to get from
Kennedy airport to my brother's birthday party in Long Island. Guilty!

But Hiro Yamagata's got one good idea and's accomplished it:

cleaned up in perfect condition, painted over with vegetation, cars don't belong running around the earth, cars belong in museums along with stuffed dinosaurs, whose ghosts they've devoured.

WRITTEN: July 31, 1994

FIRST PUBLISHED: Hiro Yamagata, *Earthly Paradise* (Boston: Journey Editions, 1994).

ERIC DROOKER

———

Drooker's Illuminations

I first glimpsed Eric Drooker's odd name on posters pasted on fire-alarm sides, construction walls checkered with advertisements, and lamppost junction boxes in the vortex of Lower East Side Avenues leading to Tompkins Square Park, where radical social dislocation mixed homeless plastic tents with Wigstock[9] transvestite dress-up anniversaries, Rastas sitting on benches sharing spliff, kids with purple Mohawks, rings in their noses ears eyebrows and bellybuttons, adorable or nasty skinheads, wives with dogs and husbands with children strolling past jobless outcasts, garbage, and a bandshell used weekly for folk-grunge concerts, anti-war rallies, squatters' rights protests, shelter for blanket-wrapped junkies and winos and political thunder music by Missing Foundation, commune-rockers whose logo, an overturned champagne glass with slogan "The Party's Over," was spray-painted on sidewalks, apartments, brownstone and brick walled streets.

Eric Drooker's numerous block-print-like posters announced much local action, especially squatters' struggles and various mayoral-police attempts to destroy the bandshell and close the Park at night, driving the homeless into notoriously violence-corrupted city shelters. Tompkins Park had a long history of political protest going back before Civil War anti-draft mob violence, memorialized as ". . . a mixed surf of muffled sound, the atheist roar of riot," in Herman Melville's "The Housetop: A Night Piece (July 1863)."

I began collecting Drooker's posters soon after overcoming shock, seeing in contemporary images the same dangerous class conflict I'd remembered from childhood, pre-Hitler block print wordless novels by Frans Masereel and Lynd Ward. Ward's images of the solitary artist dwarfed by the canyons of a Wall Street Megalopolis lay shadowed behind my own vision of Moloch. What "shocked" me in Drooker's scratchboard prints was his graphic illustration of economic crisis similar to Weimar-American 1930s Depressions.

In our own era, as one Wall Street stockbroker noted, "Reagan put the nation in hock to the military," with resulting collapse of human values and social stability. Drooker illuminated the widely-noted impoverishment of underclass, "diminishing expectations" of middleclass city dwellers, and transfer of disproportionate shares of common wealth to those already rich. This economic information, including facts of multibillion savings and loan bankruptcies paid for by federal funds, was reported in neutral tones by newspapers of record but Drooker illustrated the city's infrastructural stress, housing decay, homelessness, garbage-hunger and bitter suffering of marginalized families, blacks and youth, with such vivid detail that the authoritarian reality horror of our contemporary dog-eat-dog Malthusian technoeconomic class-war became immediately visible.

"It is a question of genuine values, human worth, trustworthiness," Thomas Mann commented, introducing Frans Masereel's novel in woodcuts *Passionate Journey*. Drooker spent his childhood on East 14th Street and Avenue B, exploring the city early, observing "shopping bag ladies, stretch-Cadillacs, screaming unshaven men, junkies nodding, Third Avenue prostitutes looking at themselves in rearview mirrors of parked cars." His maternal grandparents were 1930s socialists, his mother taught in the neighborhood's PS 19, on 11th Street and First Avenue, his father, white-collar computer programmer, tripped him to art museums all over city.

1970s he attended Henry Street Settlement art classes, graduated from Cooper Union, moved permanently to East 10th Street close to Tompkins Park. Following family tradition he organized rent strikes, supported local squats and tenant organizing against police brutality. By 1980s working as freelance artist for many leftist groups, with reputation as radical street art-provocateur, he was arrested and thrown in District of Columbia jail for postering. In "denial" of economic crisis, city bureaucrats cracked down on Punk and political postering as a "public nuisance." Xeroxed flyers were considered "illegal graffiti."

By 1990s observant Op-ed editors at *N.Y. Times* invited him to contribute art for their pages, as did the *Nation, Village Voice* and *Newsweek*. Under a new post-modern regime at *The New Yorker*, he published many illustrations, even covers, including a celebrated image of two bums sitting huddled round a bright garbage-can fire as big snowflakes fell under the Brooklyn Bridge. His novel in pictures, *FLOOD!*, with its fantastic social dreams, won an American Book Award.

Our collaboration volume began as byproduct of an illustration of my poem "The Lion For Real" for his St. Mark's Poetry Project New Year's Day 1993 Benefit poster.

As I'd followed his work over a decade, I was flattered that so radical an artist of later generations found the body of my poetry still relevant, even inspiring. Our paths crossed often, we took part in various political rallies and poetical-musical entertainments, the idea of a sizable volume of illustrated poem-pictures rose. Eric Drooker himself did all the work choosing texts (thankfully including many odd lesser-known scribings) and labored several years to complete these *Illuminated Poems.*

WRITTEN: Dec. 28, 1995

FIRST PUBLISHED: Introduction to Allen Ginsberg, *Illuminated Poems* (New York: Four Walls Eight Windows, 1996).

CHAIM GROSS

Remembering Chaim Gross

"Art gives me great happiness," Chaim Gross confessed to *New York Times* reporter Israel Shenker on the occasion of his seventieth birthday and it is the persistence of that happiness and its transmutation into material fact that is his abiding achievement. No small thing for a child, youngest of ten, who had half his family wiped out by an epidemic of diphtheria, who, at the outbreak of World War I, witnessed first hand the brutal treatment of his parents at the hands of the invading Cossacks, who aged twelve, was forced to assist the Austro-Hungarian army by picking up battlefield dead.

Chaim's early life was a catalog of misfortunes; buffeted by the forces of an extremely volatile Eastern Europe, deported from Hungary to Austria, from Austria to Poland. Even after he arrived in America, though no longer actively persecuted, he suffered, like so many fellow immigrants, years of extraordinary poverty, first doing a variety of odd jobs (delivery boy, floor cleaner, dish washer) to support his art, later living entirely from hand to mouth. One story has it that when the apple and pear that were being used by the still-life class at his home-away-from-home, the Educational Alliance, went missing, the common assumption was Chaim must have eaten them! Even more bittersweet are the circumstances of his first sale (two water-colors and one sculpture) in the early thirties. Finally disheartened, he had left town with a note ("good-bye boys") which his friends had erroneously assumed to be a suicide note. The sale took place in the interim, ninety dollars. Imagine the surprise when the artist "came back from the dead"!

The company of his fellow artists—one might mention such life-long friends as the Soyer brothers (Isaac, Moses, and Raphael), Peter Blume, Elias Newman, and many others; the significance of the Alliance (where he was first pupil, then teacher, for almost seven decades!); a fortuitous marriage to Renee and her remarkable daughter, the painter Mimi

Gross; these are some of the things that sustained him.

Perhaps more sustaining, though, was his own dedication, right to the end. "Don't wait till the muse wakes you up at night and says do this and that. Make a point of working all the time," he advised his students. What was exemplary was his commitment to his craft—sculpture. "I'm a sculptor not a painter but I'm one of those sculptors who knows how to draw and how to paint" was his own clear self-appraisal. Sculpture was a natural for him, a vocation. It was his friend and fellow-student at the Educational Alliance, Leo Jackinson, who first pointed him on his way (he subsequently studied briefly with Robert Laurent at the Art Students League) but his knowledge, as Raphael Soyer once observed, was already there, "instinctive not deliberate."

The son of a timber appraiser, following his father to the timber yards in remote Galicia, in the forests of the Carpathian Mountains, growing up watching the local peasant families whittling figures in wood, it is perhaps not so surprising that he would develop a particular affinity for direct wood carving. Chaim was a master in stone, in bronze, but it was wood that ultimately held the greatest appeal. His re-discovery of wood, his early expressionistic carvings, in the late twenties and early thirties, those airy joyful human bodies, acrobats and tight rope dances, are now recognized as seminal in the history of American art. He almost single-handedly revived the form. No one else was doing such work at the time. A "haltz hacker" (wood chopper) was how Renee's alarmed parents first disparagingly described him!—and they were right!—up to a point (but only up to a point!). Chaim's extraordinary respect for the physical properties of wood was essential to his work—the very choices that he made (by as early as 1930 he had experimented in over forty types)—hard woods, like lignum vitae, ebony, snakewood, woods that would retain their character. He would skillfully use the natural conformations of the grain to enrich the movement of the form within a specific piece. He was reverential. "I have never wanted a single piece of my wood sculpture to lose the feeling of the tree it came from—its natural origin," he once remarked. "What people consider to be out of proportion is not so. I do not want to carve too much away. Each piece has its own truth."

Chaim's articulate understanding of his own processes, of course, made him the consummate teacher that he was (not only at the Alliance but also at the New School whose faculty he joined in 1948). Generations of artists are indebted to his clarity and mindfulness, his practical wisdom. His book, *The Technique of Wood Sculpture* (1957), remains, over thirty years after its publication, an invaluable compendium and primer. His knowledge (not only of wood sculpture, not only of sculpture, but of all the visual arts), so helpful and inspiring to his students, was the result of a dutiful self-education ("It's my business to know the artists"), an appreciation for beauty and worth (irrespective of the vagaries of fashion), a truly unbiased eye.

This essential unflinching probity meant that recognition of his own work came slowly. His first one-man show took place in 1932 at Manfred Schwarz's 144 Gallery on West 13th Street (he exhibited sculptures and drawings). Earlier he had contributed to the group shows at Edith Halpert's Downtown Gallery (one of the first New York galleries to handle contemporary American art) but had quit when he came in one day and discovered a piece of his being used as a doorstop! Even though, paradoxically, the thirties, the era of the Depression, represented the breakthrough decade in Chaim's art, it did not translate into sales. As late as 1942 he could still count on his fingers every piece of sculpture that he had sold. No matter that the work was appearing in some significant collections (in 1937, for instance, the Museum of Modern Art acquired his typically graceful and exuberant study in balance, *Handlebar Riders*; *Lilian Leitzel*, completed in 1938, a figure sculpture, a similarly sensuous work, won a $3000 purchase prize from the Metropolitan Museum of Art, New York, in 1942).

The godsend was the W.P.A. (Works Progress Administration), as it was for so many later-to-be prominent American artists. The Public Works of Art Project, an off-shoot of Roosevelt's New Deal, permitted those on the program (Chaim was one of them) the luxury of an income while making their art. It also opened up possibilities in the commission of murals, reliefs and to a certain extent freestanding sculptures for the new government buildings. One such building was the new Post Office Department building in Washington, D.C. In 1936, the Section of Painting and Sculpture of the Treasury Department sponsored an open competition and Chaim's design won. He was one of twelve selected to execute their designs in full scale. His winning sculpture, *Alaskan Mail Carrier*, cast in aluminum and placed in the Postmaster General's office, won him $3000. Two years later he won a similar amount for a second commission, for a stone lintel piece for the Pennsylvania Avenue doorway of the offices of the F.T.C. (Federal Trade Commission), on the so-called Apex Building. Following this he was able to obtain work at the 1939 New York World's Fair. He worked on a fourteen foot high family group for the French Pavilion (the celebration of the human family was to be one of Chaim's most prominent themes) as well as the figure of a linesman for the Finland building. He was also "on display" himself, demonstrating his craft. He may not have sold many sculptures at this time but his pre-eminence was assured. His singularity meant that, even in the era of Social Realism, Chaim was thematically somewhat at odds. For all their apparent context, his figures, the daring acrobats say, posited, not so much commitment to each other, as the *human* quality, the interdependence of the *human*—Chaim's abiding theme. Similarly in the 1950s (and after) when the emphasis shifted to the artist's individual (subjective) vision, Chaim's art stood unaffected, he was what he was.

The immediately sensed rhythm of the body, the body as a recognized while also transcendent form, the continuous expressive interplay between "reality" (the natural bodily movement) and "abstraction" (the abstract play of lines and curves) is an essential and remains constant in his work. His acrobats, his ballerinas *are* virtuosi, but so is a mother and her children, so, in greater or lesser degrees, are we all! The miracle of balance and the no lesser miracle of movement are both celebrated by Chaim in every work he made—simultaneously, with the 'pure' detachment of the gifted esthetician and the vital engagement of the survivor recognizing the joy of life, recognizing the absolute miracle of being here at all. In his latter years Chaim worked in bronze (usually working first in plaster then casting in bronze—earlier bronzes had been cast from his wood sculpture). Representative works like the ten foot *Birds of Peace* (commissioned for the campus of Hebrew University, Jerusalem, 1959–66) and *The Ten Commandments* (unveiled 1972 at the International Synagogue at Kennedy Airport) show his mastery of the large scale, the ambitious undertaking. Nothing was lost. In fact, on the contrary, it permitted an even greater freedom and openness, an animation and exploration of space, an augmenting, of his already demonstrated skill.

Mention should also be made of Chaim's drawings, not as some incidental note but as, perhaps, the very key to his art. He was an inveterate draughtsman, throughout his life, from his earliest days of exile to his last days here in New York, filling countless sketchbooks and hundreds of sheets with his accomplished pencil, pen and ink, and ink and wash, studies—studies from nature, studies of the human form (many of them in preparation for sculptures) but also independent images, recollected or imagined—among them the so-called "fantasy drawings" (a collection of these appeared in book form under that title in 1956), unmediated examinations of his own psyche, dark in the early years and increasingly more characteristically lyrical as he finally found his home.

The reputation—the international reputation—of Chaim Gross is now assured. Those of you who were fortunate enough to visit the major retrospective of his work (at the Jewish Museum in 1977) will remember the astonishing versatility, the astonishing fecundity, (and for the remaining 14 years he kept on working). Those of you who are only familiar with selected works will, I think, be pleasantly surprised when the *catalogue raisonné* (complete catalog) comes out! Chaim's work appears in the permanent collections of the Met, MOMA, the Whitney, the Jewish Museum, the Brooklyn Museum, Newark Museum, the Art Institute of Chicago, Brooklyn College (who gave him an honorary degree in 1986) and over seventy other universities and museums.

The American Academy of Arts and Letters honored him in 1956 with an Arts and Letters Award and in 1963 with the Award of Merit Medal. In 1964 he was inducted into the National Institute of Arts and Letters and in 1983 to the American Academy of Arts and Letters (taking over the chair, 44, previously filled by another "comprehensive realizer," Buckminster Fuller!). *The New York Times* on that occasion blandly described him as one "whose art depicts Jewish themes" (Chaim's commitment to Israel and to his Jewish identity was of course profound, but surely it ranged further to *universal* dimensions?), and as one who "teaches at the Educational Alliance and the New School for Social Research in New York" (a similarly flat and limited biographical note). Chaim Gross *inspired* (as his works continue to do), having a direct reverence for beauty and human life, and he is now sitting drinking tea with Marc Chagall and Pablo Picasso in heaven.

WRITTEN: Dec. 3, 1991

FIRST PUBLISHED: *Provincetown Arts*, vol. 8 (1992) pp. 121–122 and *Proceedings of the American Academy and Institute of Arts and Letters*, 2nd series, no. 42 (1991) pp. 63–66.

JOHN CAGE

John Cage: 1912–1992

As John Cage proposed certain rigid parameters of time discipline
      within his music,
   This eulogy, altogether ten minutes, divides ideally into three
      parts:
1) Brief outline of his career, (3'67")
     2) Exposition of sitting practice of meditation, (2')
     and 3) The practice itself, (4'33").

I

First, a brief rundown on John Cage's career: Henry Cowell's classes in
non-Western Music; counterpoint with Arnold
      Schoenberg.
     Cornish Institute, Seattle, 1938, met Merce Cunningham; per-
      cussion concerts with Lou Harrison;
  prepared piano transformed ad hoc into percussion instrument by in-
      serting various objects between the strings for a dance
    of African character, lacking other orchestral means for per-
      cussion on one occasion.
Cited 1949 by our Academy for "having extended the boundaries of
      art":
     Electrically produced sounds. Influence of rhythmic struc-
      tures of some Eastern music.
Inclusion of Eastern aesthetic philosophy, the "Permanent Emotions"
      such as in
     Seasons, 1947: *Quiescence* (winter); *Creation* (spring); *Pres-
      ervation* (summer); *Destruction* (autumn);
     I Ching adapted for chance operation in musical compositions.
Zen Buddhist studies at Columbia University with D. T. Suzuki;
      thenceforth, lifelong inventions in *Dharma* art.

Result of meditation insight 1952, his *4'33" of Silence* "may be
         performed by any instrument or combination of instru-
         ments."
Studied, collaborated, worked with and/or influenced Jackson MacLow,
         Morton Feldman, David Tudor, Christian Wolff, Earle Brown,
         Nam June Paik, Luciano Berio, Karlheinz Stockhausen, Arthur
         Russell, Philip Glass,
         Robert Motherwell, Robert Rauschenberg, Jasper Johns, Alan
         Kaprow, Dick Higgins of Fluxus, George Brecht, Al Hansen.
At Black Mountain College Cage created ur-"Happenings"; among the
         earliest for the U.S. art world.
Co-founded the New York Mycological Society; Connoisseur and in-
         novator in macrobiotic cooking and eating.
Youthful epiphanous apprehension of the multiplicity of simulta-
         neous visual and audible events on a streetcorner in Se-
         ville
         later manifested aurally through exploration of consciousness
         of sound:
Innovator in music in the use of Astronomic charts; amplified plant
         sounds; sounds of places in *Finnegans Wake*;
         appropriations of Thoreau and Joyce, Satie, and Duchamp, on
         tape and cut in/cut up and mixed together.
"Everything has its own vibration," he was recalled to Hindu
         theory, Shabda yoga:
         the universe itself based on sound vibration, according to
         Eastern thought;
         sensory experience a form of vibration, beginning with sound
         itself.
Thus he concluded, "the purpose of music is to sober and quiet the
         mind."
His meditation was the practice of "non intention" with "humor,
         intransigence and detachment."
Silence "not the absence of sound but the sound of the unintended
         operation of nervous system and circulation of his blood."
"Music without beginning middle or end," . . . "Music as weather." . . .
         "I write in order to hear the music I haven't yet heard."

II

To cut thru to the classical Buddhist bones of Cage's art, one may
        try *Samatha* (quieting the mind) and
    Vipassana (clear seeing and hearing):
The following rudimentary instruction in sitting meditation may be
        practiced on the spot by those who wish to do so.
        Those of us interested in experiencing the pragmatic basis of
            Cage's art
        might sit up straight forward on our chairs:
Posture erect with back and spine straight, top of the head sup-
        porting heaven,
        arms resting palms down on thighs . . . so that the back bone's
            elevated straight,
        abdomen and belly relaxed,
        paying attention to breath exhaled from tip of nostril till
            breath dissolves in space in front of the face . . .
        Mouth closed, body balanced, shoulders relaxed, no special at-
            tention to in-breath.
When we catch ourselves thinking, it's possible to take a friendly
        attitude toward thoughts,
        acknowledging thought as thought,
not pushing thoughts away, not inviting thoughts in to tea,
        thoughts can take care of themselves.
        So return attention to the next breath outward from nostrils.

In the Western tradition of observing a minute of silence let's
        perform John Cage's *4 minutes and 33 seconds* of silence.
As David Tudor opened and closed the piano lid for the first per-
        formance,
        we'll use the ring of a traditional meditation hall bronze bell:

4'33"
[Sound of Gong]

[Sound of Gong]

FIRST PUBLISHED: *Proceedings of the American Academy and Institute of Arts and Letters,* 2nd series, no. 43 (1992) pp. 61–64.

THE LIVING THEATRE

Living Theatre and Its U.S. Critics

Brecht adapted Sophocles' *Antigone* for post-Hitler 1946 in small-town Switzerland, unable, with actress Helene Weigel, to find other work. The Living Theatre adapted *Antigone* from Brecht's playbook which they found in a book shop in Athens.

Antigone's initial lawless act is her insistence on burying her brother's corpse in defiance of King Creon's decree that Polynices be left to the dogs. Brecht's treatment, for the latter and greater part of the play, emphasizes the blind acquiescence of the people of Thebes to Creon's increasingly insane demands. They follow him to war, they accept his sacrilegious treatment of Polynices' corpse, they remain silent as Antigone is condemned to death for doing as the gods require of the bereaved and they follow him even as the city falls around them. Much of Antigone's speech is an appeal to her fellow citizens for sense and right conduct which takes the form of a running commentary on the mad king's actions and the folly of blind obedience to the tyrant.

Now the Living Theatre has returned to play *Antigone* to the US audience and media who are conditioned to go along with violent Big Brother centralized US military government's adventures. Hitler-and-the-Germans, Creon-and-the-Thebans, Presidential America goes along with murderous tyrants, with acts of newspeak "law and justice" perpetrated by our trainee client generals.

Outrage! Public outrage! But how gently, at the end of the play, the Living Theatre, vulnerable and truly inspired, shrinks back from the armed critics, Argives on the war fields of media.

Who will listen to Antigone defying the mad ruler, our waking sleep, our inertia, our powerlessness, our alienation from our own government? Her anarchist-pacifist position is now pronounced "outmoded" in a time of macho cold war, mass starvation and bloodshed, as Creon chases Argives in the Middle East, El Salvador, Guatemala, Honduras and Nicaragua.

Ms Malina, as Antigone, was trying to bury the body of Granada, she says, with due sacramental theater. This may not fit the politics or the understanding of some critics, or Reagan, or the Republican Party, or the Heritage Foundation, which happens to run (or be a front for whoever runs) the country, now hypermilitarized in nihilistic mad Creonic cold war against Russia as "the focus of world evil" for the last year or so.

Clive Barnes got personal, calling Ms Malina's Antigone "a woman who has been bumped out of order in the delicatessen line at Zabar's." His account of the play ends "standing across the stage making faces at the audience—a few are interesting, most merely silly." That's the very scene that made me cry! The cast of Living looking into the audience, into America, horrified at the advance of the Argives, a gesture appropriate to their situation (facing American *New York Times*) and to the situation of all of us in the USA. A panic trip? No, the expression of grief, disbelief, appeal, anguish, fear, compassion and retreat, which all of us feel.

Bravo for a public act such as this to deepen our awareness of our compulsive participation in cold war aggression and murder!

Critic Edith Oliver points out: (re: Living Theatre) "intruding on the audience, this can be a pain, although it is less so this time than it has been in the past." So why did Frank Rich get so upset at this late date? This critic is outraged by a conditional approach toward his thigh—a contact never actually occurred, according to Mr Beck's memory, because of the critic's reaction to his physical presence. "You're getting there," said Mr Rich, so the actor withdrew his hand. Critic Rich grasped this poignant moment and transformed it, his own catharsis, to a denunciation of the Living Theatre as "riffraff." He performed a public act of murder on *The Archaeology of Sleep*—certainly a Creonic declaration of "cultural warfare," as radical critic Bob Fass interprets *NY Times* review.

For all I know, Mr Rich may be liberal anarchist pacifist Libertarian himself, against Big Government just like William Buckley, President Reagan, and the inspired Judith Malina. Maybe it's all a New York tempest in a teapot. But it doesn't help the Living financially. They are a rare permanent theater company practicing free enterprise in New York, unlike their situation in Europe where their brand of culture is government subsidized. Here we subsidize military brass bands and the nuclear industry for the benefit of capitalist multinationals with cost overruns on their own businesses for which they get government subsidies. And who gets tax write-offs subsidizing neo-conservative Heritage Foundation to lobby against subsidies for their cultural rivals, poets and Living Theatres? Coors![10] Let's hear three cheers for drunk driving!

One critic shrewdly perceived the Snake Oil Salesman aspect of Beck's portrayal of the mad "objectively rational" insinuations and experiments of the modern scientist in white coat—an excellent parody of American nuclear science and neoconservative or Reagan era theater criticism.

In this context critic John Simon denounced Gertrude Stein as "a consummate phony," Paul Goodman as "a theatrical no talent," and the Becks' productions as "militant messes posing as pacifist propaganda." Great theater on all sides!

Critic Howard Kissel called Paris a "cultural backwater." Yahoo all the way! Three cheers for 1984 U.S.A.! Bravo for the Living Theatre for breaking the ice, a real breakthrough of public consciousness.

Most critics understood, approved, respected the attempt. A minority didn't get it, but even they got touched.

FIRST PUBLISHED: *Third Rail,* no. 7 (1985/86) pp. 32–33.

ST. MARK'S POETRY PROJECT

Foreword for *Out of This World*
[An Anthology from the St. Mark's Poetry Project]

St. Mark's has always been a culture church, and as a venue for poetry it has an old history. I first went to a poetry reading at St. Mark's in the thirties with my father, Louis, who was once secretary of the Poetry Society of America. W. H. Auden was a member of the congregation in the fifties, but long before that Isadora Duncan had danced there, Frank Lloyd Wright had lectured, Houdini'd given a magic show. There had been jazz in the late fifties, even theater.

Our postmodern era began with a series of open readings that took place in a basement, formerly a rare gay place, the MacDougal Street Bar, renamed The Gaslight Café by owner John Mitchell in '58 or '59—with LeRoi Jones, Gregory Corso, Ray Bremser, myself and Peter Orlovsky, José Garcia Villa, others. These were predated by a year by readings given by Jack Kerouac, Philip Lamantia, Howard Hart, Steve Tropp, and others at Circle in the Square, as well as at various lofts and parties. Initial events were so extraordinary that readings sprang up all along MacDougal Street, with Café Wha?, Café Figaro, Rienzi's; the first Gaslight Café reading was such an unheard-of event that it made the front page of the New York *Daily News*. In a way, it was an imitation of the San Francisco scene, supposedly brought west from Existentialist Paris, maybe ancient Rome.

The late 1950s New York readings, ignited by the San Francisco Renaissance readings, in turn continued the traditions of the "Berkeley Renaissance." The latter wave crested in 1948, with Jack Spicer, Tom Parkinson, Kenneth Rexroth, Robert Duncan, Philip Lamantia, Robin Blaser—a group of poets, an elite (not alienated, but an elite)—reading to one another in private houses, an intimate Buddhist anarchist hermetic circle that prepared the way for later generations. Grad psychologist Timothy Leary and hermetic artist-filmmaker Harry Smith were present, same community, same era. In 1955, our "famous" Gallery Six reading was held in a very small venue, an art gallery that was formerly a garage—maybe 150 people could fit in. The readings were thereafter carried on by the San Francisco State College Poetry Center.

Thus, the genealogy extends from San Francisco through the Gaslight to St. Mark's Church in New York. After the Gaslight, poets floated from joint to joint—from Circle in the Square to a couple of small cafés up and down the Lower East Side, then over to the Seven Arts Café on Ninth Avenue and 43rd Street, near Times Square. Seven Arts flourished for about a year and a half, with Ray Bremser, Janine Pommy-Vega, myself, Gregory and Peter, LeRoi, Jack Kerouac, Diane di Prima, Ed Sanders—and many other poets. As the "Beatnik" era ended, around 1963 or so, we wound up at The Metro, which was the final surge before the St. Mark's Poetry Project. The Metro was attended by everybody: Paul Blackburn was around, di Prima, Ted Berrigan, Frank O'Hara and Jackson MacLow attended, and readings were for a long while organized by Allen DeLoach, who started a little "ditto" magazine, *Poetry at Le Metro.* Later Ted Berrigan hosted the readings. Bob Dylan came once, I remember, to listen; regulars like Ishmael Reed, David Henderson and the Umbra group, A. B. Spellman, Steve and Gloria Tropp came to read. There had been an era of good feeling between blacks and whites, 1958–1962, when one literary center was LeRoi Jones's house with his wife Hettie Cohen. *The Floating Bear* magazine, an early mimeo edited by LeRoi and Diane di Prima, had circulated, as well as LeRoi's omniscient *Yugen. Evergreen Review* was flourishing and *Chicago Review* had begun printing Burroughs, Kerouac, Corso; after censorship troubles, the latter went independent as *Big Table* and fought Post Office censorship successfully in 1959.

The Metro suffered through two crises, which continue to this day, in one form or another. You had to have a "cabaret license" to have so-called "entertainment." In those days, the crucial questions concerned cost: forty, fifty, sixty thousand dollars, not to mention all the bureaucratic problems attached to a cabaret license—you had to put in an extra fire escape or an extra fire door, as well. The Metro was not a place with liquor, it was just a coffee shop with poets, and the real and legal point was freedom of speech.

Someone also wanted to hold a poetry reading in Washington Square Park. The police said no and refused to allow it; we defied the police and held the reading one Sunday. There were lots of European and Japanese camerapeople there, and the image of poets declaiming in the grass went all over the world. So-called "profanity" seemed the underlying problem—but again, the real issue was freedom of speech. This was the early sixties, but city regulations still insisted there could be no entertainment in the parks without a license, and bureaucrats said this was "entertainment," so you had to get a license. It was a classic First Amendment case. The ACLU intervened and said no, it's not "entertainment," it's public speech, free speech, soapbox.

Now, the cabaret-licensing problem was a hangover from a Draconian dope law that said that anybody who'd been busted, had any kind of conviction—misdemeanor or felony—couldn't get a cabaret license to play at a New York City café. That barred geniuses like Charlie Parker, Thelonious Monk, and Billie Holiday from performing in New York clubs for decades. We abolished the poet's cabaret-license requirement through intervention of the City Council—by that time, we'd organized a public committee. Central to it was Ed Sanders, who then edited his elegant *Fuck You: A Magazine of the Arts.*

A New York City District Attorney, one Richard Kuh, had been prosecuting D. H. Lawrence's *Lady Chatterley's Lover,* Henry Miller's *Tropic of Cancer,* Jean Genet's *Our Lady of the Flowers,* and finally William Burroughs' *Naked Lunch.* By 1962, that censorship was broken by the courts, but Kuh went on to prosecute Lenny Bruce for his Greenwich Village nightclub act, and there was a strong literary reaction to that prosecution.

All at once came the emergence of underground films, synchronous with attempts at literary censorship, cabaret card licensing, Lenny Bruce persecution, underground newspapers like *The East Village Other* (which carried poetry) and *The Village Voice,* more or less at its height as a crusading bohemian paper. The literary, musical, and cinematic avant-garde, as well as civil rights, censorship, and minority problems, all came together at one point, one spot in time, in the early sixties. So it was a glorious ferment, as the old-fashioned littérateurs say, good as anything in the thirties or twenties. Race problems arose with The Metro proprietors, so we moved to St. Mark's Church—led by Joel Oppenheimer and Paul Blackburn.

St. Mark's has become my church, my religion place. I've been living nearby on the Lower East Side for thirty-five years. Certainly by the sixties it was my church in the sense that that's where my community was, my *sangha,* my peers. I could pass out information, find out the latest gossip, what's new, follow the latest art spurt. It was part of my education, part of my resources. Networking in that open community was intricately involved with private and public life. High-school kids coming to the church could enter a very sophisticated atmosphere and get an education they wouldn't get in grammar schools or even colleges: education in the advanced standards of bohemia.

Officially, The Poetry Project began in 1966. According to Anne Waldman, the sociologist Harry Silverstein applied for the founding grant, through the New School of Social Research across town. Money came through the Office of Economic Opportunity (OEO) under Lyndon Johnson, for a pilot program to help "alienated youth" on the Lower East Side. So the church started housing the Black Panthers' breakfast program, the Motherfuckers' dinner program.[11] Anne remembers "huge pots always cooking"; there was a child-care project too. The Lower East Side hadn't any counterculture center, and given the alienation of different minority groups, some center was needed with sensitive antennae for white, black, brown, and hippie post-Beat groups.

One interesting fringe benefit of this gathering was the margin of old bohemians left over from the thirties and forties still living on the Lower East Side and in the Village—antique "delicatessen intellectuals." Politically, there were remnants of the Old Left among the poets. Another node on the Lower East Side at that time, older than The Poetry Project, was the War Resisters' League. The war was central to everybody's preoccupations in the sixties. Many of the poems of the time expressed outrage or sympathy or violence or fright or grief. Primarily grief or fear. So there was a community, a forum where people could articulate their relationship to the big national problem of the Vietnam War and the hyper-militarization of Whitman's America. Questions of ecology had also entered into poetry through the 1950s San Francisco Renaissance; Kerouac and Gary Snyder and Lew Welch used their verse as a vehicle for expressing fright or shock or information for all mankind on the planet. Sixties' mouths could meet people who had been pacifists in World War I, people who knew *Catholic Worker* saint Dorothy Day. You got a taste of prior eras, prior movements, prior communities and their moments of glory: publications, parties, social activities, and love affairs, decades old.

For a person without an extended family in New York—my brother was living on Long Island, my father in New Jersey, and my mother was dead—St. Mark's served as immediate neighborhood community and family. "Rootless cosmopolitans," urbanized, sophisticated artists and writers gathered at The Poetry Project. It served and still serves to formulate local public opinion. Barriers were removed between inner and outer, between subjective worlds and objective social worlds. Here was space where people could proclaim to society what they wanted—and in a church, which lent their address proper dignity.

Liberation of the word. Liberation of minority groups, questions of race. The famous "sexual revolution." The celebrated women's liberation—women writing and reading brilliantly, led by poets Anne Waldman and Diane di Prima, Alice Notley, Maureen Owen, Denise Levertov, Joanne Kyger, also Diane Wakoski and Rochelle Owens and Carol Bergé, others. At least in my circle these were among the stars who gave expression to new independence. There were angry denunciations, manifestos, gay liberation performance pieces; there was romantic love poetry, there were prose poetry journals like Taylor Mead's excellent *Diary of a New York Youth* (Kerouac liked Mead's free style and frankness). *The World* mimeo publications were acknowledging the changed role of sex, and all these themes could be expressed—even put to music. None of this was particularly "committed" poetry, *engagé* in the old Marxist or newer existentialist sense. Put simply, the mode of poetry was subjective, so that any rumination that might engage you alone in bed would enter your poetry, and that could include what you read in *The New York Times* or saw on television or heard on the radio or thought in bathtub solitude or saw on the streets if you were tear-gassed. Very often, while making national pronouncements in poetry, I wondered if the FBI sat in the audience listening (as they did later in Chicago in '68).

Beginning with Great Society sixties Johnson policies, followed by Carter's, the government spent a great deal of money on the arts through OEO, as it had through the 1930s WPA. In 1966–68, money was spent on art. With that came some democratization of the intelligentsia, and some local poverty workers became intelligentsia. Everyone realized that heretofore this subsidy money for the arts had been going to institutional millionaires who operated symphonies and museums. Suddenly, small, decentralized, individual community projects could be subsidized by the government. There was a big push for minority and multicultural arts, bohemian arts, for individual arts, for poetry readings around the country, poetry in the schools, little maga-zines with their coordinating councils, and a number of strong provin-cial centers of poetic activity.

Monday-night readings at St. Mark's were open to everyone. And then, for bardic soapbox stars of their own romance, subjectivity, pas-sions, and political prophecy, you had the Wednesday-night readings. On New Year's Day readings, everybody in the community would come out, perhaps two or three hundred people, to do a one-, two-, three-, or four-minute shot—maybe their most intense perception of the year, or the one piece they'd prepared that they could show off to the entire community, and that would include everybody from John Cage up to Grand Master Xylophone. Yoko Ono came once, completely dressed in white, and breathed into the microphone with her "Formula in Awe of the Air"—was that it?—a piece mostly of silence. The audience was, and is, a regular community, unlike those at university readings—this audi-ence had been going to the same place to hear readers for ten, twenty years, so accumulated much granny wisdom about poetry, familiarity, and gossip. The audience, totally attuned, might know prior work from prior readings. Let's say Robert Creeley comes and reads a special poem dedicated to René Ricard, or I read an epilogue to "Kaddish" in the form of "White Shroud," hearers know these texts resonate with old history, because everyone's familiar with earlier texts and styles.

In later years, St. Mark's became a cradle for some higher rock 'n' roll, New Wave, and performance language. Patti Smith, Jim Carroll, William Burroughs, Laurie Anderson, Lou Reed, Philip Glass, Steven Taylor—all were at one time either apprentice poets at St. Mark's or par-ticipated in year-round activities or performed occasional work. So it had tremendous impact on the centralized progression of rock 'n' roll intel-ligentsia. Interestingly enough, St. Mark's was only ten blocks away from CBGB's, the bedraggled punk mecca of the early eighties.

With the age of Reagan, a deliberate, Federal concerted anti-democratic attack on small, individualistic, community-led arts groups began. The present attack on the NEA is an attack on decentralized ini-tiative and diversity. "Why should the general public support, with tax-payers' money, dirty poems, anti-American poems, 'immoral' poems?" Kill the classic U.S. avant-garde that helped with the Cold War in Eastern Europe! "What good is this avant-garde? Why should the public be forced to pay for it?" This is the voice of the demagogue bureaucrat and can be answered simply:

The avant-garde has a healthy role to play in any culture. The Green Revolution and notions of ecology were proclaimed by the avant-garde in America before scientific popular notions of ecology became part of majority opinion. The green movement was fostered in 1950s poetry by savants like Gary Snyder and Michael McClure. More poignantly, it was the avant-garde, the very same artists who would be censored by the so-called "anti-Communist" fundamentalists in America, who were censored in totalitarian Eastern Europe. Deconstruction of the German, Czechoslovakian, Hungarian, Bulgarian, and Romanian Communist bureaucracies was spearheaded by members of the literary avant-garde who were allied, historically and by personal connection, to the very same avant-garde here in America censored by neo-conservatives. Ed Sanders and his band, the Fugs, with their "Coca-Cola Douche" or "Police State Blues," would never be subsidized under the demagogue censor's 1990s NEA new rules, nor would The Mothers of Invention, led by Frank Zappa, or Andy Warhol's Velvet Underground, Lou Reed, Dylan, Burroughs, Kerouac be approved—though all are heroes now in free Czechoslovakia. For myself, my own poetry has been chilled off public broadcast in parallel censorship by the Federal Communications Commission.

The age of Reagan-Bush, then, cracked down on the liberation of the Word, lowering St. Mark's NEA grants funds as well as diminishing funds previously granted to other decentralized arts groups, including Intersection for the Arts in San Francisco. In 1989, St. Mark's funds were reduced to $5,000, not enough to pay one person to move chairs for a year. Neo-con politicians are talking as if they had a monopoly on God, with gas-bag "moral majority" and "born-again" political groups hyping money off airwaves for promotion of what the American Founding Fathers denounced: the domination of State policy by an intolerant Church. These neo-con cults try to make the nation legislate parochial Church morality, aiming to restrict political humor and liberty of expression. The Bush Era's permissive manipulation of fundamentalist political mania has already led to withdrawal of appropriate subsidy and encouragement for the spiritual liberation that the St. Mark's Poetry Project manifests. Either way poets rather than fundamentalist betrayers of the spirit will win the world, because the planet needs imagination, the avant-garde spirit of poetry, to survive.

FIRST PUBLISHED: Anne Waldman, ed., *Out of This World* (New York: Crown, 1991).

NOTES

PART 1   POLITICS AND PROPHECIES

1. Reference to satirist Jonathan Swift who wrote *A Modest Proposal for Preventing the Children of Poor People in Ireland from being a Burden to Their Parents or Country; and for making them beneficial to their Publick* (1729) in which he suggests fattening and eating them.

2. Reference to Henry David Thoreau who was imprisoned overnight in his native Concord, Massachusetts, for refusing to pay his state poll taxes, which would have supported the Mexican War. This prompted him to write his famous *Essay on Civil Disobedience*.

3. "Universal Soldier," song by Donovan popular at the time (1965).

4. San Francisco Mime Troupe, avant-garde theater group in the Bay area.

5. "Eve of Destruction," popular song by Barry McGuire, songwriter and star of *Hair*.

6. Col. Sutton Smith—a pseudonym for William Burroughs.

7. Samsara—the Buddhist cycle of birth, suffering, death, and rebirth.

8. Bodhisattva—in Buddhist belief, one who forgoes nirvana in order to save others.

9. MKULTRA—a super-secret CIA operation that experimented with the effects of LSD and other mind-control drugs, begun in 1953 during the Cold War, headed by Richard Helms. Originally established as a funding organ of ARTICHOKE (see below), it soon began to parallel and compete with ARTICHOKE in the range of experiments.

10. Project ARTICHOKE—the umbrella organization of secret CIA projects

experimenting with mind-control drugs, searching for the perfect truth serum. Until 1951 the operation was known as BLUEBIRD.

11. FDA—Federal Drug Administration.

12. (Poets, Essayists, Novelists).

13. Weathermen—underground radical extremist revolutionary organization from the 1960s, a splinter group of the SDS (Students for a Democratic Society).

14. COINTELPRO—FBI's Counterintelligence Program.

15. *New York Times* (April 14, 1966) p. 35 article entitled "U.S. Plot To 'Set Up' Ginsberg For Arrest Is Described To Jury."

16. Burroughs' cut-up method—a method devised by Burroughs, Gysin, Beiles, and Corso in which written text is cut up and rearranged on the page to expose meanings that were previously unseen.

17. Aum—universal mantra of all sounds brought together.

18. Columbia University, New York City.

19. Upaya—Sanskrit word meaning a skillful means or method.

20. William S. Burroughs' "Academy 23: A Deconditioning" first appeared in the *Village Voice* (July 6, 1967).

21. Gandharva—Sanskrit, a Hindu deity who knows and reveals the secrets of the celestial and divine truth.

22. Diggers—group originating in San Francisco dedicated to communal living with free stores, food programs, etc.

23. Daily Mayor—light-hearted reference to Mayor Richard Daley of Chicago.

24. Jawaharlal Nehru—first prime minister of India, 1947–1964.

25. Ghat—flight of steps down to bank of a river in India.

26. Lassi—a cool drink made with rosewater and yogurt.

27. CID—Criminal Investigation Department of the Indian government.

PART 3   MINDFULNESS AND SPIRITUALITY

1. Alternative Eastern philosophy–based group of the 1960s.

2. Being in the presence of great teachers or holy persons.

3. Inspiring power of consciousness, depicted in Tibetan iconography as a wrathful naked female figure.

4. Priestesses of Bacchus.

5. The practice of expanding the breath.

6. See part 6 (p. 267), part 7 (pp. 297, 373).

PART 4   CENSORSHIP AND SEX LAWS

1. NAMBLA—North American Man Boy Love Association.

2. *A Witch Hunt Foiled*—(1985), p. 53, North American Man Boy Love Association, Box 174, Midtown Station, New York, NY 10018.

PART 5   AUTOBIOGRAPHICAL AND FRAGMENTS

1. The community of Buddhists monks, nuns, and lay followers.

2. Untermeyer, Louis, ed. *Modern American Poetry: A Critical Anthology*, 3rd rev. ed. Harcout Brace and Company, 1925.

3. *American Poetry*, edited with Introduction, Notes, Questions and Biographical Sketches by A. B. DeMille, Simmons College, Boston, Secretary of the New England Association of Teachers of English. Boston: Allyn and Bacon, 1923. Academy Classic Series.

PART 6   LITERARY TECHNIQUE AND THE BEAT GENERATION

1. Ann Charters, ed., *The Portable Beat Reader* (New York: Viking, 1992).

2. Charles Olson—see selection in Don Allen, ed., *The New American Poetry: 1945–1960* (New York: Grove, 1960).

3. Robert Creeley, *A Form of Women* (New York: Jargon/Corinth Books, 1959).

4. See some of the long sentences in Jack Kerouac, *Visions of Cody* (New York: New Directions, 1960) or *Doctor Sax* (New York: Grove Press, 1959).

5. *Kirtan*—sung mantra repetition.

6. Sandinistas—Nicaraguan revolutionary socialist government under President Daniel Ortega forced into Soviet communist sphere by U.S. Latin American policies.

PART 7   WRITERS

1. John Keats: "negative capability is when a man is capable of being in uncertainties, mysteries, doubts, without any irritable reaching out after fact and reason."

2. For Buddhist account of development of separate ego parallel to Blake's, q.v. Chögyam Trungpa, "Cutting Through Spiritual Materialism," in *On the Five Skandhas* (Boston: Shambhala, 1973), pp. 122–128.

3. Cherry Valley—in the late 1960s Ginsberg bought an old farmhouse near this upstate New York town as a retreat for city poets.

4. Benzadrine—an amphetamine stimulant.

5. Larimer Street—street in run-down Denver's skid row district where Neal Cassady grew up.

6. Probably a reference to the critic Norman Podhoretz, whose article "The Know-Nothing Bohemians" putting down the Beats was popular with the academics of the time.

7. Highest form of meditative state.

8. The interpretations of Buddha Dharma are modeled after expositions by Chögyam Trungpa Rinpoche in *Cutting Through Spiritual Materialism* (Boston:

Shambhala Press, 1973) and his other books and discourses. The translation of *Prajnaparamita Sutra* is adapted from that of the late Suzuki Roshi of the San Francisco Zen Center.

9. William S. Burroughs, *Naked Lunch* (Paris: Olympia Press, 1959).

10. Joan Vollmer Adams (1924–1951).

11. The Interzone City Market Meet Cafe passage was published by Robert Creeley in *Black Mountain Review*, no. 7 (1957) pp. 144–148, the first Burroughs prose (since *Junky*, 1952) related to *Naked Lunch* and subsequent grand style to be printed in America.

12. Wobblies—members of the International Workers of the World labor group.

13. Charles Olson in conversation with Ted Berrigan, Gloucester, 1966.

14. Raymond Foye.

PART 8   FURTHER APPRECIATIONS

1. Fosters—cafeteria in San Francisco.

2. Rue Git-Le-Coeur was famous as the home of the "Beat Hotel."

3. La Coupole—an expensive restaurant.

4. Author's Note: Later work by Lennon/Ono is equally eccentric, that is, personal. [Jan. '74]

5. Dom—popular nightclub in New York City's East Village on St. Mark's Place between Second and Third Avenues.

6. That's Kerouac's wish-fulfilling gem, "110th Chorus" in *Mexico City Blues* (New York: Grove Press, 1959).

7. *The Kalevala*, trans. F. P. MaGoun Jr. (Cambridge, Mass.: Harvard University Press, 1963) poem . . . "up to his teeth behind a rotten tree trunk."

8. Chögyam Trungpa, "The Spontaneous Song of the White Banner," *Rain of Wisdom*, trans. Nalanda Translation Committee (Boulder and London: Shambhala Publications, 1980) p. 285.

9. Wigstock—annual festival/parade of transvestite beauty.

10. Coors brewing company—a supporter of right-wing causes.

11. Motherfuckers—black skirt and shirt psychedelic anarchist lunatic fringe left-hand politics commune—romantic nuisance youth extremists of the late sixties.

GLOSSARY

Ahab—fictional captain of the *Pequod* in Herman Melville's classic tale, *Moby-Dick*.

Alcott, Bronson—(1799–1888) educator and philosopher.

Amram, David—(b. 1933) classically trained jazz musician and composer, accompanied Jack Kerouac and others in early poetry and jazz readings.

Anderson, Sherwood—(1876–1941) novelist, author of *Winesburg, Ohio*.

Anger, Kenneth—(b. 1930) avant-garde filmmaker and author of *Hollywood Babylon*.

Anslinger, Harry J.—longtime Narcotics Bureau commissioner (1930–1962); a harsh critic of marijuana legalization efforts.

Apollinaire, Guillaume—(1880–1918) Polish-born French poet, author of *Alcools* (1913).

Artaud, Antonin—(1896–1948) French surrealist poet and dramatist.

Ashbery, John—(b. 1927) New York School poet, author of *Rivers and Mountains* and *Self-Portrait in a Convex Mirror*.

Baez, Joan—(b. 1941) popular American folksinger.

Baraka, Amiri—(b. 1934) black activist poet and playwright, author of *Preface to a Twenty Volume Suicide Note*; originally known as LeRoi Jones.

Barger, Sonny—one of the founders of the Hell's Angels.

Beck, Julian—(1925–1985) anarchist, poet, actor, director and cofounder of the Living Theatre, with wife Judith Malina, 1947.

Beiles, Sinclair—South African Beat poet and friend of Burroughs, co-inventor of the cut-up method of writing.

Berrigan, Daniel—(b. 1921) Catholic priest, activist, Vietnam War protestor.

Berrigan, Ted—(1934–1983) poet active in the St. Mark's Poetry Project, author of *The Sonnets.*

Bhaktivedanta, Swami—(1896–1977) founder of the Hare Krishna movement in the United States.

Blackburn, Paul—(1926–1971) American poet, author of *In, On, Or About the Premises* and *The Cities.*

Blake, William—(1757–1827) English poet and engraver, author of *Songs of Innocence and Experience.*

Bonnefoi, Genevieve—French writer.

Brakhage, Stan—(b. 1933) underground filmmaker.

Bremser, Ray—(1934–1998) Beat poet, author of *Poems of Madness* and *Angel,* much admired by Bob Dylan.

Breton, André—(1896–1966) French poet.

Brown, Jerry—(b. 1938) governor of California and frequent candidate for president.

Bruce, Lenny—(1926–1966) controversial comedian, arrested several times on obscenity charges.

Buber, Martin—(1878–1965) German Jewish religious philosopher.

Bukowski, Charles—(1920–1994) American novelist, often associated with the Beats.

Bunting, Basil—(1900–1985) British poet, author of epic poem *Briggflats,* peer of Ezra Pound.

Burroughs, William S.—(1914–1997) author of *Naked Lunch* and founding member of the Beat Generation literary movement.

Campion, Thomas—(1567–1620) English poet, author of songs and verse.

Cardenal, Ernesto—(b. 1925) Nicaraguan poet and priest.

Carr, Lucien—(b. 1925) classmate and friend of the early Beat writers at Columbia, one of the original dedicatees of *Howl.*

Cassady, Neal—(1926–1968) author of *The First Third* and inspiration for central characters in Ginsberg's and Kerouac's works.

Cayce, Edgar—(1877–1945) spiritual leader, often considered the greatest psychic of the twentieth century.

Céline, Louis Ferdinand—(1894–1961) French writer.

Cézanne, Paul—(1839–1906) French Impressionist painter.

Charlatans—UK rock group popular in the 1990s.

Charles, Ray—(b. 1930) popular singer.

Cherne, Leo—head of Freedom House and chairman of the International Rescue Committee.

Chicago Seven—organizers of the protests staged at the 1968 Democratic National Convention, tried for conspiracy; included Abbie Hoffman, and Jerry Rubin.

Chuang, Tzu—(399–295 B.C.) Taoist Pantheist poet.

Clausen, Andy—(b. 1943) Belgian-born American poet.

Cocteau, Jean—(1891–1963) French poet.

Conner, Bruce—(b. 1933) California underground filmmaker.

Corso, Gregory—(b. 1930) American poet, author of *Gasoline,* Beat founder.

Costello, Frank—(1891–1973) replaced Lucky Luciano in 1930s as an organized crime leader, head of the Genovese crime family.

Creeley, Robert—(b. 1926) poet associated with the Black Mountain School, author of *The Gold Diggers.*

Crevel, René—French author of *Babylone.*

Damon, S. Foster—(1893–1971) Blake scholar, author of *The Blake Dictionary.*

Darío, Rubén—(1867–1916) Nicaraguan diplomat, journalist, and poet.

Davis, Angela—(b. 1944) 1960s radical black activist.

Debs, Eugene V.—(1855–1926) American labor leader, union organizer, and Socialist candidate for president.

de Gaulle, Charles—(1890–1970) French general and president.

Dellinger, Dave—(b. 1915) anti–Vietnam War activist, chairman of the national Mobilization to End the War in Vietnam, author of *From Yale to Jail.*

Deng Xiaoping—(1904–1997) premier of China 1975–1997.

Desnos, Robert—(1900–1945) French poet.

di Prima, Diane—(b. 1934) American poet, author of *Revolutionary Letters.*

Dostoyevsky, Fyodor Mikhailovich—(1821–1881) Russian novelist.

Dudjom, Rinpoche—(1904–1987) former lama head of Nyingmapa sect of Tibetan Buddhism.

Dulles, John Foster—(1888–1959) American diplomat, secretary of state under Eisenhower.

Duncan, Robert—(1919–1988) American poet, taught at Black Mountain College.

Dylan, Bob (b. 1941)—folksinger and rock 'n' roll star.

Eichmann, Adolf—(1906–1962) German Nazi leader, captured and returned to Israel, then executed for war crimes.

Eisenhower, Dwight—(1890–1969) American general and president.

Emerson, Ralph Waldo—(1803–1882) essayist and poet from Concord, Massachusetts.

Family Dogg—San Francisco–based five-member pop group of the 1960s and 1970s.

Fearing, Kenneth—(1902–1961) American novelist, editor of *Partisan Review.*

Ferlinghetti, Lawrence—(b. 1919) American poet and painter, author of *A Coney Island of the Mind,* publisher of City Lights Books.

Flaubert, Gustave—(1821–1880) French novelist, author of *Madame Bovary.*

Fonda, Jane—(b. 1937) American actress and activist.

Fourcade, Tom—Underground Press Syndicate founder.

Frank, Robert—(b. 1924) Zurich-born photographer, filmmaker of *Pull My Daisy* (1959).

Fugs—1960s rock group formed by Ed Sanders, Tuli Kupferberg, Ken Weaver.

Gelek, Rinpoche—(b. 1939) founder of Jewel Heart Tibetan Buddhist centers and friend of Ginsberg.

Genet, Jean—(1910–1986) French writer.

Goldwater, Barry—(1909–1998) conservative U.S. senator and Republican presidential candidate in 1964.

Goodman, Paul—(1911–1972) social critic and author of *Growing Up Absurd,* 1960.

Guthrie, Woody—(1912–1967) American folksinger and songwriter.

Gysin, Brion—(1916–1986) author and Burroughs' collaborator.

Hartley, Marsden—(1877–1943) artist and writer, associated with scenes of the American Southwest.

Hayden, Tom—(b. 1940) anti–Vietnam War activist, cofounder of the SDS (Students for a Democratic Society), later U.S. congressman from California.

Hearn, Lafcadio—(1850–1904) American writer influenced by his life in Japan.

Hell's Angels—sometimes violent motorcycle gang.

Helms, Jesse—(b. 1921) conservative senator from North Carolina.

Heritage Foundation—conservative PAC (Political Action Committee), "committed to rolling back the liberal welfare state."

Hiroshige, Utagaw—(1797–1858) Japanese printmaker, famous for scenes of Japan.

Hoffman, Abbie—(1936–1989) Vietnam War peace activist, cofounder of the Youth International Party (YIP).

Hofmann, Albert—(b. 1906) Swiss research scientist who invented LSD in 1938.

Holmes, John Clellon—(1926–1988) author of *Go*, the first Beat novel.

Hoover, J. Edgar—(1895–1972) director of the FBI from 1924 to 1972.

Huncke, Herbert—(1915–1996) writer who introduced the Beats to the Times Square underworld and a central figure in their writings.

Jackson, Natalie—(193?–1956) girlfriend of Neal Cassady, victim of amphetamine paranoia suicide.

Jagger, Mick—(b. 1943) leader of the Rolling Stones rock 'n' roll band.

Jeffers, Robinson—(1887–1962) American poet.

Jefferson Airplane—rock 'n' roll group with Grace Slick as lead singer.

Johnson, Lee Otis—political activist who, like John Sinclair, was imprisoned on marijuana charges.

Johnson, Lyndon Baines—(1908–1973) president of the United States (1963–1969).

Jones, LeRoi—see Baraka, Amiri.

Keats, John—(1795–1821) English poet.

Kennedy, John—(1917–1963) assassinated president of the United States.

Kennedy, Robert—(1925–1968) U.S. attorney general, assassinated during campaign for the presidency.

Kerouac, Jack—(1922–1969) author and central figure in the Beat Generation, author of *On the Road, Dharma Bums,* and others.

Kesey, Ken—(b. 1935) author of *One Flew Over the Cuckoo's Nest,* organizer of the Merry Pranksters' LSD trips.

Khomeini, Ayatollah Ruhollah—(1900–1989) Iranian religious and political leader.

King, Martin Luther, Jr.—(1929–1968) civil-rights leader and Nobel Peace Prize recipient.

Koch, Kenneth—(b. 1925) poet, member of the New York School.

Kunstler, William—(1919–1995) attorney and activist, defended the Chicago Seven among others.

Kupferberg, Tuli—(b. 1923) poet and member of the Fugs rock 'n' roll band.

Kyger, Joanne—(b. 1934) poet, author of *The Japan and India Journals.*

Lamantia, Philip—(b. 1927) American surrealist poet, author of *The Blood of the Air.*

Lansky, Meyer—(1902–1983) Russian-born American gangster and organized crime chief.

Lawrence, D. H.—(1885–1930) English author of *Lady Chatterley's Lover.*

Leary, Timothy—(1920–1996) psychologist and drug activist, made famous the statement "Tune in, turn on, drop out."

LeMar—Legalize Marijuana organization of the 1960s.

Lennon, John—(1940–1980) musician, member of the Beatles.

Lerner, Max—(b. 1902) author of *It Is Later Than You Think* and *The Need for a Militant Democracy.*

Leslie, Alfred—(b. 1927) artist and filmmaker, collaborator with Robert Frank on *Pull My Daisy.*

Levertov, Denise—(1923–1998) poet frequently associated with the Beats.

Luce, Henry R.—(1898–1967) multimillionaire founder and publisher of *Time, Life,* and *Fortune* magazines.

MacDiarmid, Hugh—(1892–1978) British poet, author of *A Drunk Man Looks at the Thistle.*

Mailer, Norman—(b. 1923) author of *The Naked and the Dead.*

Malina, Judith—(b. 1926) actress, director, and cofounder of the Living Theatre, with husband Julian Beck.

Mansour, Joyce—(b. 1928) French writer.

Mao Tse-tung—(1893–1976) Chinese Communist leader and party chairman.

McCartney, Paul—(b. 1942) musician, member of the Beatles.

McClure, Michael—(b. 1932) poet, author of *Hymns to St. Geryon and Other Poems*.

Mead, Taylor—New York author, actor in Andy Warhol films.

Mekas, Jonas—(b. 1922) filmmaker of *Guns of the Trees* and founder of the Film Anthology Archives.

Michaux, Henri—(1899–1984) French surrealist poet.

Micheline, Jack—(1929–1998) poet, author of *River of Red Wine* with Jack Kerouac introduction.

Miller, Henry—(1891–1980) American author of *Tropic of Capricorn*.

Minh, Ho Chi—(1890–1969) president of Communist North Vietnam.

Mirabai, Shiva Krishna Chaitanya—Hindu saint who spent her life composing songs of love for Krishna.

Monk, Thelonious—(1918–1982) genius of piano jazz.

Moore, Marianne—(1887–1972) American poet.

Nixon, Richard—(1913–1994) U.S. president, resigned over Watergate scandal.

Ochs, Phil—(1940–1976) folksinger.

O'Hara, Frank—(1926–1966) New York poet, author of *Second Avenue* and *Lunch Poems*.

Olson, Charles—(1910–1970) Gloucester poet associated with "Projective Verse," author of *The Maximus Poems*.

Ono, Yoko—(b. 1933) artist, musician, wife of John Lennon.

Orlovsky, Peter—(b. 1933) poet and longtime companion of Allen Ginsberg.

Paine, Thomas—(1737–1809) essayist during the American Revolution, author of *The Federalist Papers*.

Poe, Edgar Allen—(1809–1849) American writer and poet, author of "The Raven."

Pound, Ezra—(1885–1972) American poet, author of *The Cantos*.

Ramakrishna—(1834–1886) central leader of modern Hinduism.

Rebozo, Charles Gregory (Bebe)—(1912–1998) banker and real estate businessman, close friend of Richard Nixon.

Rexroth, Kenneth—(1905–1982) American poet and essayist, influential leader of the San Francisco Renaissance.

Reznikoff, Charles—(1894–1976) American poet.

Rice, Ron—1960s avant-garde filmmaker.

Rimbaud, Arthur—(1854–1891) French poet.

Rochester, John Wilmont, 2nd earl of—(1647–1680) British nobleman, writer, contemporary of Milton, subject to censorship in the 1960s.

Rockefeller, Nelson—(1908–1979) New York governor and U.S. vice president.

Rogers, Buck—comic strip hero of a futuristic world.

Rubin, Jerry—(1938–1994) radical anti-Vietnam War activist, one of the Chicago Seven and author of *Do It!*

Rusk, Dean—(1909–1994) secretary of state under Kennedy and Johnson (1961–1969).

Sandburg, Carl—(1878–1967) American poet and biographer of Lincoln.

Sanders, Ed—(b. 1939) poet, writer, musician, and founder of the Fugs.

Saroyan, Aram—(b. 1943) American writer.

Schwitters, Kurt—(1887–1948) German artist and poet.

Selby, Hubert, Jr.—(b. 1928) author of *Last Exit to Brooklyn,* 1964.

Shivananda—(1887–1962) famous Swami and friend of Ginsberg.

Sinclair, John—(b. 1941) Detroit-based activist, poet, publisher, and writer, jailed on drug charges in 1969.

Smart, Christopher—(1722–1771) British poet.

Smith, Bessie—(1894–1937) black American blues singer.

Smith, Harry—(1923–1991) filmmaker and editor of Folkways *Anthology of American Folk Music.*

Smith, Jack—(1932–1989) filmmaker and performer whose *Flaming Creatures* was censored in New York City; died of AIDS at age 57.

Snyder, Gary—(b. 1930) poet, author of *Riprap* and *Mountains and Rivers Without End.*

Solomon, Carl—(1928–1993) author, friend of Ginsberg, dedicatee of *Howl.*

Spellman, Francis Cardinal—(1889–1967) New York Catholic Church leader.

Starr, Ringo—(b. 1940) musician and one of the Beatles.

Summerfield, Arthur Ellsworth—(1899–1972) Republican postmaster general (1953–1961).

Sunday, Billy—(1862–1935) evangelist minister popular during the religious revival at the last turn of the century.

Swift, Jonathan—(1667–1745) British writer and satirist, author of *Gulliver's Travels* (1726).

Swinburne, Algernon Charles—(1837–1909) English poet and critic.

Thoreau, Henry David—(1817–1862) American essayist and poet, author of *Walden*.

Traubel, Horace—(1858–1919) friend, editor, and biographer of Walt Whitman.

Trilling, Lionel—(1905–1976) critic and writer, Ginsberg's teacher at Columbia University.

Trungpa Vajracharya, Chögyam—(1939–1987) Ginsberg's Mantrayana-style meditation teacher, founder of Shambhala and Naropa Institute.

Tzara, Tristan—(1896–1963) French Dadaist poet.

Van Doren, Mark—(1894–1972) critic, writer, and Ginsberg's teacher at Columbia University.

Vega, Janine Pommy—(b. 1942) poet, author of *Poems to Fernando*.

Vivekenanda, Swami—(1863–1902) disciple of Sri Ramakrishna, introduced Vedanta philosophy to the West.

Voznesensky, Andrei—(b. 1933) Russian poet, author of *Dogalypse*.

Waldman, Anne—(b. 1945) New York poet and cofounder of the Jack Kerouac School of Disembodied Poetics with Allen Ginsberg.

Welch, Lew—(1926–1971) poet, author of *I Remain*.

Whalen, Philip—(b. 1923) poet, author of *Scenes of Life at the Capital*.

Whitman, Walt—(1819–1892) American poet, author of *Leaves of Grass*.

Wieners, John—(b. 1934) poet, author of *The Hotel Wentley Poems*.

Williams, Jonathan—(b. 1929) poet, publisher of Jargon Books.

Williams, William Carlos—(1883–1963) New Jersey poet, author of *Paterson*.

Wittgenstein, Ludwig—(1889–1951) Influential modern philosopher.

Wordsworth, William—(1770–1850) English poet.

Wyatt, Thomas—(1503–1542) English poet.

Yahoo—member of a race of brutes invented by Jonathan Swift in his *Gulliver's Travels*.

Yeats, William Butler—(1865–1939) Irish poet and playwright.

Yevtuchenko, Yevgeny—(b. 1933) Russian poet, author of *Stolen Apples*.

Zappa, Frank—(1940–1993) lead singer for the rock 'n' roll group Mothers of Invention.

Zukofsky, Louis—(1904–1978) editor and objectivist poet.

INDEX

515